PRESIDENTIAL DOCUMENTS

Professor J. F. Watts joined The City College of New York faculty in 1965. At The College he served as chairman of the History Department for ten years, won the Outstanding Teacher Award, and contributed to innumerable academic and governance assignments. He has written on American political and social history and, most recently, on comparative world history. He lives in New York City with his wife and two cats.

Fred L. Israel is professor emeritus of American history at The City College of New York. He is the author of *Nevada's Key Pittman* and has edited *The War Diary of Breckinridge Long* and *Major Peace Treaties of Modern History, 1648–1975* (5 vols.). He holds the Scribe's Award from the American Bar Association for his joint editorship of *The Justices of the United States Supreme Court* (4 vols.). For the past 25 years Professor Israel has compiled and edited the Gallup Poll into annual reference volumes.

PRESIDENTIAL

DOCUMENTS

The Speeches, Proclamations, and Policies That Have
Shaped the Nation from Washington to Clinton

Edited by

J. F. Watts
Fred L. Israel

Routledge
New York and London

Published in 2000 by
Routledge
29 West 35th Street
New York, NY 10001

Published in Great Britain by
Routledge
11 New Fetter Lane
London, EC4P 4EE

Copyright © 2000 by Routledge
Interior design by Sencor

Printed in the United States of America on acid-free paper.

10 9 8 7 6 5 4 3 2 1

Library of Congress Cataloging-in-Publication Data

Presidential documents / [compiled by] J. F. Watts and Fred L. Israel.
    p. cm.
    Includes index.
    ISBN 0-415-92037-X (hardback)
    1. Presidents—United States—History Sources. 2. United States—Politics and government
Sources. 3. United States—History Sources. I. Watts, J. F. (Jim F.) II. Israel, Fred L., 1935-
    E176. 1.P889   1999
  973'.099—dc21   99-20927
                                                                        CIP

CONTENTS

PREFACE

In the Declaration of Independence of 1776, Thomas Jefferson listed more than thirty grievances against the King of England. A decade later, in writing the Constitution of the United States, the Founding Fathers quite naturally rejected a hereditary monarch or powerful head of state. Instead, they established an elected chief executive with a specific term of office. Article II, Section 1 of the Constitution explains: "The executive Power shall be vested in a President of the United States of America. He shall hold his Office during the Term of four Years."

The United States was the first nation to have an elected president—and a president with a stated term of office. Every four years since the adoption of the Constitution in 1789, the nation has held a presidential election. Elections have been held even during major economic disruptions and war.

The forty presidents seem to have had very little in common. Five were never elected. John Tyler, Millard Fillmore, Andrew Johnson, Chester Arthur, and Gerald Ford entered office through the death, assassination or resignation of their predecessor. Each failed to remain in office, either through personal choice or political fate.

Some of these forty men were surprisingly strong-willed, while others were simply miscast. Although Abraham Lincoln prevented the permanent break-up of the Union and Woodrow Wilson and Franklin D. Roosevelt each confronted a world war, most presidents were average men doing the best they could in a complicated job.

In understanding the legacy of our presidents, we note that the stature of a president is largely determined by the times in which he served. Crises demand a criterion of transcendent leadership, ordinary times shroud the presidency in convention. Likewise, there does not seem to be a pattern in the kind of person whom the voters have chosen to be their leader. They have been as young as John F. Kennedy (43) and as old as Ronald Reagan (69), intellectuals like Madison and Monroe and plain thinkers like the great Jackson and the failed Harding. Personality types have run the gamut, from the ebullient spirits of the two Roosevelts and Truman to the taciturn Coolidge and dour Nixon. They have come from states across the country, from Vermont to California. Mostly they have come to the White House from the Congress and from governors' mansions. Six generals have been elected to the presidency. And, except for the tragic Civil War which followed the 1860 election of Lincoln, the electorate always has accepted the peaceful transfer of power.

Many of these men sought the responsibilities of the presidency. Others landed there by accident. The former sincerely believed themselves to be the best

1

qualified for dealing wisely with the multitudinous problems facing the nation. The "accidental" presidents attempted to cope with the office—some rather successfully. Regardless, each man occupied a position of power and did his best to exercise leadership as he understood the situation. Each had the opportunity to make major decisions both in foreign and domestic matters which affected the direction of the nation.

Our assignment was to select a representative collection of presidential statements or decisions which shaped or reflected American history. We began by identifying what had to be included in this collection—Washington's inaugural address (1789) and those of Franklin Roosevelt (1933) and John F. Kennedy (1961); Lincoln's Emancipation Proclamation (1863); and various declarations of war and peace. We watched with delight as our list grew in number. Eventually we agreed on choosing thirty-seven "must documents."

But what about the remainder? This required a careful rereading, and indeed a mutual rethinking, of the discipline which we have taught and written about for many years. Each document provides a window into the world of many nearly-forgotten men who were in their time accorded all the honors of "Mr. President" when they lived in the White House on Pennsylvania Avenue in Washington, D.C. James Garfield, Benjamin Harrison, Martin Van Buren, Zachary Taylor, Chester Arthur, Calvin Coolidge, and Franklin Pierce lived there amidst the splendor and anxiety of the presidency, in the same house occupied in other years by Jefferson and Jackson, the Roosevelts and Wilson, Truman and Eisenhower, Kennedy and Nixon, Reagan and Clinton.

Beyond the "must documents" essential to American history, there are indispensable moments in the history of the American presidency which produced effects both breathtaking and disastrous. Andrew Jackson, the great democratic leader, was the first to order federal troops to suppress a labor strike (1834), establishing a precedent for nearly a century. Martin Van Buren's Proclamation of Neutrality in the Caroline Affair (1838) avoided another war with Great Britain. James K. Polk's 1848 confirmation that gold had been discovered in California set off an unprecedented westward movement. In 1877, Rutherford B. Hayes believed that reason and good will among Southern whites would end racial conflict, and thus he removed federal troops which had protected freed slaves. Grover Cleveland and Herbert Hoover each believed that the federal government should avoid direct benefits to citizens, whatever the disaster or depravation. Woodrow Wilson believed that the American Government should reconfigure the entire world. Calvin Coolidge agreed with Cleveland and Hoover, Harry Truman sided with Wilson and Franklin Roosevelt. Thus the documents reflect the patterns and themes of our two centuries under the Constitution.

Our next goal was to excerpt these documents so that they were readable in a reference volume aimed at a wide audience. Of course, we never thought of editing Lincoln's 270-word Gettysburg Address (1863). But Washington's Farewell Address (1796), indeed a most important blueprint for the nation, runs to over 4000 words and Jackson's Proclamation to the People of South Carolina (1832) is more than five times that in length. In the necessary editing, we carefully included the most relevant paragraphs of each document, always remembering the importance of presidential words which shaped the growth of the American republic and the destiny of this great nation.

Finally, we wrote an introduction for each document explaining the background and its pertinence in American history.

The late Charles E. Smith challenged us with this project. Smith, formerly President of the Academic Reference Division of Simon and Schuster and then President of Charles E. Smith Books, offered us invaluable suggestions. We hope we completed this manuscript maintaining his high standards.

J. F. WATTS
FRED L. ISRAEL
THE CITY COLLEGE OF NEW YORK
3 OCTOBER 1999

PRESIDENT GEORGE WASHINGTON'S
FIRST INAUGURAL ADDRESS
30 April 1789

George Washington presided over a new nation forged out of revolution. Could a republic endure? Could a political system rooted in "the people" remain stable? Washington himself conceded that the "destiny" of elected government was "staked on the experiment entrusted to the hands of the American people."

In 1789, the United States had vast empty spaces. Stretching from the Atlantic Ocean to the Mississippi River and from the Great Lakes to Spanish held Florida, America possessed an enormous domain. But less than half of this area had yet come under the effective jurisdiction of the United States or of any state. The population stood at just under 4 million, including 700,000 slaves. Ninety percent of these overwhelming rural people lived east of the Appalachians. There were only six cities (Philadelphia, New York, Boston, Charleston, Baltimore, and Salem) with a population of 8,000 or more; and their combined numbers included only 3 per cent of the total.

Washington faced the tremendous task of launching the new government. Enormously moved by the warm confidence placed in him by the people, the modest President wrote that he foresaw only "an ocean of difficulties . . . Integrity and firmness are all I can promise." On 30 April 1789, a festive crowd assembled before Federal Hall in New York to witness the inauguration. State Chancellor Robert R. Livingston, administered the oath of office to Washington on a balcony overlooking Wall Street. Then turning to the people, Livingston proclaimed in a loud voice, "Long live George Washington, the President of the United States." The crowd took up the cry and roared its approval as cannons boomed. Washington then entered the small senate chamber, where, embarrassed but solemn, he delivered the first inaugural address.

Among the vicissitudes incident to life no event could have filled me with greater anxieties than that of which the notification was transmitted by your order, and received on the 14th day of the present month. On the one hand, I was summoned by my country, whose voice I can never hear but with veneration and love, from a retreat which I had chosen with the fondest predilection, and, in my flattering hopes, with an immutable decision, as the asylum of my declining years—a retreat which was rendered every day more necessary as well as more dear to me by the addition of habit to inclination, and of frequent interruptions in my health to the gradual waste committed on it by time. On the other hand, the magnitude and difficulty of the trust to which the voice of my country called me, being sufficient to awaken in the wisest and most experienced of her citizens a distrustful scrutiny into his qualifications, could not but overwhelm with despondence one who (inheriting inferior endowments from nature and unpracticed in the duties of civil administration) ought to be peculiarly conscious of his own deficiencies. In this conflict of emotions all I dare aver is that it has been my faithful study to collect my duty from a just appreciation of every circumstance by which it might be affected. All I dare hope is that if, in executing this task, I have been too much swayed by a grateful remembrance of former instances, or by an affectionate sensibility to this transcendent proof of the confidence of my fellow-citizens, and have thence too little consulted my incapacity as well as disinclination for the weighty and untried cares before me, my error will be palliated by the motives which mislead me, and its consequences be judged by my country with some share of the partiality in which they originated.

Such being the impressions under which I have, in obedience to the public summons, repaired to the present station, it would be peculiarly improper to omit in this first official act my fervent supplications to that Almighty Being who rules over the universe, who presides in the councils of nations, and whose providential aids can supply every human defect, that His benediction may consecrate to the liberties and happiness of the people of the United States a Government instituted by themselves for these essential purposes, and may enable every instrument employed in its administration to execute with success the functions allotted to his

charge. In tendering this homage to the Great Author of every public and private good, I assure myself that it expresses your sentiments not less than my own, nor those of my fellow-citizens at large less than either. No people can be bound to acknowledge and adore the Invisible Hand which conducts the affairs of men more than those of the United States. Every step by which they have advanced to the character of an independent nation seems to have been distinguished by some token of providential agency; and in the important revolution just accomplished in the system of their united government the tranquil deliberations and voluntary consent of so many distinct communities from which the event has resulted can not be compared with the means by which most governments have been established without some return of pious gratitude, along with an humble anticipation of the future blessings which the past seem to presage. These reflections, arising out of the present crisis, have forced themselves too strongly on my mind to be suppressed. You will join with me, I trust, in thinking that there are none under the influence of which the proceedings of a new and free government can more auspiciously commence.

By the article establishing the executive department it is made the duty of the President "to recommend to your consideration such measures as he shall judge necessary and expedient." The circumstances under which I now meet you will acquit me from entering into that subject further than to refer to the great constitutional charter under which you are assembled, and which, in defining your powers, designates the objects to which your attention is to be given. It will be more consistent with those circumstances, and far more congenial with the feelings which actuate me, to substitute, in place of a recommendation of particular measures, the tribute that is due to the talents, the rectitude, and the patriotism which adorn the characters selected to devise and adopt them. In these honorable qualifications I behold the surest pledges that as on one side no local prejudices or attachments, no separate views nor party animosities, will misdirect the comprehensive and equal eye which ought to watch over this great assemblage of communities and interests, so, on another, that the foundation of our national policy will be laid in the pure and immutable principles of private morality, and the preeminence of free government be exemplified by all the attributes which can win the affections of its citizens and command the respect of the world. I dwell on this prospect with every satisfaction which an ardent love for my country can inspire, since there is no truth more thoroughly established than that there exists in the economy and course of nature an indissoluble union between virtue and happiness; between duty and advantage; between the genuine maxims of an honest and magnanimous policy and the solid rewards of public prosperity and felicity; since we ought to be no less persuaded that the propitious smiles of Heaven can never be expected on a nation that disregards the eternal rules of order and right which Heaven itself has ordained; and since the preservation of the sacred fire of liberty and the destiny of the republican model of government are justly considered, perhaps, as *deeply,* as *finally,* staked on the experiment intrusted to the hands of the American people. . . .

To the foregoing observations I have one to add, which will be most properly addressed to the House of Representatives. It concerns myself, and will therefore be as brief as possible. When I was first honored with a call into the service of my country, then on the eve of an arduous struggle for its liberties, the light in which I contemplated my duty required that I should renounce every pecuniary compensation. From this resolution I have in no instance departed; and being still under the impressions which produced it, I must decline as inapplicable to myself any share in the personal emoluments which may be indispensably included in a permanent provision for the executive department, and must accordingly pray that the pecuniary estimates for the station in which I am placed may during my continuance in it be limited to such actual expenditures as the public good may be thought to require.

Having thus imparted to you my sentiments as they have been awakened by the occasion which brings us together, I shall take my present leave; but not without resorting once more to the benign Parent of the Human Race in humble supplication that, since He has been pleased to favor the American people with opportunities for deliberating in perfect tranquillity, and dispositions for deciding with unparalleled unanimity on a form of government for the security of their union and the advancement of their happiness, so His divine blessing may be equally *conspicuous* in the enlarged views, the temperate consultations, and the wise measures on which the success of this Government must depend.

PRESIDENT GEORGE WASHINGTON TO SECRETARY OF THE TREASURY ALEXANDER HAMILTON
16 February 1791 – The Evolution of the Cabinet

PRESIDENT GEORGE WASHINGTON TO SECRETARY OF STATE THOMAS JEFFERSON
25 November 1791 – The Evolution of the Cabinet

Article II, Section 2 of the Constitution states that the President "may require the Opinion in writing, of the principal Officer in each of the executive Departments, upon any Subject relating to their Duties of their respective Offices." These " offices" were created by Congress and their holders were considered to be the personal assistants of the President in carrying out the work of his administration.

At first, Washington tried to abide by the intentions of the Framers that the Senate should serve as a privy council on the British model. However, he stopped attending Senate meetings and conferences with Senators when he realized that he was creating friction within that body. In 1793, he tried to obtain the advice of the Supreme Court at the time of a crisis with France. He submitted to the Court a series of questions about interpretations of treaties with France. The justices refused to answer on the ground that this was not their duty.

The President now turned to his three secretaries or department Heads of State, War, and Navy—the three departments involved with France—and called them, along with the attorney general, into a "council meeting." In time, the public recognized such meetings of the President's assistants as the "official council" or cabinet of the President. The name cabinet was first used in 1793. Congressional debates show that the term was used in Congress in 1798 and again in 1802. The name "cabinet" does not appear in a federal statute until 1907.

In the first document below, President Washington requested the views of Secretary of the Treasury Alexander Hamilton on the legality of the Bank of the United States.

This is among the earliest documents in which the President requests guidance from his principal assistants on the constitutionality of a Congressional bill.

The second document, dated 25 November 1791, notes the first cabinet meeting called by the President of the United States. President Washington, in his memo, set the agenda.

. . . "An act to incorporate the subscribers to the Bank of the United States" is now before me for consideration.

The Constitutionality of it is objected to. It therefore becomes more particularly my duty to examine the ground on which the objection is built. As a mean of investigation I have called upon the Attorney General of the United States, in whose line it seemed more particularly to be, for his official examination and opinion. His report is, that the Constitution does not warrant the Act. I then applied to the Secretary of State for his sentiments on the subject. These coincide with the Atty. General's, and the reasons for their opinions having been submitted in writing, I now require, in like manner, yours, on the validity and propriety of the above recited Act: and that you may know the points on which the Secretary of State and the Attorney General dispute the constitutionality of the Act; and that I may be fully possessed of the argument *for* and *against* the measure, before I express any opinion of my own, I give you an opportunity of examining and answering the objections contained in the enclosed papers. I require the return of them, when your own sentiments are handed me (which I wish may be as soon as is convenient;) and further, that no copies of them be taken as it is for my own satisfaction they have been called for.

* * *

As the meeting, proposed to be held (at nine o'clock tomorrow morning) with the heads of the Great Departments, is to consider important Subjects belonging (more immediately) to the Department of State, The President desires Mr. Jefferson would commit the several points on which opinions will be asked to Paper, and in the order they ought to be taken up.

PRESIDENT GEORGE WASHINGTON'S PROCLAMATION ON RESISTANCE TO THE EXCISE TAX
15 September 1792

The American back-country in the 1790s was intensely democratic. They resented the way in which Secretary of the Treasury Alexander Hamilton's fiscal policies concentrated power in the hands of the upper classes. Other grievances accentuated Western displeasure with the new federal government—the failure to open the Mississippi River to navigation; the dilatory conduct of the Indian wars; the speculative prices for land; and the scarcity of specie. The Excise Act of 1791 that taxed whisky, the chief bartable western product, furnished a convenient peg on which to hang these grievances. For three years, the opposition to this measure increased.

The Excise Act appeared as unjust to westerners as the Stamp Act had been to the colonist. Beyond the Appalachian mountains, distillation was the only practical way to dispose of surplus corn. Whiskey also served as currency—one-gallon jugs passed for a quarter in probably every western store. In western Pennsylvania especially, covenants were formed never to pay the hated tax. In addition, the new tax added to the growing resentment of government meddling. Opponents of the tax, meeting in Pittsburgh (21 August 1792), resolved that "it is insulting to the feelings of the people to have their vessels marked, houses . . . ransacked, to the subject to informers." They declared legal means would be used to obstruct collections of the tax.

Opposition to the Excise Tax centered in the central counties of North Carolina and in the four Pennsylvania counties west of the Alleghenies. Pennsylvania's governor virtually ignored the situation. Washington saw these protests as a movement to overthrow the government. On 29 September 1792, he issued a proclamation warning against unlawful "combinations," stating that the excise provisions would be enforced by the federal government.

Whereas certain violent and unwarrantable proceedings have lately taken place tending to obstruct the operation of the laws of the United States for raising a revenue upon spirits distilled within the same, enacted pursuant to express authority delegated in the Constitution of the United States, which proceedings are subversive of good order, contrary to the duty that every citizen owes to his country and to the laws, and of a nature dangerous to the very being of a government; and

Whereas such proceedings are the more unwarrantable by reason of the moderation which has been heretofore shown on the part of the Government and of the disposition which has been manifested by the Legislature (who alone have authority to suspend the operation of laws) to obviate causes of objection and to render the laws as acceptable as possible; and

Whereas it is the particular duty of the Executive "to take care that the laws be faithfully executed," and not only that duty but the permanent interests and happiness of the people require that every legal and necessary step should be pursued as well to prevent such violent and unwarrantable proceedings as to bring to justice the infractors of the laws and secure obedience thereto:

Now, therefore, I, George Washington, President of the United States, do by these presents most earnestly admonish and exhort all persons whom it may concern to refrain and desist from all unlawful combinations and proceedings whatsoever having for object or tending to obstruct the operation of the laws aforesaid, inasmuch as all lawful ways and means will be strictly put in execution for bringing to justice the infractors thereof and securing obedience thereto.

And I do moreover charge and require all courts, magistrates, and officers whom it may concern, according to the duties of their several offices, to exert the powers in them respectively vested by law for the purposes aforesaid, hereby also enjoining and requiring all persons whomsoever, as they tender the welfare of their country, the just and due authority of Government, and the preservation of the public peace, to be aiding and assisting therein according to law. . .

PRESIDENT GEORGE WASHINGTON'S PROCLAMATION OF NEUTRALITY
22 April 1793

News reached the United States in April 1793, that France had declared war on Great Britain. The wars of the Revolution had now been transformed into a great maritime conflict. Most Americans had followed events of the French Revolution with the keenest interest, and up to a point with complete sympathy. However, now most Americans believed the United States must remain neutral.

President Washington hurried to Philadelphia from Mount Vernon, and after earnest discussions with his Cabinet, decided on a policy of strict neutrality. A proclamation to that effect was drawn up by Attorney General Edmund Randolph and signed by the President and Secretary of State Thomas Jefferson. At the latter's suggestion, the proclamation studiously avoided the word neutrality, hoping that the absence of this would be noted by Great Britain and persuade that power to make maritime concessions to the United States in order to keep it neutral.

Nevertheless, the belligerent powers regarded it as a genuine proclamation of neutrality as indeed it was. The policy fixed was carefully carried out, in adherence to the rigid letter of treaty obligations. The executive regulations issued to enforce the proclamation were soon legislated into the Neutrality Act of 5 June 1794.

The proclamation of 22 April 1793 is a landmark in the history of international law. It set American precedent. The ensuing problems connected with neutrality have constituted a major part of the diplomatic history of the United States.

Whereas it appears that a state of war exists between Austria, Prussia, Sardinia, Great Britain, and the United Netherlands of the one part and France on the other, and the duty and interest of the United States require that they should with sincerity and good faith adopt and pursue a conduct friendly and impartial toward the belligerent powers:

I have therefore thought fit by these presents to declare the disposition of the United States to observe the conduct aforesaid toward those powers respectively, and to exhort and warn the citizens of the United States carefully to avoid all acts and proceedings whatsoever which may in any manner tend to contravene such disposition.

And I do hereby also make known that whosoever of the citizens of the United States shall render himself liable to punishment or forfeiture under the law of nations by committing, aiding, or abetting hostilities against any of the said powers, or by carrying to any of them those articles which are deemed contraband by the modern usage of nations, will not receive the protection of the United States against such punishment or forfeiture; and further, that I have given instructions to those officers to whom it belongs to cause prosecutions to be instituted against all persons who shall, within the cognizance of the courts of the United States, violate the law of nations with respect to the powers at war, or any of them. . . .

PRESIDENT GEORGE WASHINGTON'S PROCLAMATIONS ON THE WHISKEY INSURRECTION
7 August; 25 September 1794

Discontent over enforcement of the whiskey excise tax continued throughout 1793 and 1794. Non-complying distillers from western Pennsylvania had to go to York or Philadelphia for trial, a most costly procedure. In June 1794, Congress passed a law making such offenses triable in state courts. But, while the bill was in Congress, the U.S. District Court of Pennsylvania issued a series of processes returnable to Philadelphia. Citizens of the southwestern counties were outraged. A federal marshal was attacked in Allegheny County while serving a process. On 17 July, several hundred men, led by members of a local "Democratic society" attacked and burned the home of General John Neville, the regional collector of the excise. Rebellious leaders robbed the mails. Pittsburgh seemed on the verge of civil anarchy. A Monongahela Valley convention almost declared independence from the United States.

President Washington issued a proclamation (7 August) ordering all insurgents to return to their homes. He called for 12,900 militia from Virginia, Maryland, New Jersey, and Pennsylvania. Negotiations with the leaders of the insurrection proved fruitless. Washington now issued a second proclamation (24 September) ordering the suppression of the rebellion. Government forces under the command of General Henry Lee, who was accompanied by Secretary of the Treasury Alexander Hamilton and President Washington quelled the demonstrations. (President Washington rode with the troops as far as Bedford, Pennsylvania, before returning to Philadelphia. This was the first and only time in American history when a President took the field with his troops.) The western counties of Pennsylvania were occupied by November. More than a score of prisoners were sent to Philadelphia. All of them were acquitted, pardoned, or dismissed for lack of evidence.

The results of the insurrection strengthened the political power of the Federalists. The defeat of the "democrats" also encouraged investors to accelerate the economic development of the region. Henceforth, those who had a grievance against federal law, had to evolve the doctrine of state's rights as a shelter against national authority.

Whereas combinations to defeat the execution of the laws laying duties upon spirits distilled within the United States and upon stills have from the time of the commencement of those laws existed in some of the western parts of Pennsylvania; and

Whereas the said combinations, proceeding in a manner subversive equally of the just authority of government and of the rights of individuals, have hitherto effected their dangerous and criminal purpose by the influence of certain irregular meetings whose proceedings have tended to encourage and uphold the spirit of opposition by misrepresentations of the laws calculated to render them odious; by endeavors to deter those who might be so disposed from accepting offices under them through fear of public resentment and of injury to person and property, and to compel those who had accepted such offices by actual violence to surrender or forbear the execution of them; by circulating vindictive menaces against all those who should otherwise, directly or indirectly, aid in the execution of the said laws, or who, yielding to the dictates of conscience and to a sense of obligation, should themselves comply therewith; by actually injuring and destroying the property of persons who were understood to have so complied; by inflicting cruel and humiliating punishments upon private citizens for no other cause than that of appearing to be the friends of the laws; by intercepting the public officers on the highways, abusing, assaulting, and otherwise ill treating them; by going to their houses in the night, gaining admittance by force, taking away their papers, and committing other outrages, employing for these unwarrantable purposes the agency of armed banditti disguised in such manner as for the most part to escape discovery; and

Whereas the endeavors of the Legislature to obviate objections to the said laws by lowering the duties and by other alterations conducive to the convenience of those whom they immediately affect (though they have given satisfaction in other quarters), and the endeavors of the executive officers to conciliate a compliance with the laws by explanations, by forbearance, and even by particular accommodations founded on the suggestion of local considerations, have been disappointed of their effect by the machinations of persons whose industry to excite resistance has increased with every appearance of a disposition among the people to relax in their opposition and to acquiesce in the laws, insomuch that many persons in the said western parts of Pennsylvania have at length been hardy enough to perpetrate acts which I am advised amount to treason, being overt acts of levying war against the United States, the said persons having on the 16th and 17th July last past proceeded in arms (on the second day amounting to several hundreds) to the house of John Neville, inspector of the revenue for the fourth survey of the district of Pennsylvania; having repeatedly attacked the said house with the persons therein, wounding some of them; having seized David Lenox, marshal of the district of Pennsylvania, who previous thereto had been fired upon while in the execution of his duty by a party of armed men, detaining him for some time prisoner, till for the preservation of his life and the obtaining of his liberty he found it necessary to enter into stipulations to forbear the execution of certain official duties touching processes issuing out of a court of the United States; and having finally obliged the said inspector of the said revenue and the said marshal from considerations of personal safety to fly from that part of the country, in order, by a circuitous route, to proceed to the seat of Government, avowing as the motives of these outrageous proceedings an intention to prevent by force of arms the execution of the said laws, to oblige the said inspector of the revenue to renounce his said office, to withstand by open violence the lawful authority of the Government of the United States, and to compel thereby an alteration in the measures of the Legislature and a repeal of the laws aforesaid; and

Whereas by a law of the United States entitled "An act to provide for calling forth the militia to execute the laws of the Union, suppress insurrections, and repel invasions," it is enacted "that whenever the laws of the United States shall be opposed or the execution thereof obstructed in any State by combinations too powerful to be suppressed by the ordinary course of judicial proceedings or by the powers vested in the marshals by that act, the same being notified by an associate justice or the district judge, it shall be lawful for the President of the United States to call forth the militia of such State to suppress such combinations and to cause the laws to be duly executed. And if the militia of a State where such combinations may happen shall refuse or be insufficient to suppress the same, it shall be lawful for the President, if the Legislature of the United States shall not be in session, to call forth and employ such numbers of the militia of any other State or States most convenient thereto as may be necessary; and the use of the militia so to be called forth may be continued, if necessary, until the expiration of thirty days after the commencement of the ensuing session: *Provided always,* That whenever it may be necessary in the judgment of the President to use the military force hereby directed to be called forth, the President shall forthwith, and previous thereto, by proclamation, command such insurgents to disperse and retire peaceably to their respective abodes within a limited time;" and

Whereas James Wilson, an associate justice, on the 4th instant, by writing under his hand, did from evidence which had been laid before him notify to me that "in the counties of Washington and Allegany, in Pennsylvania, laws of the United States are opposed and the execution thereof obstructed by combinations too powerful to be suppressed by the ordinary course of judicial proceedings or by the powers vested in the marshal of that district;" and

Whereas it is in my judgment necessary under the circumstances of the case to take measures for calling forth the militia in order to suppress the combinations aforesaid, and to cause the laws to be duly executed; and I have accordingly determined so to do,

feeling the deepest regret for the occasion, but withal the most solemn conviction that the essential interests of the Union demand it, that the very existence of Government and the fundamental principles of social order are materially involved in the issue, and that the patriotism and firmness of all good citizens are seriously called upon, as occasions may require, to aid in the effectual suppression of so fatal a spirit:

Wherefore, and in pursuance of the proviso above recited, I, George Washington, President of the United States, do hereby command all persons being insurgents as aforesaid, and all others whom it may concern, on or before the 1st day of September next to disperse and retire peaceably to their respective abodes. And I do moreover warn all persons whomsoever against aiding, abetting, or comforting the perpetrators of the aforesaid treasonable acts, and do require all officers and other citizens, according to their respective duties and the laws of the land, to exert their utmost endeavors to prevent and suppress such dangerous proceedings. . . .

* * *

Whereas from a hope that the combinations against the Constitution and laws of the United States in certain of the western counties of Pennsylvania would yield to time and reflection I thought it sufficient in the first instance rather to take measures for calling forth the militia than immediately to embody them, but the moment is now come when the overtures of forgiveness, with no other condition than a submission to law, have been only partially accepted; when every form of conciliation not inconsistent with the being of Government has been adopted without effect; when the well-disposed in those counties are unable by their influence and example to re-claim the wicked from their fury, and are compelled to associate in their own defense; when the proffered lenity has been perversely misinterpreted into an apprehension that the citizens will march with reluctance; when the opportunity of examining the serious consequences of a treasonable opposi-tion has been employed in propagat-ing principles of anarchy, endeavoring through emissaries to alienate the friends of order from its support, and inviting its enemies to perpetrate sim-ilar acts of insurrection; when it is manifest that violence would continue to be exercised upon every attempt to enforce the laws; when, therefore, Gov-ernment is set at defiance, the contest being whether a small portion of the United States shall dictate to the whole Union, and, at the expense of those who desire peace, indulge a desperate ambition:

Now, therefore, I, George Washing-ton, President of the United States, in obedience to that high and irresistible duty consigned to me by the Constitu-tion "to take care that the laws be faithfully executed," deploring that the American name should be sullied by the outrages of citizens on their own Government, commiserating such as

remain obstinate from delusion, but resolved, in perfect reliance on that gracious Providence which so signally displays its goodness towards this country, to reduce the refractory to a due subordination to the law, do hereby declare and make known that, with a satisfaction which can be equaled only by the merits of the militia summoned into service from the States of New Jersey, Pennsylvania, Maryland, and Virginia, I have received intelligence of their patriotic alacrity in obeying the call of the present, though painful, yet commanding necessity; that a force which, according to every rea-sonable expectation, is adequate to the exigency is already in motion to the scene of disaffection; that those who have confided or shall confide in the protection of Government shall meet full succor under the standard and from the arms of the United States; that those who, having offended against the laws, have since entitled them-selves to indemnity will be treated with the most liberal good faith if they shall not have forfeited their claim by any subsequent conduct, and that instruc-tions are given accordingly.

And I do moreover exhort all indi-viduals, officers, and bodies of men to contemplate with abhorrence the mea-sures leading directly or indirectly to those crimes which produce this re-sort to military coercion; to check in their respective spheres the efforts of misguided or designing men to substi-tute their misrepresentation in the place of truth and their discontents in the place of stable government, and to call to mind that, as the people of the United States have been permitted, under the Divine favor, in perfect freedom, after solemn deliberation, and in an enlightened age, to elect their own government, so will their gratitude for this inestimable blessing be best distinguished by firm exertions to maintain the Constitution and the laws.

And, lastly, I again warn all persons whomsoever and wheresoever not to abet, aid, or comfort the insurgents aforesaid, as they will answer the contrary at their peril; and I do also require all officers and other citizens, according to their several duties, as far as may be in their power, to bring under the cognizance of the laws all offenders in the premises. . .

WASHINGTON ON THE ROLE OF THE ARMY – PRESIDENT GEORGE WASHINGTON TO MAJOR GENERAL DANIEL MORGAN
27 March 1795

President George Washington took a view of the Army that few such leaders have adopted. In 1794, General Daniel Morgan assisted in suppressing the Whiskey insurrection in western Pennsylvania. After the withdrawal of the main army, districts remained under military control. Morgan successfully pursued a policy of conciliation.

Washington's advice on the role of the army in such a situation was contained in a personal letter to the General. Always polite to a fault, the President told Morgan that he did "not communicate these things to you for any other purpose, than that you may weigh them."

. . . It has afforded me great pleasure to learn, that the general conduct and character of the Army has been temperate and indulgent; and that your attention to the quiet and comfort of the western inhabitants has been well received by them. Still it may be proper constantly and strongly to impress upon the Army that they are mere agents of Civil power: that out of Camp, they have no other authority, than other citizens that offenses against the laws are to be examined, not by a military officer, but by a Magistrate; that they are not exempt from arrests and indictments for violations of the law; that officers out to be careful, not to give orders, which may lead the agents into infractions of law; that no compulsion be used towards the inhabitants in the traffic, carried on between them and the army: that disputes be avoided, as much as possible, and be adjusted as quickly as may be, without urging them to an extreme: and that the whole country is not to be considered as within the limits of the camp.

I do not communicate these things to you for any other purpose, than that you may weigh them; and, without referring to any instructions from me, adopt the measures, necessary for accomplishing the foregoing objects. . . .

PRESIDENT GEORGE WASHINGTON'S FAREWELL ADDRESS
17 September 1796

George Washington could have held the presidency for life had he so desired. But, he had grown weary of politics. He looked forward to returning to his beloved Mount Vernon plantation. On 17 September 1796, Washington issued his famous Farewell Address in which he gave his reasons for retiring. By refusing to run for a third term, he contributed to the two-term tradition in presidential politics broken only by Franklin D. Roosevelt in 1940 and again in 1944.

In his Address, Washington warned the American people against what he believed were the principal internal dangers to the new republic—sectional jealousies and partisan political parties. He then proceeded to urge a foreign policy "clear of permanent alliances." While temporary alliances might prove necessary, he wrote, the nation must remain neutral in the age-old European political struggles and chart its own independent course in world affairs. Ignoring the circumstances in which these words were written, later generations used Washington's valedictory to justify an isolationist foreign policy. But placed in the context of the 1790s, Washington summarized the foreign and domestic dangers facing the young nation as he perceived them.

The Address was never publicly read by Washington. Rather, the President asked his friend David C. Claypoole, editor of the Philadelphia Daily American Advertiser *to print his statement. Other newspapers then copied it. The presidential election (1796) which followed Washington's withdrawal is important because it was the first time in modern history that an elected chief executive of an independent nation had voluntarily surrendered his office and his successor was chosen in accordance with a plan detailed in a written constitution.*

The period for a new election of a citizen to administer the executive government of the United States being not far distant, and the time actually arrived when your thoughts must be employed in designating the person who is to be clothed with that important trust, it appears to me proper, especially as it may conduce to a more distinct expression of the public voice, that I should now apprise you of the resolution I have formed to decline being considered among the number of those out of whom a choice is to be made. . . .

The acceptance of and continuance hitherto in the office to which your suffrages have twice called me have been a uniform sacrifice of inclination to the opinion of duty and to a deference for what appeared to be your desire. I constantly hoped that it would have been much earlier in my power, consistently with motives which I was not at liberty to disregard, to return to that retirement from which I had been reluctanly drawn. The strength of my inclination to do this previous to the last election had even led to the preparation of an address to declare it to you; but mature reflection on the then perplexed and critical posture of our affairs with foreign nations and the unanimous advice of persons entitled to my confidence impelled me to abandon the idea. . . .

In contemplating the causes which may disturb our Union it occurs as matter of serious concern that any ground should have been furnished for characterizing parties by geographical discriminations—Northern and Southern, Atlantic and Western—whence designing men may endeavor to excite a belief that there is a real difference of local interest and views. One of the expedients of party to acquire influence within particular districts is to misrepresent the opinions and aims of other districts. You cannot shield yourselves too much against the jealousies and heartburnings which spring from these misrepresentations; they tend to render alien to each other those who ought to be bound together by fraternal affection. The inhabitants of our Western country have lately had a useful lesson on this head. They have seen in the negotiation by the executive and in the unanimous ratification by the Senate of the treaty with Spain, and in the universal satisfaction at that event through-out the United States, a decisive proof how unfounded were the suspicions propagated among them of a policy in the general government and in the Atlantic states unfriendly to their interests in regard to the Mississippi. They have been witnesses to the formation of two treaties—that with Great Britain and that with Spain—which secure to them everything they could desire in respect to our foreign relations toward confirming their prosperity. Will it not be their wisdom to rely for the preservation of these advantages on the union by which they were procured? Will they not henceforth be deaf to those advisers, if such there are, who would sever them from their brethren and connect them with aliens?

To the efficacy and permanency of your union a government for the whole is indispensable. No alliances, however strict, between the parts can be an adequate substitute. They must inevitably experience the infractions and interruptions which all alliances in all times have experienced. Sensible of this momentous truth, you have improved upon your first essay by the adoption of a Constitution of government better calculated than your former for an intimate union and for the efficacious management of your common concerns. This government, the offspring of our own choice, uninfluenced and unawed, adopted upon full investigation and mature deliberation, completely free in its principles, in the distribution of its powers, uniting security with energy, and containing within itself a provision for its own amendment, has a just claim to your confidence and your support. Respect for its authority, compliance with its laws, acquiescence in its measures, are duties enjoined by the fundamental maxims of true liberty. The basis of our political systems is the right of the people to make and to alter their constitutions of government. But the constitution which at any time exists till changed by an explicit and authenticact of the whole people is sacredly obligatory upon all. The very idea of the power and the right of the people to establish government presupposes the duty of every individual to obey the established government. . . .

However combinations or associations of the above description may now and then answer popular ends, they are likely in the course of time and things to become potent engines by which cunning, ambitious, and unprincipled men will be enabled to subvert the power of the people, and to usurp for themselves the reins of government, destroying afterwards the very engines which have lifted them to unjust dominion.

Toward the preservation of your government and the permanency of your present happy state, it is requisite not only that you steadily discountenance irregular oppositions to its acknowledged authority, but also that you resist with care the spirit of innovation upon its principles, however specious the pretexts. One method of assault may be to effect in the forms of the Constitution alterations which will impair the energy of the system, and thus to undermine what can not be directly overthrown. In all the changes to which you may be invited remember that time and habit are at least as necessary to fix the true character of governments as of other human institutions; that experience is the surest standard by which to test the real tendency of the existing constitution of a country; the facility in changes upon the credit of mere hypothesis and opinion exposes to perpetual change, from the endless variety of hypothesis and opinion; and remember especially that for the efficient management of your common interests in a country so extensive as ours a government of as much vigor as is consistent with the perfect security of liberty is indispensable. Liberty itself will find in such a government, with powers properly distributed and adjusted, its surest guardian. It is, indeed, little else than a name where the government is too feeble to withstand the enterprises of faction, to confine each member of the society within the limits prescribed by the laws, and to maintain all in the secure and tranquil enjoyment of the rights of person and property.

I have already intimated to you the danger of parties in the state, with particular reference to the founding of them on geographical discriminations. Let me now take a more comprehensive view, and warn you in the most solemn manner against the baneful effects of the spirit of party generally.

This spirit, unfortunately, is inseparable from our nature, having its root in the strongest passions of the human mind. It exists under different shapes in all governments, more or less stifled, controlled, or repressed; but in those of the popular form it is seen in its greatest rankness and is truly their worst enemy.

The alternate domination of one faction over another, sharpened by the spirit of revenge natural to party dissension, which in different ages and countries has perpetrated the most horrid enormities, is itself a frightful despotism. But this leads at length to a more formal and permanent despotism. The disorders and miseries which result gradually incline the minds of men to seek security and repose in the absolute power of an individual, and sooner or later the chief of some prevailing faction, more able or more fortunate than his competitors, turns this disposition to the purposes of his own elevation on the ruins of public liberty.

Without looking forward to an extremity of this kind (which nevertheless ought not to be entirely out of sight), the common and continual mischiefs of the spirit of party are sufficient to make it the interest and duty of a wise people to discourage and restrain it.

It serves always to distract the public councils and enfeeble the public administration. It agitates the community with ill-founded jealousies and false alarms; kindles the animosity of one part against another; foments occasionally riot and insurrection. It opens the door to foreign influence and corruption, which find a facilitated access to the government itself through the channels of party passion. Thus the policy and the will of one country are subjected to the policy and will of another.

There is an opinion that parties in free countries are useful checks upon the administration of the government, and serve to keep alive the spirit of liberty. This within certain limits is probably true; and in governments of a monarchical cast patriotism may look with indulgence, if not with favor, upon the spirit of party. But in those of the popular character, in governments purely elective, it is a spirit not to be encouraged. From their natural tendency it is certain there will always be enough of that spirit for every salutary purpose; and there being constant danger of excess, the effort ought to be by force of public opinion to mitigate and assuage it. A fire not to be quenched, it demands a uniform vigilance to prevent its bursting into a flame, lest, instead of warming, it should consume.

It is important, likewise, that the habits of thinking in a free country should inspire caution in those intrusted with its administration to confine themselves within their respective constitutional spheres, avoiding in the exercise of the powers of one department to encroach upon another. The spirit of encroachment tends to consolidate the powers of all the departments in one, and thus to create, whatever the form of government, a real despotism. A just estimate of that love of power and proneness to abuse it which predominates in the human heart is sufficient to satisfy us of the truth of this position. The necessity of reciprocal checks in the exercise of political power, by dividing and distributing it into different depositories, and constituting each the guardian of the public weal against invasions by the others, has been evinced by experiments ancient and modern, some of them in our country and under our own eyes. To preserve them must be as necessary as to institute them. If in the opinion of the people the distribution or modification of the constitutional powers be in any particular wrong, let it be corrected by an amendment in the way which the Constitution designates. But let there be no change by usurpation; for though this in one instance may be the instrument of good, it is the customary weapon by which free govern-

ments are destroyed. The precedent must always greatly overbalance in permanent evil any partial or transient benefit which the use can at any time yield.

Of all the dispositions and habits which lead to political prosperity, religion and morality are indispensable supports. In vain would that man claim the tribute of patriotism who should labor to subvert these great pillars of human happiness—these firmest props of the duties of men and citizens. The mere politician, equally with the pious man, ought to respect and to cherish them. A volume could not trace all their connections with private and public felicity. Let it simply be asked, Where is the security for property, for reputation, for life, if the sense of religious obligation desert the oaths which are the instruments of investigation in courts of justice? And let us with caution indulge the supposition that morality can be maintained without religion. Whatever may be conceded to the influence of refined education on minds of peculiar structure, reason and experience both forbid us to expect that national morality can prevail in exclusion of religious principle.

It is substantially true that virtue or morality is a necessary spring of popular government. The rule indeed extends with more or less force to every species of free government. Who that is a sincere friend to it can look with indifference upon attempts to shake the foundation of the fabric? Promote, then, as an object of primary importance, institutions for the general diffusion of knowledge. In proportion as the structure of a government gives force to public opinion, it is essential that public opinion should be enlightened. . . .

Observe good faith and justice toward all nations. Cultivate peace and harmony with all. Religion and morality enjoin this conduct. And can it be that good policy does not equally enjoin it? It will be worthy of a free, enlightened, and at no distant period a great nation to give to mankind the magnanimous and too novel example of a people always guided by an exalted justice and benevolence. Who can doubt that in the course of time and things the fruits of such a plan would richly repay any temporary advantages which might be lost by a steady adherence to it? Can it be that Providence has not connected the permanent felicity of a nation with its virtue? The experiment, at least, is recommended by every sentiment which ennobles human nature. Alas! is it rendered impossible by its vices?

In the execution of such a plan nothing is more essential than that permanent, inveterate antipathies against particular nations and passionate attachments for others should be excluded, and that in place of them just and amicable feelings toward all should be cultivated. The nation which indulges toward another an habitual hatred or an habitual fondness is in some degree a slave. It is a slave to its animosity or to its affection, either of

which is sufficient to lead it astray from its duty and its interest. Antipathy in one nation against another disposes each more readily to offer insult and injury, to lay hold of slight causes of umbrage, and to be haughty and intractable when accidental or trifling occasions of dispute occur.

Hence frequent collisions, obstinate, envenomed, and bloody contests. The nation prompted by ill will and resentment sometimes impels to war the government contrary to the best calculations of policy. The government sometimes participates in the national propensity, and adopts through passion what reason would reject. At other times it makes the animosity of the nation subservient to projects of hostility, instigated by pride, ambition, and other sinister and pernicious motives. The peace often, sometimes perhaps the liberty, of nations has been the victim.

So, likewise, a passionate attachment of one nation for another produces a variety of evils. Sympathy for the favorite nation, facilitating the illusion of an imaginary common interest in cases where no real common interest exists, and infusing into one the enmities of the other, betrays the former into a participation in the quarrels and wars of the latter without adequate inducement or justification. It leads also to concessions to the favorite nation of privileges denied to others, which is apt doubly to injure the nation making the concessions by unnecessarily parting with what ought to have been retained, and by exciting jealousy, ill will, and a disposition to retaliate in the parties from whom equal privileges are withheld; and it gives to ambitious, corrupted, or delude citizens (who devote themselves to the favorite nation) facility to betray or sacrifice the interests of their own country without odium, sometimes even with popularity, gilding with the appearances of a virtuous sense of obligation, a commendable deference for public opinion, or a laudable zeal for public good the base or foolish compliances of ambition, corruption, or infatuation. . . .

Europe has a set of primary interests which to us have none or a very remote relation. Hence she must be engaged in frequent controversies, the causes of which are essentially foreign to our concerns. Hence, therefore, it must be unwise in us to implicate ourselves by artificial ties in the ordinary vicissitudes of her politics or the ordinary combinations and collisions of her friendships or enmities.

Our detached and distant situation invites and enables us to pursue a different course. If we remain one people, under an efficient government, the period is not far off when we may defy material injury from external annoyance; when we may take such an attitude as will cause the neutrality we may at any time resolve upon to be scrupulously respected; when belligerent nations, under the impossibility of making acquisitions upon us, will not lightly hazard the giving us provocation; when we may choose peace or war, as our interest, guided by justice, shall counsel.

Why forego the advantages of so peculiar a situation? Why quit our own to stand upon foreign ground? Why, by interweaving our destiny with that of any part of Europe, entangle our peace and prosperity in the toils of European ambition, rivalship, interest, humor, or caprice?

It is our true policy to steer clear of permanent alliances with any portion of the foreign world, so far, I mean, as we are now at liberty to do it; for let me not be understood as capable of patronizing infidelity to existing engagements. I hold the maxim no less applicable to public than to private affairs that honesty is always the best policy. I repeat, therefore, let those engagements be observed in their genuine sense. But in my opinion it is unnecessary and would be unwise to extend them.

Taking care always to keep ourselves by suitable establishments on a respectable defensive posture, we may safely trust to temporary alliances for extraordinary emergencies.

Harmony, liberal intercourse with all nations are recommended by policy, humanity, and interest. But even our commercial policy should hold an equal and impartial hand, neither seeking nor granting exclusive favors or preferences; consulting the natural course of things; diffusing and diversifying by gentle means the screams of commerce, but forcing nothing; establishing with powers so disposed, in order to give trade a stable course, to define the rights of our merchants, and to enable the government to support them, conventional rules of intercourse, the best that present circumstances and mutual opinion will permit, but temporary and liable to be from time to time abandoned or varied as experience and circumstances shall dictate; constantly keeping in view that it is folly in one nation to look for disinterested favors from another; that it must pay with a portion of its independence for whatever it may accept under that character; that by such acceptance it may place itself in the condition of having given equivalents for nominal favors, and yet of being reproached with ingratitude for not giving more.

There can be no greater error than to expect or calculate upon real favors from nation to nation. It is an illusion which experience must cure, which a just pride ought to discard. . . .

Relying on its kindness in this as in other things, and actuated by that fervent love toward it which is so natural to a man who views in it the native soil of himself and his progenitors for several generations, I anticipate with pleasing expectation that retreat in which I promise myself to realize without alloy the sweet enjoyment of partaking in the midst of my fellow citizens the benign influence of good laws under a free government—the ever-favorite object of my heart, and the happy reward, as I trust, of our mutual cares, labors, and dangers.

PRESIDENT JOHN ADAMS' REPORT TO CONGRESS ON THE XYZ AFFAIR
19 March 1798

The XYZ affair was a dramatic incident in the bitter dispute between the French Directory and the United States. France issued decrees against American shipping and refused to receive C. C. Pinckney, the newly appointed American minister. President Adams now sent a mission to Paris composed of Pinckney, then in Holland, John Marshall and Elbridge Gerry.

The three commissioners arrived in Paris on 4 October 1797. The French foreign minister Tallyrand stated they would have an audience with the Directory as soon as a report could be prepared on American affairs. Weeks of official silence followed. Meanwhile, three unofficial agents of the foreign minister called on the Americans, later designated in dispatches as X, Y, and Z, suggesting a bribe of $250,000 for Tallyrand, a loan to France, and an indemnity for Adams' criticism of France in his speech to Congress on 15 May 1797. The Americans refused to make such concessions.

On 19 March 1798, President Adams reported to Congress on the failure of negotiations. Only Gerry remained in Paris. Tallyrand intimated that if he departed, a French declaration of war against the United States would ensue.

The publication of the ministers' dispatches by the American government aroused public opinion against France. The incident was given a mysterious quality by the substitution of the letters X, Y, and Z for the names of Tallyrand's agents. Congress suspended commercial relations with France and strengthened the nation's naval and military forces. Tallyrand, now thoroughly alarmed, sought to prevent war. The wise policies he and President Adams then pursued led to the Convention of 1800, which ended the misunderstanding.

The dispatches from the envoys extraordinary of the United States to the French Republic, which were mentioned in my message to both Houses of Congress of the 5th instant, have been examined and maturely considered.

While I feel a satisfaction in informing you that their exertions for the adjustment of the differences between the two nations have been sincere and unremitted, it is incumbent on me to declare that I perceive no ground of expectation that the objects of their mission can be accomplished on terms compatible with the safety, the honor, or the essential interests of the nation.

This result can not with justice be attributed to any want of moderation on the part of this Government, or to any indisposition to forego secondary interests for the preservation of peace. Knowing it to be my duty, and believing it to be your wish, as well as that of the great body of the people, to avoid by all reasonable concessions any participation in the contentions of Europe, the powers vested in our envoys were commensurate with a liberal and pacific policy and that high confidence which might justly be reposed in the abilities, patriotism, and integrity of the characters to whom the negotiation was committed. After a careful review of the whole subject, with the aid of all the information I have received, I can discern nothing which could have insured or contributed to success that has been omitted on my part, and nothing further which can be attempted consistently with maxims for which our country has contended at every hazard, and which constitute the basis of our national sovereignty.

Under these circumstances I can not forbear to reiterate the recommendations which have been formerly made, and to exhort you to adopt with promptitude, decision, and unanimity such measures as the ample resources of the country afford for the protection of our seafaring and commercial citizens, for the defense of any exposed portions of our territory, for replenishing our arsenals, establishing foundries and military manufactures, and to provide such efficient revenue as will be necessary to defray extraordinary expenses and supply the deficiencies which may be occasioned by depredations on our commerce.

The present state of things is so essentially different from that, in which instructions were given to the collectors to restrain vessels of the United States from sailing in an armed condition that the principle on which those orders were issued has ceased to exist. I therefore deem it proper to inform Congress that I no longer conceive myself justifiable in continuing them, unless in particular cases where there may be reasonable ground of suspicion that such vessels are intended to be employed contrary to law.

In all your proceedings it will be important to manifest a zeal, vigor, and concert in defense of the national rights proportioned to the danger with which they are threatened.

PRESIDENT JOHN ADAMS' COMMISSION OF JOHN MARSHALL AS CHIEF JUSTICE
31 January 1801

In retrospect, President Adams' most important decision was his nomination of John Marshall as Chief Justice of the United States Supreme Court. Marshall served from 1801–1835. His thirty-four years on the bench established the prestige of the Court. Taking upon himself the task of writing most of the important opinions, Marshall used the Court to set aside state laws that he determined to be contrary to the federal Constitution. His assertion of the right of judicial review, the doctrine of implied powers, and his broad interpretation of the commerce clause rank him as one of the most important jurists in American history.

The actual circumstances of Adams' nomination of Marshall to the chief justiceship are recounted by Marshall himself in an autobiographical sketch. "On the resignation of Chief Justice Ellsworth," Marshall, then secretary of State, wrote, "I recommended Judge Patterson [William Paterson] as his successor. The President [Adams] objected to him, and assigned as his ground of objection that the feelings of Judge Cushing would be wounded by passing him and selecting a junior member of the bench . . . The President himself mentioned Mr. Jay [John Jay, the first Chief Justice who now was finishing his term as governor of New York] . . . When I waited on the President with Mr. Jay's letter declining the appointment he said thoughtfully 'who shall I nominate now?' I replied that I could not tell . . . After a moment's hesitation he said 'believe I must nominate you.' I had never before heard myself named for the office and had not even thought of it. I was pleased as well as surprised, and bowed in silence."

Adams nominated Marshall on 20 January 1801, the Senate confirmed the appointment on 27 January and the President signed Marshall's commission on 31 January.

To all who shall see these Presents,— GREETING: KNOW YE, That reposing special Trust and Confidence in the Wisdom, Uprightness and Learning of JOHN MARSHALL, of Virginia, I have nominated, and by and with the advice and consent of the Senate DO appoint him CHIEF JUSTICE OF THE SUPREME COURT OF THE UNITED STATES, and do authorize and empower him to execute and fulfill the Duties of that Office according to the constitution and Laws of the said United States; and to HAVE and to HOLD the said Office, with all the powers, privileges and Emoluments to the same of Right appertaining unto him the said JOHN MARSHALL during his good behaviour. . .

PRESIDENT THOMAS JEFFERSON'S
FIRST INAUGURAL ADDRESS
4 March 1801

The 1800 presidential election was a major turning point in American history. For the first time, power peacefully passed from one ruling party to another through a free election. This was a significant accomplishment for the new nation.

Congressional party caucuses selected candidates for President and Vice President— the Republicans chose Thomas Jefferson and Aaron Burr, and the Federalists John Adams and C. C. Pinckney. The Republicans made limited government and personal liberties their main issues while the Federalists described Jefferson as a madman who would bring on a class war and a reign of terror. The bitter campaign was waged through letter writing and newspaper articles. Each side masterfully mobilized its forces, marking the beginning of modern political elections.

Republican electors dutifully cast their votes for Jefferson and Burr. They tied, each receiving 73 votes; Adams obtained 65 and Pinckney 64. The Constitution mandated that the House of Representatives, with each state delegation casting one vote, had to choose between Jefferson and Burr for the presidency. (The Twelfth Amendment to the Constitution, adopted in 1804, requires electors to vote separately for President and Vice President.) On the 36th ballot, Jefferson won a majority of the states and became the third President of the United States.

It had long been popularly believed that at noon, 4 March 1801, Jefferson, unattended by a living soul, rode up the Capitol hill, tied his horse to the picket fence, entered the Senate chamber, and took the oath of office as President. Although this story is not true, it served for many generations to illustrate the inauguration of the "Man of the People." In reality, Jefferson, surrounded by a crowd and some militiamen, left his boarding-house and walked across the open space between it and the unfinished Capitol—the first President to take the oath in the new city of Washington. The ceremony was held in the small Senate chamber. Afterward, the President read his address in a low, almost inaudible voice.

Called upon to undertake the duties of the first executive office of our country, I avail myself of the presence of that portion of my fellow-citizens which is here assembled to express my grateful thanks for the favor with which they have been pleased to look toward me, to declare a sincere consciousness that the task is above my talents, and that I approach it with those anxious and awful presentiments which the greatness of the charge and the weakness of my powers so justly inspire. A rising nation, spread over a wide and fruitful land, traversing all the seas with the rich productions of their industry, engaged in commerce with nations who feel power and forget right, advancing rapidly to destinies beyond the reach of mortal eye—when I contemplate these transcendent objects, and see the honor, the happiness, and the hopes of this beloved country committed to the issue, and the auspices of this day, I shrink from the contemplation, and humble myself before the magnitude of the undertaking. Utterly, indeed, should I despair did not the presence of many whom I here see remind me that in the other high authorities provided by our Constitution I shall find resources of wisdom, of virtue, and of zeal on which to rely under all difficulties. To you, then, gentlemen, who are charged with the sovereign functions of legislation, and to those associated with you, I look with encouragement for that guidance and support which may enable us to steer with safety the vessel in which we are all embarked amidst the conflicting elements of a troubled world.

During the contest of opinion through which we have passed the animation of discussions and of exertions has sometimes worn an aspect which might impose on strangers unused to think freely and to speak and to write what they think; but this being now decided by the voice of the nation, announced according to the rules of the Constitution, all will, of course, arrange themselves under the will of the law, and unite in common efforts for the common good. All, too, will bear in mind this sacred principle, that though the will of the majority is in all cases to prevail, that will to be rightful must be reasonable; that the minority possesses their equal rights, which equal law must protect, and to violate would be oppression. Let us, then, fellow-citizens, unite with one heart and one mind. Let us restore to social intercourse that harmony and affection without which liberty and even life itself are but dreary things. And let us reflect that, having banished from our land that religious intolerance under which mankind so long bled and suffered, we have yet gained little if we countenance a political intolerance as despotic, as wicked, and capable of as bitter and bloody persecutions. During the throes and convulsions of the ancient world, during the agonizing spasms of infuriated man, seeking through blood and slaughter his long-lost liberty, it was not wonderful that the agitation of the billows should reach even this distant and peaceful shore; that this should be more felt and feared by some and less by others, and should divide opinions as to measures of safety. But every difference of opinion is not a difference of principle. We have called by different names brethren of the same principle. We are all Republicans, we are all Federalists. If there be any among us who would wish to dissolve this Union or to change its republican form, let them stand undisturbed as monuments of the safety with which error of opinion may be tolerated where reason is left free to combat it. I know, indeed, that some honest men fear that a republican government can not be strong, that this Government is not strong enough; but would the honest patriot, in the full tide of successful experiment, abandon a government which has so far kept us free and firm on the theoretic and visionary fear that this Government,

the world's best hope, may by possibility want energy to preserve itself? I trust not. I believe this, on the contrary, the strongest Government on earth. I believe it the only one where every man, at the call of the law, would fly to the standard of the law, and would meet invasions of the public order as his own personal concern. Sometimes it is said that man can not be trusted with the government of himself. Can he, then, be trusted with the government of others? Or have we found angels in the forms of kings to govern him? Let history answer this question. . . .

About to enter, fellow-citizens, on the exercise of duties which comprehend everything dear and valuable to you, it is proper you should understand what I deem the essential principles of our Government, and consequently those which ought to shape its Administration. I will compress them within the narrowest compass they will bear, stating the general principle, but not all its limitations. Equal and exact justice to all men, of whatever state or persuasion, religious or political; peace, commerce, and honest friendship with all nations, entangling alliances with none; the support of the State governments in all their rights, as the most competent administrations for our domestic concerns and the surest bulwarks against antirepublican tendencies; the preservation of the General Government in its whole constitutional vigor, as the sheet anchor of our peace at home and safety abroad; a jealous care of the right of election by the people—a mild and safe corrective of abuses which are lopped by the sword of revolution where peaceable remedies are unprovided; absolute acquiescence in the decisions of the majority, the vital principle of republics, from which is no appeal but to force, the vital principle and immediate parent of despotism; a well-disciplined militia, our best reliance in peace and for the first moments of war, till regulars may relieve them; the supremacy of the civil over the military authority; economy in the public expense, that labor may be lightly burthened; the honest payment of our debts and sacred preservation of the public faith; encouragement of agriculture, and of commerce as its handmaid; the diffusion of information and arraignment of all abuses at the bar of the public reason; freedom of religion; freedom of the press, and freedom of person under the protection of the habeas corpus, and trial by juries impartially selected. These principles form the bright constellation which has gone before us and guided our steps through an age of revolution and reformation. The wisdom of our sages and blood of our heroes have been devoted to their attainment. They should be the creed of our political faith, the text of civic instruction, the touchstone by which to try the services of those we trust; and should we wander from them in moments of error or of alarm, let us hasten to retrace our steps and to regain the road which alone leads to peace, liberty, and safety. . . .

Relying, then, on the patronage of your good will, I advance with obedience to the work, ready to retire from it whenever you become sensible how much better choice it is in your power to make. And may that Infinite Power which rules the destinies of the universe lead our councils to what is best, and give them a favorable issue for your peace and prosperity.

PRESIDENT THOMAS JEFFERSON'S FIRST ANNUAL MESSAGE TO CONGRESS
8 December 1801

President Jefferson's First Annual Message to Congress broke the precedent established by Washington and continued by Adams. They had addressed Congress in person. Jefferson sent a written version of his message to each house. This remained the custom until Woodrow Wilson reverted to the original practice in 1913.

Jefferson told the President of the Senate that construction on the new Capitol building made it "inconvenient" for him to personally appear before the Congress. However, his low voice could hardly be heard upon a public occasion anyway and so he used the unfinished Capitol as the excuse. "By sending a message, instead of making a speech," he told a friend, "I have prevented the bloody conflict which the making an answer would have committed them. They consequently were able to set into real business at once." Above all, he confided to another, his "great anxiety" was "to avail ourselves of our ascendancy [the Democratic–Republican party] to establish good principles and good practices; to fortify republicanism behind as many barriers as possible, that the outworks may give time to rally and save the citadel."

It is a circumstance of sincere gratification to me that on meeting the great council of our nation I am able to announce to them on grounds of reasonable certainty that the wars and troubles which have for so many years afflicted our sister nations have at length come to an end, and that the communications of peace and commerce are once more opening among them. . . .

Among our Indian neighbors also a spirit of peace and friendship generally prevails, and I am happy to inform you that the continued efforts to introduce among them the implements and the practice of husbandry and of the household arts have not been without success; that they are becoming more and more sensible of the superiority of this dependence for clothing and subsistence over the precarious resources of hunting and fishing, and already we are able to announce that instead of that constant diminution of their numbers produced by their wars and their wants, some of them begin to experience an increase of population.

To this state of general peace with which we have been blessed, one only exception exists. Tripoli, the least considerable of the Barbary States, had come forward with demands unfounded either in right or in compact, and had permitted itself to denounce war on our failure to comply before a given day. The style of the demand admitted but one answer. I sent a small squadron of frigates into the Mediterranean, with assurances to that power of our sincere desire to remain in peace, but with orders to protect our commerce against the threatened attack. The measure was seasonable and salutary. The Bey had already declared war. His cruisers were out. Two had arrived at Gib-raltar. Our commerce in the Mediterranean was blockaded and that of the Atlantic in peril. The arrival of our squadron dispelled the danger. One of the Tripolitan cruisers having fallen in with and engaged the small schooner *Enterprise,* commanded by Lieutenant Sterret, which had gone as a tender to our larger vessels, was captured, after a heavy slaughter of her men, without the loss of a single one on our part. The bravery exhibited by our citizens on that element will, I trust, be a testimony to the world that it is not the want of that virtue which makes us seek their peace, but a conscientious desire to direct the energies of our nation to the multiplication of the human race, and not to its destruction. Unauthorized by the Constitution, without the sanction of Congress, to go beyond the line of defense, the vessel, being disabled from committing further hostilities, was liberated with its crew. The Legislature will doubtless consider whether, by authorizing measures of offense also, they will place our force on an equal footing with that of its adversaries. I communicate all material information on this subject, that in the exercise of this important function confided by the Constitution to the Legislature exclusively their judgment may form itself on a knowledge and consideration of every circumstance of weight. . . .

Agriculture, manufactures, commerce, and navigation, the four pillars of our prosperity, are then most thriving when left most free to individual enterprise. Protection from casual embarrassments, however, may sometimes be seasonably interposed. If in the course of your observations or inquiries they should appear to need any aid within the limits of our constitutional powers, your sense of their importance is a sufficient assurance they will occupy your attention. We can not, indeed, but all feel an anxious solicitude for the difficulties under which our carrying trade will soon be placed. How far it can be relieved, otherwise than by time, is a subject of important consideration. . . .

PRESIDENT THOMAS JEFFERSON ON THE IMPORTANCE OF NEW ORLEANS
18 April 1802

Jefferson's first administration won the approval of the nation and brought him to the height of his popularity. The major policies of Washington and Adams had not been upset; a social revolution had not occurred.

Jefferson's greatest triumph was the acquisition of the Louisiana Territory, a purchase that doubled the size of the United States. Napoleon had acquired the vast area from France's ally Spain and here he planned to establish a new empire in the Western Hemisphere. Americans shuddered with apprehension. New Orleans was an indispensable port for the shipment of crops grown in the Ohio Valley. If a strong power occupied the city, would the mouth of the Mississippi River forever be closed to American commerce? "There is on the globe one single spot, the possessor of which is our natural and habitual enemy," wrote Jefferson to Robert Livingston, the American Minister to France. "It is New Orleans, through which the produce of three-eighths of our territory must pass to market." Jefferson's fears seemed confirmed when the Spanish in 1802, still in authority, suspended the "right of deposit."

The President now sent James Monroe to Paris; together with Livingston, he had instructions to purchase the city of New Orleans. To their complete surprise, Napoleon offered the whole province. For 80,000,000 francs, or about $15,000,000, the United States obtained some 828,000 square miles lying between the Mississippi River and the Rocky Mountains. An exuberant Livingston exclaimed: "We have lived long, but this is the noblest work of our whole lives. . . From this day the United States take their place among the powers of the first rank."

The news of the great purchase came as a shock to the perplexed Jefferson since Livingston and Monroe had exceeded their instructions. Yet here was an opportunity to double the size of the nation. Did the President have the authority to purchase foreign territory? The flexible Jefferson broadly construed his treaty-making power and approved the sale: "If our friends think differently, certainly I shall acquiesce with satisfaction." On 20 December 1803, the United States formally took possession of the Louisiana Territory.

. . . The cession of Louisiana and the Floridas by Spain to France, works most sorely on the United States. On this subject the Secretary of State has written to you fully, yet I cannot forbear recurring to it personally, so deep is the impression it makes on my mind. It completely reverses all the political relations of the United States, and will form a new epoch in our political course. Of all nations of any consideration, France is the one which, hitherto, has offered the fewest points on which we could have any conflict of right, and the most points of a communion of interest. From these causes, we have ever looked to her as our natural friend, as one with which we could never have an occasion of difference. Her growth, therefore, we viewed as our own, her misfortunes ours. There is on the globe one single spot, the possessor of which is our natural and habitual enemy. It is New Or-leans, through which the produce of three-eighths of our territory must pass to market, and from its fertility it will ere long yield more than half of our whole produce and contain more than half of our inhabitants. France, placing herself in that door, assumes to us the attitude of defiance. Spain might have retained it quietly for years. Her pacific dispositions, her feeble state, would induce her to increase our facilities there so that her possession of the place would hardly be felt by us, and it would not, perhaps, be very long before some circumstance might arise, which might make the cession of it to us the price of something of more worth to her. Not so can it ever be in the hands of France: the impetuosity of her temper, the energy and restlessness of her character, placed in a point of eternal friction with us, and our character, which, though quiet and loving peace and the pursuit of wealth, is high-minded, despising wealth in competition with insult or injury, enterprising and energetic as any nation on earth; these circumstances render it impossible that France and the United States can continue long friends, when they meet in so irritable a position. They, as well as we, must be blind if they do not see this; and we must be very improvident if we do not begin to make arrangements on that hypothesis. The day that France takes possession of New Orleans, fixes the sentence which is to restrain her forever within her low-water mark. It seals the union of two nations, who, in conjunction, can maintain exclusive possession of the ocean. From that moment, we must marry ourselves to the British fleet and nation. We must turn all our attention to a maritime force, for which our resources place us on very high ground; and having formed and connected together a power which may render reinforcement of her settlements here impossible to France, make the first cannon which shall be fired in Europe the signal for the tearing up of any settlement she may have made, and for holding the two continents of America in sequestration for the common purposes of the United British and American nations. This is not a state of things we seek or desire. . . .

President Thomas Jefferson's Request for Appropriations for the Lewis and Clark Expedition
18 January 1803

In his message to Congress on 18 January 1803, President Jefferson asked for an appropriation for an expedition to the Pacific northwest for the purpose of cultivating friendly relations with the Indians. Captain Meriwether Lewis, Jefferson's private secretary was appointed to command the expedition. Lewis chose his friend Lieutenant William Clark as his associate. Both were officers of the regular army. Jefferson instructed them to keep careful journals about the plants, minerals, and animals they found. They also were told to record all information about Indian tribes, trading possibilities, and possible routes for overland migration.

The Lewis and Clark expedition took more than two years (1804–1806). It was a stunning success. More than forty men accompanied them. Each had vigorous outdoor training and were variously skilled in botany, meteorology, zoology, Indian sign language, carpentry, gun repair, and boat handling.

The expedition became a great epic in human advancement. Thousands of miles of wilderness had been traversed and mapped. Important additions to existing geographical and scientific knowledge had been made. The explorers crossed the Rockies and descended along the Columbia River to the Pacific Ocean. Lewis and Clark added greatly to the knowledge of the West and they demonstrated that overland travel was possible in those enormous expanses. Their expedition also strengthened American claims to the vaguely defined "Oregon country" and to the Pacific coast.

. . . The Indian tribes residing within the limits of the United States have for a considerable time been growing more and more uneasy at the constant diminution of the territory they occupy, although effected by their own voluntary sales, and the policy has long been gaining strength with them of refusing absolutely all further sale on any conditions, insomuch that at this time it hazards their friendship and excites dangerous jealousies and perturbations in their minds to make any overture for the purchase of the smallest portions of their land. A very few tribes only are not yet obstinately in these dispositions. In order peaceably to counteract this policy of theirs and to provide an extension of territory which the rapid increase of our numbers will call for, two measures are deemed expedient. First. To encourage them to abandon hunting, to apply to the raising stock, to agriculture, and domestic manufacture, and thereby prove to themselves that less land and labor will maintain them in this better than in their former mode of living. The extensive forests necessary in the hunting life will then become useless, and they will see advantage in exchanging them for the means of improving their farms and of increasing their domestic comforts. Secondly. To multiply trading houses among them, and place within their reach those things which will contribute more to their domestic comfort than the possession of extensive but uncultivated wilds. Experience and reflection will develop to them the wisdom of exchanging what they can spare and we want for what we can spare and they want. In leading them thus to agriculture, to manufactures, and civilization; in bringing together their and our sentiments, and in preparing them ultimately to participate in the benefits of our Government, I trust and believe we are acting for their greatest good. . . .

While the extension of the public commerce among the Indian tribes may deprive of that source of profit such of our citizens as are engaged in it, it might be worthy the attention of Congress in their care of individual as well as of the general interest to point in another direction the enterprise of these citizens, as profitably for themselves and more usefully for the public. The river Missouri and the Indians inhabiting it are not as well known as is rendered desirable by their connection with the Mississippi, and consequently with us. It is, however, understood that the country on that river is inhabited by numerous tribes, who furnish great supplies of furs and peltry to the trade of another nation, carried on in a high latitude through an infinite number of portages and lakes shut up by ice through a long season. The commerce on that line could bear no competition with that of the Missouri, traversing a moderate climate, offering, according to the best accounts, a continued navigation from its source, and possibly with a single portage from the Western Ocean, and finding to the Atlantic a choice of channels through the Illinois or Wabash, the Lakes and Hudson, through the Ohio and Susquehanna, or Potomac or James rivers, and through the Tennessee and Savannah rivers. An intelligent officer, with ten or twelve chosen men, fit for the enterprise and willing to undertake it, taken from our posts where they may be spared without inconvenience, might explore the whole line, even to the Western Ocean, have conferences with the natives on the subject of commercial intercourse, get admission among them for our traders as others are admitted, agree on convenient deposits for an interchange of articles, and return with the information acquired in the course of two summers. Their arms and accouterments, some instruments of observation, and light and cheap presents for the Indians would be all the apparatus they could carry, and with an expectation of a soldier's portion of land on their return would constitute the whole expense. Their pay would be going on whether here or there. While other civilized nations have encountered great expense to enlarge the boundaries of knowledge by undertaking voyages of discovery, and for other literary purposes, in various parts and directions, our nation seems to owe to the same object, as well as to its own interests, to explore this the only line of easy communication across the continent, and so directly traversing our own part of it. The interests of commerce place the principal object within the constitutional powers and care of Congress, and that it should incidentally advance the geographical knowledge of our own continent can not but be an additional gratification. The nation claiming the territory, regarding this as a literary pursuit, which it is in the habit of permitting within its dominions, would not be disposed to view it with jealousy, even if the expiring state of its interests there did not render it a matter of indifference. The appropriation of $2,500 "for the purpose of extending the external commerce of the United States," while understood and considered by the Executive as giving the legislative sanction, would cover the undertaking from notice and prevent the obstructions which interested individuals might otherwise previously prepare in its way.

PRESIDENT THOMAS JEFFERSON'S RECOMMENDATION TO END THE AFRICAN SLAVE TRADE
2 December 1806

By the outbreak of the American Revolution, most colonies had restricted the slave trade. Virginia had forbade importation of slaves in 1768 and other colonies shortly followed. Jefferson condemned the slave trade in the original draft of the Declaration of Independence but the New England traders joined the planters of Georgia and South Carolina to strike out the clause. The Articles of Confederation made no mention of the slave trade.

The Constitution of the United States (Article I, Section 9) forbid congressional interference with the foreign slave trade before 1808. In keeping with Jefferson's recommendation (2 December 1806), Congress officially stopped (2 March 1807) slave importation into the United States after 1 January 1808. The law provided a penalty of forfeiture of vessel and cargo, with disposal of the seized slaves to be left to the state in which the ship was condemned.

The importation of slaves did not stop. Both New England traders and southern planters opposed the action of Congress and smuggling soon became a profitable enterprise. It is estimated that between 1808 and 1816, more than 15,000 slaves were annually smuggled into the United States. Congress at first made little attempt to enforce the law. However, after 1820, when the slave trade was made piracy, an agency was set up to enforce it.

... I congratulate you, fellow-citizens, on the approach of the period at which you may interpose your authority constitutionally to withdraw the citizens of the United States from all further participation in those violations of human rights which have been so long continued on the unoffending inhabitants of Africa, and which the morality, the reputation, and the best interests of our country have long been eager to proscribe. Although no law you may pass can take prohibitory effect till the first day of the year 1808, yet the intervening period is not too long to prevent by timely notice expeditions which can not be completed before that day. . . .

PRESIDENT THOMAS JEFFERSON'S EMBARGO MESSAGE
18 December 1807

President Jefferson faced tremendous difficulties during his second administration as the leader of a neutral nation at a time of a ruthless general European war. He decided to rely on economic pressure to bring the belligerent powers to terms.

The underlying cause for the Embargo was a series of restrictions upon American commerce imposed by the European warring factions. In the early years of the

Napoleonic wars, the United States had grown wealthy as the chief neutral carrier trading with both England and France. Roughly speaking, this period of prosperity lasted from 1793 to 1805. Restrictions then cut these profits. Subsequently the British Orders in Council (1807) and the French Berlin and Milan Decrees (1806, 1807) threatened direct penalties to any neutral ship entering a port of the enemy of either.

Jefferson never considered taking sides with either of the European rivals. He relied on diplomacy supplemented by the threat of economic pressure. When diplomacy failed, he fell back on economic pressure.

The Embargo was perhaps Jefferson's most original and daring measure of statesmanship. It also proved to be his greatest failure. The aim was to suspend foreign commerce for an indefinite period. Attempts to enforce this arbitrary power by the federal government led to an infringement on individual rights, which was contrary to Jefferson's most cherished ideals. But Jefferson was determined to bring the proud belligerents to their knees by withholding from them the raw materials and finished products that they normally received from the United States. The President opposed war but he did not realize that his peaceful substitute posed a galling dilemma.

The communications now made, showing the great and increasing dangers with which our vessels, our seamen, and merchandise are threatened on the high seas and elsewhere from the belligerent powers of Europe, and it being of the greatest importance to keep in safety these essential resources, I deem it my duty to recommend the subject to the consideration of Congress, who will doubtless perceive all the advantages which may be expected from an inhibition of the departure of our vessels from the ports of the United States.

Their wisdom will also see the necessity of making every preparation for whatever events may grow out of the present crisis.

President Thomas Jefferson Discusses the Non-Intercourse Act
1 March 1809

Jefferson to Pierre Samuel du Pont de Nemours
2 March 1809

Jefferson's Embargo failed to achieve its objective. The President had calculated that war-causing incidents would stop and that, in addition, hundreds of thousands of British laborers would be thrown out of work as foreign importations halted. This, he felt, would cause England to re-evaluate the policies of seizing of American ships and impressment of American seamen.

Within one year though, this unilateral attempt to secure a peaceful redress of grievances created an economic depression in the United States. Letters to Jefferson from all parts of the country reveal an astonishing bitterness toward him and the embargo. The commercial counties of New England talked of secession—damning Jefferson and his embargo. Annual exports fell from $108,000,000 to $22,000,000. Businesses failed. Shipbuilding stopped. Wheat plunged from $2.00 a bushel to $.75. Tobacco glutted the idle wharves. On 1 March 1809, three days before the end of his second term, Jefferson signed a congressional resolution repealing his attempt at economic coercion. "The embargo act," admitted the President, "is certainly the most embarrassing we ever had to execute."

Jefferson defended his economic policies in a letter to his friend Pierre Samuel du Pont de Nemours two days before his term expired. The outgoing President also expressed his relief at "shaking off the shackles of power."

. . . After using every effort which could prevent or delay our being entangled in the war of Europe, that seems now our only resource. The edicts of the two belligerents, forbidding us to be seen on the ocean, we met by an embargo. This gave us time to call home our seamen, ships and property, to levy men and put our seaports into a certain state of defense. We have now taken off the embargo, except as to France & England & their territories, because 50 millions of exports, annually sacrificed, are the treble of what war would cost us. Besides that by war we shall take something, & lose less than at present. But to give you a true description of the state of things here, I must refer you to Mr. Coles, the bearer of this, my Secretary, a most worthy, intelligent & well-informed young man, whom I recommend to your notice, and conversation on our affairs. His discretion and fidelity may be relied on. I expect he will find you with Spain at your feet, but England still afloat, & a barrier to the Spanish colonies. But all these concerns I am now leaving to be settled by my friend Mr. Madison. Within a few days I retire to my family, my books, and farms & having gained the harbor myself, shall look on my friends still buffeting the storm, with anxiety indeed, but not with envy. Never did a prisoner, released from his chains, feel such relief as I shall on shaking off the shackles of power. Nature intended me for the tranquil pursuits of science, by rendering them my supreme delight. But the enormities of the times in which I have lived, have forced me to take a part in resisting them, and to commit myself on the boisterous ocean of political passions. I thank God for the opportunity of retiring from them without censure, and carrying with me the most consoling proofs of public approbation. I leave everything in the hands of men so able to take care of them, that if we are destined to meet misfortunes, it will be because no human wisdom could avert them. Should you return to the U.S. perhaps your curiosity may lead you to visit the hermit of Monticello. . . .

PRESIDENT JAMES MADISON'S PROCLAMATION ON WEST FLORIDA
27 October 1810

During President Madison's administration, the two Floridas, East and West, belonged to Spain, a nation that controlled only the area around Pensacola and St. Augustine. The total population included about 12, 000 blacks and whites and about 5,000 Indians. It was a poor area. Nevertheless, Madison was eager to acquire Florida while Spain wanted to retain it. Great Britain opposed American annexation. The Indian population considered it their land. Throughout Madison's presidency, these contenders kept Florida in constant turmoil.

The Louisiana Treaty of 1803 with France made no reference to the status of Spanish-ruled East and West Florida. Jefferson maintained that the Louisiana Purchase included that portion of Spanish Florida between the Mississippi River to the west and the Perdido River to the east. In 1810, Southern expansionists led a revolt in the Spanish dominion. On 26 September they proclaimed the independent state of the Republic of West Florida. Madison issued a Proclamation (27 October) announcing United States possession of West Florida from the Mississippi to the Perdido and authorized its military occupation as part of the Orleans Territory.

Florida remained in turmoil throughout Madison's administration. Finally, the Adams-Onis Treaty of 1819 provided for the cession of Florida by Spain to the United States. In return, the United States assumed some $5 million in claims by American citizens against Spain.

Whereas the territory south of the Mississippi Territory and eastward of the river Mississippi, and extending to the river Perdido, of which possession was not delivered to the United States in pursuance of the treaty concluded at Paris on the 30th April 1803, has at all times, as is well known, been considered and claimed by them as being within the colony of Louisiana conveyed by the said treaty in the same extent that it had in the hands of Spain and that it had when France originally possessed it; and

Whereas the acquiescence of the United States in the temporary continuance of the said territory under the Spanish authority was not the result of any distrust of their title, as has been particularly evinced by the general tenor of their laws and by the distinction made in the application of those laws between that territory and foreign countries, but was occasioned by their conciliatory views and by a confidence in the justice of their cause and in the success of candid discussion and amicable negotiation with a just and friendly power; and

Whereas a satisfactory adjustment, too long delayed, without the fault of the United States, has for some time been entirely suspended by events over which they had no control; and

Whereas a crisis has at length arrived subversive of the order of things under the Spanish authorities, whereby a failure of the United States to take the said territory into its possession may lead to events ultimately contravening the views of both parties, whilst in the meantime the tranquillity and security of our adjoining territories are endangered and new facilities given to violations of our revenue and commercial laws and of those prohibiting the introduction of slaves;

Considering, moreover, that under these peculiar and imperative circumstances a forbearance on the part of the United States to occupy the territory in question, and thereby guard against the confusions and contingencies which threaten it, might be construed into a dereliction of their title or an insensibility to the importance of the stake; considering that in the hands of the United States it will not cease to be a subject of fair and friendly negotiation and adjustment; considering, finally, that the acts of Congress, though contemplating a present possession by a foreign authority, have contemplated also an eventual possession of the said territory by the United States, and are accordingly so framed as in that case to extend in their operation to the same:

Now be it known that I, James Madison, President of the United States of America, in pursuance of these weighty and urgent considerations, have deemed it right and requisite that possession should be taken of the said territory in the name and behalf of the United States. William C.C. Claiborne, governor of the Orleans Territory, of which the said Territory is to be taken as part, will accordingly proceed to execute the same and to exercise over the said Territory the authorities and functions legally appertaining to his office; and the good people inhabiting the same are invited and enjoined to pay due respect to him in that character, to be obedient to the laws, to maintain order, to cherish harmony, and in every manner to conduct themselves as peaceable citizens, under full assurance that they will be protected in the enjoyment of their liberty, property, and religion. . . .

PRESIDENT JAMES MADISON'S PROCLAMATION RESUMING TRADE WITH FRANCE
2 November 1810

Under the administrations of Jefferson and Madison, the United States was treated as a pawn in the wars between Great Britain and France. Both nations attempted to control American oceanic trade through a series of orders in council and decrees. These acts subjected neutral American shipping to illegal searches and seizures. Jefferson and Madison both believed that the halting of American products to the belligerents would force them to acknowledge America's maritime rights as a neutral nation. They were wrong. Both the Embargo of 1807–1809, followed by the Non-Intercourse Act of 1809 hurt American economic interests more than those of Great Britain and France.

In May 1810, Congress made another attempt at economic coercion. Macon's Bill No. 2 authorized the President to reopen trade with Great Britain and France. If either nation ceased its violation of American shipping, the President could prohibit trade with the other. Napoleon gladly seized the opportunity offered by the bill to gain an advantage against his English adversary. The French foreign minister wrote to the American Minister that the Berlin and Milan Decrees (1806, 1807) were now revoked. Madison quickly accepted the statement as a genuine change in French policy. On 2 November 1810, the President instituted a trade blockade against Great Britain.

Whereas by the fourth section of the act of Congress passed on the 1st day of May 1810, entitled "An act concerning the commercial intercourse between the United States and Great Britain and France and their dependencies, and for other purposes," it is provided "that in case either Great Britain or France shall before the 3d day of March next so revoke or modify her edicts as that they shall cease to violate the neutral commerce of the United States, which fact the President of the United States shall declare by proclamation and if the other nation shall not within three months thereafter so revoke or modify her edicts in like manner, then the third, fourth, fifth, sixth, seventh, eighth, ninth, tenth, and eighteenth sections of the act entitled 'An act to interdict the commercial intercourse between the United States and Great Britain and France and their dependencies, and for other purposes,' shall from and after the expiration of three months from the date of the proclamation aforesaid be revived and have full force and effect so far as relates to the dominions, colonies, and dependencies, and to the articles the growth, produce, or manufacture of the dominions, colonies, and dependencies, of the nation thus refusing or neglecting to revoke or modify her edicts in the manner aforesaid.

And the restrictions imposed by this act shall, from the date of such proclamation cease and be discontinued in relation to the nation revoking or modifying her decrees in the manner aforesaid;" and

Whereas it has been officially made known to this Government that the edicts of France violating the neutral commerce of the United States have been so revoked as to cease to have effect on the 1st of the present month:

Now, therefore, I, James Madison, President of the United States, do hereby proclaim that the said edicts of France have been so revoked as that they ceased on the said 1st day of the present month to violate the neutral commerce of the United States, and that from the date of these presents all the restrictions imposed by the aforesaid act shall cease and be discontinued in relation to France and their dependencies. . . .

PRESIDENT JAMES MADISON'S WAR MESSAGE TO CONGRESS
1 June 1812

On 1 June 1812, President Madison recommended a declaration of war against Great Britain. The causes of the War of 1812, like those of most wars, are varied and complex. In his message to Congress, Madison cited the impressment of seamen and the repeated violation of America's neutral rights as major causes. In addition, spokesmen for the West held England responsible for encouraging Indian attacks by supplying them with powder and rifles. Also, land-hungry Westerners coveted the fertile plains of Canada. Henry Clay, the young Speaker of the House Representatives, boasted that the Kentucky militia alone could capture Montreal and Quebec. Even Jefferson thought that the taking of Canada was only a matter of marching. In the South, hostile Indians and runaway slaves took refuge in Spanish Florida. The frontiersmen of Georgia and Louisiana said they would fight for the annexation of Canada with the assumption that Northwesterners would assist in capturing Florida from England's ally. Ironically, the greatest opposition to war came from the maritime sections of New England that suffered the most from impressment and seizures. These areas had endured arbitrary British acts but the profits of successful voyages made confiscation bearable.

Congress acted upon the advice of the President and declared war on Great Britain on 18 June 1812. Madison knew that the United States was not prepared for another conflict with England. Years later, he told the historian George Bancroft he decided upon war by throwing "forward the flag of the country, sure that the people would press forward and defend it."

I communicate to Congress certain documents, being a continuation of those heretofore laid before them on the subject of our affairs with Great Britain.

Without going back beyond the renewal in 1803 of the war in which Great Britain is engaged, and omitting unrepaired wrongs of inferior magnitude, the conduct of her Government presents a series of acts hostile to the United States as an independent and neutral nation.

British cruisers have been in the continued practice of violating the American flag on the great highway of nations, and of seizing and carrying off persons sailing under it, not in the exercise of a belligerent right founded on the law of nations against an enemy, but of a municipal prerogative over British subjects. British jurisdiction is thus extended to neutral vessels in a situation where no laws can operate but the law of nations and the laws of the country to which the vessels belong, and a self-redress is assumed which, if British subjects were wrongfully detained and alone concerned, is that substitution of force for a resort to the responsible sovereign which falls within the definition of war. Could the seizure of British subjects in such cases be regarded as within the exercise of a belligerent right, the acknowledged laws of war, which forbid an article of captured property to be adjudged without a regular investigation before a competent tribunal, would imperiously demand the fairest trial where the sacred rights of persons were at issue. In place of such a trial these rights are subjected to the will of every petty commander.

The practice, hence, is so far from affecting British subjects alone that, under the pretext of searching for these, thousands of American citizens, under the safeguard of public law and of their national flag, have been torn from their country and from everything dear to them; have been dragged on board ships of war of a foreign nation and exposed, under the severities of their discipline, to be exiled to the most distant and deadly climes, to risk their lives in the battles of their oppressors, and to be the melancholy instruments of taking away those of their own brethren.

Against this crying enormity, which Great Britain would be so prompt to avenge if committed against herself, the United States have in vain exhausted remonstrances and expostulations, and that no proof might be wanting of their conciliatory dispositions, and no pretext left for a continuance of the practice, the British Government was formally assured of the readiness of the United States to enter into arrangements such as could not be rejected if the recovery of British subjects were the real and the sole object. The communication passed without effect.

British cruisers have been in the practice also of violating the rights and the peace of our coasts. They hover over and harass our entering and departing commerce. To the most insulting pretensions they have added the most lawless proceedings in our very harbors, and have wantonly spilt American blood within the sanctuary of our territorial jurisdiction. The principles and rules enforced by that nation, when a neutral nation, against armed vessels of belligerents hovering near her coasts and disturbing her commerce are well known. When called on, nevertheless, by the United States to punish the greater offenses committed by her own vessels, her Government has bestowed on their commanders additional marks of honor and confidence. . . .

Not content with these occasional expedients for laying waste our neutral trade, the cabinet of Britain resorted at length to the sweeping system of blockades, under the name of orders in council, which has been molded and managed as might best suit its political views, its commercial jealousies, or the avidity of British cruisers. . . .

When deprived of this flimsy veil for a prohibition of our trade with her enemy by the repeal of his prohibition of our trade with Great Britain, her cabinet, instead of a corresponding repeal or a practical discontinuance of its orders, formally avowed a determination to persist in them against the United States until the markets of her enemy should be laid open to British products, thus asserting an obligation on a neutral power to require one belligerent to encourage by its internal regulations the trade of another belligerent, contradicting her own practice toward all nations, in peace as well as in war, and betraying the insincerity of those professions which inculcated a belief that,

having resorted to her orders with regret, she was anxious to find an occasion for putting an end to them.

Abandoning still more all respect for the neutral rights of the United tates and for its own consistency, the British Government now demands as prerequisites to a repeal of its orders as they relate to the United States that a formality should be observed in the repeal of the French decrees nowise necessary to their termination nor exemplified by British usage, and that the French repeal, besides including that portion of the decrees which operates within a territorial jurisdiction, as well as that which operates on the high seas, against the commerce of the United States should not be a single and special repeal in relation to the United States, but should be extended to whatever other neutral nations unconnected with them may be affected by those decrees. And as an additional insult, they are called on for a formal disavowal of conditions and pretensions advanced by the French Government for which the United States are so far from having made themselves responsible that, in official explanations which have been published to the world, and in a correspondence of the American minister at London with the British minister for foreign affairs such a responsibility was explicitly and emphatically disclaimed.

It has become, indeed, sufficiently certain that the commerce of the United States is to be sacrificed, not as interfering with the belligerent rights of Great Britain; not as supplying the wants of her enemies, which she herself supplies; but as interfering with the monopoly which she covets for her own commerce and navigation. She carries on a war against the lawful commerce of a friend that she may the better carry on a commerce with an enemy—a commerce polluted by the forgeries and perjuries which are for the most part the only passports by which it can succeed. . . .

In reviewing the conduct of Great Britain toward the United States our attention is necessarily drawn to the warfare just renewed by the savages on one of our extensive frontiers—a warfare which is known to spare neither age nor sex and to be distinguished by feature peculiarly shocking to humanity. It is difficult to account for the activity and combinations which have for some time been developing themselves among tribes in constant intercourse with British traders and garrisons without connecting their hostility with that influence and without recollecting the authenticated examples of such interpositions heretofore furnished by the officers and agents of that Government. . . .

Whether the United States shall continue passive under these progressive usurpations and these accumulating wrongs, or, opposing force to force in defense of their national rights, shall commit a just cause into the hands of the Almighty Disposer of Events, avoiding all connections which might entangle it in the contest or views of other powers, and preserving a constant readiness to concur in an honorable reestablishment of peace and friendship, is a solemn question which the Constitution wisely confides to the legislative department of the Government. In recommending it to their early deliberations I am happy in the assurance that the decision will be worthy the enlightened and patriotic councils of a virtuous, a free, and a powerful nation. . . .

PRESIDENT JAMES MADISON'S VETO OF THE SECOND BANK OF THE UNITED STATES
30 January 1815

PRESIDENT JAMES MADISON'S RECOMMENDATION FOR A SECOND BANK OF THE UNITED STATES
5 December 1815

Two generations of Americans debated the constitutionality of the Bank of the United States. Secretary of the Treasury Alexander Hamilton had argued that a national bank was essential for the nation's prosperity and the Bank became a major part of his economic program (1790). In 1811, Congress refused to recharter the First Bank because many representatives seriously doubted that the government had such authority.

The War of 1812 created financial havoc and emphasized anew the need for a national bank. On 30 January 1815, President Madison vetoed a recharter bill because he felt it inadequate for "reviving the public credit," "providing for a national medium of circulation," and "aiding the Treasury" in collecting taxes. In 1791, Madison had argued that the Framers of the Constitution never envisioned such sweeping national powers. However, a quarter of a century later, the "Father of the Constitution" seems to have accepted that the nation's frame of government was a "living" Constitution. He now conceded the legal authority of Congress to enact such legislation.

Madison's Annual Message of 5 December 1815 noted that if state banks could not restore a uniform national currency, "the probable operation of a national bank will merit consideration." Jefferson also retreated from his 1791 position on the Bank and endorsed Madison's recommendation. Congressional debate witnessed a Republican reversal of objections to a national bank on constitutional grounds.

The Second Bank of the United States began operations on 1 January 1817. It was authorized to act as a depository for government funds without paying interest for their use. In most other respects, the provisions followed the First Bank charter. The central office remained in Philadelphia, and in time had twenty-five branches throughout the country.

. . . Having bestowed on the bill entitled "An act to incorporate the subscribers to the Bank of the United States of America" that full consideration which is due to the great importance of the subject, and dictated by the respect which I feel for the two Houses of Congress, I am constrained by a deep and solemn conviction that the bill ought not to become a law to return it to the Senate, in which it originated, with my objections to the same.

Waiving the question of the constitutional authority of the Legislature to establish an incorporated bank as being precluded in my judgment by repeated recognitions under varied circumstances of the validity of such an institution in acts of the legislative, executive, and judicial branches of the Government, accompanied by indications, in different modes, of a concurrence of the general will of the nation, the proposed bank does not appear to be calculated to answer the purposes of reviving the public credit, of providing a national medium of circulation, and of aiding the Treasury by facilitating the indispensable anticipations of the revenue and by affording to the public more durable loans. . . .

Public credit might indeed be expected to derive advantage from the establishment of a national bank, without regard to the formation of its capital, if the full aid and cooperation of the institution were secured to the Government during the war and during the period of its fiscal embarrassments. But the bank proposed will be free from all legal obligation to cooperate with the public measures, and whatever might be the patriotic disposition of its directors to contribute to the removal of those embarrassments, and to invigorate the prosecution of the war, fidelity to the pecuniary and general interest of the institution according to their estimate of it might oblige them to decline a connection of their operations with those of the National Treasury during the continuance of the war and the difficulties incident to it. Temporary sacrifices of interest, though overbalanced by the future and permanent profits of the charter, not being requirable of right in behalf of the public, might not be gratuitously made, and the bank would reap the full benefit of the grant, whilst the public would lose the equivalent expected from it; for it must be kept in view that the sole inducement to such a grant on the part of the public would be the prospect of substantial aids to its pecuniary means at the present crisis and during the sequel of the war. It is evident that the stock of the bank will on the return of peace, if not sooner, rise in the market to a value which, if the bank were established in a period of peace, would authorize and obtain for the public a bonus to a very large amount. In lieu of such a bonus the Government is fairly entitled to and ought not to relinquish or risk the needful services of the bank under the pressing circumstances of war . . . .

On the whole, when it is considered that the proposed establishment will enjoy a monopoly of the profits of a national bank for a period of twenty years; that the monopolized profits will be continually growing with the progress of the national population and wealth; that the nation will during the same period be dependent on the notes of the bank for that species of circulating medium whenever the precious metals may be wanted, and at all times for so much thereof as may be an eligible substitute for a specie medium, and that the extensive employment of the notes in the collection of the augmented taxes will, moreover, enable the bank greatly to extend its profitable issues of them without the expense of specie capital to support their circulation, it is as reasonable as it is requisite that the Government, in return for these extraordinary concessions to the bank, should have a greater security for attaining the public objects of the institution than is presented in the bill, and particularly for every practicable accommodation, both in the temporary advances necessary to anticipate the taxes and in those more durable loans which are equally necessary to diminish the resort to taxes.

In discharging this painful duty of stating objections to a measure which has undergone the deliberations and received the sanction of the two Houses of the National Legislature. I console myself with the reflection that if they have not the weight which I attach to them they can be constitutionally overruled, and with a confidence that in a contrary event the wisdom of Congress will hasten to substitute a more commensurate and certain provision for the public exigencies.

* * *

... The arrangements of the finances with a view to the receipts and expenditures of a permanent peace establishment will necessarily enter into the deliberations of Congress during the present session. It is true that the improved condition of the public revenue will not only afford the means of maintaining the faith of the Government with its creditors inviolate, and of prosecuting successfully the measures of the most liberal policy, but will also justify an immediate alleviation of the burdens imposed by the necessities of the war. It is, however, essential to every modification of the finances that the benefits of an uniform national currency should be restored to the community. The absence of the precious metals will, it is believed, be a temporary evil, but until they can again be rendered the general medium of exchange it devolves on the wisdom of Congress to provide a substitute which shall equally engage the confidence and accommodate the wants of the citizens throughout the Union. If the operation of the State banks can not produce this result, the probable operation of a national bank will merit consideration; and if neither of these expedients be deemed effectual it may become necessary to ascertain the terms upon which the notes of the Government (no longer required as an instrument of credit) shall be issued upon motives of general policy as a common medium of circulation ...

PRESIDENT JAMES MONROE COMMENTS ON THE MISSOURI COMPROMISE – MONROE TO THOMAS JEFFERSON
19 February 1820

A notable feature of the constitutional and economic growth of the nation was the orderly admission of new states into the Union. However, the easy procession of admitting new states was suddenly interrupted by a controversy over Missouri, a controversy which reopened the issue of the extension of slavery.

Prior to 1819, new states had entered the Union without much debate over slavery. Now, there were eleven slave and eleven free states. The admission of Missouri threatened to upset this balance. At the core of the argument was the growing conviction that human bondage violated the very ethos of the Revolution and of the Republic.

On the issue of slavery, President James Monroe's sympathies were with the South. However, his concept of his presidential duties led him to abstain from all interference with the struggle over the Missouri bill until it came to him for his signature. The measure which Congress sent him provided for the admission of Missouri as a slave state but prohibited slavery north of the 36° 30′ parallel in the future. He was by no means certain that Congress had the constitutional power to exclude slavery from states to be formed at some distant date. He submitted the question to the cabinet. Most shared his apprehensions. Monroe finally decided to permit this issue to remain unsettled. He signed the several measures, no doubt the most momentous act of his administration.

. . . The *Intelligencer* will communicate to you some account of the proceedings of Congress on the Missouri Question, & particularly of the late votes taken on different propositions in the Senate. It seems, that a resolution was adopted on the 17th, which establishes a line, to commence, from the western boundary of Missouri, in Lat: 36. 30. & run westward indefinitely, north of which slavery should be prohibited; but permitted South of it. Missouri & Arkansas, as is presum'd, to be admitted, without restraint. By the terms applied to the restriction "for ever" it is inferr'd that it is intended, that the restraint should apply to territories, after they become States, as well as before.

This will increase the difficulty incident to an arrangement of this subject, otherwise sufficiently great, in any form, in which it can be presented. Many think that the right exists in one instance & not in the other. I have never known a question so menacing to the tranquility and even the continuance of our Union as the present one. All other subjects have given way to it, & appear to be almost forgotten. As however there is a vast portion of intelligence & virtue in the body of the people, & the bond of Union has heretofore prov'd sufficiently strong to triumph over all attempts against it, I have great confidence that this effort will not be less unavailing.

PRESIDENT JAMES MONROE'S VETO OF THE CUMBERLAND ROAD BILL
4 May 1822

The growth of the United States stimulated the demand for better internal transportation facilities. Roads, for the most part, were rutted dirt ones which followed older Indian trails. By 1800, however, stone or macadam—spread ten inches deep—was being used to make a nearly flat and stronger road. No state could afford the construction and repair of any extensive road system.

In 1806 Congress authorized the President to appoint three commissioners to survey a road from the Potomac to the Ohio Rivers. By 1816, a road linked Cumberland, Maryland with Wheeling in the western part of Virginia. (In later years, the National Road as it was commonly called, was constructed westwardly through Ohio and Indiana to central Illinois. It eventually became part of U.S. Highway No. 40 in the automobile era.)

By the 1820s, the road was crowded with emigrants pushing westward, their wagons laden with household goods. It was equally crowded with wagons bringing the produce of western farms to eastern markets.

Federal expenditures for roads and other internal improvements became a major domestic issue. Did the Constitution authorize such projects? Both Presidents Jefferson and Madison thought not and supported a constitutional amendment granting such power. President Monroe, in his first Annual Message to Congress (1817), declared that he, likewise, was concerned that the national government did not have the right to spend monies for internal improvements. (The interstate commerce clause of the Constitution had not then been interpreted allowing the federal government to do whatever it wanted so long as its project crossed a state line.)

President Monroe vetoed every bill which came before him involving federal construction projects. On 4 May 1822, in vetoing a bill for repairs on the Cumberland (national) Road, he sent Congress a detailed explanation of his thoughts on internal improvements. He again recommended an amendment authorizing the government to make such expenditures. This debate underscored the sharp differences between a strict interpretation of the Constitution—that is, the federal government could do only what the document literally stated—and those who supported implied powers or a broader interpretation of its clauses.

Having duly considered the bill entitled "An act for the preservation and repair of the Cumberland road," it is with deep regret, approving as I do the policy, that I am compelled to object to its passage and to return the bill to the House of Representatives, in which it originated, under a conviction that Congress do not possess the power under the Constitution to pass such a law.

A power to establish turnpikes with gates and tolls, and to enforce the collection of tolls by penalties, implies a power to adopt and execute a complete system of internal improvement. A right to impose duties to be paid by all persons passing a certain road, and on horses and carriages, as is done by this bill, involves the right to take the land from the proprietor on a valuation and to pass laws for the protection of the road from injuries, and if it exist as to one read it exists as to any other, and to as many roads as Congress may think proper to establish. A right to legislate for one of these purposes is a right to legislate for the others. It is a complete right of jurisdiction and sovereignty for all the purposes of internal improvement, and not merely the right of applying money under the power vested in Congress to make appropriations, under which power, with the consent of the States through which this road passes, the work was originally commenced, and has been so far executed. I am of opinion that Congress do not possess this power; that the States individually can not grant it, for although they may assent to the appropriation of money within their limits for such purposes, they can grant no power of jurisdiction or sovereignty by special compacts with the United States. This power can be granted only by an amendment to the Constitution and in the mode prescribed by it.

If the power exist, it must be either because it has been specifically granted to the United States or that it is incidental to some power which has been specifically granted. If we examine the specific grants of power we do not find it among them, nor is it incidental to any power which has been specifically granted.

It has never been contended that the power was specifically granted. It is claimed only as being incidental to some one or more of the powers which are specifically granted. The following are the powers from which it is said to be derived:

First, from the right to establish post-offices and post-roads; second, from the right to declare war; third, to regulate commerce; fourth, to pay the debts and provide for the common defense and general welfare; fifth, from the power to make all laws necessary and proper for carrying into execution all the powers vested by the Constitution in the Government of the United States or in any department or officer thereof; sixth and lastly, from the power to dispose of and make all needful rules and regulations respecting the territory and other property of the United States.

According to my judgment it can not be derived from either of those powers, nor from all of them united, and in consequence it does not exist.

Having stated my objections to the bill, I should now cheerfully communicate at large the reasons on which they are founded if I had time to reduce them to such form as to include them in this paper. The advanced stage of the session renders that impossible. Having at the commencement of my service in this high trust considered it a duty to express the opinion that the United States do not possess the power in question, and to suggest for the consideration of Congress the propriety of recommending to the States an amendment to the Constitution to vest the power in the United States, my attention has been often drawn to the subject since, in consequence whereof I have occasionally committed my sentiments to paper respecting it. The form which this exposition has assumed is not such as I should have given it had it been intended for Congress, nor is it concluded. Nevertheless, as it contains my views on this subject, being one which I deem of very high importance, and which in many of its bearings has now become peculiarly urgent, I will communicate it to Congress, if in my power, in the course of the day, or certainly on Monday next.

THE MONROE DOCTRINE
2 December 1823

An event in President Monroe's second administration has made his name immortal. In his Annual Message to Congress in December 1823, the President enunciated the so-called Monroe Doctrine, which has become a sacrosanct part of American foreign policy. Europe, declared the Chief Executive, would be forbidden to establish any new dependencies in the Western Hemisphere and could no longer interfere in the affairs of New World nations in any way as to threaten their independence. In future years, corollaries and interpretations would be added to Monroe's statements, making them cardinal principles of the nation's unwritten constitution. No other presidential statement, with the possible exception of Washington's Farewell Address, has won such acceptance from the American people.

There were only two completely independent nations in the Americas in 1815, the United States and Haiti. The next seven years saw rebellious Spanish colonies establish new republics throughout Latin America. During the fall of 1823, Richard Rush, minister to England, advised Monroe that the European powers contemplated destroying these republics by reconquering Spain's former colonies. Russia's Tsar Alexander, in an October 1823 memorandum to the American government, further encouraged such speculation.

Long cabinet discussions followed in which Secretary of State John Quincy Adams played an undeniable influential part. But it was President Monroe who thought of dealing with the Spanish colonial question in his forthcoming Annual Message to Congress.

The President drafted the now famous paragraphs of his 1823 message. Both the initiative and the responsibility of the Doctrine belong to him. But, the principle that the American continents are no longer subject to European colonization had been enunciated by Secretary Adams in his negotiations with Russia over claims their explorers had made along the Pacific coast. It also should be noted that Monroe carefully avoided making any definite commitments when invited by the Colombian government to implement the language of the Doctrine into a treaty of alliance.

Americans cheered the President's message. Editorial comments were overwhelmingly favorable. But the President's words had little practical influence upon Europe's diplomacy. For the next twenty years, Great Britain and France violated the Doctrine with impunity. It was not until the late nineteenth century, when the United States had become a major power, did the Old World finally respect the Monroe Doctrine. By this time, however, the United States managed to turn Monroe's words into a justification for American meddling with the internal affairs of Latin American nations.

. . . It was stated at the commencement of the last session that a great effort was then making in Spain and Portugal to improve the condition of the people of those countries, and that it appeared to be conducted with extraordinary moderation. It need scarcely be remarked that the result has been so far very different from what was then anticipated. Of events in that quarter of the globe, with which we have so much intercourse and from which we derive our origin, we have always been anxious and interested spectators. The citizens of the United States cherish sentiments the most friendly in favor of the liberty and happiness of their fellow-men on that side of the Atlantic. In the wars of the European powers in matters relating to themselves we have never taken any part, nor does it comport with our policy so to do. It is only when our rights are invaded or seriously menaced that we resent injuries or make preparation for our defense. With the movements in this hemisphere we are of necessity more immediately connected, and by causes which must be obvious to all enlightened and impartial observers. The political system of the allied powers is essentially different in this respect from that of America. This difference proceeds from that which exists in their respective Governments; and to the defense of our own, which has been achieved by the loss of so much blood and treasure, and matured by the wisdom of their most enlightened citizens, and under which we have enjoyed unexampled felicity, this whole nation is devoted. We owe it, therefore, to candor and to the amicable relations existing between the United States and those powers to declare that we should consider any attempt on their part to extend their system to any portion of this hemisphere as dangerous to our peace and safety. With the existing colonies or dependencies of any European power we have not interfered and shall not interfere. But with the Governments who have declared their independence and maintained it, and whose independence we have, on great consideration and on just principles, acknowledged, we could not view any interposition for the purpose of oppressing them, or controlling in any other manner their destiny, by any European power in any other light than as the manifestation of an unfriendly disposition toward the United States. In the war between those new Governments and Spain we declared our neutrality at the time of their recognition, and to this we have adhered, and shall continue to adhere, provided no change shall occur which, in the judgment of the competent authorities of this Government, shall make a corresponding change on the part of the United States indispensable to their security.

The late events in Spain and Portugal shew that Europe is still unsettled. Of this important fact no stronger proof can be adduced than that the allied powers should have thought it proper, on any principle satisfactory to themselves, to have interposed by force in the internal concerns of Spain. To what extent such interposition may be carried, on the same principle, is a question in which all independent powers whose governments differ from theirs are interested, even those most remote, and surely none more so than the United States. Our policy in regard to Europe, which was adopted at an early stage of the wars which have so long agitated that quarter of the globe, nevertheless remains the same, which is, not to interfere in the internal concerns of any of its powers; to consider the government *de facto* as the legitimate government for us; to cultivate friendly relations with it, and to preserve those relations by a frank, firm, and manly policy, meeting in all instances the just claims of every power, submitting to injuries from none. But in regard to those continents circumstances are eminently and conspicuously different. It is impossible that the allied powers should extend their political system to any portion of either continent without endangering our peace and happiness; nor can anyone believe that our southern brethren, if left to themselves, would adopt it of their own accord. It is equally impossible, therefore, that we should behold such interposition in any form with indifference. If we look to the comparative strength and resources of Spain and those new Governments, and their distance from each other, it must be obvious that she can never subdue them. It is still the true policy of the United States to leave the parties to themselves, in the hope that other powers will pursue the same course. . . .

President John Quincy Adams' Broad Plan of Internal Improvements
6 December 1825

In his inaugural address, President John Quincy Adams stated his broad plan of internal improvements: "The great object of the institution of civil government is the improvement of those who are parties social to the compact." In his first Annual Message (6 December 1825), the President specifically described his ideas to promote the arts and sciences. He proposed a national university, an astronomical observatory— a "lighthouse of the sky," national roads and canals, sending out scientific expeditions to map the country, in short, to do whatever would improve the lives of the people. Adams expected to finance these programs from the sale of public lands. Northern strict con-

structionists were alarmed. Adams was proposing to transcend the nationalism of Hamilton. Likewise, Southerners thought such extensive executive powers could lead to the end of slavery.

Many sound recommendations by Adams were rudely rejected by Congress, only to be adopted years later. The failure of Adams domestic programs probably had profound consequences for the nation. His ideas could have strengthened American nationality and worked against the growing forces of sectionalism. A vast system of roads and canals, for example, might have tied the Union together. Instead, as Adams predicted, "the clanking chain of the slave" was riveted "into perpetuity."

Adams recommended a national naval academy following the outline John Paul Jones had made during the Revolution. A small appropriation for starting one was placed in the 1827 naval appropriations bill only to be struck out after a raucous debate. Senator William Smith of South Carolina even pointed out that neither Julius Caesar nor Lord Nelson had attended a naval academy. He predicted such a school would produce "effeminate leaders." It was not until 1845, on the eve of the Mexican War, that Secretary of the Navy George Bancroft obtained funds to establish the "Naval School."

. . . Upon this first occasion of addressing the Legislature of the Union, with which I have been honored, in presenting to their view the execution so far as it has been effected of the measures sanctioned by them for promoting the internal improvement of our country, I can not close the communication without recommending to their calm and persevering consideration the general principle in a more enlarged extent. The great object of the institution of civil government is the improvement of the condition of those who are parties to the social compact, and no government, in whatever form constituted, can accomplish the lawful ends of its institution but in proportion as it improves the condition of those over whom it is established. Roads and canals, by multiplying and facilitating the communications and intercourse between distant regions and multitudes of men, are among the most important means of improvement. But moral, political, intellectual improvement are duties assigned by the Author of Our Existence to social no less than to individual man. For the fulfillment of those duties governments are invested with power, and to the attainment of the end—the progressive improvement of the condition of the governed—the exercise of delegated powers is a duty as sacred and indispensable as the usurpation of powers not granted is criminal and odious. Among the first, perhaps the very first, instrument for the improvement of the condition of men is knowledge, and to the acquisition of much of the knowledge adapted to the wants, the comforts, and enjoyments of human life public institutions and seminaries of learning are essential. So convinced of this was the first of my predecessors in this office, now first in the memory, as, living, he was first in the hearts, of our countrymen, that once and again in his addresses to the Congresses with whom he cooperated in the public service he earnestly recommended the establishment of seminaries of learning, to prepare for all the emergencies of peace and war—a national university and a military academy. With respect to the latter, had he lived to the present day, in turning his eyes to the institution at West Point he would have enjoyed the gratification of his most earnest wishes; but in surveying the city which has been honored with his name he would have seen the spot of earth which he had destined and bequeathed to the use and benefit of his country as the site for an university still bare and barren.

In assuming her station among the civilized nations of the earth it would seem that our country had contracted the engagement to contribute her share of mind, of labor, and of expense to the improvement of those parts of knowledge which lie beyond the reach of individual acquisition, and particularly to geographical and astronomical science. Looking back to the history only of the half century since the declaration of our independence, and observing the generous emulation with which the Governments of France, Great Britain, and Russia have devoted the genius, the intelligence, the treasures of their respective nations to the common improvement of the species in these branches of science, is it not incumbent upon us to inquire whether we are not bound by obligations of a high and honorable character to contribute our portion of energy and exertion to the common stock? The voyages of discovery prosecuted in the course of that time at the expense of those nations have not only redounded to their glory, but to the improvement of human knowledge. We have been partakers of that improvement and owe for it a sacred debt, not only of gratitude, but of equal or proportional exertion in the same common cause. Of the cost of these undertakings, if the mere expenditures of outfit, equipment, and completion of the expeditions were to be considered the only charges, it would be unworthy of a great and generous nation to take a second thought. One hundred expeditions of circumnavigation like those of Cook and La Pérouse would not burden the exchequer of the nation fitting them out so much as the ways and means of defraying a single campaign in war. But if we take into the account the lives of those benefactors of mankind of which their services in the cause of their species were the purchase, how shall the cost of those heroic enterprises be estimated, and what compensation can be made to them or to their countries for them? Is it not by bearing them in affectionate remembrance? Is it not still more by imitating their example—by enabling countrymen of our own to pursue the same career and to hazard their lives in the same cause?

In inviting the attention of Congress to the subject of internal improvements upon a view thus enlarged it is not my design to recommend the equipment of an expedition for circumnavigating the globe for purposes of scientific research and inquiry. We have objects of useful investigation nearer home, and to which our cares may be more beneficially applied. The interior of our own territories has yet been very imperfectly explored. Our coasts along many degrees of latitude upon the shores of the Pacific Ocean, though much frequented by our spirited commercial navigators, have been barely visited by our public ships. The River of the West, first fully discovered and navigated by a countryman of our own, still bears the name of the ship in which he ascended its waters, and claims the protection of our armed national flag at its mouth. With the establishment of a military post there or at some other point of that coast, recommended by my predecessor and already matured in the deliberations of the last Congress, I would suggest the expediency of connecting the equipment of a public ship for the exploration of the whole northwest coast of this continent. . . .

Connected with the establishment of an university, or separate from it, might be undertaken the erection of an astronomical observatory, with provision for the support of an astronomer, to be in constant attendance of observation upon the phenomena of the heavens, and for the periodical publication of his observations. It is with no feeling of pride as an American that the remark may be made that on the comparatively small territorial surface of Europe there are existing upward of 130 of these light-houses of the skies, while throughout the whole American hemisphere there is not one. If we reflect a moment upon the discoveries which in the last four centuries have been made in the physical constitution of the universe by the means of these buildings and of observers stationed in them, shall we doubt of their usefulness to every nation? And while scarcely a year passes over our heads without bringing some new astronomical discovery to light, which we must fain receive at second hand from Europe, are we not cutting ourselves off from the means of returning light for light while we have neither observatory nor observer upon our half of the globe and the earth revolves in perpetual darkness to our unsearching eyes? . . .

PRESIDENT ANDREW JACKSON'S FIRST INAUGURAL ADDRESS
4 March 1829

In 1828, all but two states sanctioned popular voting for the electors, forcing politics to take on a new tone as the campaign was fought in newspapers, journals, and before mass meetings. Caucuses of several state legislatures put forth only two candidates—John Quincy

Adams and Andrew Jackson. Very little mention was made of the problems of the day as advocates of each man shunted aside the tariff, internal improvements, and foreign policy, concentrating instead on slanderous statements to arouse partisan hate. In a disgraceful exhibition of unfair tactics, both sides engaged in publishing vituperative pamphlets containing unsubstantiated character assaults. However, an alliance of the West, the South, and the lower classes of the Middle Atlantic states, won the election for Jackson, who was portrayed as the champion of the plain people. The indomitable Indian fighter and military hero received 171 ballots to 83 for Adams—Jackson polled 647,231 votes to Adams' 509,097. In addition, the Democrats controlled both houses of Congress. For the first time since the founding of the republic, a President hailed from an inland state.

As Inauguration Day drew closer, towns and cities along the way from Tennessee to Washington planned elaborate welcoming ceremonies. But the death of Mrs. Jackson on 8 January changed the joy to mourning. Jackson arrived in the capital after a quiet and uneventful trip. On 4 March 1829, surrounded by "gigs, wood wagons, vehicles of every sort crowded with women eager to be near the chief, and followed by the officers of his suite, worthies of the Revolution, and hundreds of strangers without distinction of rank," Jackson walked to the Capitol, and at noon, on the East Portico, took the oath of office.

About to undertake the arduous duties that I have been appointed to perform by the choice of a free people, I avail myself of this customary and solemn occasion to express the gratitude which their confidence inspires and to acknowledge the accountability which my situation enjoins. While the magnitude of their interests convinces me that no thanks can be adequate to the honor they have conferred, it admonishes me that the best return I can make is the zealous dedication of my humble abilities to their service and their good.

As the instrument of the Federal Constitution it will devolve on me for a stated period to execute the laws of the United States, to superintend their foreign and their confederate relations, to manage their revenue, to command their forces, and, by communications to the Legislature, to watch over and to promote their interests generally. And the principles of action by which I shall endeavor to accomplish this circle of duties it is now proper for me briefly to explain.

In administering the laws of Congress I shall keep steadily in view the limitations as well as the extent of the Executive power, trusting thereby to discharge the functions of my office without transcending its authority. With foreign nations it will be my study to preserve peace and to cultivate friendship on fair and honorable terms, and in the adjustment of any differences that may exist or arise to exhibit the forbearance becoming a powerful nation rather than the sensibility belonging to a gallant people.

In such measures as I may be called on to pursue in regard to the rights of the separate States I hope to be animated by a proper respect for those sovereign members of our Union, taking care not to confound the powers they have reserved to themselves with those they have granted to the Confederacy. . . .

Considering standing armies as dangerous to free governments in time of peace, I shall not seek to enlarge our present establishment nor disregard that salutary lesson of political experience which teaches that the military should be held subordinate to the civil power. The gradual increase of our Navy, whose flag has displayed in distant climes our skill in navigation and our fame in arms; the preservation of our forts, arsenals, and dockyards, and the introduction of progressive improvements in the discipline and science of both branches of our military service are so plainly prescribed by prudence that I should be excused for omitting their mention sooner than for enlarging on their importance. But the bulwark of our defense is the national militia, which in the present state of our intelligence and population must render us invincible. As long as our Government is administered for the good of the people, and is regulated by their will; as long as it secures to us the rights of person and of property, liberty of conscience and of the press, it will be worth defending; and so long as it is worth defending a patriotic militia will cover it with an impenetrable ægis. Partial injuries and occasional mortifications we may be subjected to, but a million of armed freemen, possessed of the means of war, can never be conquered by a foreign foe. To any just system, therefore, calculated to strengthen this natural safeguard of the country I shall cheerfully lend all the aid in my power. . . .

PRESIDENT ANDREW JACKSON'S VOLUNTEER TOAST
13 April 1830

The Jefferson Day Dinner, held at Brown's Indian Queen Hotel in Washington, was planned to align the Democratic party with Jeffersonian principles and to celebrate the new alliance between the West and the South. President Jackson gave much thought to the phrasing of his volunteer toast, given after he had heard twenty-four prepared toasts, many of them alluding to state sovereignty and hinting at nullification. Delivered in a most dramatic setting, with John C. Calhoun, the chief exponent of nullification at the table, and described by those present as ringing through the banquet hall like one of the General's strident battlefield commands, it clarified Jackson's position on nullification. His toast also served to strengthen the hearts of Unionists throughout the nation.

Calhoun responded: "The Union, next to our liberty, most dear. May we always remember that it can only be preserved by distributing equally the benefits and burdens of the Union." At the request of Senator Robert Y. Hayne of South Carolina, Jackson agreed to amend his toast for publication to read: "Our Federal Union: It must and shall be preserved." But supporters of nullification could find only small comfort in this concession.

"OUR UNION: IT MUST BE PRESERVED."

PRESIDENT ANDREW JACKSON'S VETO OF THE MAYSVILLE ROAD BILL
27 May 1830

In his first Annual Message to Congress (8 December 1829), President Jackson questioned the constitutionality of federal funds being used for internal improvements. He recommended the distribution of any surplus revenue among the states according to their congressional apportionment. The states could then use these funds at their discretion.

One of Jackson's most outstanding vetoes killed the Maysville Road Bill of 1830. This bill would have required the federal government to buy stock in a private corporation for the construction of a sixty mile road in Kentucky. The President declared that the road lay entirely within the limits of a single state and it had no connection with any national system of internal improvements. If federally subsidized roads and canals were thought desirable, reasoned Jackson, they should be sanctioned by a constitutional amendment.

Jackson's position was easy to justify. He also was well aware that he would be strongly supported by such states as New York and Pennsylvania as they had developed internal transportation systems at their own expense. Likewise, southern states, committed to states' rights and slavery, now opposed federal money for internal improvements.

Jackson vetoed more legislation than all former Presidents combined. He believed that the Constitution, through the veto power, gave him the right to participate in making—or unmaking—the law as well as executing it.

I have maturely considered the bill proposing to authorize "a subscription of stock in the Maysville, Washington, Paris, and Lexington Turnpike Road Company," and now return the same to the House of Representatives, in which it originated, with my objections to its passage. . . .

The constitutional power of the Federal Government to construct or promote works of internal improvement presents itself in two points of view—the first as bearing upon the sovereignty of the States within whose limits their execution is contemplated, if jurisdiction of the territory which they may occupy be claimed as necessary to their preservation and use; the second as asserting the simple right to appropriate money from the National Treasury in aid of such works when undertaken by State authority, surrendering the claim of jurisdiction. In the first view the question of power is an open one, and can be decided without the embarrassments attending the other, arising from the practice of the Government. Although frequently and strenuously attempted, the power to this extent has never been exercised by the Government in a single instance. It does not, in my opinion, possess it; and no bill, therefore, which admits it can receive my official sanction.

But in the other view of the power the question is differently situated. The ground taken at an early period of the Government was "that whenever money has been raised by the general authority and is to be applied to a particular measure, a question arises whether the particular measure be within the enumerated authorities vested in Congress. If it be, the money requisite for it may be applied to it; if not, no such application can be made." The document in which this principle was first advanced is of deservedly high authority, and should be held in grateful remembrance for its immediate agency in rescuing the country from much existing abuse and for its conservative effect upon some of the most valuable principles of the Constitution. The symmetry and purity of the Government would doubtless have been better preserved if this restriction of the power of appropriation could have been maintained without weakening its ability to fulfill the general objects of its institution, an effect so likely to attend its admission, notwithstanding its apparent fitness, that every subsequent Administration of the Government, embracing a period of thirty out of the forty-two years of its existence, has adopted a more enlarged construction of the power. It is not my purpose to detain you by a minute recital of the acts which sustain this assertion, but it is proper that I should notice some of the most prominent in order that the reflections which they suggest to my mind may be better understood. . . .

The bill before me does not call for a more definite opinion upon the particular circumstances which will warrant appropriations of money by Congress to aid works of internal improvement, for although the extension of the power to apply money beyond that of carrying into effect the object for which it is appropriated has, as we have seen, been long claimed and exercised by the Federal Government, yet such grants have always been professedly under the control of the general principle that the works which might be thus aided should be "of a general, not local, national, not State," character. A disregard of this distinction would of necessity lead to the subversion of the federal system. That even this is an unsafe one, arbitrary in its nature, and liable, consequently, to great abuses, is too obvious to require the confirmation of experience. It is, however, sufficiently definite and imperative to my mind to forbid my approbation of any bill having the character of the one under consideration. I have given to its provisions all the reflection demanded by a just regard for the interests of those of our fellow-citizens who have desired its passage, and by the respect which is due to a coordinate branch of the Government, but I am not able to view it in any other light than as a measure of purely local character; or, if it can be considered national, that no further distinction between the appropriate duties of the General and State Government used be attempted, for there can be no local interest that may not with equal propriety be denominated national. It has no connection with any established system of improvements; is exclusively within the limits of a State, starting at a point on the Ohio River and running out 60 miles to an interior town, and even as far as the State is interested conferring partial instead of general advantages.

Considering the magnitude and importance of the power, and the embarrassments to which, from the very nature of the thing, its exercise must

necessarily be subjected, the real friends of internal improvement ought not to be willing to confide it to accident and chance . . . .

In the other view of the subject, and the only remaining one which it is my intention to present at this time, is involved the expediency of embarking in a system of internal improvement without a previous amendment of the Constitution explaining and defining the precise powers of the Federal Government over it. Assuming the right to appropriate money to aid in the construction of national works to be warranted by the contemporaneous and continued exposition of the Constitution, its insufficiency for the successful prosecution of them must be admitted by all candid minds. If we look to usage to define the extent of the right, that will be found so variant and embracing so much that has been overruled as to involve the whole subject in great uncertainty and to render the execution of our respective duties in relation to it replete with difficulty and embarrassment. It is in regard to such works and the acquisition of additional territory that the practice obtained its first footing. In most, if not all, other disputed questions of appropriation the construction of the Constitution may be regarded as unsettled if the right to apply money in the enumerated cases is placed on the ground of usage. . . .

If it be the desire of the people that the agency of the Federal Government should be confined to the appropriation of money in aid of such undertakings, in virtue of State authorities, then the occasion, the manner, and the extent of the appropriations should be made the subject of constitutional regulation. This is the more necessary in order that they may be equitable among the several States, promote harmony between different sections of the Union and their representatives, preserve other parts of the Constitution from being undermined by the exercise of doubtful powers or the too great extension of those which are not so, and protect the whole subject against the deleterious influence of combinations to carry by concert measures which, considered by themselves, might meet but little countenance.

That a constitutional adjustment of this power upon equitable principles is in the highest degree desirable can scarcely be doubted, nor can it fail to be promoted by every sincere friend to the success of our political institutions. In no government are appeals to the source of power in cases of real doubt more suitable than in ours. No good motive can be assigned for the exercise of power by the constituted authorities, while those for whose benefit it is to be exercised have not conferred it and may not be willing to confer it. It would seem to me that an honest application of the conceded powers of the General Government to the advancement of the common weal present a sufficient scope to satisfy a reasonable ambition. The difficulty and supposed impracticability of obtaining an amendment of the Constitution in this respect is, I firmly believe, in a great degree unfounded. The time has never yet been when the patriotism and intelligence of the American people were not fully equal to the greatest exigency, and it never will when the subject calling forth their interposition is plainly presented to them. To do so with the questions involved in this bill, and to urge them to an early, zealous, and full consideration of their deep importance, is, in my estimation, among the highest of our duties. . . .

President Andrew Jackson's Veto of the Bank Bill
10 July 1832

The second Bank of the United States had been granted a twenty-year federal charter in 1816. A private corporation with immense financial powers, the Bank, originally part of Hamilton's financial program, served as the depository for United States funds without paying interest for their use. In return, the Bank and its several branches paid out government drafts and transferred public money free of charge. Its notes were exempt from taxation. But for these privileges, the Bank gave the government a sizable bonus. Through sound programs, the Bank established a reliable and more uniform currency. To those farmers and merchants who favored liberal borrowing policies combined with inflationary programs, the unwarrantable actions of the "monster bank" seemed to resemble a gigantic octopus "sucking the blood from the arteries of the toilers on the farm and in the shop." As the Bank grew, its branches vigorously competed with local banks for business. When several states taxed the branch offices, as they did every other commercial concern, the Supreme Court intervened. In McCulloch vs. Maryland (1819), the Court ruled that a state could not tax a corporation chartered by the United States; as Chief Justice John Marshall said, "the power to tax involves the power to destroy." Thus, the Bank and its branches had still another advantage in their competition with local financial institutions—another reason why animosity increased against the "monster."

In his lengthy first Annual Message to Congress in 1829, Jackson attacked the Bank as being monopolistic and unconstitutional. Proposing a national bank "founded upon the credit of the Government and its revenues . . . which would avoid all constitutional difficulties and at the same time secure all the advantages to the Government and country that were expected to result from the present bank," the President served notice to the directors and shareholders that he would not recommend renewal of the charter.

Jackson vetoed the recharter bill on 10 July 1832. In a stinging message, the President repudiated Marshall and Hamilton and lashed out at the rich men who "have besought us to make them richer by act of Congress. By attempting to gratify their desires we have in the results of our legislation arrayed section against section, interest against interest, and man against man, in a fearful commotion which threatens to shake the foundations of our Union." Nicholas Biddle, the director of the Bank of the United States, described the message as "a manifesto of anarchy, such as Marat or Robespierre might have issued." Beyond any doubt, the Bank now would be the major issue in the 1832 campaign.

The bill "to modify and continue" the act entitled "An act to incorporate the subscribers to the Bank of the United States" was presented to me on the 4th July instant. Having considered it with that solemn regard to the principles of the Constitution which the day was calculated to inspire, and come to the conclusion that it ought not to become a law, I herewith return it to the Senate, in which it originated, with my objections.

A bank of the United States is in many respects convenient for the Government and useful to the people. Entertaining this opinion, and deeply impressed with the belief that some of the powers and privileges possessed by the existing bank are unauthorized by the Constitution, subversive of the rights of the States, and dangerous to the liberties of the people, I felt it my duty at an early period of my Administration to call the attention of Congress to the practicability of organizing an institution combining all its advantages and obviating these objections. I sincerely regret that in the act before me I can perceive none of those modifications of the bank charter which are necessary, in my opinion, to make it compatible with justice, with sound policy, or with the Constitution of our country.

The present corporate body, denominated the president, directors, and company of the Bank of the United States, will have existed at the time this act is intended to take effect twenty years. It enjoys an exclusive privilege of banking under the authority of the General Government, a monopoly of its favor and support, and, as a necessary consequence, almost a monopoly of the foreign and domestic exchange. The powers, privileges, and favors bestowed upon it in the original charter, by increasing the value of the stock far above its par value, operated as a gratuity of many millions to the stockholders.

An apology may be found for the failure to guard against this result in the consideration that the effect of the original act of incorporation could not be certainly foreseen at the time of its passage. The act before me proposes another gratuity to the holders of the same stock, and in many cases to the same men, of at least seven millions more. This donation finds no apology in any uncertainty as to the effect of the act. On all hands it is conceded that its passage will increase at least 20

or 30 per cent more the market price of the stock, subject to the payment of the annuity of $200,000 per year secured by the act, thus adding in a moment one-fourth to its par value. It is not our own citizens only who are to receive the bounty of our Government. More than eight millions of the stock of this bank are held by foreigners. By this act the American Republic proposes virtually to make them a present of some millions of dollars. For these gratuities to foreigners and to some of our own opulent citizens the act secures no equivalent whatever. They are the certain gains of the present stockholders under the operation of this act, after making full allowance for the payment of the bonus.

Every monopoly and all exclusive privileges are granted at the expense of the public, which ought to receive a fair equivalent. The many millions which this act proposes to bestow on the stockholders of the existing bank must come directly or indirectly out of the earnings of the American people. It is due to them, therefore, if their Government sell monopolies and exclusive privileges, that they should at least exact for them as much as they are worth in open market. The value of the monopoly in this case may be correctly ascertained. The twenty-eight millions of stock would probably be at an advance of 50 per cent, and command in market at least $42,000,000, subject to the payment of the present bonus. The present value of the monopoly, therefore, is $17,000,000, and this the act proposes to sell for three millions, payable in fifteen annual installments of $200,000 each.

It is not conceivable how the present stockholders can have any claim to the special favor of the Government. The present corporation has enjoyed its monopoly during the period stipulated in the original contract. If we must have such a corporation, why should not the Government sell out the whole stock and thus secure to the people the full market value of the privileges granted? Why should not Congress create and sell twenty-eight millions of stock, incorporating the purchasers with all the powers and privileges secured in this act and putting the premium upon the sales into the Treasury?

But this act does not permit competition in the purchase of this monopoly. It seems to be predicated on the erroneous idea that the present stockholders have a prescriptive right not only to the favor but to the bounty of Government. It appears that more than a fourth part of the stock is held by foreigners and the residue is held by a few hundred of our own citizens, chiefly of the richest class. For their benefit does this act exclude the whole American people from competition in the purchase of this monopoly and dispose of it for many millions less than it is worth. This seems the less excusable because some of our citizens not now stockholders petitioned that the door of competition might be opened, and offered to take a charter on terms much more favorable to the Government and country.

But this proposition, although made by men whose aggregate wealth is believed to be equal to all the private stock in the existing bank, has been set aside, and the bounty of our Government is proposed to be again bestowed on the few who have been fortunate enough to secure the stock and at this moment wield the power of the existing institution. I can not perceive the justice or policy of this course. If our Government must sell monopolies, it would seem to be its duty to take nothing less than their full value, and if gratuities must be made once in fifteen or twenty years let them not be bestowed on the subjects of a foreign government nor upon a designated and favored class of men in our own country. It is but justice and good policy, as far as the nature of the case will admit, to confine our favors to our own fellow citizens, and let each in his turn enjoy an opportunity to profit by our bounty. In the bearings of the act before me upon these points I find ample reasons why it should not become a law.

It has been urged as an argument in favor of rechartering the present bank that the calling in its loans will produce great embarrassment and distress. The time allowed to close its concerns is ample, and if it has been well managed its pressure will be light, and heavy only in case its management has been bad. If, therefore, it shall produce distress, the fault will be its own, and it would furnish a reason against renewing a power which has been so obviously abused. But will there ever be a time when this reason will be less powerful? To acknowledge its force is to admit that the bank ought to be perpetual, and as a consequence the present stockholders and those inheriting their rights as successors be established a privileged order, clothed both with great political power and enjoying immense pecuniary advantages from their connection with the Government. . . .

On two subjects only does the Constitution recognize in Congress the power to grant exclusive privileges or monopolies. It declares that "Congress shall have power to promote the progress of science and useful arts by securing for limited times to authors and inventors the exclusive right to their respective writings and discoveries." Out of this express delegation of power have grown our laws of patents and copyrights. As the Constitution expressly delegates to Congress the power to grant exclusive privileges in these cases as the means of executing the substantive power "to promote the progress of science and useful arts," it is consistent with the fair rules of construction to conclude that such a power was not intended to be granted as a means of accomplishing any other end. On every other subject which comes within the scope of Congressional power there is an ever-living discretion in the use of proper means, which can not be restricted or abolished without an amendment of the Constitution. Every act of Congress, therefore, which attempts by grants of

monopolies or sale of exclusive privileges for a limited time, or a time without limit, to restrict or extinguish its own discretion in the choice of means to execute its delegated powers is equivalent to a legislative amendment of the Constitution, and palpably unconstitutional.

This act authorizes and encourages transfers of its stock to foreigners and grants them an exemption from all State and national taxation. So far from being "*necessary and proper*" that the bank should possess this power to make it a safe and efficient agent of the Government in its fiscal operations, it is calculated to convert the Bank of the United States into a foreign bank, to impoverish our people in time of peace, to disseminate a foreign influence through every section of the Republic, and in war to endanger our independence. . . .

Experience should teach us wisdom. Most of the difficulties our Government now encounters and most of the dangers which impend over our Union have sprung from an abandonment of the legitimate objects of Government by our national legislation, and the adoption of such principles as are embodied in this act. Many of our rich men have not been content with equal protection and equal benefits, but have besought us to make them richer by act of Congress. By attempting to gratify their desires we have in the results of our legislation arrayed section against section, interest against interest, and man against man, in a fearful commotion which threatens to shake the foundation of our Union. It is time to pause in our career to review our principles, and if possible revive that devoted patriotism and spirit of compromise which distinguished the sages of the Revolution and the fathers of our Union. If we can not at once, in justice to interests vested under improvident legislation, make our Government what it ought to be, we can at least take a stand against all new grants of monopolies and exclusive privileges, against any prostitution of our Government to the advancement of the few at the expense of the many, and in favor of compromise and gradual reform in our code of laws and system of political economy. . . .

President Andrew Jackson's Proclamation to the People of South Carolina
10 December 1832

Nullification was the act by which a state suspended a federal law. The right of nullification was first asserted by Virginia and Kentucky in their Resolutions of 1798 and 1799. These resolutions boldly stated that the Union was a compact between sovereign states. Therefore, the states could rightfully decide when the national government had exceeded its delegated powers—and nullify federal legislation within its borders. The most noted example of nullification occurred in South Carolina. Opposition to the protective tariff developed in the South during the 1820s. This hostility grew to such proportions that the South Carolina legislature carried the issue to the voters. After Congress passed the Tariff Act of 1832, the legislature called a state convention (19 November 1832). This body adopted an Ordinance of Nullification declaring the Tariff Acts of 1828 and 1832 oppressive, unconstitutional, null and void, and not binding on the people of South Carolina. Appeals to the federal courts were forbidden and state officials were required to take an oath to support the Ordinance.

A furious President Jackson issued a proclamation (10 December 1832) in which he denounced nullification as rebellion and treason. He warned the people of South Carolina that he would use every power at his command to enforce the laws. Before the date for the Ordinance to take effect (1 February 1833), measures for reducing the tariff were introduced into Congress. On 11 March 1833, another convention called by the South Carolina legislature rescinded the Ordinance of Nullification. A crisis between South Carolina and the national government had been averted. Both sides claimed victory but most Americans welcomed the fact that the Union had survived a major constitutional crisis. The idea of nullification appeared to be dead.

Whereas a convention assembled in the State of South Carolina have passed an ordinance by which they declare "that the several acts and parts of acts of the Congress of the United States purporting to be laws for the imposing of duties and imposts on the importation of foreign commodities, and now having actual operation and effect within the United States, and more especially" two acts for the same purposes passed on the 29th of May 1828, and on the 14th of July 1832, "are unauthorized by the Constitution of the United States, and violate the true meaning and intent thereof, and are null and void and no law," nor binding on the citizens of that State or its officers; and by the said ordinance it is further declared to be unlawful for any of the constituted authorities of the State or of the United States to enforce the payment of the duties imposed by the said acts within the same State, and that it is the duty of the legislature to pass such laws as may be necessary to give full effect to the said ordinance; and

Whereas by the said ordinance it is further ordained that in no case of law or equity decided in the courts of said State wherein shall be drawn in question the validity of the said ordinance, or of the acts of the legislature that may be passed to give it effect, or of the said laws of the United States, no appeal shall be allowed to the Supreme Court of the United States, nor shall any copy of the record be permitted or allowed for that purpose, and that any person attempting to take such appeal shall be

punished as for contempt of court; and, finally, the said ordinance declares that the people of South Carolina will maintain the said ordinance at every hazard, and that they will consider the passage of any act by Congress abolishing or closing the ports of the said State or otherwise obstructing the free ingress or egress of vessels to and from the said ports, or any other act of the Federal Government to coerce the State, shut up her ports, destroy or harass her commerce, or to enforce the said acts otherwise than through the civil tribunals of the country, as inconsistent with the longer continuance of South Carolina in the Union, and that the people of the said State will thenceforth hold themselves absolved from all further obligation to maintain or preserve their political connection with the people of the other States, and will forth—with proceed to organize a separate government and do all other acts and things which sovereign and independent states may of right do; and

Whereas the said ordinance prescribes to the people of South Carolina a course of conduct in direct violation of their duty as citizens of the United States, contrary to the laws of their country, subversive of its Constitution and having for its object the destruction of the Union— that Union which, coeval with our political existence, led our fathers, without any other ties to unite them than those of patriotism and a common cause, through a sanguinary struggle to a glorious independence; that sacred Union, hitherto inviolate, which, perfected by our happy Constitution, has brought us, by the favor of Heaven, to a state of prosperity at home and high consideration abroad rarely, if ever, equaled in the history of nations:

To preserve this bond of our political existence from destruction, to maintain inviolate this state of national honor and prosperity, and to justify the confidence my fellow-citizens have reposed in me, I, Andrew Jackson, President of the United States, have thought proper to issue this my proclamation, stating my views of the Constitution and laws applicable to the measures adopted by the convention of South Carolina and to the reasons they have put forth to sustain them, declaring the course which duty will require me to pursue, and, appealing to the understanding and patriotism of the people, warnt hem of the consequences that must inevitably result from an observance of the dictates of the convention. . . .

The ordinance is founded, not on the indefeasible right of resisting acts which are plainly unconstitutional and too oppressive to be endured, but on the strange position that any one State may not only declare an act of Congress void, but prohibit its execution; that they may do this consistently with the Constitution; that the true construction of that instrument permits a State to retain its place in the Union and yet be bound by no other of its laws than those it may choose to consider as constitutional. It is true, they add, that to justify this abrogation of a law it must be palpably contrary to the

Constitution; but it is evident that to give the right of resisting laws of that description, coupled with the uncontrolled right to decide what laws deserve that character, is to give the power of resisting all laws; for as by the theory there is no appeal, the reasons alleged by the State, good or bad, must prevail. If it should be said that public opinion is a sufficient check against the abuse of this power, it may be asked why it is not deemed a sufficient guard against the passage of an unconstitutional act by Congress? There is, however, a restraint in this last case which makes the assumed power of a State more indefensible, and which does not exist in the other. There are two appeals from an unconstitutional act passed by Congress— one to the judiciary, the other to the people and the States. There is no appeal from the State decision in theory, and the practical illustration shows that the courts are closed against an application to review it, both judges and jurors being sworn to decide in its favor. But reasoning on this subject is superfluous when our social compact, in express terms, declares that the laws of the United States, its Constitution, and treaties made under it are the supreme law of the land, and, for greater caution, adds "that the judges in every State shall be bound thereby, anything in the constitution or laws of any State to the contrary notwithstanding." And it may be asserted without fear of refutation that no federative government could exist without a similar provision. Look for a moment to the consequence. If South Carolina considers the revenue laws unconstitutional and has a right to prevent their execution in the port of Charleston, there would be a clear constitutional objection to their collection in every other port; and no revenue could be collected anywhere, for all imposts must be equal. It is no answer to repeat that an unconstitutional law is no law so long as the question of its legality is to be decided by the State itself, for every law operating injuriously upon any local interest will be perhaps thought, and certainly represented, as unconstitutional, and, as has been shown, there is no appeal. . . .

The Constitution has given, expressly, to Congress the right of raising revenue and of determining the sum the public exigencies will require. The States have no control over the exercise of this right other than that which results from the power of changing the representatives who abuse it, and thus procure redress. Congress may undoubtedly abuse this discretionary power; but the same may be said of others with which they are vested. Yet the discretion must exist somewhere. The Constitution has given it to the representatives of all the people, checked by the representatives of the States and by the Executive power. The South Carolina construction gives it to the legislature or the convention of a single State, where neither the people of the different States, nor the States in their separate capacity, nor the Chief Magistrate elected by the people have any representation. Which is the most discreet disposition of the power? I do not ask you, fellow-citizens, which is the constitutional disposition; that instrument speaks a language not to be misunderstood. But if you were assembled in general convention, which would you think the safest depository of this discretionary power in the last resort? Would you add a clause giving it to each of the State, or would you sanction the wise provisions already made by your Constitution? If this should be the result of your deliberations when providing for the future, are you, can you, be ready to risk all that we hold dear, to establish, for a temporary and a local purpose, that which you must acknowledge to be destructive, and even absurd, as a general provision? Carry out the consequences of this right vested in the different States, and you must perceive that the crisis your conduct presents at this day would recur whenever any law of the United States displeased any of the States, and that we should soon cease to be a nation. . . .

These are the allegations contained in the ordinance. Examine them seriously, my fellow-citizens; judge for yourselves. I appeal to you to determine whether they are so clear, so convincing, as to leave no doubt of their correctness; and even if you should come to this conclusion, how far they justify the reckless, destructive course which you are directed to pursue. Review these objections and the conclusions drawn from them once more. What are they? Every law, then, for raising revenue, according to the South Carolina ordinance, may be rightfully annulled, unless it be so framed as no law ever will or can be framed. Congress have a right to pass laws for raising revenue and each State have a right to oppose their execution—two rights directly opposed to each other; and yet is this absurdity supposed to be contained in an instrument drawn for the express purpose of avoiding collisions between the States and the General Government by an assembly of the most enlightened statesmen and purest patriots ever embodied for a similar purpose. . . .

This right to secede is deduced from the nature of the Constitution, which, they say, is a compact between sovereign States who have preserved their whole sovereignty and therefore are subject to no superior; that because they made the compact they can break it when in their opinion it has been departed from by the other States. Fallacious as this course of reasoning is, it enlists State pride and finds advocates in the honest prejudices of those who have not studied the nature of our Government sufficiently to see the radical error on which it rests.

The people of the United States formed the Constitution, acting through the State legislatures in making the compact, to meet and discuss its provisions, and acting in separate conventions when they ratified those provisions; but the terms used in its construction show it to be a Govern-

ment in which the people of all the States, collectively, are represented. We are *one people* in the choice of President and Vice-President. Here the States have no other agency than to direct the mode in which the votes shall be given. The candidates having the majority of all the votes are chosen. The electors of a majority of States may have given their votes for one candidate, and yet another may be chosen. The people, then, and not the States, are represented in the executive branch. . . .

The Constitution of the United States, then, forms a *government,* not a league; and whether it be formed by compact between the States or in any other manner, its character is the same. It is a Government in which all the people are presented, which operates directly on the people individually, not upon the States; they retained all the power they did not grant. But each State, having expressly parted with so many powers as to constitute, jointly with the other States, a single nation, can not, from that period, possess any right to secede, because such secession does not break a league, but destroys the unity of a nation; and any injury to that unity is not only a breach which would result from the contravention of a compact, but it is an offense against the whole Union. To say that any State may at pleasure secede from the Union is to say that the United States are not a nation, because it would be a solecism to contend that any part of a nation might dissolve its connection with the other parts, to their injury or ruin, without committing any offense. Secession, like any other revolutionary act, may be morally justified by the extremity of oppression; but to call it a constitutional right is confounding the meaning of terms, and can only be done through gross error or to deceive those who are willing to assert a right, but would pause before they made a revolution or incur the penalties consequent on a failure.

Because the Union was formed by a compact, it is said the parties to that compact may, when they feel themselves aggrieved, depart from it; but it is precisely because it is a compact that they can not. A compact is an agreement or binding obligation. . . .

Fellow-citizens of my native State, let me not only admonish you, as the First Magistrate of our common country, not to incur the penalty of its laws, but use the influence that a father would over his children whom he saw rushing to certain ruin. In that paternal language, with that paternal feeling, let me tell you, my countrymen, that you are deluded by men who are either deceived themselves or wish to deceive you. Mark under what pretenses you have been led on to the brink of insurrection and treason on which you stand. First, a diminution of the value of your staple commodity, lowered by overproduction in other quarters, and the consequent diminution in the value of your lands were the sole effect of the tariff laws. The effect of those laws was confessedly injurious, but the evil was greatly exaggerated by the unfounded theory you were taught to

believe—that its burthens were in proportion to your exports, not to your consumption of imported articles. Your pride was roused by the assertion that a submission to those laws was a state of vassalage and that resistance to them was equal in patriotic merit to the opposition our fathers offered to the oppressive laws of Great Britain. You were told that this opposition might be peaceably, might be constitutionally, made; that you might enjoy all the advantages of the Union and bear none of its burthens. Eloquent appeals to your passions, to your State pride, to your native courage, to your sense of real injury, were used to prepare you for the period when the mask which concealed the hideous features of *disunion* should be taken off. It fell, and you were made to look with complacency on objects which not long since you would have regarded with horror. Look back to the arts which have brought you to this state; look forward to the consequences to which it must inevitably lead! Look back to what was first told you as an inducement to enter into this dangerous course. The great political truth was repeated to you that you had the revolutionary right of resisting all laws that were palpably unconstitutional and intolerably oppressive. It was added that the right to nullify a law rested on the same principle, but that it was a peaceable remedy. This character which was given to it made you receive with too much confidence the assertions that were made of the unconstitutionality of the law and its oppressive effects. Mark, my fellow-citizens, that by the admission of your leaders the unconstitutionality must be *palpable,* or it will not justify either resistance or nullification. What is the meaning of the word *palpable* in the sense in which it is here used? That which is apparent to everyone; that which no man of ordinary intellect will fail to perceive. Is the unconstitutionality of these laws of that description? Let those among your leaders who once approved and advocated the principle of protective duties answer the question; and let them choose whether they will be considered as incapable then of perceiving that which must have been apparent to every man of common understanding, or as imposing upon your confidence and endeavoring to mislead you now. In either case they are unsafe guides in the perilous path they urge you to tread. Ponder well on this circumstance, and you will know how to appreciate the exaggerated language they address to you. They are not champions of liberty, emulating the fame of our Revolutionary fathers, nor are you an oppressed people, contending, as they repeat to you, against worse than colonial vassalage.

You are free members of a flourishing and happy Union. There is no settled design to oppress you. . . .

. . . Snatch from the archives of your State the disorganizing edict of its convention; bid its members to reassemble and promulgate the decided expressions of your will to remain in the path which alone can conduct you to safety, prosperity, and honor. Tell them that compared to disunion all other evils are light, because that brings with it an accumulation of all. Declare that you will never take the field unless the star-spangled banner of your country shall float over you; that you will not be stigmatized when dead, and dishonored and scorned while you live, as the authors of the first attack on the Constitution of your country. Its destroyers you can not be. You may disturb its peace, you may interrupt the course of its prosperity, you may cloud its reputation for stability; but its tranquillity will be restored, its prosperity will return, and the stain upon its national character will be transferred and remain an eternal blot on the memory of those who caused the disorder. . . .

PRESIDENT ANDREW JACKSON ORDERS FEDERAL TROOPS TO SUPPRESS A LABOR STRIKE
29 January 1834

For most of the nation's first century, the federal government rarely participated in shaping labor policy. Under the then prevailing constitutional interpretations, labor issues remained within the jurisdiction of the states.

A rare exception to such noninvolvement occurred on 29 January 1834. President Andrew Jackson ordered the War Department to send federal troops to suppress "riotous assembly" among Irish immigrant workers then constructing the Chesapeake and Ohio Canal near Williamsport, Maryland. Jackson claimed that the incident fell within federal jurisdiction under the interstate commerce clause of the Constitution. This was the first time in American history that federal troops were used to intervene in a labor dispute.

The Secretary of War will forthwith order such military as will be able to aid the civil authority of Maryland to put down the riotous assembly named within [on the Chesapeake and Ohio Canal]—at least two companies of regulars with as much expedition as possible.

PRESIDENT ANDREW JACKSON'S MESSAGE ON THE REMOVAL OF SOUTHERN INDIANS
7 December 1835

The idea of removing Indians, the Native American population, to lands west of the Mississippi River seems to have originated with Thomas Jefferson. While contemplating the purchase of the Louisiana Territory in 1803, Jefferson drafted a constitutional amendment authorizing Congress to exchange lands west of the Mississippi for lands owned by Indians east of it. He never submitted his amendment to Congress but the idea of Indian removal was not abandoned. The Act of 1804, which established the Territory of Louisiana, contained a clause that authorized the President "to stipulate with any Indian tribes owning land on the east side of the Mississippi, and residing thereon, for an exchange of lands, the property of the United States, on the west side of the Mississippi, in case the said tribes shall remove and settle thereon." However, for the next two decades, the old practice continued of extinguishing Indian land titles by treaties which made no provision for the displaced peoples.

President Andrew Jackson relentlessly pursued the complete removal of Indians living east of the Mississippi. In 1830, at his insistence, Congress authorized the President to exchange lands held by tribes within the states for land in the Great Plains, an area then thought to be unsuited for white habitation. Forceful Indian cessions now accelerated as American settlers swept westward.

However, it was in the South that the removal policy encountered its most stubborn resistance, a resistance which led to tragic results. Here the tribes, especially the Cherokee and the Creeks, had permanent homes and farms on which they maintained cattle

herds, raised varied crops, built grist mills, sent their children to missionary schools, and
had representative governments. They opposed the arguments, threats and bribes
offered by agents sent to induce them to remove to the Great Plains.

In 1828, Georgia declared the laws of the Cherokee Nation would be void after
1 June 1830. White residents living within the Nation, notably missionaries, had to ob-
tain a license from the Governor of Georgia and take an allegiance to the state. Chief
Justice John Marshall held for the Supreme Court in 1832 that the Cherokee Nation had
exclusive jurisdiction within its own territory and Georgia law "can have no force"
there. Georgia defied the Court and was supported by Jackson who is reported to have
said: "John Marshall has made his decision, now let him enforce it."

Jackson pursued a sweeping policy of removing the Indian population to the Great
Plains. During his two terms, at least 94 treaties were concluded under coercion. Finally,
under the Treaty of 29 December 1835, the Cherokees surrendered to the United States
all their lands east of the Mississippi in return for transportation costs and land in the
new Indian territory.

Jackson explained his removal policy of the southern Indians in his Seventh Annual
Message to Congress.

. . . The plan of removing the aboriginal people who yet remain within the settled portions of the United States to the country west of the Mississippi River approaches its consummation. It was adopted on the most mature consideration of the condition of this race, and ought to be persisted in till the object is accomplished, and prosecuted with as much vigor as a just regard to their circumstances will permit, and as fast as their consent can be obtained. All preceding experiments for the improvement of the Indians have failed. It seems now to be an established fact that they can not live in contact with a civilized community and prosper. Ages of fruitless endeavors have at length brought us to a knowledge of this principle of intercommunication with them. The past we can not recall, but the future we can provide for. Independently of the treaty stipulations into which we have entered with the various tribes for the usufructuary rights they have ceded to us, no one can doubt the moral duty of the Government of the United States to protect and if possible to preserve and perpetuate the scattered remnants of this race which are left within our borders. In the discharge of this duty an extensive region in the West has been assigned for their permanent residence. It has been divided into districts and allotted among them. Many have already removed and others are preparing to go, and with the exception of two small bands living in Ohio and Indiana, not exceeding 1,500 persons, and of the

Cherokees, all the tribes on the east side of the Mississippi, and extending from Lake Michigan to Florida, have entered into engagements which will lead to their transplantation.

The plan for their removal and reestablishment is founded upon the knowledge we have gained of their character and habits, and has been dictated by a spirit of enlarged liberality. A territory exceeding in extent that relinquished has been granted to each tribe. Of its climate, fertility, and capacity to support an Indian population the representations are highly favorable. To these districts the Indians are removed at the expense of the United States, and with certain supplies of clothing, arms, ammunition, and other indispensable articles; they are also furnished gratuitously with provisions for the period of a year after their arrival at their new homes. In that time, from the nature of the country and of the products raised by them, they can subsist themselves by agricultural labor, if they choose to resort to that mode of life; if they do not they are upon the skirts of the great prairies, where countless herds of buffalo roam, and a short time suffices to adapt their own habits to the changes which a change of the animals destined for their food may require. Ample arrangements have also been made for the support of schools; in some instances council houses and churches are to be erected, dwellings constructed for the chiefs, and mills for common use. Funds have been set apart for the maintenance of the poor; the most necessary mechanical arts have been introduced, and blacksmiths, gunsmiths, wheelwrights, millwrights, etc., are supported among them. Steel and iron, and sometimes salt, are purchased for them, and plows and other farming utensils, domestic animals, looms, spinning wheels, cards, etc., are presented to them. And besides these beneficial arrangements, annuities are in all cases paid, amounting in some instances to more than $30 for each individual of the tribe, and in all cases sufficiently great, if justly divided and prudently expended, to enable them, in addition to their own exertions, to live comfortably. And as a stimulus for exertion, it is now provided by law that "in all cases of the appointment of interpreters or other persons employed for the benefit of the Indians a preference shall be given to persons of Indian descent, if such can be found who are properly qualified for the discharge of the duties."

Such are the arrangements for the physical comfort and for the moral improvement of the Indians. The necessary measures for their political advancement and for their separation from our citizens have not been neglected. The pledge of the United States has been given by Congress that the country destined for the residence of this people shall be forever "secured and and guaranteed to them." A country west of Missouri and Arkansas has been assigned to them, into which the white settlements are not to be pushed. No political communities can be formed in that extensive region, except those which are established by the Indians themselves or by the United States for them and with their concurrence. A barrier has thus been raised for their protection against the encroachment of our citizens, and guarding the Indians as far as possible from those evils which have brought them to their present condition. . . .

Some general legislation seems necessary for the regulation of the relations which will exist in this new state of things between the Government and people of the United States and these transplanted Indian tribes, and for the establishment among the latter, and with their own consent, of some principles of intercommunication which their juxtaposition will call for; that moral may be substituted for physical force, the authority of a few and simple laws for the tomahawk, and that an end may be put to those bloody wars whose prosecution seems to have made part of their social system. . . .

PRESIDENT ANDREW JACKSON'S FAREWELL ADDRESS
4 March 1837

President Andrew Jackson's administration ranks as one of the most important in American history. He was not a theorist. He met issues as they arose, sometimes acting on his own initiative but more often on the suggestions of his advisors. He had little understanding of the democratic movement that bears his name. He supported it primarily because it supported him. Jackson lived in a time of heroes—and he must be considered one of America's greatest heroes with all of the glamour that goes with such a colorful personality. On 4 March 1837, Jackson, now nearing his seventieth birthday, witnessed the inauguration of his heir. Seated beside Martin Van Buren, he rode to the Capitol as the thousands who lined Pennsylvania Avenue wildly cheered. "For once," wrote Senator Thomas Hart Benton "the rising was eclipsed by the setting sun." As the new President read his long, boring inaugural, copies of Jackson's Farewell Address circulated among the crowd.

On the morning he left office (4 March 1837), Jackson published his Farewell Address. He reviewed his two terms. Obviously writing about slavery, Jackson warned of the dangers emanating from sectional differences that based party differences only on geographical distinctions. He appealed for loyalty to the Union. On this issue he never equivocated or compromised.

Being about to retire finally from public life, I beg leave to offer you my grateful thanks for the many proofs of kindness and confidence which I have received at your hands. It has been my fortune in the discharge of public duties, civil and military, frequently to have found myself in difficult and trying situations, where prompt decision and energetic action were necessary, and where the interest of the country required that high responsibilities, should be fearlessly encountered; and it is with the deepest emotions of gratitude that I acknowledge the continued and unbroken confidence with which you have sustained me in every trial . . .

We have now lived almost fifty years under the Constitution framed by the sages and patriots of the Revolution. The conflicts in which the nations of Europe were engaged during a great part of this period, the spirit in which they waged war against each other, and our intimate commercial connections with every part of the civilized world rendered a time of much difficulty for the Government of the United States. We have had our seasons of peace and of war, with all the evils which precede or follow a state of hostility with powerful nations. We encountered these trials with our Constitution yet in its infancy, and under the disadvantages which a new and untried government must always feel when it is called upon to put forth its whole strength without the lights of experience to guide it or the weight of precedents to justify its measures. But we have passed triumphantly through all these difficulties. Our Constitution is no longer a doubtful experiment, and at the end of nearly half a century we find that it has preserved unim-

paired the liberties of the people, secured the rights of property, and that our country has improved and is flourishing beyond any former example in the history of nations . . .

We behold systematic efforts publicly made to sow the seeds of discord between different parts of the United States and to place party divisions directly upon geographical distinctions; to excite the *South* against the *North* and the *North* against the *South*, and to force into the controversy the most delicate and exciting topics—topics upon which it is impossible that a large portion of the Union can ever speak without strong emotion. Appeals, too, are constantly made to sectional interests in order to influence the election of the Chief Magistrate, as if it were desired that he should favor a particular quarter of the country instead of fulfilling the duties of his station with impartial justice to all; and the possible dissolution of the Union has at length become an ordinary and familiar subject of discussion. Has the warning voice of Washington been forgotten,or have designs already been formed to sever the Union? Let it not be supposed that I impute to all of those who have taken an active part in these unwise and unprofitable discussions a want of patriotism or of public virtue. The honorable feeling of State pride and local attachments finds a place in the bosoms of the most enlightened and pure. But while such men are conscious of their own integrity and honesty of purpose, they ought never to forget that the citizens of other States are their political brethren, and that however mistaken they may be in their views, the great body of them are equally honest and upright with themselves. Mutual suspicions and reproaches may in time create mutual hostility, and artful and designing men will always be found who are ready to foment these fatal divisions and to inflame the natural jealousies of different sections of the country. The history of the world is full of such examples, and especially the history of republics.

What have you to gain by division and dissension? Delude not yourselves with the belief that a breach once made maybe afterwards repaired. If the Union is once severed, the line of separation will grow wider and wider, and the controversies which are now debated and settled in the halls of legislation will then be tried in fields of battle and determined by the sword. Neither should you deceive yourselves with the hope that the first line of separation would be the permanent one, and that nothing but harmony and concord would be found in the new associations formed upon the dissolution of this Union. . . . It is impossible to look on the consequences that would inevitably follow the destruction of this Government and not feel indignant when we hear cold calculations about the value of the Union and have so constantly before us a line of conduct so well calculated to weaken its ties.

There is too much at stake to allow pride or passion to influence your decision. . . .

But in order to maintain the Union unimpaired it is absolutely necessary that the laws passed by the constituted authorities should be faithfully executed in every part of the country, and that every good citizen should at all times stand ready to put down, with the combined force of the nation, every attempt at unlawful resistance, under whatever pretext it may be made or whatever shape it may assume. Unconstitutional or oppressive laws may no doubt be passed by Congress, either from erroneous views or the want of due consideration; if they are within the reach of judicial authority, the remedy is easy and peaceful; and if, from the character of the law, it is an abuse of power not within the control of the judiciary, then free discussion and calm appeals to reason and to the justice of the people will not fail to redress the wrong. But until the law shall be declared void by the courts or repealed by Congress no individual or combination of individuals can be justified in forcibly resisting its execution. It is impossible that any government can continue to exist upon any other principles. It would cease to be a government and be unworthy of the name if it had not the power to enforce the execution of its own laws within its own sphere of action. . . .

There is, perhaps, no one of the powers conferred on the Federal Government so liable to abuse as the taxing power. The most productive and convenient sources of revenue were necessarily given to it, that it might be able to perform the important duties imposed upon it; and the taxes which it lays upon commerce being concealed from the real payer in the price of the article, they do not so readily attract the attention of the people as smaller sums demanded from them directly by the taxgatherer. But the tax imposed on goods enhances by so much the price of the commodity to the consumer, and as many of these duties are imposed on articles of necessity which are daily used by the great body of the people, the money raised by these imposts is drawn from their pockets. Congress has no right under the Constitution to take money from the people unless it is required to execute some one of the specific powers intrusted to the Government; and if they raise more than is necessary for such purposes, it is an abuse of the power of taxation, and unjust and oppressive. . . .

In reviewing the conflicts which have taken place between different interests in the United States and the policy pursued since the adoption of our present form of Government, we find nothing that has produced such deep-seated evil as the course of legislation in relation to the currency. The Constitution of the United States unquestionably intended to secure to the people a circulating medium of gold and silver. But the establishment of a national bank by Congress, with the privilege of issuing paper money receivable in the payment of the public dues, and the unfortunate course of legislation in the several States upon the same subject, drove from general circulation the constitutional currency and substituted one of paper in its place.

It was not easy for men engaged in the ordinary pursuits of business, whose attention had not been particularly drawn to the subject, to foresee all the consequences of a currency exclusively of paper, and we ought not on that account to be surprised at the facility with which laws were obtained to carry into effect the paper system. Honest and even enlightened men are sometimes misled by the specious and plausible statements of the designing. But experience has now proved the mischiefs and dangers of a paper currency, and it rests with you to determine whether the proper remedy shall be applied.

The paper system being founded on public confidence and having of itself no intrinsic value, it is liable to great and sudden fluctuations, thereby rendering property insecure and the wages of labor unsteady and uncertain. The corporations which create the paper money can not be relied upon to keep the circulating medium uniform in amount. In times of prosperity, when confidence is high, they are tempted by the prospect of gain or by the influence of those who hope to profit by it to extend their issues of paper beyond the bounds of discretion and the reasonable demands of business; and when these issues have been pushed on from day to day, until public confidence is at length shaken, then a reaction takes place, and they immediately withdraw the credits they have given, suddenly curtail their issues, and produce an unexpected and ruinous contraction of the circulating medium, which is felt by the whole community. The banks by this means save themselves, and the mischievous consequences of their imprudence or cupidity are visited upon the public. Nor does the evil stop here. These ebbs and flows in the currency and these indiscreet extensions of credit naturally engender a spirit of speculation injurious to the habits and character of the people. . . .

Recent events have proved that the paper-money system of this country may be used as an engine to undermine your free institutions, and that those who desire to engross all power in the hands of the few and to govern by corruption or force are aware of its power and prepared to employ it. Your banks now furnish your only circulating medium, and money is plenty or scarce according to the quantity of notes issued by them. While they have capitals not greatly disproportioned to each other, they are competitors in business, and no one of them can exercise dominion over the rest; and although in the present state of the currency these banks may and do operate injuriously upon the habits of business, the pecuniary concerns, and the moral tone of society, yet, from their number and dispersed situation, they can not combine for the purposes of political influence, and whatever may be the dispositions of some of them their power of mischief must necessarily be confined to a narrow space and felt only in their immediate neighborhoods.

But when the charter for the Bank of the United States was obtained from Congress it perfected the schemes of the paper system and gave to its advocates the position they have struggled to obtain from the commencement of the Federal Government to the present hour. The immense capital and peculiar privileges bestowed upon it enabled it to exercise despotic sway over the other banks in every part of the country. From its superior strength it could seriously injure, if not destroy, the business of any one of them which might incur its resentment; and it openly claimed for itself the power of regulating the currency throughout the United States. In other words, it asserted (and it undoubtedly possessed) the power to make money plenty or scarce at its pleasure, at any time and in any quarter of the Union, by controlling the issues of other banks and permitting an expansion or compelling a general contraction of the circulating medium, according to its own will. The other banking institutions were sensible of its strength, and they soon generally became its obedient instruments, ready at all times to execute its mandates; and with the banks necessarily went also that numerous class of persons in our commercial cities who depend altogether on bank credits for their solvency and means of business, and who are therefore obliged, for their own safety, to propitiate the favor of the money power by distinguished zeal and devotion in its service. The result of the ill-advised legislation which established this great monopoly was to concentrate the whole moneyed power of the Union, with its boundless means of corruption and its numerous dependents, under the direction and command of one acknowledged head, thus organizing this particular interest as one body and securing to it unity and concert of action throughout the United States, and enabling it to bring forward upon any occasion its entire and undivided strength to support or defeat any measure of the Government. In the hands of his formidable power, thus perfectly organized, was also placed unlimited dominion over the amount of the circulating medium, giving it the power to regulate the value of property and the fruits of labor in every quarter of the Union, and to bestow prosperity or bring ruin upon any city or section of the country as might best comport with its own interest or policy.

We are not left to conjecture how the moneyed power, thus organized and with such a weapon in its hands, would be likely to use it. The distress and alarm which pervaded and agitated the whole country when the Bank of the United States waged war upon the people in order to compel them to submit to its demands can not yet be forgotten. The ruthless and unsparing temper with which whole cities and communities were oppressed, individuals impoverished and ruined, and a scene of cheerful prosperity suddenly changed into one of gloom and despondency ought to be indelibly impressed on the memory of the people of the United States. If such was its power in a time of peace, what would it not have been in a season of war, with an enemy at your doors? . . .

It is one of the serious evils of our present system of banking that it enables one class of society—and that by no means a numerous one—by its control over the currency, to act injuriously upon the interests of all the others and to exercise more than its just proportion of influence in political affairs. The agricultural, the mechanical, and the laboring classes have little or no share in the direction of the great moneyed corporations, and from their habits and the nature of their pursuits they are incapable of forming extensive combinations to act together with united force. Such concert of action may sometimes be produced in a single city or in a small district of country by means of personal communications with each other, but they have no regular or active correspondence with those who are engaged in similar pursuits in distant places; they have but little patronage to give to the press, and exercise but a small share of influence over it; they have no crowd of dependents about them who hope to grow rich without labor by their countenance and favor, and who are therefore always ready to execute their wishes. The planter, the farmer, the mechanic, and the laborer all know that their success depends upon their own industry and economy, and that they must not expect to become suddenly rich by the fruits of their toil. Yet these classes of society form the great body of the people of the United States; they are the bone and sinew of the country—men who love liberty and desire nothing but equal rights and equal laws, and who, moreover, hold the great mass of our national wealth, although it is distributed in moderate amounts among the millions of freemen who possess it. But with overwhelming numbers and wealth on their side they are in constant danger of losing their fair influence in the Government, and with difficulty maintain their just rights against the incessant efforts daily made to encroach upon them. The mischief springs from the power which the moneyed interest derives from a paper currency which they are able to control, from the multitude of corporations with exclusive privileges which they have succeeded in obtaining in the different States, and which are employed altogether for their benefit; and unless you become more watchful in your States and check this spirit of monopoly and thirst for exclusive privileges you will in the end find that the most important powers of Government have been

given or bartered away, and the control over your dearest interests has passed into the hands of these corporations . . . .

In presenting to you, my fellow-citizens, these parting counsels, I have brought before you the leading principles upon which I endeavored to administer the Government in the high office with which you twice honored me. Knowing that the path of freedom is continually beset by enemies who often assume the disguise of friends, I have devoted the last hours of my public life to warn you of the dangers. The progress of the United States under our free and happy institutions has surpassed the most sanguine hopes of the founders of the Republic. Our growth has been rapid beyond all former example in numbers, in wealth, in knowledge, and all the useful arts which contribute to the comforts and convenience of man, and from the earliest ages of history to the present day there never have been thirteen millions of people associated in one political body who enjoyed so much freedom and happiness as the people of these United States. You have no longer any cause to fear danger from abroad; your strength and power are well known throughout the civilized world, as well as the high and gallant bearing of your sons. It is from within, among yourselves—from cupidity, from corruption, from disappointed ambition and inordinate thirst for power—that factions will be formed and liberty endangered. It is against such designs, whatever disguise the actors may assume, that you have especially to guard yourselves. You have the highest of human trusts committed to your care. Providence has showered on this favored land blessings without number, and has chosen you as the guardians of freedom, to preserve it for the benefit of the human race. May He who holds in His hands the destinies of nations make you worthy of the favors He has bestowed and enable you, with pure hearts and pure hands and sleepless vigilance, to guard and defend to the end of time the great charge He has committed to your keeping.

My own race is nearly run; advanced age and failing health warn me that before long I must pass beyond the reach of human events and cease to feel the vicissitudes of human affairs. I thank God that my life has been spent in a land of liberty and that He has given me a heart to love my country with the affection of a son. And filled with gratitude for your constant and unwavering kindness, I bid you a last and affectionate farewell.

PRESIDENT MARTIN VAN BUREN'S INDEPENDENT TREASURY MESSAGE
4 September 1837

President Van Buren planned to follow Jackson's lead by endorsing programs to help both southern and western farmers and the growing working class of the North. But within two months of his inauguration, a general financial and business collapse caused by overspeculative investments in land and industry confronted the President. Stock prices tumbled. Imports fell and customs revenue dwindled. By May 1837, banks had suspended specie payments so that no one could redeem paper money in gold or silver. In New York City, unemployed workers demonstrated against high rents and inflated food prices. In the South, cotton prices halved.

Van Buren blamed the problem on overbanking and overtrading. On 4 September 1837, he asked Congress to enact an independent treasury system. This would enable the federal government to keep its funds in its own depositories entirely separate from the banking system. His proposal would completely separate banking from the government. This would sharply reduce speculation since bankers would no longer have the government's funds to use as backing for issuing loans and making investments. Van Buren's advisors believed that an independent treasury system would stabilize the economy and reduce financial panics. In January 1840, after more than two years of debate, the Independent Treasury Act finally was passed.

The act of the 23d of June 1836, regulating the deposits of the public money and directing the employment of State, District, and Territorial banks for that purpose, made it the duty of the Secretary of the Treasury to discontinue the use of such of them as should at any time refuse to redeem their notes in specie, and to substitute other banks, provided a sufficient number could be obtained to receive the public deposits upon the terms and conditions therein prescribed. The general and almost simultaneous suspension of specie payments by the banks in May last rendered the performance of this duty imperative in respect to those which had been selected under the act, and made it at the same time impracticable to employ the requisite number of others upon the prescribed conditions. The specific regulations established by Congress for the deposit and safe-keeping of the public moneys having thus unexpectedly become inoperative, I felt it to be my duty to afford you an early opportunity for the exercise of your supervisory powers over the subject.

I was also led to apprehend that the suspension of specie payments, increasing the embarrassments before existing in the pecuniary affairs of the country, would so far diminish the public revenue that the accruing receipts into the Treasury would not, with the reserved five millions, be sufficient to defray the unavoidable expenses of the Government until the usual period for the meeting of Congress, whilst the authority to call upon the States for a portion of the sums deposited with them was too restricted to enable the Department to realize a sufficient amount from that source. These apprehensions have been justified by subsequent results, which render it certain that this deficiency will occur if additional means be not provided by Congress.

The difficulties experienced by the mercantile interest in meeting their engagements induced them to apply to me previously to the actual suspension of specie payments for indulgence upon their bonds for duties, and all the relief authorized by law was promptly and cheerfully granted. The dependence of the Treasury upon the avails of these bonds to enable it to make the deposits with the States required by law led me in the outset to limit this indulgence to the 1st of September, but it has since been extended to the 1st of October, that the matter might be submitted to your further direction. . . .

During the earlier stages of the revulsion through which we have just passed much acrimonious discussion arose and great diversity of opinion existed as to its real causes. This was not surprising. The operations of credit are so diversified and the influences which affect them so numerous, and often so subtle, that even impartial and well-informed persons are seldom found to agree in respect to them. . . . I proceed to state my views, so far as may be necessary to a clear understanding of the remedies I feel it my duty to propose and of the reasons by which I have been led to recommend them. . . .

They are, to regulate by law the safe-keeping, transfer, and disbursement of the public moneys; to designate the funds to be received and paid by the Government; to enable the Treasury to meet promptly every demand upon it; to prescribe the terms of indulgence and the mode of settlement to be adopted, as well in collecting from individuals the revenue that has accrued as in withdrawing it from former depositories; and to devise and adopt such further measures, within the constitutional competency of Congress, as will be best calculated to revive the enterprise and to promote the prosperity of the country.

For the deposit, transfer, and disbursement of the revenue national and State banks have always, with temporary and limited exceptions, been heretofore employed; but although advocates of each system are still to be found, it is apparent that the events of the last few months have greatly augmented the desire, long existing among the people of the United States, to separate the fiscal operations of the Government from those of individuals or corporations.

Again to create a national bank as a fiscal agent would be to disregard the popular will, twice solemnly and unequivocally expressed. On no question of domestic policy is there stronger evidence that the sentiments of a large majority are deliberately fixed, and I can not concur with those who think they see in recent events a proof that these sentiments are, or a reason that they should be, changed. . . .

A danger difficult, if not impossible, to be avoided in such an arrangement is made strikingly evident in the very event by which it has now been defeated. A sudden act of the banks intrusted with the funds of the people deprives the Treasury, without fault or agency of the Government, of the ability to pay its creditors in the currency they have by law a right to demand. This circumstance no fluctuation of commerce could have produced if the public revenue had been collected in the legal currency and kept in that form by the officers of the Treasury. The citizen whose money was in bank receives it back since the suspension at a sacrifice in its amount, whilst he who kept it in the legal currency of the country and in his own possession pursues without loss the current of his business. The Government, placed in the situation of the former, is involved in embarrassments it could not have suffered had it pursued the course of the latter. These embarrassments are, moreover, augmented by those salutary and just laws which forbid it to use a depreciated currency, and by so doing take from the Government the ability which individuals have of accommodating their transactions to such a catastrophe.

A system which can in a time of profound peace, when there is a large revenue laid by, thus suddenly prevent the application and the use of the money of the people in the manner and for the objects they have directed can not be wise; but who can think without painful reflection that under it the same unforeseen events might have befallen us in the midst of a war and taken from us at the moment when most wanted the use of those very means which were treasured up to promote the national welfare and guard our national rights? To such embarrassments and to such dangers will this Government be always exposed whilst it takes the moneys raised for and necessary to the public service out of the hands of its own officers and converts them into a mere right of action against corporations intrusted with the possession of them. Nor can such results be effectually guarded against in such a system without investing the Executive with a control over the banks themselves, whether State or national, that might with reason be objected to. Ours is probably the only Government in the world that is liable in the management of its fiscal concerns to occurrences like these. . . .

The foregoing views, it seems to me, do but fairly carry out the provisions of the Federal Constitution in relation to the currency, as far as relates to the public revenue. At the time that instrument was framed there were but three or four banks in the United States, and had the extension of the banking system and the evils growing out of it been foreseen they would probably have been specially guarded against. The same policy which led to the prohibi-

tion of bills of credit by the States would doubtless in that event have also interdicted their issue as a currency in any other form. The Constitution, however, contains no such prohibition; and since the States have exercised for nearly half a century the power to regulate the business of banking, it is not to be expected that it will be abandoned. The whole matter is now under discussion before the proper tribunal—the people of the States. Never before has the public mind been so thoroughly awakened to a proper sense of its importance; never has the subject in all its bearings been submitted to so searching an inquiry. It would be distrusting the intelligence and virtue of the people to doubt the speedy and efficient adoption of such measures of reform as the public good demands. All that can rightfully be done by the Federal Government to promote the accomplishment of that important object will without doubt be performed. . . .

The plan proposed will be adequate to all our fiscal operations during the remainder of the year. Should it be adopted, the Treasury, aided by the ample resources of the country, will be able to discharge punctually every pecuniary obligation. For the future all that is needed will be that caution and forbearance in appropriations which the diminution of the revenue requires and which the complete accomplishment or great forwardness of many expensive national undertakings renders equally consistent with prudence and patriotic liberality. . . .

PRESIDENT MARTIN VAN BUREN'S PROCLAMATION OF NEUTRALITY IN THE CAROLINE AFFAIR
5 January 1838

In November 1837, William Lyon Mackenzie began a rebellion in Upper Canada. Defeated by British forces, Mackenzie and his followers took refuge on Navy Island on the Canadian side of the Niagara River. American sympathizers supplied them with arms, food, and recruits. A small steamboat, the Caroline, was used to ferry supplies from the American side to Navy Island. On 29 December, Canadian militia crossed to the American side and seized the Caroline. The steamer was towed into midstream and set afire.

President Van Buren ordered the State Department to protest vigorously to the British Minister in Washington. But this protest was ignored. Patriotic indignation ignited violent Anglophobe sentiment along the Canadian border. The President called out the New York militia to prevent violence. He also ordered General Winfield Scott to take immediate command of U.S. forces in the area. On 5 January 1838, Van Buren, fearful of another war with Great Britain, issued a neutrality proclamation warning Americans to desist from hostile actions. Nevertheless, a continuing number of violent acts kept anti-British feeling at a high pitch. The various Canadian boundary disputes were finally settled by the Webster-Ashburton Treaty of 1842. However, the movement to annex Canada continued. The last such resolution was introduced into the House of Representatives in 1911.

Whereas information having been received of a dangerous excitement on the northern frontier of the United States in consequence of the civil war begun in Canada, and instructions having been given to the United States officers on that frontier and applications having been made to the governors of the adjoining States to prevent any unlawful interference on the part of our citizens in the contest unfortunately commenced in the British Provinces, additional information has just been received that, notwithstanding the proclamations of the governors of the States of New York and Vermont exhorting their citizens to refrain from any unlawful acts within the territory of the United States, and notwithstanding the presence of the civil officers of the United States, who by my directions have visited the scenes of commotion with a view of impressing the citizens with a proper sense of their duty, the excitement, instead of being appeased, is every day increasing in degree; that arms and munitions of war and other supplies have been procured by the insurgents in the United States; that a military force, consisting in part, at least, of citizens of the United States, had been actually organized, had congregated at Navy Island, and were still in arms under the command of a citizen of the United States, and that they were constantly receiving accessions and aid:

Now, therefore, to the end that the authority of the laws may be maintained and the faith of treaties observed, I, Martin Van Buren, do most earnestly exhort all citizens of the United States who have thus violated their duties to return peaceably to their respective homes; and I hereby warn them that any persons who shall compromit the neutrality of this Government by interfering in an unlawful manner with the affairs of the neighboring British Provinces will render themselves liable to arrest and punishment under the laws of the United States, which will be rigidly enforced; and, also, that they will receive no aid or countenance from their Government, into whatever difficulties they may be thrown by the violation of the laws of their country and the territory of a neighboring and friendly nation. . . .

PRESIDENT JOHN TYLER'S REQUEST FOR RATIFICATION OF THE WEBSTER-ASHBURTON TREATY BETWEEN THE UNITED STATES AND GREAT BRITAIN
11 August 1842

A notable achievement of the Tyler administration was the successful conclusion of the Webster-Ashburton Treaty. This treaty made great headway in the settlement of a number of vexing Anglo-American issues. Of these, boundary disputes with British Canada were the most important.

Secretary of State Daniel Webster usually has been given all the credit for the settlement of the nation's boundary disputes with Great Britain but many provisions were proposed by President Tyler. One treaty section included joint naval squadrons to operate off the coast of west Africa to suppress the slave trade. Both men successfully concluded the complicated negotiations with skill, tact, and dignity.

On 11 August 1842, Tyler submitted the treaty to the Senate who approved it on 20 August—by a vote of 39–9.

I have received your excellency's communication of the 25th instant, informing me of efforts making Mr. Dorr and others to embody a force in the contiguous States for the invasion of the State of Rhode Island, and calling upon the Executive of the United States for military's aid.

In answer I have to inform your excellency that means have been taken to ascertain the extent of the dangers of any armed invasion by the citizens of other States of the State of Rhode Island, either to put down her government or to disturb her peace. The apparent improbability of a violation so flagrant ad unprecedented of all our laws and institutions makes me, I confess, allow to believe that any serious attempts will be made to execute the designs which some evil-minded persons may have formed.

But should the necessity of the case require the interposition of the authority of the United States it will be rendered in the manner prescribed by the laws.

In the meantime I indulge a confident expectation, founded upon the recent manifestations of public opinion in your State in favor of law and order, that your own resources and means will be abundantly adequate to preserve the public peace, and that the difficulties which have arisen will be soon amicably and permanently adjusted by the exercise of a spirit of liberality and forbearance.

President John Tyler's Response to Governor Samuel W. King of Rhode Island
28 May 1842

As late as 1841, Rhode Island was still using as its constitution the charter granted by King Charles II in 1663. Although revised in 1776 and in 1790, less than half of the state's white males could vote. In 1842, Thomas Dorr campaigned to implement a new constitution that had been ratified by a majority of white, adult males but lacked the consent of the state government. The existing government feared an extension of the franchise. As a result, the state had two governments claiming authority. Each side refused to compromise. Many thought that only force would settle the issue.

Both sides appealed to Washington for recognition. President John Tyler announced that he would act, if required, in defense of the charter government. He relied on Article IV, Section 4 of the Constitution, which guarantees to all states a republican form of government. However, he urged both sides to settle their differences peacefully. While no federal troops were used against Dorr and the reformers, Tyler did order measures to prepare for all contingencies.

Dorr was arrested after his followers attacked an arsenal in Providence. Convicted of treason, he eventually was pardoned. In 1843, Rhode Island adopted a new state constitution that substantially broadened the right to vote. The Supreme Court case of Luther vs. Borden (1849) grew out of the so-called Dorr War. Chief Justice Roger Taney held, in part, that President Tyler had acted appropriately under the Constitu-

tion when he supported the charter government. Further, he ruled that every state government had the right to protect itself against domestic violence even if from a majority of its own citizens.

I have the satisfaction to communicate to the Senate the results of the negotiations recently had in this city with the British minister, special and extraordinary.

These results comprose—

First. A treaty to settle and define the boundaries between the territories of the United States and the possessions of Her Britannic Majesty in North America, for the suppression of the African slave trade, and the surrender of criminals fugitive from justice in certain cases.

Second. A correspondence on the subject of the interference of the colonial authorities of the British West Indies with American merchant vessels driven by stress of weather or carried by violence into the ports of those colonies.

Third. A correspondence upon the subject of the attack and destruction of the steamboat *Caroline*.

Fourth. A correspondence on the subject of impressment.

If this treaty shall receive the approbation of the Senate, it will terminate a difference respecting boundary which has long subsisted between the two Governments, has been the subject of several ineffectual attempts at settlement, and has sometimes led to great irritation, not without danger of disturbing the existing peace. Both the United States and the States more immediately concerned have entertained no doubt of the validity of the American title to all the territory which has been in dispute, but that title was controverted and the Government of the United States had agreed to make the dispute a subject of arbitration. One arbitration had been actually had, but had failed to settle the controversy, and it was found at the commencement of last year that a correspondence had been in progress between the two Governments for a joint commission, with an ultimate reference to an umpire or arbitrator with authority to make a final decision. That correztarded by various occurrences, and had come to no definite result when the special mission of Lord Ashburton was announced. This movement on the part of England afforded in the judgment of the Executive a favorable opportunity for making an attempt to settle this long-existing controversy by some agreement or treaty without further reference to arbitration. . . .

Ordinarily it would be no easy task to reconcile and bring together such a variety of interests in a matter in itself difficult and perplexed, but the efforts of the Government in attempting to accomplish this desirable object have been seconded and sustained by a spirit of accommodation and conciliation on the part of the States concerned, to which much of the success of these efforts is to be ascribed. . . .

The treaty obligations subsisting between the two countries for the suppression of the African slave trade and the complaints made to this Government within the last three or four years, many of them but too well founded, of the visitation, seizure, and detention of American vessels on that coast by British cruisers could not but form a delicate and highly important part of the negotiations which have now been held.

The early and prominent part which the Government of the United States has taken for the abolition of this unlawful and inhuman traffic is well known. By the tenth article of the treaty of Ghent it is declared that the traffic in slaves is irreconcilable with the principles of humanity and justice, and that both His Majesty and the United States are desirous of continuing their efforts to promote its entire abolition; and it is thereby agreed that both the contracting parties shall use their best endeavors to accomplish so desirable an object. . . .

The impressment of seamen from merchant vessels of this country by British cruisers, although not practiced in time of peace, and therefore not at present a productive cause of difference and irritation, has, nevertheless, hitherto been so prominent a topic of controversy and is so likely to bring on renewed contentions at the first breaking out of a European war that it has been thought the part of wisdom now to take it into serious and earnest consideration. The letter from the Secretary of State to the British minister explains the ground which the Government has assumed and the principles which it means to uphold. For the defense of these grounds and the maintenance of these principles the most perfect reliance is placed on the intelligence of the American people and on their firmness and patriotism in whatever touches the honor of the country or its great and essential interests.

President John Tyler's Message Urging the Annexation of Texas
22 April 1844

The United States had followed a distinctly unneutral policy during the Texas War for Independence (1835–1836). Both Texans and many Americans favored immediate annexation by the United States. However, since Mexico refused to recognize Texan independence, annexation might provoke war. Also, the incorporation of a slave territory into the Union would aggravate the growing antislavery sentiment in the North. President Andrew Jackson waited until his last day in office (4 March 1837) before recognizing the new Texas Republic. President Martin Van Buren avoided the annexation issue.

Admitting Texas into the Union was revived in 1842. President John Tyler enthusiastically supported it. A slaveholder, Tyler believed that the expansion of slavery was vital to the southern economy. He ordered his Secretary of State Abel Upshur to draft the necessary treaty with Texas. After Upshur's death, the new Secretary of State John C. Calhoun completed the arrangements. The treaty was submitted to the Senate on 22 April 1844 accompanied by a message from Tyler urging annexation. Tyler cited national interest, the security of Southern states, and the danger posed by abolitionist Great Britain.

The Senate rejected the treaty on 8 June 1844 by a vote of 35–16. Abolitionists had argued that President Tyler and Secretary Calhoun were part of a slaveholders' conspiracy. Tyler then unsuccessfully tried to incorporate Texas into the Union by proposing a joint resolution of both houses of Congress. After the 1844 presidential election but before the inauguration of the expansionist James K. Polk, Tyler again appealed for a joint resolution of annexation. This time he succeeded as Congress regarded Polk's election as a plebiscite. The February 1845 joint resolution annexing Texas was the first time such a procedure was used to approve a treaty or to acquire territory.

I transmit herewith, for your approval and ratification, a treaty which I have caused to be negotiated between the United States and Texas, whereby the latter, on the conditions therein set forth, has transferred and conveyed all its right of separate and independent sovereignty and jurisdiction to the United States. In taking so important as step I have been influenced by what appeared to me to be the most controlling considerations of public policy and the general good, and in having accomplished it, should it meet with your approval, the Government will have succeeded in reclaiming a territory which formerly constituted a portion, as it is confidently believed, of its domain under the treaty of cession of 1803 by France to the United States.

The country thus proposed to be annexed has been settled principally by persons from the United States, who emigrated on the invitation of both Spain and Mexico, and who carried with them into the wilderness which they have partially reclaimed the laws, customs, and political and domestic institutions of their native land. They are deeply indoctrinated in all the principles of civil liberty, and will bring along with them in the act of reassociation devotion to our Union and a firm and inflexible resolution to assist in maintaining the public liberty unimpaired—a consideration which, as it appears to me, is to be regarded as of no small moment. The country itself thus obtained is of incalculable value in an agricultural and commercial point of view. To a soil of inexhaustible fertility it unites a genial and healthy climate, and is destined at a day not distant to make large contributions to the commerce of the world. . . .

To Mexico the Executive is disposed to pursue a course conciliatory in its character and at the same time to render her the most ample justice by conventions and stipulations not inconsistent with the rights and dignity of the Government. It is actuated by no spirit of unjust aggrandizement, but looks only to its own security. It has made known to Mexico at several periods its extreme anxiety to witness the termination of hostilities between that country and Texas. Its wishes, however have been entirely disregarded. It has ever been ready to urge an adjustment of the dispute upon terms mutually advantageous to both. It will be ready at all times to hear and discuss any claims Mexico may think she has on the justice of the United States and to adjust any that may be deemed to be so on the most liberal terms. There is no desire on the part of the Executive to wound her pride or affect injuriously her interest, but at the same time it can not compromit by any delay in its action the essential interests of the United States. Mexico has no right to ask or expect this of us; we deal rightfully with Texas as an independent power. The war which has been waged for eight years has resulted only in the conviction with all others than herself that Texas can not be reconquered. I can not but repeat the opinion expressed in my message at the opening of Congress that it is time it had ceased. The Executive, while it could not look upon its longer continuance without the greatest un-

easiness, has, nevertheless, for all past time preserved a course of strict neutrality. It could not be ignorant of the fact of the exhaustion which a war of so long a duration had produced. Least of all was it ignorant of the anxiety of other powers to induce Mexico to enter into terms of reconciliation with Texas, which, affecting the domestic institutions of Texas, would operate most injuriously upon the United States and might most seriously threaten the existence of this happy Union. . . .

In full view, then, of the highest public duty, and as a measure of security against evils incalculably great, the Executive has entered into the negotiation, the fruits of which are now submitted to the Senate. Independent of the urgent reasons which existed for the step it has taken, it might safely invoke the fact (which it confidently believes) that there exists no civilized government on earth having a voluntary tender made it of a domain so rich and fertile, so replete with all that can add to national greatness and wealth, and so necessary to its peace and safety that would reject the offer. Nor are other powers, Mexico inclusive, likely in any degree to be injuriously affected by the ratification of the treaty. The prosperity of Texas will be equally interesting to all: in the increase of the general commerce of the world that prosperity will be secured by annexation.

But one view of the subject remains to be presented. It grows out of the proposed enlargement of our territory.

From this, I am free to confess, I see no danger. The federative system is susceptible of the greatest extension compatible with the ability of the representation of the most distant State or Territory to reach the seat of Government in time to participate in the functions of legislation and to make known the wants of the constituent body. Our confederated Republic consisted originally of thirteen members. It now consists of twice that number, while applications are before Congress to permit other additions. This addition of new States has served to strengthen rather than to weaken the Union. New interests have sprung up, which require the united power of all, through the action of the common Government, to protect and defend upon the high seas and in foreign parts. Each State commits with perfect security to that common Government those great interests growing out of our relations with other nations of the world, and which equally involve the good of all the States. Its domestic concerns are left to its own exclusive management. But if there were any force in the objection it would seem to require an immediate abandonment of territorial possessions which lie in the distance and stretch to a far-off sea, and yet no one would be found, it is believed, ready to recommend such an abandonment. Texas lies at our very doors and in our immediate vicinity.

Under every view which I have been able to take of the subject, I think that the interests of our common constituents, the people of all the States, and a love of the Union left the Executive no other alternative than to negotiate the treaty. The high and solemn duty of ratifying or rejecting it is wisely devolved on the Senate by the Constitution of the United States.

PRESIDENT JOHN TYLER'S VETO OF THE REVENUE CUTTERS AND STEAMERS BILL
20 February 1845

The power to veto legislation is one of the few powers granted by the Constitution to the President, which involves the Chief Executive in legislative affairs. Early Presidents used the veto power sparingly. George Washington used the veto twice in his two terms as President—once for constitutional reasons and once for a policy reason. From Washington in 1789 through William Henry Harrison in 1841, nine Presidents used their veto power twenty-three times with Andrew Jackson invoking the veto twelve times. (Most of Jackson's vetoes focused attention on a major issue of the time—government involvement in public works and other internal improvement projects.)

On 20 February 1845, President John Tyler vetoed a bill that prohibited payment for some naval craft that Tyler had ordered built. The Senate and the House passed the measure over his veto on 3 March 1845, the last day of his administration. This was the first time a presidential veto was overridden.

I herewith return the bill entitled "An act relating to revenue cutters and steamers," with the following objections to its becoming a law:

The executive has found it necessary and esteemed it important to the public interests to direct the building of two revenue boats, to be propelled by wind or steam, as occasion may require—the one for the coast of Georgia and the other for Mobile Bay, to be used as dispatch vessels if necessary. The models have been furnished by the Navy Department and side wheels have been ordered, as being best tested and least liable to failure. The one boat is directed to be built at Richmond, Va., the other at Pittsburg, Pa., and contracts have been regularly entered into for their construction. The contractors have made and are making all necessary arrangements in procuring materials and sites for building, etc., and have doubtless been at considerable expense in the necessary preparations for completing their engagements. It was no part of the intention of the Senate in originating the bill, I am well convinced, to violate the sanctity of contracts regularly entered into by the Government. The language of the act, nevertheless, is of a character to produce in all probability that effect. Its language is "that no revenue cutter or revenue steamer shall hereafter be built (*excepting such as are now in the course of building or equipment*) nor purchased unless an appropriation be first made by law therefor." The *building* of the two cutters under contract can not be said properly to have commenced, although preparations have been made for building; but even if the construction be ambiguous, it is better that all ambiguity should be removed and thus the hazard of violating the pledged faith of the country be removed along with it.

I am free to confess that, existing contracts being guarded and protected, the law to operate *in futuro* would be regarded as both proper and wise.

With these objections, I return the bill to the House in which it originated for its final constitutional action.

PRESIDENT JAMES K. POLK'S COMMENTS ON TEXAS AND OREGON IN HIS INAUGURAL ADDRESS
4 March 1845

In 1844, James K. Polk won an extremely close election. He failed to capture a majority of the popular vote but he gained a clear majority of the electoral votes. Polk's victory was an endorsement that the United States would extend its boundaries westward.

On 4 March 1845, Polk was inaugurated. The crowd gathered before the Capitol stood in a pouring rain and heard the President reaffirm the Democratic platform declaration on Texas. Polk slowly read these statements, emphasizing each word: "I regard the question of annexation as belonging exclusively to the United States and Texas as the prerogative of two independent powers." Two days later though, Mexico formally protested against the annexation of Texas, calling it the "most unjust act of aggression in the annals of modern history." At the end of March, the Mexican government broke diplomatic relations with the United States and took steps to augment its armed forces. Polk's inaugural address also asserted the American title to Oregon to be "clear and unquestionable."

The Republic of Texas has made known her desire to come into our Union, to form a part of our Confederacy and enjoy with us the blessings of liberty secured and guaranteed by our Constitution. Texas was once a part of our country was unwisely ceded away to a foreign power is now independent, and possesses an undoubted right to dispose of a part or the whole of her territory and to merge her sovereignty as a separate and independent state in ours. I congratulate my country that by an act of the late Congress of the United States the assent of this Government has been given to the reunion, and it only remains for the two countries to agree upon the terms to consummate an object so important to both.

I regard the question of annexation as belonging exclusively to the United States and Texas. They are independent powers competent to contract, and foreign nations have no right to interfere with them or to take exceptions to their reunion. Foreign powers do not seem to appreciate the true character of our Government. Our Union is a confederation of independent States, whose policy is peace with each other and all the world. To enlarge its limits is to extend the dominions of peace over additional territories and increasing millions. The world has nothing to fear from military ambition in our Government. While the Chief Magistrate and the popular branch of Congress are elected for short terms by the suffrages of those millions who must in their own persons bear all the burdens and miseries of war, our Government can not be otherwise than pacific. Foreign powers should therefore look on the annexation of Texas to the United States not as the conquest of a nation seeking to extend her dominions by arms and violence, but as the peaceful acquisition of a territory once her own, by adding another member to our confederation, with the consent of that member, thereby diminishing the chances of war and opening to them new and ever-increasing markets for their products.

To Texas the reunion is important, because the strong protecting arm of our Government would be extended over her, and the vast resources of her fertile soil and genial climate would be speedily developed, while the safety of New Orleans and of our whole southwestern frontier against hostile aggression, as well as the interests of the whole Union, would be promoted by it. . . .

None can fail to see the danger to our safety and future peace if Texas remains an independent state or becomes an ally or dependency of some foreign nation more powerful than herself. Is there one among our citizens who would not prefer perpetual peace with Texas to occasional wars, which so often occur between bordering independent nations? Is there one who would not prefer free intercourse with her to high duties on all our products and manufactures which enter her ports or cross her frontiers? Is there one who would not prefer an unrestricted communication with her citizens to the frontier obstructions which must occur if she remains out of the Union? Whatever is good or evil in the local institutions of Texas will remain her own whether annexed to the United States or not. None of the present States will be responsible for them any more than they are for the local institutions of each other. They have confederated together for certain specified objects. Upon the same principle that they would refuse to form a perpetual union with Texas because of her local institutions our forefathers would have been prevented from forming our present Union. Perceiving no valid objection to the measure and many reasons for its adoption vitally affecting the peace, the safety, and the prosperity of both countries, I shall on the broad principle which formed the basis and produced the adoption of our Constitution, and not in any narrow spirit of sectional policy, endeavor by all constitutional, honorable, and appropriate means to consummate the expressed will of the people and Government of the United States by the reannexation of Texas to our Union at the earliest practicable period.

Nor will it become in a less degree my duty to assert and maintain by all constitutional means the right of the United States to that portion of our territory which lies beyond the Rocky Mountains. Our title to the country of the Oregon is "clear and unquestionable," and already are our people preparing to perfect that title by occupying it with their wives and children. But eighty years ago our population was confined on the west by the ridge of the Alleghenies. Within that period—within the lifetime, I might say, of some of my hearers—our people, increasing to many millions, have filled the eastern valley of the Mississippi, adventurously ascended the Missouri to its headsprings, and are already engaged in establishing the blessings of self-government in valleys of which the rivers flow to the Pacific. The world beholds the peaceful triumphs of the industry of our emigrants. To us belongs the duty of protecting them adequately wherever they may be upon our soil. The jurisdiction of our laws and the benefits of our republican institutions should be extended over them in the distant regions which they have selected for their homes. The increasing facilities of intercourse will easily bring the States, of which the formation in that part of our territory can not be long delayed, within the sphere of our federative Union. In the meantime every obligation imposed by treaty or conventional stipulations should be sacredly respected.

PRESIDENT JAMES K. POLK'S COROLLARIES TO THE MONROE DOCTRINE
2 December 1845

Shortly after James K. Polk was inaugurated (4 March 1845), Mexico broke diplomatic relations with the United States over the annexation of Texas. From the Mexican view, Texas was a providence in rebellion. Polk ordered American troops to the new state to protect it against a possible Mexican attack. Above all though, Polk now wanted to annex the Mexican provenance of California. He knew little about the area except that it had several superb ports—San Francisco, Monterey, and San Diego. The President feared that a possible war with Mexico over Texas could cause either England, France or even Russia, to seize California from Mexico. The American consulate at Liverpool reported to Polk that "all Europe" coveted California.

Polk was determined to obtain California. The United States had no claim to it except desire. Mexico ignored Polk's offer to buy the territory as they had comparable offers during the administration of Jackson and Tyler. Attempts to stir up a local revolution failed. War with Mexico (1846) eventually will lead to American annexation. However, before that dramatic event occurred, Polk expanded the Monroe Doctrine. In his First Annual Message to Congress on 2 December 1845, the President stated that "the people of this continent alone have the right to decide their own destiny" and "no future European colony or dominion" could be established in North America without United States approval. These corollaries enunciated by Polk became an integral part of American foreign policy.

. . . The rapid extension of our settlements over our territories heretofore unoccupied, the addition of new States to our Confederacy, the expansion of free principles, and our rising greatness as a nation are attracting the attention of the powers of Europe, and lately the doctrine has been broached in some of them of a "balance of power" on this continent to check our advancement. The United States, sincerely desirous of preserving relations of good understanding with all nations, can not in silence permit any European interference on the North American continent, and should any such interference be attempted will be ready to resist it at any and all hazards.

It is well known to the American people and to all nations that this Government has never interfered with the relations subsisting between other governments. We have never made ourselves parties to their wars or their alliances; we have not sought their territories by conquest; we have not mingled with parties in their domestic struggles; and believing our own form of government to be the best, we have never attempted to propagate it by intrigues, by diplomacy, or by force. We may claim on this continent a like exemption from European interference. The nations of America are equally sovereign and independent with those of Europe. They possess the same rights, independent of all foreign interposition, to make war, to conclude peace, and to regulate their internal affairs. The people of the United States can not, therefore, view with indifference attempts of European powers to interfere with the independent action of the nations on this continent. The American system of government is entirely different from that of Europe. Jealousy among the different sovereigns of Europe, lest any one of them might become too powerful for the rest, has caused them anxiously to desire the establishment of what they term the "balance of power." It can not be permitted to have any application on the North American continent, and especially to the United States. We must ever maintain the principle that the people of this continent alone have the right to decide their own destiny. Should any portion of them, constituting an independent state, propose to unite themselves with our Confederacy, this will be a question for them and us to determine without any foreign interposition. We can never consent that European powers shall interfere to prevent such a union because it might disturb the "balance of power" which they may desire to maintain upon this continent. Near a quarter of a century ago the principle was distinctly announced to the world, in the annual message of one of my predecessors, that—

The American continents, by the free and independent condition which they have assumed and maintain, are henceforth not to be considered as subjects for future colonization by any European powers.

This principle will apply with greatly increased force should any European power attempt to establish any new colony in North America. In the existing circumstances of the world the present is deemed a proper occasion to reiterate and reaffirm the principle avowed by Mr. Monroe and to state my cordial concurrence in its wisdom and sound policy. The reassertion of this principle, especially in reference to North America, is at this day but the promulgation of a policy which no European power should cherish the disposition to resist. Existing rights of every European nation should be respected, but it is due alike to our safety and our interests that the efficient protection of our laws should be extended over our whole territorial limits, and that it should be distinctly announced to the world as our settled policy that no future European colony or dominion shall with our consent be planted or established on any part of the North American continent. . . .

PRESIDENT JAMES K. POLK'S WAR MESSAGE TO CONGRESS
11 May 1846

President James K. Polk wholeheartedly supported the concept of Manifest Destiny. This was the belief that the United States was destined to expand its territory to the Pacific Ocean.

In September 1845, Polk appointed former Congressman John Slidell of Louisiana as envoy-minister on a secret mission to Mexico. His instructions were to secure Upper California and the territory of New Mexico for fifteen to twenty million dollars if possible, or for forty million if necessary. Slidell also was authorized to settle the southern boundary of Texas at the Rio Grande River. In addition, the United States would assume the claims of its nationals against Mexico. The Mexican government refused to receive Slidell. They considered the American offer both an insult to their national honor and a threat to their territorial integrity.

When Slidell's report reached Washington on 12 January 1846, President Polk immediately ordered General Zachary Taylor to take his army across the Nueces River and to occupy the area up to the left bank of the Rio Grande. (In reality, the authority of Texas, either as a republic or as a state, had never been exercised beyond the Nueces.) Taylor carried out his orders by the end of March with his guns aimed across the Rio Grande at the Mexican town of Matamoros. This show of force, reasoned Polk, might force the Mexicans to reconsider their refusal to negotiate a purchase.

A new Mexican government offered to negotiate the single issue of Texas. But Polk dismissed this offer as insincere. On 9 May 1846, the President informed the cabinet that he had begun to draft a war message to Congress. All nodded approval except Secretary of the Navy George Bancroft, who thought that war should not be declared until Mexico initiated some hostile act. Later that day, news reached Washington that Mexican cavalry had crossed the Rio Grande and had engaged in a skirmish with United States soldiers. The conscience of Bancroft was now satisfied. The cabinet unanimously agreed that a war message should be presented to Congress documenting the "wrongs and injuries" the United States had suffered from Mexico. All day Sunday, 10 May except for two hours at church, Polk prepared his war message. "It was a day of great anxiety to me," wrote the President in his diary. "And I regretted the necessity which had existed to make it necessary for me to spend the Sabbath in the manner I have." At noon on Monday, 11 May 1846, the war message was sent to Congress.

The existing state of the relations between the United States and Mexico renders it proper that I should bring the subject to the consideration of Congress. . . .

In my message at the commencement of the present session I informed you that upon the earnest appeal both of the Congress and convention of Texas I had ordered an efficient military force to take a position "between the Nueces and the Del Norte." This had become necessary to meet a threatened invasion of Texas by the Mexican forces, for which extensive military preparations had been made. The invasion was threatened solely because Texas had determined in accordance with a solemn resolution of the Congress of the United States, to annex herself to our Union, and under these circumstances it was plainly our duty to extend our protection over her citizens and soil.

This force was concentrated at Corpus Christi, and remained there until after I had received such information from Mexico as rendered it probable, if not certain, that the Mexican Government would refuse to receive our envoy.

Meantime Texas, by the final action of our Congress, had become an integral part of our Union. The Congress of Texas, by its act of 19 December 1836, had declared the Rio del Norte to be the boundary of that Republic. Its jurisdiction had been extended and exercised beyond the Nueces. The country between that river and the Del Norte had been represented in the Congress and in the convention of Texas, had thus taken part in the act of annexation itself, and is now included within one of our Congressional districts. Our own Congress had, moreover, with great unanimity, by the act approved 31 December 1845, recognized the country beyond the Nueces as a part of our territory by including it within our own revenue system, and a revenue officer to reside within that district has been appointed by and with the advice and consent of the Senate. It became, therefore, of urgent necessity to provide for the defense of that portion of our country. Accordingly, on the 13th of January last instructions were issued to the general in command of these troops to occupy the left bank of the Del Norte. This river, which is the southwestern boundary of the State of Texas, is an exposed frontier. . . .

The movement of the troops to the Del Norte was made by the commanding general under positive instructions to abstain from all aggressive acts toward Mexico or Mexican citizens and to regard the relations between that Republic and the United States as peaceful unless she should declare war or commit acts of hostility indicative of a state of war. . . .

The Mexican forces at Matamoras assumed a belligerent attitude, and on the

12th of April General Ampudia, then in command, notified General Taylor to break up his camp within twenty-four hours and to retire beyond the Nueces River, and in the event of his failure to comply with these demands announced that arms, and arms alone, must decide the question. But no open act of hostility was committed until the 24th of April. On that day General Arista, who had succeeded to the command of the Mexican forces, communicated to General Taylor that "he considered hostilities commenced and should prosecute them." A party of dragoons of 63 men and officers were on the same day dispatched from the American camp up the Rio del Norte on, its left bank, to ascertain whether the Mexican troops had crossed or were preparing to cross the river, "became engaged with a large body of these troops, and after a short affair, in which some 16 were killed and wounded, appear to have been surrounded and compelled to surrender." . . .

Our commerce with Mexico has been almost annihilated. It was formerly highly beneficial to both nations, but our merchants have been deterred from prosecuting it by the system of outrage and extortion which the Mexican authorities have pursued against them, whilst their appeals through their own Government for indemnity have been made in vain. . . .

In the meantime we have tried every effort at reconciliation. The cup of forbearance had been exhausted even before the recent information from the frontier of the Del Norte. But now, after reiterated menaces, Mexico has passed the boundary of the United States, has invaded our territory and shed American blood upon the American soil. She has proclaimed that hostilities have commenced, and that the two nations are now at war.

As war exists, and, notwithstanding all our efforts to avoid it, exists by the act of Mexico herself, we are called upon by every consideration of duty and patriotism to vindicate with decision the honor, the rights, and the interests of our country. . . .

In further vindication of our rights and defense of our territory, I invoke the prompt action of Congress to recognize the existence of the war, and to place at the disposition of the Executive the means of prosecuting the war with vigor, and thus hastening the restoration of peace. . . .

PRESIDENT JAMES K. POLK'S ANNOUNCEMENT OF THE DISCOVERY OF GOLD IN CALIFORNIA
5 December 1848

No other event in California's history has been of such far-reaching importance as James W. Marshall's discovery of gold in the Sierra Nevada's about forty miles from present day Sacramento, on 24 January 1848. This momentous event occurred but nine days before the formal transfer of the territory from Mexico to the United States under the Treaty of Guadeloupe Hidalgo (2 February 1848). For three centuries, this area had not been settled by the Spaniards.

Marshall and his partner John A. Sutter tried to keep the discovery secret. But, the news spread rapidly. On 5 December 1848, President Polk confirmed the discovery in his annual message to Congress. The President had relied on a report by Governor R. B. Mason that stated "there is more gold in the country drained by the Sacramento and San Joaquin Rivers than will pay the cost of the present war with Mexico a hundred times over." Polk's sensational announcement stimulated the great California gold rush. Adventurers came from all parts of the United States and from places as distant as China and Australia. By the end of 1849, the population of California had grown by more than 100,000 as people took any and every route to try their luck in this unprecedented movement. It seemed as if the entire world was chanting Stephen Foster's 1848 ballad "Oh! Susanna:"

Oh! California,
That's the land for me;
I'm off for Sacramento
With my washbowl on my knee.

... It was known that mines of the precious metals existed to a considerable extent in California at the time of its acquisition. Recent discoveries render it probable that these mines are more extensive and valuable than was anticipated. The accounts of the abundance of gold in that territory are of such an extraordinary character as would scarcely command belief were they not corroborated by the authentic reports of officers in the public service who have visited the mineral district and derived the facts which they detail from personal observation. Reluctant to credit the reports in general circulation as to the quantity of gold, the officer commanding our forces in California visited the mineral district in July last for the purpose of obtaining accurate information on the subject. His report to the War Department of the result of his examination and the facts obtained on the spot is herewith laid before Congress. When he visited the country there were about 4,000 persons engaged in collecting gold. There is every reason to believe that the number of persons so employed has since been augmented. The explorations already made warrant the belief that the supply is very large and that gold is found at various places in an extensive district of country.

Information received from officers of the Navy and other sources, though not so full and minute, confirms the accounts of the commander of our military force in California. It appears also from these reports that mines of quicksilver are found in the vicinity of the gold region. One of them is now being worked, and is believed to be among the most productive in the world.

The effects produced by the discovery of these rich mineral deposits and the success which has attended the labors of those who have resorted to them have produced a surprising change in the state of affairs in California. Labor commands a most exorbitant price, and all other pursuits but that of searching for the precious metals are abandoned. Nearly the whole of the male population of the country have gone to the gold districts. Ships arriving on the coast are deserted by their crews and their voyages suspended for want of sailors. Our commanding officer there entertains apprehensions that soldiers can not be kept in the public service without a large increase of pay. Desertions in his command have become frequent, and he recommends that those who shall withstand the strong temptation and remain faithful should be rewarded.

This abundance of gold and the all-engrossing pursuit of it have already caused in California an unprecedented rise in the price of all the necessaries of life. . . .

President Zachary Taylor's Recommendation of Statehood for California
4 December 1849

With the signing of the Treaty of Guadeloupe Hidalgo (2 February 1848), California was formally annexed to the United States. The discovery of gold and the turbulent influx of people caused a clash between native Californian and Anglo-American customs. The military government established during the Mexican War proved to be inadequate to handle the crisis situation. The establishment of an effective civil authority was imperative. Yet Congress, harassed by the question of slavery in the Mexican Cession, remained deaf to California's plea for a territorial government. Finally, exasperated Californians took the initiative on 13 November 1849 by adopting a constitution that outlawed slavery.

President Taylor believed that the people of California had the right to adopt their own constitution without congressional authorization. He sent a special agent to inform them of his opinion. But before the agent arrived, Californians had acted. On 4 December 1849, Taylor recommended in his Annual Message the immediate admission of California into the Union. He urged Congress to "abstain from the introduction of those exiting topics of a sectional character." Southerners at once attacked Taylor's proposal for the admission of California with a constitution that had outlawed slavery.

... No civil government having been provided by Congress for California, the people of that Territory, impelled by the necessities of their political condition, recently met in convention for the purpose of forming a constitution and State government, which the latest advices give me reason to suppose has been accomplished; and it is believed they will shortly apply for the admission of California into the Union as a sovereign State. Should such be the case, and should their constitution be comformable to the requisitions of the Constitution of the United States, I recommend their application to the favorable consideration of Congress. The people of New Mexico will also, it is believed, at no very distant period present themselves for admission into the Union. Preparatory to the admission of California and New Mexico the people of each will have instituted for themselves a republican form of government, "laying its foundation in such principles and organizing its powers in such form as to them shall seem most likely to effect their safety and happiness." By awaiting their action all causes of uneasiness may be avoided and confidence and kind feeling preserved. With a view of maintaining the harmony and tranquillity so dear to all, we should abstain from the introduction of those exciting topics of a sectional character which have hitherto produced painful apprehensions in the public mind; and I repeat the solemn warning of the first and most illustrious of my predecessors against furnishing "any ground for characterizing parties by geographical discriminations." ...

PRESIDENT ZACHARY TAYLOR'S REQUEST FOR RATIFICATION OF THE CLAYTON-BULWER TREATY BETWEEN THE UNITED STATES AND GREAT BRITAIN
22 April 1850

When the Monroe Doctrine was first announced (1823) Great Britain had two settlements in Central America—in Belize, or British Honduras, and a protectorate over the pseudo-kingdom of the Mosquito Indians in Nicaragua. During the Mexican War, the British government quickly realized that an assured American victory would stimulate American interest in a ship canal across the Central American isthmus. Therefore, on 1 January 1848, British authorities, acting for the Mosquito King, seized the mouth of the San Juan River, the logical eastern terminus of any future canal in the region.

Strained relations at once developed between the two governments. Sir Henry Bulwer was sent to Washington, where, with Secretary of State John Clayton, he negotiated the treaty that bears their names. It provided that the two countries should jointly control and protect the canal which was expected to soon be built. Each nation guaranteed the neutrality and security of the canal.

On 22 April 1850, President Taylor requested the Senate to ratify the treaty, which it promptly did by a vote of 42–10. Almost immediately though, the treaty became very unpopular in the United States. Demand grew for abrogation to make possible the construction of an American-controlled canal. Finally, in 1902, the Hay-Pauncefote Treaty superseded the Clayton-Bulwer agreement.

I herewith transmit to the Senate, for their advice with regard to its ratification, a convention between the United States and Great Britain, concluded at Washington on the 19th instant by John M. Clayton, Secretary of State, on the part of the United States, and by the Right Hon. Sir Henry Lytton Bulwer, on the part of Great Britain.

This treaty has been negotiated in accordance with the general views expressed in my message to Congress in December last. Its object is to establish a commercial alliance with all great maritime states for the protection of a contemplated ship canal through the territory of Nicaragua to connect the Atlantic and Pacific oceans, and at the same time to insure the same protection to the contemplated railways or canals by the Tehuantepec and Panama routes, as well as to every other interoceanic communication which may be adopted to shorten the transit to or from our territories on the Pacific.

It will be seen that this treaty does not propose to take money from the public Treasury to effect any object contemplated by it. It yields protection to the capitalists who may undertake to construct any canal or railway across the Isthmus, commencing in the southern part of Mexico and terminating in the territory of New Granada. It gives no preference to any one route over another, but proposes the same measure of protection for all which ingenuity and enterprise can construct. Should this treaty by ratified, it will secure in future the liberation of all Central America from any kind of foreign aggression. . . .

If there by any who would desire to seize the annex any portion of the territories of these weak sister republics to the American Union, or to extend our dominion over them, I do not concur in their policy; and I wish it to be understood in reference to that subject that I adopt the views entertained, so far as I know, by all my predecessors.

The principles by which I have been regulated in the negotiation of this treaty are in accordance with the sentiments well expressed by my immediate predecessor on the 10th of February 1847, when he communicated to the Senate the treaty with New Granada for the protection of the railroad at Panama. It is in accordance with the whole spirit of the resolution of the Senate of the 3d of March 1835, referred to by President Polk, and with the policy adopted by President Jackson immediately after the passage of that resolution, who dispatched an agent to Central America and New Granada "to open negotiations with those Governments for the purpose of effectually protecting, by suitable treaty stipulations with them, such individuals or companies as might undertake to open a communication between the Atlantic and Pacific oceans by the construction of a ship canal across the isthmus which connects North and South America, and of securing forever by such stipulations the free and equal right of navigating such canal to all such nations on the payment of such reasonable tolls as might be established to compensate the capitalists who should engage in such undertaking and complete the work." . . .

Should the Senate in its wisdom see fit to confirm this treaty, and the treaty heretofore submitted by me for their advice in regard to its ratification, negotiated with the State of Nicaragua on the 3d day of September last, it will be necessary to amend one or both of them, so that both treaties may stand in conformity with each other in their spirit and intention. The Senate will discover by examining them both that this is a task of no great difficulty.

I have good reason to believe that France and Russia stand ready to accede to this treaty, and that no other great maritime state will refuse its accession to an arrangement so well calculated to diffuse the blessings of peace, commerce, and civilization, and so honorable to all nations which may enter into the engagement.

PRESIDENT MILLARD FILLMORE'S DEFENSE OF THE COMPROMISE OF 1850
2 December 1850

In 1850, the nation stood equally divided into fifteen slave and fifteen free states. When California petitioned for admission as a free state, the mounting sectional antagonisms threatened to disrupt the Union. Once more an adjustment resulted—the Compromise of 1850—in which both moderate northern and southern leaders rallied to avoid secession. The plan proposed the admission of California as a free state; the organization of New Mexico and Utah as territories without mention of slavery; the establishment of more efficient procedures for returning fugitive slaves to their masters; the abolition of the slave trade in the District of Columbia but the continuation of slavery there unless Maryland consented otherwise; and federal compensation to Texas for some territory ceded to New Mexico. Both sides would give up something but the Union would be preserved.

For months, Vice President Fillmore had presided over the Senate debate on the Great Compromise to save the Union. He thought that the Compromise would prevent a Civil War. In the midst of the debates, President Taylor, an opponent of the compromise measures, died. As President, Millard Fillmore supported the final passage. In the end, moderation triumphed and the nation endured—at least for another decade.

The Compromise of 1850 was the outstanding achievement of Fillmore's administration. On 2 December 1850, he explained why the preservation of the Union was above any specific settlement of the slavery question. His support for the Fugitive Slave Act, which ensured the return of runaway slaves, enraged abolitionists. His commitment to this part of the 1850 Compromise ended his political career.

. . . The act, passed at your last session, making certain propositions to Texas for settling the disputed boundary between that State and the Territory of New Mexico was, immediately on its passage, transmitted by express to the governor of Texas, to be laid by him before the general assembly for its agreement thereto. Its receipt was duly acknowledged, but no official information has yet been received of the action of the general assembly thereon. It may, however, be very soon expected, as, by the terms of the propositions submitted they were to have been acted upon on or before the first day of the present month.

It was hardly to have been expected that the series of measures passed at your last session with the view of healing the sectional differences which had sprung from the slavery and territorial questions should at once have realized their beneficent purpose. All mutual concession in the nature of a compromise must necessarily be unwelcome to men of extreme opinions. And though without such concessions our Constitution could not have been formed, and can not be permanently sustained, yet we have seen them made the subject of bitter controversy in both sections of the Republic. It required many months of discussion and deliberation to secure the concurrence of a majority of Congress in their favor. It would be strange if they had been received with immediate approbation by people and States prejudiced and heated by the exciting controversies of their representatives. I believe those measures to have been required by the circumstances and condition of the country. I believe they were necessary to allay asperities and animosities that were rapidly alienating one section of the country from another and destroying those fraternal sentiments which are the strongest supports of the Constitution. They were adopted in the spirit of conciliation and for the purpose of conciliation. I believe that a great majority of our fellow-citizens sympathize in that spirit and that purpose, and in the main approve and are prepared in all respects to sustain these enactments. I can not doubt that the American people, bound together by kindred blood and common traditions, still cherish a paramount regard for the Union of their fathers, and that they are ready to rebuke any attempt to violate its integrity, to disturb the compromises on which it is based, or to resist the laws which have been enacted under its authority.

The series of measures to which I have alluded are regarded by me as a settlement in principle and substance—a final settlement of the dangerous and exciting subjects which they embraced. Most of these subjects, indeed, are beyond your reach, as the legislation which disposed of them was in its character final and irrevocable. It may be presumed from the opposition which they all encountered that none of those measures was free from imperfections, but in their mutual dependence and connection they formed a system of compromise the most conciliatory and best for the entire country that could be obtained from conflicting sectional interests and opinions.

For this reason I recommend your adherence to the adjustment established by those measures until time and experience shall demonstrate the necessity of further legislation to guard against evasion or abuse.

By that adjustment we have been rescued from the wide and boundless agitation that surrounded us, and have a firm, distinct, and legal ground to rest upon. And the occasion, I trust, will justify me in exhorting my countrymen to rally upon and maintain that ground as the best, if not the only, means of restoring peace and quiet to the country and maintaining inviolate the integrity of the Union. . . .

PRESIDENT FRANKLIN PIERCE'S REQUEST FOR RATIFICATION OF THE TREATY OF KANAGAWA BETWEEN THE UNITED STATES AND JAPAN
12 July 1854

In January 1852, President Millard Fillmore authorized Commodore Matthew Perry to lead an expedition to Japan. Its objective was threefold: concern about shipwrecked Americans'; permission for American ships involved in the Asiatic trade to obtain emergency fuel and water; and to induce the Japanese government to open up one or more of their ports for trade.

On 31 March 1854, Commodore Perry concluded with the Japanese government a treaty of peace, friendship, and commerce. The success of the expedition, so important for Japan and the entire Western World, was mainly due to the skill with which Perry combined diplomacy and naval power in overcoming Japanese reluctance to the break-down of their isolation.

On 12 July 1854, President Pierce submitted the Treaty of Kanagawa for ratification. The Senate rapidly complied and on 22 June 1855, the treaty was officially promulgated.

I transmit to the Senate, for its consideration with a view to ratification, a treaty between the United States and the Empire of Japan, signed at Kanagawa on the 31st day of March last by the plenipotentiaries of the two Governments. The Chinese and Dutch translations of the instrument and the chart and sketch to which it refers are also herewith communicated.

President James Buchanan's Inaugural Address
4 March 1857

On Inauguration Day, 1857 James Buchanan rode to the Capitol with the outgoing Pierce. From the East Portico, he read his long address.

The new President had something to say on most great issues of the day. He recommended the construction of a national railroad to the Pacific for military purposes. He stood for economy, for the payment of the public debt, and for a small increase in the navy. Above all, he affirmed his decision to uphold the Kansas-Nebraska Act (1854), believing that the people should be free to regulate slavery as they saw fit. In an oblique reference, Buchanan predicted the Supreme Court would shortly settle the issue of slavery in the territories once and for all—although he did not reveal that he had received advance information of the fateful Dred Scott decision (1857). Most startling though, was his announcement declaring he would serve only one term. Thus, from the beginning of Buchanan's presidency, politicians sought his successor.

I appear before you this day to take the solemn oath "that I will faithfully execute the office of President of the United States and will to the best of my ability preserve, protect, and defend the Constitution of the United States." . . .

Convinced that I owe my election to the inherent love for the Constitution and the Union which still animates the hearts of the American people, let me earnestly ask their powerful support in sustaining all just measures calculated to perpetuate these, the richest political blessings which Heaven has ever bestowed upon any nation. Having determined not to become a candidate for reelection, I shall have no motive to influence my conduct in administering the Government except the desire ably and faithfully to serve my country and to live in grateful memory of my countrymen. . . .

What a happy conception, then, was it for Congress to apply this simple rule, that the will of the majority shall govern, to the settlement of the question of domestic slavery in the Territories! Congress is neither "to legislate slavery into any Territory or State nor to exclude it therefrom, but to leave the people thereof perfectly free to form and regain their domestic institutions in their own way, subject only to the Constitution of the United States."

As a natural consequence, Congress has also prescribed that when the Territory of Kansas shall be admitted as a State it "shall be received into the Union with or without slavery, as their constitution may prescribe at the time of their admission."

A difference of opinion has arisen in regard to the point of time when the people of a Territory shall decide this question for themselves.

This is, happily, a matter of but little practical importance. Besides, it is a judicial question, which legitimately belongs to the Supreme Court of the United States, before whom it is now pending, and will, it is understood, be speedily and finally settled. To their

decision, in common with all good citizens, I shall cheerfully submit, whatever this may be, though it has ever been my individual opinion that under the Nebraska-Kansas act the appropriate period will be when the number of actual residents in the Territory shall justify the formation of a constitution with a view to its admission as a State into the Union. But be this as it may, it is the imperative and indispensable duty of the Government of the United States to secure to every resident inhabitant the free and independent expression of his opinion by his vote. This sacred right of each individual must be preserved. That being accomplished, nothing can be fairer than to leave the people of a Territory free from all foreign interference to decide their own destiny for themselves, subject only to the Constitution of the United States.

The whole Territorial question being thus settled upon the principle of popular sovereignty—a principle as ancient as free government itself—everything of a practical nature has been decided. No other question remains for adjustment, because all agree that under the Constitution slavery in the States is beyond the reach of any human power except that of the respective States themselves wherein it exists. . . .

The Federal Constitution is a grant from the States to Congress of certain specific powers, and the question whether this grant should be liberally or strictly construed has more or less divided political parties from the beginning. Without entering into the argument, I desire to state at the commencement of my Administration that long experience and observation have convinced me that a strict construction of the powers of the Government is the only true, as well as the only safe, theory of the Constitution. Whenever in our past history doubtful powers have been exercised by Congress, these have never failed to produce injurious and unhappy consequences. Many such instances might be adduced if this were the proper occasion. Neither is it necessary for the public service to strain the language of the Constitution, because all the great and useful powers required for a successful administration of the Government, both in peace and in war, have been granted, either in express terms or by the plainest implication. . . .

Whilst deeply convinced of these truths, I yet consider it clear that under the war-making power Congress may appropriate money toward the construction of a military road when this is absolutely necessary for the defense of any State or Territory of the Union against foreign invasion. Under the Constitution Congress has power "to declare war," "to raise and support armies," "to provide and maintain a navy," and to call forth the militia to "repel invasions." Thus endowed, in an ample manner, with the war-making power, the corresponding duty is required that "the United States shall protect each of them [the States] against invasion." Now, how is it possi-

ble to afford this protection to California and our Pacific possessions except by means of a military road through the Territories of the United States, over which men and munitions of war may be speedily transported from the Atlantic States to meet and to repel the invader? In the event of a war with a naval power much stronger than our own we should then have no other available access to the Pacific Coast, because such a power would instantly close the route across the isthmus of Central America. It is impossible to conceive that whilst the Constitution has expressly required Congress to defend all the States it should yet deny to them, by any fair construction, the only possible means by which one of these States can be defended. Besides, the Government, ever since its origin, has been in the constant practice of constructing military roads. It might also be wise to consider whether the love for the Union which now animates our fellow-citizens on the Pacific Coast may not be impaired by our neglect or refusal to provide for them, in their remote and isolated condition, the only means by which the power of the States on this side of the Rocky Mountains can reach them in sufficient time to "protect" them "again invasion." I forbear for the present from expressing an opinion as to the wisest and most economical mode in which the Government can lend its aid in accomplishing this great and necessary work. I believe that many of the difficulties in the way, which now appear formidable, will in a great degree vanish as soon as the nearest and best

route shall have been satisfactorily ascertained. . . .

PRESIDENT JAMES BUCHANAN'S
VIEWS ON THE SECESSION
3 December 1860

Between Lincoln's electoral victory (6 November 1860) and his inauguration (4 March 1861), James Buchanan served as a "lame-duck" President—one without the will to make commitments involving the impending crisis between the states.

On 3 December 1861, Buchanan sent his last Annual Message to Congress. In it he placed the blame for the crisis squarely on the northern antislavery agitators and warned them that unless they left the slave states alone, disunion would be inevitable. One half the nation would not live "habitually and perpetually insecure," and only those who had threatened to bathe the South in blood could dissipate the fears they had aroused. He proposed a Constitutional convention that would amend the document guaranteeing slavery! At the same time Buchanan deprecated the possible breakup of the Union, he announced that the federal government could not use force to prevent secession.

Buchanan's message got a mixed and partisan reception. Voices of unqualified approval were scarce. Republicans found it outrageous in placing the blame for the crisis on their party while failing to meet head-on, the threat of disunion. Many northern Democrats agreed with the President's rebuke to antislavery agitators but were dissatisfied with his feeble attempts to prevent secession. Overall, Buchanan's statement strengthened the assumption that little could be expected from the White House to save the Union. With only three months remaining in his term, the President no longer commanded public respect or exercised much control over his defeated and divided party.

Throughout the year since our last meeting the country has been eminently prosperous in all its material interests. The general health has been excellent, our harvests have been abundant, and plenty smiles throughout the land. Our commerce and manufactures have been prosecuted with energy and industry, and have yielded fair and ample returns. In short, no nation in the tide of time has ever presented a spectacle of greater material prosperity than we have done until within a very recent period.

Why is it, then, that discontent now so extensively prevails, and the Union of the States, which is the source of all these blessings, is threatened with destruction?

The long-continued and intemperate interference of the Northern people with the question of slavery in the Southern States has at length produced its natural effect. The different sections of the Union are now arrayed against each other, and the time has arrived, so much dreaded by the Father of his Country, when hostile geographical parties have been formed.

I have long foreseen and often forewarned my countrymen of the now impending danger. This does not proceed solely from the claim on the part of Congress or the Territorial legislatures to exclude slavery from the Territories, nor from the efforts of different States to defeat the execution of the fugitive-slave law. All or any of these evils might have been endured by the South without danger to the Union (as others have been) in the hope that time and reflection might apply the remedy. The immediate peril arises not so much from these causes as from the fact that the incessant and violent agitation of the slavery question throughout the North for the last quarter of a century has at length produced its malign influence on the slaves and inspired them with vague notions of freedom. Hence a sense of security no longer exists around the family altar. This feeling of peace at home has given place to apprehensions of servile insurrections.

Many a matron throughout the South retires at night in dread of what may befall herself and children before the morning. Should this apprehension of domestic danger, whether real or imaginary, extend and intensify itself until it shall pervade the masses of the Southern people, then disunion will become inevitable. Self-preservation is the first law of nature, and has been implanted in the heart of man by his Creator for the wisest purpose; and no political union, however fraught with blessings and benefits in all other respects, can long continue if the necessary consequence be to render the homes and the firesides of nearly half the parties to it habitually and hopelessly insecure. Sooner or later the bonds of such a union must be severed. It is my conviction that this fatal period has not yet arrived, and my prayer to God is that He would preserve the Constitution and the Union throughout all generations. . . .

How easy would it be for the American people to settle the slavery question forever and to restore peace and harmony to this distracted country! They, and they alone, can do it. All that is necessary to accomplish the object, and all for which the slave States have ever contended, is to be let alone and permitted to manage their domestic institutions in their own way. As sovereign States, they, and they alone, are responsible before God and the world for the slavery existing among them. For this the people of the North are not more responsible and have no more right to interfere than with similar institutions in Russia or in Brazil.

Upon their good sense and patriotic forbearance I confess I still greatly rely. Without their aid it is beyond the power of any President, no matter what may be his own political proclivities, to restore peace and harmony among the States. Wisely limited and restrained as is his power under our Constitution and laws, he alone can accomplish but little for good or for evil on such a momentous question.

And this brings me to observe that the election of any one of our fellow-citizens to the office of President does not of itself afford just cause for dissolving the Union. This is more especially true if his election has been effected by a mere plurality, and not a majority of the people, and has resulted from transient and temporary causes, which may probably never again occur. In order to justify a resort to revolutionary resistance, the Federal Government must be guilty of "a deliberate, palpable, and dangerous exercise" of powers not granted by the Constitution. The late Presidential election, however, has been held in strict conformity with its express provisions. How, then, can the result justify a revolution to destroy this very Constitution? . . .

It is alleged as one cause for immediate secession that the Southern States are denied equal rights with the other States in the common Territories. But by what authority are these denied? Not by Congress, justly be held respon-

sible. Having been passed in violation of the Federal Constitution, they are therefore null and void. All the courts, both State and national, before whom the question has arisen have from the beginning declared the fugitive-slave law to be constitutional. The single exception is that of a State court in Wisconsin, and this has not only been reversed by the proper appellate tribunal, but has met with such universal reprobation that there can be no danger from it as a precedent. The validity of this law has been established over and over again by the Supreme Court of the United States with perfect unanimity. It is founded upon an express provision of the Constitution, requiring that fugitive slaves who escape from service in one State to another shall be "delivered up" to their masters. Without this provision it is a well-known historical fact that the Constitution itself could never have been adopted by the Convention. . . .

The Southern States, standing on the basis of the Constitution, have a right to demand this act of justice from the States of the North. Should it be refused, then the Constitution, to which all the States are parties, will have been willfully violated by one portion of them in a provision essential to the domestic security and happiness of the remainder. In that event the injured States, after having first used all peaceful and constitutional means to obtain redress, would be justified in revolutionary resistance to the Government of the Union. . . .

PRESIDENT ABRAHAM LINCOLN'S
FIRST INAUGURAL ADDRESS
4 March 1861

The 1860 election is the most important in American history. When the results were known, the Union began to shatter. During Buchanan's administration, sectional disputes had become more acrimonious, passions more excited, propagandists in both the North and South more active. The Dred Scott decision (1857) and John Brown's raid at Harper's Ferry (1859) further intensified the burning slavery issue. With the fatalism of a Greek tragedy, the nation appeared to be rushing toward destruction.

When the Democratic party assembled at Charleston in April 1860, southern delegates refused to accept any platform that did not guarantee federal protection of slavery in the territories. Stephen Douglas controlled a majority of the delegates and would not agree— but his support stopped short of the two-thirds necessary to gain the nomination. After ten days of futile balloting, the convention adjourned to meet again in Baltimore on 18 June. Upon reassembling, the party remained divided into northern and southern wings. Most southern delegates now withdrew and the Northern Democrats nominated Douglas. The bolters put forth John C. Breckinridge of Kentucky for President on a platform supporting slavery in the territories. With this crucial Democratic split, another bond holding the Union together dissolved. Republican chances for victory now brightened.

The Republican party nominated Abraham Lincoln. Now fifty-three years old, he had served as a Whig representative for one term (1847–49) and then resumed his law practice in Springfield, Illinois. In 1858, Lincoln had accepted the Republican nomination for the Senate, opposing Stephen Douglas. In the course of seven campaign debates with Douglas, Lincoln, although he lost the election, established himself as a national figure. Few who voted for Lincoln at the 1860 Republican convention realized that their greatest man had been nominated, a man who would become a towering humanitarian. To the majority of the delegates, he simply appeared to have the best chance of winning.

In addition to Lincoln, Douglas and Breckinridge, the former Whig-American party, renamed the Constitutional Union party, nominated John Bell of Tennessee on a platform advocating "the Constitution of the country, the union of the states, and enforcement of the laws." When the returns were tabulated, Lincoln received 180 of the 303 electoral votes—all from free states. Breckinridge carried eleven slave states and 72 votes; Bell ran third with 39, winning three border slave states; Douglas captured only Missouri and three New Jersey votes for a total of 12. In the popular vote column, Lincoln received only 39.9 percent of the total. The results clearly show the sectional voting pattern, almost as if two elections were being held: Lincoln vs. Douglas in the North and West, Breckinridge vs. Bell in the South. Although Lincoln pledged himself and his party to uphold the Union, its future remained in southern hands.

On 20 December 1860, South Carolina seceded. Lincoln's election, declared the state's governor, would "inevitably destroy our equality in the Union, and ultimately reduce the Southern states to mere provinces of a consolidated despotism, to be governed by a fixed majority in Congress hostile to our institutions and fatally bent upon our ruin." The Deep South followed and during January 1861, Mississippi, Florida, Alabama, Georgia, Louisiana, and Texas passed secession ordinances. With the exception of South Carolina, this movement certainly was not unanimous. In Alabama, for example, 34 of the 95 delegates to the special convention voted against immediate secession; in Georgia, 133 out of 297. Nevertheless, the zealots triumphed. And the South, which had talked about states rights for so long, now, ironically, established a national government, the Confederate States of America. Throughout this crisis, the Buchanan administration evolved no clear policy.

Lincoln left Springfield on 11 February 1861. As he moved toward Washington, he calmly explained to anxious crowds the necessity of preserving the Union. His journey became one continuous ovation. "We mean to treat you, as near as we possibly can, as Washington, Jefferson, and Madison treated you," he told a group of Kentuckians present in the Cincinnati crowd. "We mean to leave you alone, and in no way to interfere with your institutions, to abide by all and every compromise of the Constitution." At Pittsburgh, he remarked that despite the trouble "across the river," no crisis existed: "If the American people will only keep their temper on both sides of the line the troubles will come to an end and they will prosper as heretofore." He reached Washington on 23 February. Nine days later, before the stark, unfinished Capitol, Lincoln took his oath of office. In a masterly inaugural address, which had been carefully prepared, he invoked "the mystic chords of memory" in making a direct appeal to Southerners: "In your hands, my dissatisfied fellow-countrymen, and not in mine, is the momentous issue of civil war. The government will not assail you. You can have no conflict without being yourselves the aggressors."

In compliance with a custom as old as the Government itself, I appear before you to address you briefly and to take in your presence the oath prescribed by the Constitution of the United States to be taken by the President "before he enters on the execution of this office.". . .

Apprehension seems to exist among the people of the Southern States that by the accession of a Republican Administration their property and their peace and personal security are to be endangered. There has never been any reasonable cause for such apprehension. Indeed, the most ample evidence to the contrary has all the while existed and been open to their inspection. It is found in nearly all the published speeches of him who now addresses you. I do but quote from one of those speeches when I declare that—

I have no purpose, directly or indirectly, to interfere with the institution of slavery in the States where it exists. I believe I have no lawful right to do so, and I have no inclination to do so. . . .

I now reiterate these sentiments, and in doing so I only press upon the public attention the most conclusive evidence of which the case is susceptible that the property, peace, and security of no section are to be in any wise endangered by the now incoming Administration. I add, too, that all the protection which, consistently with the Constitution and the laws, can be given will be cheerfully given to all the States when lawfully demanded, for whatever cause—as cheerfully to one section as to another. . . .

I take the official oath today with no mental reservations and with no purpose to construe the Constitution or laws by any hypercritical rules; and while I do not choose now to specify particular acts of Congress as proper to be enforced, I do suggest that it will be much safer for all, both in official and private stations, to conform to and abide by all those acts which stand unrepealed than to violate any of them trusting to find impunity in having them held to be unconstitutional.

It is seventy-two years since the first inauguration of a President under our National Constitution. During that period fifteen different and greatly distinguished citizens have in succession administered the executive branch of the Government. They have conducted it through many perils, and generally with great success. Yet, with all this scope of precedent, I now enter upon the same task for the brief constitutional term of four years under great and peculiar difficulty. A disruption of the Federal Union, heretofore only menaced, is now formidably attempted.

I hold that in contemplation of universal law and of the Constitution the Union of these Sates is perpetual. Perpetuity is implied, if not expressed, in the fundamental law of all national governments. It is safe to assert that no government proper ever had a provision in its organic law for its own termination. Continue to execute all the express provisions of our National Constitution, and the Union will endure forever, as being impossible to destroy it except by some action not provided for in the instrument itself.

Again: If the United States be not a government proper, but an association of States in the nature of contract merely, can it, as a contract, be peaceably unmade by less than all the parties who made it? One party to a contract may violate it—break it, so to speak—but does it not require all to lawfully rescind it?

Descending from these general principles, we find the proposition that in legal contemplation the Union is perpetual, confirmed by the history of the Union itself. The Union is much older than the Constitution. It was formed, in fact, by the Articles of Association in 1774. It was matured and continued by the Declaration of Independence in 1776. It was further matured, and the faith of all the then thirteen States expressly plighted and engaged that it should be perpetual, by the Articles of Confederation in

1778. And finally, in 1787, one of the declared objects for ordaining and establishing the Constitution was "*to form a more perfect Union.*"

But if destruction of the Union by one or by a part only of the States be lawfully possible, the Union is *less* perfect than before the Constitution, having lost the vital element of perpetuity.

It follows from these views that no State upon its own mere motion can lawfully get out of the Union; that *resolves* and *ordinances* to that effect are legally void, and that acts of violence within any State or States against the authority of the United States are insurrectionary or revolutionary, according to circumstances.

I therefore consider that in view of the Constitution and the laws the Union is unbroken, and to the extent of my ability, I shall take care, as the Constitution itself expressly enjoins upon me, that the laws of the Union be faithfully executed in all the States. Doing this I deem to be only a simple duty on my part, and I shall perform it so far as practicable unless my rightful masters, the American people, shall withhold the requisite means or in some authoritative manner direct the contrary. I trust this will not be regarded as a menace, but only as the declared purpose of the Union that it *will* constitutionally defend and maintain itself.

In doing this there needs to be no bloodshed or violence, and there shall be none unless it be forced upon the national authority. The power confided to me will be used to hold, occupy, and possess the property and places belonging to the Government and to collect the duties and imposts; but beyond what may be necessary for these objects, there will be no invasion, no using of force against or among the people anywhere. Where hostility to the United States in any interior locality shall be so great and universal as to prevent competent resident citizens from holding the Federal offices, there will be no attempt to force obnoxious strangers among the people for that object. While the strict legal right may exist in the Government to enforce the exercise of these offices, the attempt to do so would be so irritating and so nearly impracticable withal that I deem it better to forego for the time the uses of such offices.

The mails, unless repelled, will continue to be furnished in all parts of the Union. So far as possible the people everywhere shall have that sense of perfect security which is most favorable to calm thought and reflection. The course here indicated will be followed unless current events and experience shall show a modification or change to be proper, and in every case and exigency my best discretion will be exercised, according to circumstances actually existing and with a view and a hope of a peaceful solution of the national troubles and the restoration of fraternal sympathies and affections.

That there are persons in one section or another who seek to destroy the Union at all events and are glad of any pretext to do it I will neither affirm nor deny; but if there be such, I need address no word to them. To those, however, who really love the Union may I not speak?

Before entering upon so grave a matter as the destruction of our national fabric, with all its benefits, its memories, and its hopes, would it not be wise to ascertain precisely why we do it? Will you hazard so desperate a step while there is any possibility that any portion of the ills you fly from have no real existence? Will you, while the certain ills you fly to are greater than all the real ones you fly from, will you risk the commission of so fearful a mistake?

All profess to be content in the Union if all constitutional rights can be maintained. Is it true, then, that any right plainly written in the Constitution has been denied? I think not. Happily, the human mind is so constituted that no party can reach to the audacity of doing this. Think, if you can, of a single instance in which a plainly written provision of the Constitution has ever been denied. If by the mere force of numbers a majority should deprive a minority of any clearly written constitutional right, it might in a moral point of view justify revolution; certainly would if such right were a vital one. But such is not our case. All the vital rights of minorities and of individuals are so plainly assured to them by affirmations and negations, guaranties and prohibitions, in the Constitution that controversies never arise concerning them. But no organic law can ever be framed with a provision specifically applicable to every question which may occur in practical administration. No foresight can anticipate nor any document of reasonable length contain express provisions for all possible questions. Shall fugitives from labor be surrendered by national or by State authority? The Constitution does not expressly say. *May* Congress prohibit slavery in the Territories? The Constitution does not expressly say. *Must* Congress protect slavery in the Territories? The Constitution does not expressly say.

From questions of this class spring all our constitutional controversies, and we divide upon them into majorities and minorities. If the minority will not acquiesce, the majority must, or the Government must cease. There is no other alternative, for continuing the Government is acquiescence on one side or the other. If a minority in such case will secede rather than acquiesce, they make a precedent which in turn will divide and ruin them, for a minority of their own will secede from them whenever a majority refuses to be controlled by such minority. For instance, why may not any portion of a new confederacy a year or two hence arbitrarily secede again, precisely as portions of the present Union now claim to secede from it? All who cherish disunion sentiments are now being educated to the exact temper of doing this.

Is there such perfect identity of interests among the States to compose a new union as to produce harmony only and prevent renewed secession?

Plainly the central idea of secession is the essence of anarchy. A majority held in restraint by constitutional checks and limitations, and always changing easily with deliberate changes of popular opinions and sentiments, is the only true sovereign of a free people. Whoever rejects it does of necessity fly to anarchy or to despotism. Unanimity is impossible. The rule of a minority, as a permanent arrangement, is wholly inadmissible; so that, rejecting the majority principle, anarchy or despotism in some form is all that is left.

I do not forget the position assumed by some that constitutional questions are to be decided by the Supreme Court, nor do I deny that such decisions must be binding in any case upon the parties to a suit as to the object of that suit, while they are also entitled to very high respect and consideration in all parallel cases by all other departments of the Government. And while it is obviously possible that such decision may be erroneous in any given case, still the evil effect following it, being limited to that particular case, with the chance that it may be overruled and never become a precedent for other cases, can better be borne than could the evils of a different practice. At the same time, the candid citizen must confess that if the policy of the Government upon vital questions affecting the whole people is to be irrevocably fixed by decisions of the Supreme Court, the instant they are made in ordinary litigation between parties in personal actions the people will have ceased to be their own rulers, having to that extent practically resigned their Government into the hands of that eminent tribunal. Nor is there in this view any assault upon the court or the judges. It is a duty from which they may not shrink to decide cases properly brought before them, and it is no fault of theirs if others seek to turn their decisions to political purposes.

One section of our country believes slavery is *right* and ought to be extended, while the other believes it is *wrong* and ought not to be extended. This is the only substantial dispute. The fugitive-slave clause of the Constitution and the law for the suppression of the foreign slave trade are each as well enforced, perhaps, as any law can ever be in a community where the moral sense of the people imperfectly supports the law itself. The great body of the people abide by the dry legal obligation in both cases, and a few break over in each. This, I think, can not be perfectly cured, and it would be worse in both cases *after* the separation of the sections than before. The foreign slave trade, now imperfectly suppressed, would be ultimately revived without restriction in one section, while fugitive slaves, now only partially surrendered, would not be surrendered at all by the other.

Physically speaking, we can not separate. We can not remove our respective sections from each other nor build an impassable wall between them. A husband and wife may be divorced and go out of the presence and beyond the reach of each other, but the different parts of our country can not do this. They can not but remain face to face, and intercourse, either amicable or hostile, must continue between them. Is it possible, then, to make that intercourse more advantageous or more satisfactory *after* separation than *before?* Can aliens make treaties easier than friends can make laws? Can treaties be more faithfully enforced between aliens than laws can among friends? Suppose you go to war, you can not fight always; and when, after much loss on both sides and no gain on either, you cease fighting, the identical old questions, as to terms of intercourse, are again upon you.

This country, with its institutions, belongs to the people who inhabit it. Whenever they shall grow weary of the existing Government, they can exercise their *constitutional* right of amending it or their *revolutionary* right to dismember or overthrow it. I can not be ignorant of the fact that many worthy and patriotic citizens are desirous of having the National Constitution amended. While I make no recommendation of amendments, I fully recognize the rightful authority of the people over the whole subject, to be exercised in either of the modes prescribed in the instrument itself; and I should, under existing circumstances, favor rather than oppose a fair opportunity being afforded the people to act upon it. I will venture to add that to me the convention mode seems preferable, in that it allows amendments to originate with the peo-

ple themselves, instead of only permitting them to take or reject propositions originated by others, not especially chosen for the purpose, and which might not be precisely such as they would wish to either accept or refuse. I understand a proposed amendment to the Constitution—which amendment, however, I have not seen—has passed Congress, to the effect that the Federal Government shall never interfere with the domestic institutions of the States, including that of persons held to service. To avoid misconstruction of what I have said, I depart from my purpose not to speak of particular amendments so far as to say that, holding such a provision to now be implied constitutional law, I have no objection to its being made express and irrevocable.

The Chief Magistrate derives all his authority from the people, and they have referred none upon him to fix terms for the separation of the States. The people themselves can do this if also they choose but the Executive as such has nothing to do with it. His duty is to administer the present Government as it came to his hands and to transmit it unimpaired by him to his successor.

Why should there not be a patient confidence in the ultimate justice of the people? Is there any better or equal hope in the world? In our present differences, is either party without faith of being in the right? If the Almighty Ruler of Nations, with His eternal truth and justice, be on your side of the North, or on yours of the South, that truth and that justice will surely prevail by the judgment of this great tribunal of the American people.

By the frame of the Government under which we live this same people have wisely given their public servants but little power for mischief, and have with equal wisdom provided for the return of that little to their own hands at very short intervals. While the people retain their virtue and vigilance no Administration by any extreme of wickedness or folly can very seriously injure the Government in the short space of four years.

My countrymen, one and all, think calmly and *well* upon this whole subject. Nothing valuable can be lost by taking time. If there be an object to *hurry* any of you in hot haste to a step which you would never take *deliberately,* that object will be frustrated by taking time; but no good object can be frustrated by it. Such of you as are now dissatisfied still have the old Constitution unimpaired, and, on the sensitive point, the laws of your own framing under it; while the new Administration will have no immediate power, if it would, to change either. If it were ad-mitted that you who are dissatisfied hold the right side in the dispute, there still is no single good reason for precipitate action. Intelligence, patriotism, Christianity, and a firm reliance on Him who has never yet forsaken this favored land are still competent to adjust in the best way all our present difficulty.

In *your* hands, my dissatisfied fellow-countrymen, and not in *mine,* the momentous issue of civil war. The Government will not assail *you.* You can have no conflict without being yourselves the aggressors. *You* have no oath registered in heaven to destroy the Government, while *I* shall have the most solemn one to "preserve, protect, and defend it."

I am loath to close. We are not enemies, but friends. We must not be enemies. Though passion may have strained it must not break our bonds of affection. The mystic chords of memory, stretching from every battlefield and patriot grave to every living heart and hearthstone all over this broad land, will yet swell the chorus of the Union, when again touched, as surely they will be, by the better angels of our nature.

PRESIDENT ABRAHAM LINCOLN'S MESSAGE TO CONGRESS
4 July 1861

The Civil War began on 12 April 1861 with the firing on Fort Sumter in Charleston harbor by South Carolinians. On 15 April, Lincoln declared that an "insurrection" existed and he called for 75,000 three month volunteers. At the same time, he called Congress to meet in special session on 4 July 1861.

Between April and July, Lincoln had summoned the militia into active duty, proclaimed a blockade, expanded the regular army beyond the legal limit, suspended the habeas corpus privilege, directed governmental expenditures in advance of congressional appropriations, and, in cooperation with his cabinet and the state governments, had launched a series of military measures to suppress the rebellion.

In a masterly message to Congress on 4 July 1861, Lincoln explained his policies since the firing on Fort Sumter. He recounted the steps that had led to war, stated his concept on the significance of preserving the Union, and appealed for ratification of his acts as well as for future cooperation. Congress ratified the President's actions—and the Supreme Court added its sanction by deciding, in the Prize Cases (1863), that executive proclamations were adequate to blockade Confederate ports. The Court ruled that the President could not initiate war but he was fulfilling his lawful duties in resisting insurrection, and that an insurrection was, in fact, war.

Having been convened on an extraordinary occasion, as authorized by the Constitution, your attention is not called to any ordinary subject of legislation.

At the beginning of the present presidential term, four months ago, the functions of the Federal Government were found to be generally suspended within the several States of South Carolina, Georgia, Alabama, Mississippi, Louisiana, and Florida, excepting only those of the Post-office Department.

Within these States all the forts, arsenals, dockyards, custom-houses, and the like, including the movable and stationary property in and about them, had been seized, and were held in open hostility to this government, excepting only Forts Pickens, Taylor, and Jefferson, on and near the Florida coast, and Fort Sumter, in Charleston Harbor, South Carolina. The forts thus seized had been put in improved condition, new ones had been built, and armed forces had been organized and were organizing, all avowedly with the same hostile purpose.

The forts remaining in the possession of the Federal Government in and near these States were either besieged or menaced by warlike preparations, and especially Fort Sumter was nearly surrounded by well-protected hostile batteries, with guns equal in quality to the best of its own, and outnumbering the latter as perhaps ten to one. A disproportionate share of the Federal muskets and rifles had somehow found their way into these States, and had been seized to be used against the government. Accumulations of the public revenue lying within them had been seized for the same object. The navy was scattered in distant seas, leaving but a very small part of it within the immediate reach of the government. Officers of the Federal army and navy had resigned in great numbers; and of those resigning a large proportion had taken up arms against the government. Simultaneously, and in connection with all this, the purpose to sever the Federal Union was openly avowed. In accordance with this purpose, an ordinance had been adopted in each of these States, declaring the States respectively to be separated from the National Union. A formula for instituting a combined government of these States had been promulgated; and this illegal organization, in the character of confederate States, was already invoking recognition, aid, and intervention from foreign powers.

Finding this condition of things, and believing it to be an imperative duty upon the incoming executive to prevent, if possible, the consummation of such attempt to destroy the Federal Union, a choice of means to that end became indispensable. This choice was made and was declared in the inaugural address. The policy chosen looked to the exhaustion of all peaceful measures before a resort to any stronger ones. It sought only to hold the public places and property not already wrested from the government, and to collect the revenue, relying for the rest on time, discussion, and the ballot-box. It promised a continuance of the mails, at government expense, to the very people who were resisting the government; and it gave repeated pledges against any disturbance to any of the people, or any of their rights. Of all that which a President might constitutionally and justifiably do in such a case, everything was forborne without

which it was believed possible to keep the government on foot. . . .

It was believed, however, that to so abandon that position, under the circumstances, would be utterly ruinous; that the necessity under which it was to be done would not be fully understood; that by many it would be construed as a part of a voluntary policy; that at home it would discourage the friends of the Union, embolden its adversaries, and go far to insure to the latter a recognition abroad; that, in fact, it would be our national destruction consummated. This could not be allowed. Starvation was not yet upon the garrison, and ere it would be reached Fort Pickens might be reinforced. This last would be a clear indication of policy, and would better enable the country to accept the evacuation of Fort Sumter as a military necessity. An order was at once directed to be sent for the landing of the troops from the steamship *Brooklyn* into Fort Pickens. This order could not go by land, but must take the longer and slower route by sea. The first return news from the order was received just one week before the fall of Fort Sumter. The news itself was that the officer commanding the *Sabine,* to which vessel the troops had been transferred from the *Brooklyn*, acting upon some *quasi* armistice of the late administration (and of the existence of which the present administration, up to the time the order was dispatched, had only too vague and uncertain rumors to fix attention), had refused to land the troops. To now reinforce Fort Pickens before a crisis would be reached at Fort Sumter was impossible—rendered so by the near exhaustion of provisions in the latter-named fort. In precaution against such a conjuncture, the government had, a few days before, commenced preparing an expedition as well adapted as might be to relieve Fort Sumter, which expedition was intended to be ultimately used, or not, according to circumstances. The strongest anticipated case for using it was now presented, and it was resolved to send it forward. As had been intended in this contingency, it was also resolved to notify the governor of South Carolina that he might expect an attempt would be made to provision the fort; and that, if the attempt should not be resisted, there would be no effort to throw in men, arms, or ammunition, without further notice, or in case of an attack upon the fort. This notice was accordingly given; whereupon the fort was attacked and bombarded to its fall, without even awaiting the arrival of the provisioning expedition.

It is thus seen that the assault upon and reduction of Fort Sumter was in no sense a matter of self-defense on the part of the assailants. They well knew that the garrison in the fort could by no possibility commit aggression upon them. They knew—they were expressly notified—that the giving of bread to the few brave and hungry men of the garrison was all which would on that occasion be attempted, unless themselves, by resisting so much, should provoke more. They knew that this government desired to keep the garrison in the fort, not to assail them, but merely to maintain visible possession, and thus to preserve the Union from actual and immediate dissolution—trusting, as hereinbefore stated, to time, discussion, and the ballot-box for final adjustment; and they assailed and reduced the fort for precisely the reverse object—to drive out the visible authority of the Federal Union, and thus force it to immediate dissolution. . . .

Unquestionably the States have the powers and rights reserved to them in and by the National Constitution; but among these surely are not included all conceivable powers, however mischievous or destructive, but, at most, such only as were known in the world at the time as governmental powers; and certainly a power to destroy the government itself had never been known as a governmental, as a merely administrative power. This relative matter of national power and State rights, as a principle, is no other than the principle of generality and locality. Whatever concerns the whole should be confided to the whole—to the General Government; while whatever concerns only the State should be left exclusively to the State. This is all there is of original principle about it. Whether the National Constitution in defining boundaries between the two has applied the principle with exact accuracy, is not to be questioned. We are all bound by that defining, without question.

What is now combated is the position that secession is consistent with the Constitution—is lawful and peaceful. It is not contended that there is any express law for it; and nothing should ever be implied as law which leads to unjust or absurd consequences. The nation purchased with money the countries out of which several of these States were formed. Is it just that they shall go off without leave and without refunding? The nation paid very large sums (in the aggregate, I believe, nearly a hundred millions) to relieve Florida of the aboriginal tribes. Is it just that she shall now be off without consent or without making any return? The nation is now in debt for money applied to the benefit of these so-called seceding States in common with the rest. Is it just either that creditors shall go unpaid or the remaining States pay the whole? A part of the present national debt was contracted to pay the old debts of Texas. Is it just that she shall leave and pay no part of this herself?

Again, if one State may secede, so may another; and when all shall have seceded, none is left to pay the debts. Is this quite just to creditors? Did we notify them of this sage view of ours when we borrowed their money?

If we now recognize this doctrine by allowing the seceders to go in peace, it is difficult to see what we can do if others choose to go or to extort terms upon which they will promise to remain.

The seceders insist that our Constitution admits of secession. They have assumed to make a national constitution of their own, in which of necessity they have either discarded or retained the right of secession as they insist it exists in ours. If they have discarded it, they thereby admit that on principle it ought not to be in ours. If they have retained it by their own construction of ours, they show that to be consistent they must secede from one another whenever they shall find it the easiest way of settling their debts, or effecting any other selfish or unjust object. The principle itself is one of disintegration, and upon which no government can possibly endure.

If all the States save one should assert the power to drive that one out of the Union, it is presumed the whole class of seceder politicians would at once deny the power and denounce the act as the greatest outrage upon State rights. But suppose that precisely the same act, instead of being called "driving the one out," should be called "the seceding of the others from that one," it would be exactly what the seceders claim to do, unless, indeed, they make the point that the one, because it is a minority, may rightfully do what the others, because they are a majority, may not rightfully do. These politicians are subtle and profound on the rights of minorities. They are not partial to that power which made the Constitution and speaks from the preamble called itself "We, the People."

It may well be questioned whether there is today a majority of the legally qualified voters of any State, except perhaps South Carolina, in favor of disunion. There is much reason to believe that the Union men are the majority in many, if not in every other one, of the so-called seceded States. . . .

This is essentially a people's contest. On the side of the Union it is a struggle for maintaining in the world that form and substance of government whose leading object is to elevate the condition of men—to lift artificial weights from all shoulders; to clear the paths of laudable pursuit for all; to afford all an unfettered start, and a fair chance in the race of life. Yielding to partial and temporary departures, from necessity, this is the leading object of the government for whose existence we contend. . . .

It was with the deepest regret that the executive found the duty of employing the war power in defense of the government forced upon him. He could but perform this duty or surrender the existence of the government. No compromise by public servants could, in this case, be a cure; not that compromises are not often proper, but that no popular government can long survive a marked precedent that those who carry an election can only save the government from immediate destruction by giving up the main point upon which the people gave the election. The people themselves, and not their servants, can safely reverse their own deliberate decisions. . . .

THE EMANCIPATION PROCLAMATION
1 January 1863

From the day he took office, Lincoln "struggled," as he said, with the issue of freeing the slaves without compensating their owners. Every kind of pressure—religious, political, and personal—was brought on him to make such a declaration. However, Lincoln's policy dealing with slavery was a matter of slow development.

Lincoln finally reached his decision during the summer of 1862—and on 22 September, he declared that "persons held as slaves" within areas "in rebellion against the United States" would be free on 1 January 1863. When that day arrived, the final proclamation specifically designated those areas "wherein the people . . . are this day in rebellion . . ." and ordered "that all persons held as slaves . . . [within those areas] are, and henceforward shall be, free . . ."

The Proclamation was far from an abolition document as it did not apply to Tennessee, nor to specially excepted portions of Virginia and Louisiana, nor to the border states within the Union. Since liberation took place in areas not under Union military control, the Proclamation had negligible effect on the immediate freeing of any individuals. Nevertheless, abolitionists hailed the Proclamation. Through his action, Lincoln ensured the death of slavery when the war was won. In fact, many slaves had already seized their own freedom in parts of the South occupied by Federal troops.

Whereas on the 22d day of September A.D. 1862, a proclamation was issued by the President of the United States, containing among other things, the following, to wit:

"That on the 1st day of January, A.D. 1863, all persons held as slaves within any State or designated part of a State the people whereof shall then be in rebellion against the United States shall be then, thenceforward, and forever free; and the executive government of the United States including the military and naval authority thereof, will recognize and maintain the freedom of such persons and will do no act or acts to repress such persons, or any of them, in any efforts they may make for their actual freedom.

"That the executive will on the 1st day of January aforesaid, by proclamation, designate the States and parts of States, if any, in which the people thereof, respectively, shall then be in rebellion against the United States; and the fact that any State or the people thereof shall on that day be in good faith represented in the Congress of the United States by members chosen thereto at elections wherein a majority of the qualified voters of such States shall have participated shall, in the absence of strong countervailing testimony, be deemed conclusive evidence that such State and the people thereof are not then in rebellion against the United States."

Now, therefore, I, Abraham Lincoln, President of the United States, by virtue of the power in me vested as Commander-in-Chief of the Army and Navy of the United States in time of actual armed rebellion against the authority and government of the United States, and as a fit and necessary war measure for suppressing said rebellion, do, on this 1st day of January, A.D. 1863, and in accordance with my purpose so to do, publicly proclaimed for the full period of one hundred days from the first day above mentioned, order and designate as the States and parts of States wherein the people thereof, respectively, are this day in rebellion against the United States the following, to wit:

Arkansas, Texas, Louisiana (except the parishes of St. Bernard, Plaquemines, Jefferson, St. John, St. Charles, St. James, Ascension, Assumption, Terrebonne, Lafourche, St. Mary, St. Martin, and Orleans, including the city of New Orleans), Mississippi, Alabama, Florida, Georgia, South Carolina, North Carolina, and Virginia (except the forty-eight counties designated as West Virginia, and also the counties of Berkeley, Accomac, Northhampton, Elizabeth City, York, Princess Anne, and Norfolk, including the cities of Norfolk and Portsmouth), and which excepted parts are for the present left precisely as if this proclamation were not issued.

And by virtue of the power and for the purpose aforesaid, I do order and declare that all persons held as slaves within said designated States and parts of States are, and henceforward shall be, free; and that the Executive Government of the United States, including the military and naval authorities thereof, will recognize and maintain the freedom of said persons.

And I hereby enjoin upon the people so declared to be free to abstain from all violence, unless in necessary self-defense; and I recommend to them that, in all cases when allowed, they labor faithfully for reasonable wages.

And I further declare and make known that such persons of suitable condition will be received into the armed service of the United States to garrison forts, positions, stations, and other places, and to man vessels of all sorts in said service.

And upon this act, sincerely believed to be an act of justice, warranted by the Constitution upon military necessity, I invoke the considerate judgment of mankind and the gracious favor of Almighty God.

President Abraham Lincoln's
Gettysburg Address
19 November 1863

On 19 November 1863, the national cemetery at the Gettysburg (PA) battlefield was dedicated. The principal oration was delivered by Edward Everett but Lincoln's brief remarks, in the course of which he referred to "a new birth of freedom," is the most memorable of all American addresses.

Lincoln, as President, made very few public addresses, the chief examples being his inaugurals, his Gettysburg Address, and his last speech on 11 April 1865. Rather than addresses, Lincoln used the art of correspondence. When answering criticism or appealing to the people, he would prepare a letter which, while addressed to an individual or delegation, would be intended for the nation.

Four score and seven years ago our fathers brought forth on this continent, a new nation, conceived in Liberty, and dedicated to the proposition that all men are created equal.

Now we are engaged in a great civil war testing whether that nation or any nation so conceived and so dedicated, can long endure. We are met on a great battle-field of that war. We have come to dedicate a portion of that field, as a final resting place for those who here gave their lives that that nation might live. It is altogether fitting and proper that we should do this.

But, in a larger sense, we can not dedicate—we can not consecrate— we can not hallow—this ground. The brave men, living and dead, who struggled here, have consecrated it, far above our poor power to add or detract. The world will little note, nor long remember what we say here, but it can never forget what they did here. It is for us the living, rather, to be dedicated here to the unfinished work which they who fought here have thus far so nobly advanced. It is rather for us to be here dedicated to the great task remaining before us—that from these honored dead we take increased devotion to that cause for which they gave the last full measure of devotion—that we here highly resolve that these dead shall not have died in vain—that this nation, under God, shall have a new birth of freedom—and that government of the people, by the people, for the people, shall not perish from the earth.

President Abraham Lincoln's Plan for Reconstruction
8 December 1863

In his proclamation of 8 December 1863, President Lincoln offered amnesty, with certain exceptions, to those who would take an oath to support the Constitution and abide by federal laws and proclamations involving the freedmen. When oathtakers equaled one-tenth of the state's voters in the 1860 election, they could proceed to "re-establish" a lawful government in a seceded state. Lincoln promised executive recognition to such governments.

Radical Republicans denounced both the plan and Lincoln's whole Southern policy as far too lenient to the Confederates. They accurately reflected the widespread feeling that, as the war became more bitter, southerners should be punished for secession. Since the Radicals controlled Congress, they prevented any settlement of the reconstruction issue during Lincoln's life. The deadlock between the President and Congress can be seen in the Wade-Davis bill that Lincoln killed by a pocket veto (4 July 1864). On 8 July 1864, Lincoln issued a proclamation explaining that he could not accept the radical plan as the only method of reconstructing the former Confederacy. Radical Republicans now excoriated Lincoln as being too lenient on those who had caused the war.

No state was actually restored to the Union in accordance with Lincoln's plan, though he considered his terms fulfilled in Tennessee, Arkansas, and Louisiana. In his last public speech (11 April 1865), Lincoln urged generosity in restoring the states. And, in his last cabinet meeting (14 April 1865), he advised leniency to the defeated South.

Whereas in and by the Constitution of the United States it is provided that the President "shallhave power to grant reprieves and pardons for offenses against the United States, except in cases of impeachment;" and

Whereas a rebellion now exists whereby the loyal State governments of several States have for a long time been subverted, and many persons have committed and are now guilty of treason against the United States; and

Whereas, with reference to said rebellion and treason, laws have been enacted by Congress declaring forfeitures and confiscation of property and liberation of slaves, all upon terms and conditions therein stated, and also declaring that the President was thereby authorized at any time thereafter, by proclamation, to extend to persons who may have participated in the existing rebellion in any State or part thereof pardon and amnesty, with such exceptions and at such times and on such conditions as he may deem expedient for the public welfare; and

Whereas the Congressional declaration for limited and conditional pardon accords with well-established judicial exposition of the pardoning power; and

Whereas, with reference to said rebellion, the President of the United States has issued several proclamations with provisions in regard to the liberation of slaves; and

Whereas it is now desired by some persons heretofore engaged in said rebellion to resume their allegiance to the United States and to reinaugurate loyal State governments within and for their respective States:

Therefore, I, Abraham Lincoln, President of the United States, do proclaim, . . . to all persons who have, directly or by implication, participated in the existing rebellion, except as hereinafter excepted, that a full pardon is hereby granted to them and each of them, with restoration of all rights of property, except as to slaves and in property cases where rights of third parties shall have intervened, and upon the condition that every such person shall take and subscribe an oath and thenceforward keep and maintain said oath inviolate, and which oath shall be registered for permanent preservation and shall be of the tenor and effect following, to wit:

I, ——, do solemnly swear, in presence of Almighty God, that I will henceforth faithfully support, protect, and defend the Constitution of the United States and the Union of the States thereunder; and that I will in like manner abide by and faithfully support all acts of Congress passed during the existing rebellion with reference to slaves, so long and so far as not repealed, modified, or held void by Congress or by decision of the Supreme Court; and that I will in like manner abide by and faithfully support all proclamations of the President made during the existing rebellion having reference to slaves, so long and so far as not modified or declared void by decision of the Supreme Court. So help me God.

The persons excepted from the benefits of the foregoing provisions are all who are or shall have been civil or diplomatic officers or agents of the so-called Confederate Government; all who have left judicial stations under the United States to aid the rebellion; all who are or shall have been military or naval officers of said so-called Confederate Government above the rank of colonel in the army or of lieutenant in the navy; all who left seats in the United States Congress to aid the rebellion; all who resigned commissions in the Army or Navy of the United States and afterwards aided the rebellion; and all who have engaged in any way in treating colored persons, or white persons in charge of such, otherwise than lawfully as prisoners of war, and which persons may have been found in the United States service as soldiers, seamen, or in any other capacity.

And I do further proclaim, declare, and make known that whenever, in any of the States of Arkansas, Texas, Louisiana, Mississippi, Tennessee, Alabama, Georgia, Florida, South Carolina, and North Carolina, a number of persons, not less than one-tenth in number of the votes cast in such State at the Presidential election of the year

A. D. 1860, each having taken oath aforesaid, and not having since violated it, and being a qualified voter by the election law of the State existing immediately before the so-called act of secession, and excluding all others, shall re-establish a State government which shall be republican and in nowise contravening said oath, such shall be recognized as the true government of the State, and the State shall receive thereunder the benefits of the constitutional provision which declares that "the United States shall guarantee to every State in this Union a republican form of government and shall protect each of them against invasion, and, on application of the legislature, or the executive (when the legislature can not be convened), against domestic violence."

And I do further proclaim, declare, and make known that any provision which may be adopted by such State government in relation to the freed people of such State which shall recognize and declare their permanent freedom, provide for their education, and which may yet be consistent as a temporary arrangement with their present condition as a laboring, landless, and homeless class, will not be objected to by the National Executive.

And it is suggested as not improper that in constructing a loyal State government in any State the name of the State, the boundary, the subdivisions, the constitution, and the general code of laws as before the rebellion be maintained, subject only to the modifications made necessary by the conditions hereinbefore stated, and such others, if any, not contravening said conditions and which may be deemed expedient by those framing the new State government.

To avoid misunderstanding, it may be proper to say that this proclamation, so far as it relates to State governments, has no reference to States wherein loyal State governments have all the while been maintained. And for the same reason it may be proper to further say that whether members sent to Congress from any State shall be admitted to seats constitutionally rests exclusively with the respective Houses, and not to any extent with the Executive. And, still further, that this proclamation is intended to present the people of the States wherein the national authority has been suspended and loyal State governments have been subverted a mode in and by which the national authority and loyal State governments may be re-established within said States or in any of them; and while the mode presented is the best the Executive can suggest, with his present impressions, it must not be understood that no other possible mode would be acceptable.

PRESIDENT ABRAHAM LINCOLN'S SECOND INAUGURAL ADDRESS
4 March 1865

Lincoln delivered his short but brilliant Second Inaugural Address—just a little under seven hundred words—on 4 March 1865. For four years, the crusade to save the Union had raged and now it neared a successful conclusion. Four years of death and destruction had created an atmosphere of vindictiveness. But Lincoln's memorable address stands above the hate that preceded, accompanied, and followed this horrible war: "With malice toward none, with charity for all." In four paragraphs, he soared above momentary passions to capture something of the larger tragedy involved, embracing that feeling of renewed confidence so necessary in facing the future problems of reconstruction. There was one new and striking feature in the simple inaugural ceremony— the presence of a battalion of African-American troops in the escort party.

At this second appearing to take the oath of the Presidential office there is less occasion for an extended address than there was at the first. Then a statement somewhat in detail of a course to be pursued seemed fitting and proper. Now, at the expiration of four years, during which public declarations have been constantly called forth on every point and phase of the great contest which still absorbs the attention and engrosses the energies of the nation, little that is new could be presented. The progress of our arms, upon which all else chiefly depends, is as well known to the public as to myself, and it is, I trust, reasonably satisfactory and encouraging to all. With high hope for the future, no prediction in regard to it is ventured.

On the occasion corresponding to this four years ago all thoughts were anxiously directed to an impending civil war. All dreaded it, all sought to avert it. While the inaugural address was being delivered from this place, devoted altogether to *saving* the Union without war, insurgent agents were in the city seeking to *destroy* it without war—seeking to dissolve the Union and divide effects by negotiation. Both parties deprecated war, but one them would *make* war rather than let the nation survive, and the other would *accept* war rather than let it perish, and the war came.

One-eighth of the whole population were colored slaves, not distributed generally over the Union, but localized in the southern part of it. These slaves constituted a peculiar and powerful interest. All knew that this interest was somehow the cause of the war. To strengthen, perpetuate, and extend this interest was the object for which the insurgents would rend the Union even by war, while the Government claimed no right to do more than to restrict the ter-

ritorial enlargement of it. Neither party expected for the war the magnitude or the duration which it has already attained. Neither anticipated that the *cause* of the conflict might cease with or even before the conflict itself should cease. Each looked for an easier triumph, and a result less fundamental and astounding. Both read the same Bible and pray to the same God, and each invokes His aid against the other. It may seem strange that any men should dare to ask a just God's assistance in wringing their bread from the sweat of other men's faces, but let us judge not, that we be not judged. The prayers of both could not be answered. That of neither has been answered fully. The Almighty has His own purposes. "Woe unto the world because of offenses; for it must needs be that offenses come, but woe to that man by whom the offense cometh." If we shall suppose that American slavery is one of those offenses which, in the providence of God, must needs come, but which, having continued through His appointed time, He now wills to remove, and that He gives to both North and South this terrible war as the woe due to those by whom the offense came, shall we discern therein any departure from those divine attributes which the believers in a living God always ascribe to Him? Fondly do we hope, fervently do we pray, that this mighty scourge of war may speedily pass away. Yet, if God wills that it continue until all the wealth piled by the bondsman's two hundred and fifty years of unrequited toil shall be sunk, and until every drop of blood drawn with the lash shall be paid by another drawn with the sword, as was said three thousand years ago, so still it must be said "the judgments of the Lord are true and righteous altogether."

With malice toward none, with charity for all, with firmness in the right as God gives us to see the right, let us strive on to finish the work we are in, to bind up the nation's wounds, to care for him who shall have borne the battle and for his widow and his orphan, to do all which may achieve and cherish a just and lasting peace among ourselves and with all nations.

PRESIDENT ANDREW JOHNSON INFORMS CONGRESS THAT THE UNION IS RESTORED
4 December 1865

President Andrew Johnson generally followed Lincoln's plan of leniency to the defeated South much to the chagrin of the Radical Republicans. By December 1865, every former Confederate state, except Texas, had conformed to Johnson's requirements for reestablishing civil government. On 4 December, the President informed Congress that the Union was restored.

... I have sought to solve the momentous questions and overcome the appalling difficulties that met me at the very commencement of my Administration. It has been my stead-fast object to escape from the sway of momentary passions and to derive a healing policy from the fundamental and unchanging principles of the Constitution.

I found the States suffering from the effects of a civil war. Resistance to the General Government appeared to have exhausted itself. The United States had recovered possession of their forts and arsenals, and their armies were in the occupation of every State which had attempted to secede. Whether the territory within the limits of those States should be held as conquered territory, under military authority emanating from the President as the head of the Army, was the first question that presented itself for decision.

Now military governments, established for an indefinite period, would have offered no security for the early suppression of discontent, would have divided the people into the vanquishers and the vanquished, and would have envenomed hatred rather than have restored affection. Once established, no precise limit to their continuance was conceivable. They would have occasioned an incalculable and exhausting expense. Peaceful emigration to and from that portion of the country is one of the best means that can be thought of for the restoration of harmony, and that emigration would have been prevented; for what emigrant from abroad, what industrious citizen at home, would place himself willingly under military rule? The chief persons who would have followed in the train of the Army would have been dependents on the General Government or men who expected profit from the miseries of their erring fellow-citizens. The powers of patronage and rule which would have been exercised under the President, over a vast and populous and naturally wealthy region are greater than, unless under extreme necessity, I should be willing to intrust to any one man. They are such as, for myself, I could never, unless on occasions of great emergency, consent to exercise. The willful use of such powers, if continued through a period of years, would have endangered the purity of the general administration and the liberties of the States which remained loyal.

Besides, the policy of military rule over a conquered territory would have implied that the States whose inhabitants may have taken part in the rebellion had by the act of those inhabitants ceased to exist. But the true theory is that all pretended acts of secession were from the beginning null and void. The States can not commit treason nor screen the individual citizens who may have committed treason any more than

they can make valid treaties or engage in lawful commerce with any foreign power. The States attempting to secede placed themselves in a condition where their vitality was impaired, but not extinguished; their functions suspended, but not destroyed.

But if any State neglects or refuses to perform its offices there is the more need that the General Government should maintain all its authority and as soon as practicable resume the exercise of all its functions. On this principle I have acted, and have gradually and quietly, and by almost imperceptible steps, sought to restore the rightful energy of the General Government and of the States. To that end provisional governors have been appointed for the States, conventions called, governors elected, legislatures assembled, and Senators and Representatives chosen to the Congress of the United States. At the same time the courts of the United States, as far as could be done, have been reopened, so that the laws of the United States may be enforced through their agency. The blockade has been removed and the custom-houses reestablished in ports of entry, so that the revenue of the United States may be collected. The Post-Office Department renews its ceaseless activity, and the General Government is thereby enabled to communicate promptly with its officers and agents. The courts bring security to persons and property; the opening of the ports invites the restoration of industry and commerce; the post-office renews the facilities of social intercourse and of business. And is it not happy for us all that the restoration of each one of these functions of the General Government brings with it a blessing to the States over which they are extended? Is it not a sure promise of harmony and renewed attachment to the Union that after all that has happened the return of the General Government is known only as a beneficence?

I know very well that this policy is attended with some risk; that for its success it requires at least the acquiescence of the States which it concerns; that it implies an invitation to those States, by renewing their allegiance to the United States, to resume their functions as States of the Union. But it is a risk that must be taken. In the choice of difficulties it is the smallest risk; and to diminish and if possible to remove all danger, I have felt it incumbent on me to assert one other power of the General Government—the power of pardon. As no State can throw a defense over the crime of treason, the power of pardon is exclusively vested in the executive government of the United States. In exercising that power I have taken every precaution to connect it with the clearest recognition of the binding force of the laws of the United States and an unqualified acknowledgment of the great social change of condition in regard to slavery which has grown out of the war. . . .

PRESIDENT ANDREW JOHNSON'S VETO OF THE FREEDMEN'S BUREAU
19 February 1866

The Freedmen's Bureau was a federal agency created by Congress in 1865. The purpose of the bureau was to aid the former slaves' adjustment to a life of freedom. It furnished food and clothing to the needy and aided in finding employment. It provided homesteads on public lands and supervised labor contracts to insure fairness. The bureau established hospitals and schools for the freedmen and tried to protect their civil rights in unfriendly Southern communities.

Congress proceeded to extend the Freedmen's Bureau, both as to duration and power. Johnson vetoed the bill (19 February) because he believed that care and protection of the freedmen should be left to the states. Although the President's veto was sustained, a serious breach was developing between Johnson and the Radical Republicans. On 16 July 1866, Congress overrode the President's second veto of the Freedmen's Bureau.

I have examined with care the bill, which originated in the Senate and has been passed by the two Houses of Congress, to amend an act entitled "An act to establish a bureau for the relief of freedmen and refugees," and for other purposes. Having with much regret come to the conclusion that it would not be consistent with the public welfare to give my approval to the measure, I return the bill to the Senate with my objections to its becoming a law.

I might call to mind in advance of these objections that there is no immediate necessity for the proposed measure. The act to establish a bureau for the relief of freedmen and refugees, which was approved in the month of March last, has not yet expired. It was thought stringent and extensive enough for the purpose in view in time of war. Before it ceases to have effect further experience may assist to guide us to a wise conclusion as to the policy to be adopted in time of peace.

I share with Congress the strongest desire to secure to the freedmen the full enjoyment of their freedom and property and their entire independence and equality in making contracts for their labor, but the bill before me contains provisions which in my opinion are not warranted by the Constitution and are not well suited to accomplish the end in view.

The bill proposes to establish by authority of Congress military jurisdiction over all parts of the United States containing refugees and freedmen. It would by its very nature apply with most force to those parts of the United States in which the freedmen most abound, and it expressly extends the existing temporary jurisdiction of the Freedmen's Bureau, with greatly enlarged powers, over those States "in which the ordinary course of judicial proceedings has been interrupted by the rebellion." The source from which this military jurisdiction is to emanate is none other than the President of the United States, acting through the War Department and the Commissioner of the Freedmen's Bureau. The agents to carry out this military jurisdiction are to be selected either from the Army or from civil life; the country is to be divided into districts and subdistricts, and the number of salaried agents to be employed may be equal to the number of counties or parishes in all the United States where freedmen and refugees are to be found.

The subjects over which this military jurisdiction is to extend in every part of the United States include protection to "all employees, agents, and officers of this bureau in the exercise of the duties imposed" upon them by the bill. In eleven States it is further to extend over all cases affecting freedmen and refugees discriminated against "by local law, custom, or prejudice." In those eleven States the bill subjects any white person who may be charged with depriving a freedman of "any civil rights or immunities belonging to white persons" to imprisonment or fine, or both, without, however, defining the "civil rights and immunities" which are thus to be secured to the freedmen by military law. This military jurisdiction also extends to all questions that may arise respecting contracts. The agent who is thus to exercise the office of a military judge may be a stranger, entirely ignorant of the laws of the place, and exposed to the errors of judgment to which all men are liable. The exercise of power over which there is no legal supervision by so vast a number of agents as is contemplated by the bill must, by the very nature of man, be attended by acts of caprice, injustice, and passion. . . .

In time of war it was eminently proper that we should provide for those who were passing suddenly from a condition of bondage to a state of freedom. But this bill proposes to make the Freedmen's Bureau, established by the act of 1865 as one of many great and extraordinary military measures to suppress a formidable rebellion, a permanent branch of the public administration, with its powers greatly enlarged. I have no reason to suppose, and I do not understand it to be alleged, that the act of March 1865, has proved deficient for the purpose for which it was passed, although at that time and for a considerable period thereafter the Government of the United States remained unacknowledged in most of the States whose inhabitants had been involved in the rebellion. The institution of slavery, for the military destruction of which the Freedmen's Bureau was called into ex-

istence as an auxiliary, has been already effectually and finally abrogated throughout the whole country by an amendment of the Constitution of the United States, and practically its eradication has received the assent and concurrence of most of those States in which it at any time had an existence. I am not, therefore, able to discern in the condition of the country anything to justify an apprehension that the powers and agencies of the Freedmen's Bureau, which were effective for the protection of freedmen and refugees during the actual continuance of hostilities and of African servitude, will now, in a time of peace and after the abolition of slavery, prove inadequate to the same proper ends. If I am correct in these views, there can be no necessity for the enlargement of the powers of the Bureau, for which provision is made in the bill. . . .

The third section of the bill authorizes a general and unlimited grant of support to the destitute and suffering refugees and freedmen, their wives and children. Succeeding sections make provision for the rent or purchase of landed estates for freedmen, and for the erection for their benefit of suitable buildings for asylums and schools, the expenses to be defrayed from the Treasury of the whole people. The Congress of the United States has never heretofore thought itself empowered to establish asylums beyond the limits of the District of Columbia, except for the benefit of our disabled soldiers and sailors. It has never founded schools for any class of our own people, not even for the orphans of those who have fallen in the defense of the Union, but has left the care of education to the much more competent and efficient control of the States, of communities, of private associations, and of individuals. It has never deemed itself authorized to expend the public money for the rent or purchase of homes for the thousands, not to say millions, of the white race who are honestly toiling from day to day for their subsistence. A system for the support of indigent persons in the United States was never contemplated by the authors of the Constitution; nor can any good reason be advanced why, as a permanent establishment, it should be founded for one class or color of our people more than another. . . .

In addition to the objections already stated, the fifth section of the bill proposes to take away land from its former owners without any legal proceedings being first had, contrary to that provision of the Constitution which declares that no person shall "be deprived of life, liberty, or property without due process of law." It does not appear that a part of the lands to which this section refers may not be owned by minors or persons of unsound mind, or by those who have been faithful to all their obligations as citizens of the United States. If any portion of the land is held by such persons, it is not competent for any authority to deprive them of it. If, on the other hand, it be found that the

property is liable to confiscation, even then it can not be appropriated to public purposes until by due process of law it shall have been declared forfeited to the Government.

There is still further objection to the bill, on grounds seriously affecting the class of persons to whom it is designed to bring relief. It will tend to keep the mind of the freedman in a state of uncertain expectation and restlessness, while to those among whom he lives it will be a source of constant and vague apprehension. . . .

The bill under consideration refers to certain of the States as though they had not "been fully restored in all their constitutional relations to the United States." If they have not, let us at once act together to secure that desirable end at the earliest possible moment. It is hardly necessary for me to inform Congress that in my own judgment most of those States, so far, at least, as depends upon their own action, have already been fully restored, and are to be deemed as entitled to enjoy their constitutional rights as members of the Union. Reasoning from the Constitution itself and from the actual situation of the country, I feel not only entitled but bound to assume that with the Federal courts restored and those of the several States in the full exercise of their functions the rights and interests of all classes of people will, with the aid of the military in cases of resistance to the laws, be essentially protected against unconstitutional infringement or violation. Should this expectation

unhappily fail, which I do not anticipate, then the Executive is already fully
armed with the powers conferred by
the act of March 1865, establishing the
Freedmen's Bureau, and hereafter, as
heretofore, he can employ the land and
naval forces of the country to suppress
insurrection or to overcome obstructions to the laws.

In accordance with the Constitution, I return the bill to the Senate, in
the earnest hope that a measure involving questions and interests so important to the country will not become
a law, unless upon deliberate consideration by the people it shall receive
the sanction of an enlightened public
judgment.

PRESIDENT ANDREW JOHNSON'S VETO OF THE CIVIL RIGHTS ACT
27 March 1866

The passage over President Johnson's vetoes by substantial majorities of one law after another throughout 1866–1867, demonstrated that the President could no longer inter-fere with the legislative branch. It is to his credit that he conformed with the strict con-struction of the law and with every duty Congress imposed on him.

On 27 March 1866, the split between the President and Congress intensified. The President vetoed the Civil Rights Act—Congress overrode it on 9 April. In his message, Johnson wrote that his states'—rights' principles were violated by the bills guarantee to the freedmen to preserve their rights through the federal courts. To prevent possible re-peal of the Civil Rights Act, Congress incorporated most of its provisions into the Four-teenth Amendment.

I regret that the bill, which has passed
both Houses of Congress, entitled "An
act to protect all persons in the United
States in their civil rights and furnish
the means of their vindication," contains provisions which I can not approve consistently with my sense of
duty to the whole people and my
obligations to the Constitution of the
United States. I am therefore constrained to return it to the Senate, the

House in which it originated, with my
objections to its becoming a law.

By the first section of the bill all persons born in the United States and not
subject to any foreign power, excluding Indians not taxed, are declared to
be citizens of the United States. This
provision comprehends the Chinese of
the Pacific States, Indians subject to
taxation, the people called gypsies, as
well as the entire race designated as

blacks, people of color, negroes, mulattoes, and persons of African blood. Every individual of these races born in the United States is by the bill made a citizen of the United States. It does not purport to declare or confer any other right of citizenship than Federal citizenship. It does not purport to give these classes of persons any status as citizens of States, except that which may result from their status as citizens of the United States. The power to confer the right of State citizenship is just as exclusively with the several States as the power to confer the right of Federal citizenship is with Congress. . . .

The first section of the bill also contains an enumeration of the rights to be enjoyed by these classes so made citizens "in every State and Territory in the United States." These rights are " to make and enforce contracts; to sue, be parties, and give evidence; to inherit, purchase, lease, sell, hold, and convey real and personal property," and to have "full and equal benefit of all laws and proceedings for the security of person and property as is enjoyed by white citizens." So, too, they are made subject to the same punishment, pains, and penalties in common with white citizens, and to none other. Thus a perfect equality of the white and colored races is attempted to be fixed by Federal law in every State of the Union over the vast field of State jurisdiction covered by these enumerated rights. In no one of these can any State ever exercise any power of discrimination between the different races. In the ex-

ercise of State policy over matters exclusively affecting the people of each State it has frequently been thought expedient to discriminate between the two races. By the statutes of some of the States, Northern as well as Southern, it is enacted, for instance, that no white person shall intermarry with a negro or mulatto. Chancellor Kent says, speaking of the blacks, that—

> Marriages between them and the whites are forbidden in some of the States where slavery does not exist, and they are prohibited in all the slaveholding States; and when not absolutely contrary to law, they are revolting, and regarded as an offense against public decorum.

I do not say that this bill repeals State laws on the subject of marriage between the two races, for as the whites are forbidden to intermarry with the blacks, the blacks can only make such contracts as the whites themselves are allowed to make, and therefore can not under this bill enter into the marriage contract with the whites. I cite this discrimination, however, as an instance of the State policy as to discrimination, and to inquire whether if Congress can abrogate all State laws of discrimination between the two races in the matter of real estate, of suits, and of contracts generally Congress may not also repeal the State laws as to the contract of marriage between the two races. Hitherto every subject embraced in the enumeration of rights contained in this bill has been considered as exclusively belonging to the States. They all relate to the internal police and economy of the respective States. They are matters which in each State concern the domestic condition of its people, varying in each according to its own peculiar circumstances and the safety and well-being of its own citizens. I do not mean to say that upon all these subjects there are not Federal restraints—as, for instance, in the State power of legislation over contracts there is a Federal limitation that no State shall pass a law impairing the obligations of contracts; and, as to crimes, that no State shall pass an *ex post facto* law; and, as to money, that no State shall make anything but gold and silver a legal tender; but where can we find a Federal prohibition against the power of any State to discriminate, as do most of them, between aliens and citizens, between artificial persons, called corporations, and natural persons, in the right to hold real estate? If it be granted that Congress can repeal all State laws discriminating between whites and blacks in the subjects covered by this bill, why, it may be asked, may not Congress repeal in the same way all State laws discriminating between the two races on the subjects of suffrage and office? If Congress can declare by law who shall hold lands, who shall testify, who shall have capacity to make a contract in a State, then Congress can by law also declare who, without regard to color or race, shall have the right to sit as a juror or as a judge, to hold any office, and, finally, to vote "in every State and Territory of the United States." As respects the Territo-

ries, they come within the power of Congress, for as to them the lawmaking power is the Federal power; but as to the States no similar provision exists vesting in Congress the power "to make rules and regulations" for them. . . .

The object of the second section of the bill is to afford discriminating protection to colored persons in the full enjoyment of all the rights secured to them by the preceding section. It declares—

> That any person who, under color of any law, statute, ordinance, regulation, or custom, shall subject, or cause to be subjected, any inhabitant of any State or Territory to the deprivation of any right secured or protected by this act, or to different punishment, pains, or penalties on account of such person having at any time been held in a condition of slavery or involuntary servitude, except as a punishment for crime whereof the party shall have been duly convicted, or by reason of his color or race, than is prescribed for the punishment of white persons, shall be deemed guilty of a misdemeanor, and on conviction shall be punished by fine not exceeding $1,000, or imprisonment not exceeding one year, or both, in the discretion of the court.

This section seems to be designed to apply to some existing or future law of a State or Territory which may conflict with the provisions of the bill now under consideration. It provides for counteracting such forbidden legislation by imposing fine and imprisonment upon the legislators who may pass such conflicting laws, or upon the officers or agents who shall put or attempt to put them into execution. It means an official offense, not a common crime committed against law upon the persons of property of the black race. Such an act may deprive the black man of his property, but not of the *right* to hold property. It means a deprivation of the right itself, either by the State judiciary or the State legislature. It is therefore assumed that under this section members of State legislatures who should vote for laws conflicting with the provisions of the bill, that judges of the State courts who should render judgments in antagonism with its terms, and that marshals and sheriffs who should, as ministerial officers, execute processes sanctioned by State laws and issued by State judges in execution of their judgments could be brought before other tribunals and there subjected to fine and imprisonment for the performance of the duties which such State laws might impose. The legislation thus proposed invades the judicial power of the State. It says to every State court or judge, If you decide that this act is unconstitutional; if you refuse, under the prohibition of a State law, to allow a negro to testify; if you hold that over such a subject-matter the State law is paramount, and "under color" of a State law refuse the exercise of the right to the negro, your error of judgment, however conscientious, shall subject you to fine and imprisonment. I do not apprehend that the conflicting legislation which the bill seems to contemplate is so likely to occur as to render it necessary at this time to adopt a measure of such doubtful constitutionality. . . .

I do not propose to consider the policy of this bill. To me the details of the bill seem fraught with evil. The white race and the black race of the South have hitherto lived together under the relation of master and slave—capital owning labor. Now, suddenly, that relation is changed, and as to ownership capital and labor are divorced. They stand now each master of itself. In this new relation, one being necessary to the other, there will be a new adjustment, which both are deeply interested in making harmonious. Each has equal power in settling the terms, and if left to the laws that regulate capital and labor it is confidently believed that they will satisfactorily work out the problem. Capital, it is true, has more intelligence, but labor is never so ignorant as not to understand its own interests, not to know its own value, and not to see that capital must pay that value.

This bill frustrates this adjustment. It intervenes between capital and labor and attempts to settle questions of political economy through the agency of numerous officials whose interest it will be to foment discord between the two races, for as the breach widens their employment will continue, and when it is closed their occupation will terminate.

In all our history, in all our experience as a people living under Federal and State law, no such system as that contemplated by the details of this bill has ever before been proposed or adopted. They establish for the security of the colored race safeguards which go infinitely beyond any that the General Government has ever provided for the white race. . . .

President Andrew Johnson's Defense of His Views on Reconstruction
3 December 1867

Throughout 1867, impeachment resolutions were introduced in Congress. By the end of the year, a collision between the President and Congress seemed inevitable.

On 3 December 1867, in his third Annual Message, Johnson defended his views on Reconstruction as being constitutionally sound. The President explained his interpretation of the Tenure of Office Act (1867). Johnson's violation of this act will lead to his impeachment on 24 February 1868. In a trial before the Senate, 30 March–26 May 1868, the President was acquitted of the charges against him by one vote short of the two-thirds necessary to remove him from office.

The continued disorganization of the Union, to which the President has so often called the attention of Congress, is yet a subject of profound and patriotic concern. We may, however, find some relief from that anxiety in the reflection that the painful political situation, although before untried by ourselves, is not new in the experience of nations. Political science, perhaps as highly perfected in our own time and country as in any other, has not yet disclosed any means by which civil wars can be absolutely prevented. An enlightened nation, however, with a wise and beneficent constitution of free government, may diminish their frequency and mitigate their severity by directing all its proceedings in accordance with its fundamental law. . . .

Candor compels me to declare that at this time there is no Union as our fathers understood the term, and as they meant it to be understood by us. The Union which they established can exist only where all the States are represented in both Houses of Congress; where one State is as free as another to regulate its internal concerns according to its own will, and where the laws of the central Government, strictly confined to matters of national jurisdiction, apply with equal force to all the people of every section. That such is not the present "state of the Union" is a melancholy fact, and we must all acknowledge that the restoration of the States to their proper legal relations with the Federal Government and with one another, according to the terms of the original compact, would be the greatest temporal blessing which God, in His kindest providence, could bestow upon this nation. It becomes our imperative duty to consider whether or not it is impossible to effect this most desirable consummation. . . .

To me the process of restoration seems perfectly plain and simple. It consists merely in a faithful application of the Constitution and laws. The execution of the laws is not now obstructed or opposed by physical force. There is no military or other necessity, real or pretended, which can prevent obedience to the Constitution, either North or South. All the rights and all the obligations of States and individuals can be protected and enforced by means perfectly consistent with the fundamental law. The courts may be everywhere open, and if open their process would be unimpeded. Crimes against the United States can be prevented or punished by the proper judicial authorities in a manner entirely practicable and legal. There is therefore no reason why the Constitution should not be obeyed, unless those who exercise its powers have determined that it shall be disregarded and violated. The mere naked will of this Government, or of some one or more of its branches, is the only obstacle that can exist to a perfect union of all the States.

On this momentous question and some of the measures growing out of it I have had the misfortune to differ from Congress, and have expressed my convictions without reserve, though with becoming deference to the opinion of the legislative department. Those convictions are not only unchanged, but strengthened by subsequent events and further reflection. The transcendent importance of the subject will be a sufficient excuse for calling your attention to some of the reasons which have so strongly influenced my own judgment. The hope that we may all finally concur in a mode of settlement consistent at once with our true interests and with our sworn duties to the Constitution is too natural and too just to be easily relinquished.

It is clear to my apprehension that the States lately in rebellion are still members of the National Union. When did they cease to be so? The "ordinances of secession" adopted by a portion (in most of them a very small portion) of their citizens were mere nullities. If we admit now that they were valid and effectual for the purpose intended by their authors we sweep from under our feet the whole ground upon which we justified the war. Were those States afterwards expelled from the Union by war? The direct contrary was averred by this Government to be its purpose, and was so understood by the all those who gave their blood and treasure to aid in its prosecution. It can not be that a successful war, waged for the preservation of the Union, had the legal effect of dissolving it. The victory of the nation's arms was not the disgrace of her policy; the defeat of seces-

sion on the battlefield was not the triumph of its lawless principle. Nor
could Congress, with or without the
consent of the Executive, do anything
which would have the effect, directly or
indirectly, of separating the States from
each other. To dissolve the Union is to
repeal the Constitution which holds it
together, and that is a power which
does not belong to any department of
this Government, or to all of them
united. . . .

The acts of Congress in question are
not only objectionable for their assumption of ungranted power, but many of
their provisions are in conflict with the
direct prohibitions of the Constitution.
The Constitution commands that a republican form of government shall be
guaranteed to all the States; that no
person shall be deprived of life, liberty,
or property without due process of
law, arrested without a judicial warrant,
or punished without a fair trial before
an impartial jury; that the privilege of
habeas corpus shall not be denied in time
of peace, and that no bill of attainder
shall be passed even against a single individual. Yet the system of measures established by these acts of Congress does
totally subvert and destroy the form as
well as the substance of republican government in the ten States to which they
apply. It binds them hand and foot in
absolute slavery, and subjects them to a
strange and hostile power, more unlimited and more likely to be abused than
any other now known among civilized
men. It tramples down all those rights
in which the essence of liberty consists,

and which a free government is always
most careful to protect. It denies the
habeas corpus and the trial by jury. Personal freedom, property, and life, if assailed by the passion, the prejudice, or
the rapacity of the ruler, have no security whatever. It has the effect of a bill of
attainder or bill of pains and penalties,
not upon a few individuals, but upon
whole masses, including the millions
who inhabit the subject States, and even
their unborn children. These wrongs,
being expressly forbidden, can not be
constitutionally inflicted upon any portion of our people, no matter how they
may have come within our jurisdiction,
and no matter whether they live in
States, Territories, or districts. . . .

The blacks in the South are entitled
to be well and humanely governed,
and to have the protection of just laws
for all their rights of person and property. If it were practicable at this time
to give them a Government exclusively
their own, under which they might
manage their own affairs in their own
way, it would become a grave question
whether we ought to do so, or whether
common humanity would not require
us to save them from themselves. But
under the circumstances this is only a
speculative point. It is not proposed
merely that they shall govern themselves, but that they shall rule the
white race, make and administer State
laws, elect Presidents and members of
Congress, and shape to a greater or less
extent the future destiny of the whole
country. Would such a trust and power
be safe in such hands? . . .

The plan of putting the Southern States wholly and the General Government partially into the hands of negroes is proposed at a time peculiarly unpropitious. The foundations of society have been broken up by civil war. Industry must be reorganized, justice reestablished, public credit maintained, and order brought out of confusion. To accomplish these ends would require all the wisdom and virtue of the great men who formed our institutions originally. I confidently believe that their descendants will be equal to the arduous task before them, but it is worse than madness to expect that negroes will perform it for us. Certainly we ought not to ask their assistance till we despair of our own competency.

The great difference between the two races in physical, mental, and moral characteristics will prevent an amalgamation or fusion of them together in one homogeneous mass. If the inferior obtains the ascendency over the other, it will govern with reference only to its own interests—for it will recognize no common interest—and create such a tyranny as this continent has never yet witnessed. Already the negroes are influenced by promises of confiscation and plunder. They are taught to regard as an enemy every white man who has any respect for the rights of his own race. If this continues it must become worse and worse, until all order will be subverted, all industry cease, and the fertile fields of the South grow up into a wilderness. Of all the dangers which our nation has yet encountered, none are equal to those which must result from the success of the effort now making to Africanize the half of our country.

The unrestricted power of removal from office is a very great one to be trusted even to a magistrate chosen by the general suffrage of the whole people and accountable directly to them for his acts. It is undoubtedly liable to abuse, and at some periods of our history perhaps has been abused. If it be thought desirable and constitutional that it should be so limited as to make the President merely a common informer against other public agents, he should at least be permitted to act in that capacity before some open tribunal, independent of party politics, ready to investigate the merits of every case, furnished with the means of taking evidence, and bound to decide according to established rules. This would guarantee the safety of the accuser when he acts in good faith, and at the same time secure the rights of the other party. I speak, of course, with all proper respect for the present Senate, but it does not seem to me that any legislative body can be so constituted as to insure its fitness for these functions.

It is not the theory of this Government that public offices are the property of those who hold them. They are given merely as a trust for the public benefit, sometimes for a fixed period, sometimes during good behavior, but generally they are liable to be terminated at the pleasure of the appointing power, which represents the collective majesty and speaks the will of the people. The forced retention in office of a single dishonest person may work great injury to the public interests. The danger to the public service comes not from the power to remove, but from the power to appoint. Therefore it was that the framers of the Constitution left the power of removal unrestricted, while they gave the Senate a right to reject all appointments which in its opinion were not fit to be made. A little reflection on this subject will probably satisfy all who have the good of the country at heart that our best course is to take the Constitution for our guide, walk in the path marked out by the founders of the Republic, and obey the rules made sacred by the observance of our great predecessors. . . .

PRESIDENT ULYSSES S. GRANT'S DECISION NOT TO DISPATCH FEDERAL TROOPS TO QUELL A RACE RIOT IN SOUTH CAROLINA
26 July 1876

Upon taking office in 1869, President Ulysses Grant faced the same intractable political and social issues of Reconstruction that had brought his predecessor to impeachment. Unlike Andrew Johnson, Grant did not favor an unreconstructed South able to reform itself as if the Civil War never happened. Yet the new President also refused to employ full Federal power to force fundamental change on a reconstructed South, as Radical Republicans demanded. In fact, beyond an occasional dispatch of force to support embattled Old South Republican governments, Grant did nothing. Deeply conservative and suspicious of executive power, the President hoped that circumstances would produce general social equity. In his earliest days in the White House, he unequivocally and successfully defended passage of the 15th Amendment, with its declaration that voting rights could not be denied "on account of race, color, or previous condition of servitude." Yet toward the white South, where voting rights for freedmen constituted but one of many grievances, the President sought accommodation. Like most of his countrymen, Grant wearied of solving the great American problem of race, which still faced him unresolved even after the bloodiest war in American history. Moreover, dramatic new forces in the life of the nation commanded attention. The America over which Grant presided had been hurled full tilt into a new age of technology and industrial capitalism. Trade and enterprise radiated out on the railroad tracks that spanned the nation. Oil and steel industries and their subsidiaries absorbed increasing thousands of workers while altering the environment, producing material improvements along with unprecedented capital now organized in corporations of surpassing power. The financial centers of the big cities resonated with

busy markets, secret deals and schemes, fortunes won and lost. In the midst of unprece-
dented social and economic change the White House deserted the old racial battleground
of the rural and backward South, where states rights doctrines and vigilante violence
were employed to good effect to resist change. In the summer of 1876, as black Republi-
cans in South Carolina faced murderous violence, the President responded to the pleas of
its Republican Governor. Nothing could be done.

DEAR SIR: I am in receipt of your letter of the 22d of July, and all the inclosures enumerated therein, giving an account of the late barbarous massacre of innocent men at the town of Hamburgh, S. C. The views which you express as to the duty you owe to your oath of office, and to the citizen, to secure to all their civil rights, including the right to vote according to the dictates of their own consciences, and the further duty of the Executive of the nation to give all needful aid, when properly called on to do so, to enable you to insure this inalienable right, I fully concur in. The scene at Hamburgh, as cruel, bloodthirsty, wanton, unprovoked, and as uncalled for as it was, is only a repetition of the course that has been pursued in other Southern States within the last few years, notably in Mississippi and Louisiana. Mississippi is governed today by officials chosen through fraud and violence, such as would scarcely be accredited to savages, much less to a civilized and Christian people. How long these things are to continue, or what is to be the final remedy, the Great Ruler of the Universe only knows. But I havean abiding faith that the remedy will come, and come speedily, and

earnestly hope that it will come peacefully. There has never been a desire on the part of the North to humiliate the South. Nothing is claimed for one State that is not freely accorded to all the others, unless it may be the right to kill negroes and republicans without fear of punishment, and without loss of caste or reputation. This has seemed to be a privilege claimed by a few States.

I repeat again that I fully agree with you as to the measure of your duties in the present emergency, and as to my duties. Go on, and let every governor, where the same dangers threaten the peace of his State, go on in the conscientious performance of his duties to the humblest as well as the proudest citizen, and I will give every aid for which I can find law or constitutional power. Government that cannot give protection to the life, property, and all guaranteed civil rights (in this country the greatest is an untrammeled ballot) to the citizen is in so far a failure, and every energy of the oppressed should be exerted (always within the law, and by constitutional means) to regain lost privileges or protection. Too long denial of guaranteed rights is sure to lead to revolution, bloody revolution, where suffering must fall upon the guilty as well as the innocent. Expressing the hope that the better judgment and co-operation of the citizens of the State over which you have presided so ably may enable you to secure a fair trial and punishment of all offenders, without distinction of race, color or previous condition of servitude, and without aid from the Federal Government, but with the promise of such aid on the conditions named in the foregoing, I subscribe myself, very respectfully, your obedient servant.

PRESIDENT ULYSSES S. GRANT'S ACKNOWLEDGMENT OF HIS POLITICAL MISTAKES
5 December 1876

President Grant submitted his eighth and final Annual Message to Congress on 5 December 1876. To the end of his presidency Grant, the stolid war hero and national icon, had retained popular adulation. Yet even as crowds cheered him, incompetence and corruption already marred his presidency, and he realized it. The great and bloody Civil War had preserved the Union but the Federal Government abandoned the cause of racial justice. The Grant administration allowed the South to revert to its traditions of racial separation, stripping from Freedmen their constitutional protections through legal sophistry and the brutality of the Ku Klux Klan. Out on the high plains, the Government itself waged war against other peoples of color. Fighting with Indian tribes raged across the badlands, flouting Grant's earlier professions of good will. General Philip Sheridan said, "The only good Indian is a dead Indian," and few disagreed. Grant's extraordinary capacity for loyalty also came to besmirch his administration. He trusted too widely and too well, often continuing to champion men who in dishonoring themselves had implicated him as well. Before the eight-year Grant administration had passed, scandal would touch two Vice Presidents, a Secretary of the Interior, an Attorney General, the Speaker of the House, and the President's own personal secretary. Nor did the Grant Administration bestir itself as northern industrialists and financiers created powerful and lucrative monopolies. In this "Gilded Age," corruption predominated in the absence of government interest. At the very end of his public life, self-possessed as always, President Grant took the unprecedented step of alluding to his own deficiencies in the opening passage of his last message.

In submitting my eighth and last annual message to Congress it seems proper that I should refer to and in some degree recapitulate the events and official acts of the past eight years.

It was my fortune, or misfortune, to be called to the office of Chief Executive without any previous political training. From the age of 17 I had never even witnessed the excitement attending a

Presidential campaign but twice antecedent to my own candidacy, and at but one of them was I eligible as a voter.

Under such circumstances it is but reasonable to suppose that errors of judgment must have occurred. Even had they not, differences of opinion between the Executive, bound by an oath to the strict performance of his duties, and writers and debaters must have arisen. It is not necessarily evidence of blunder on the part of the Executive because there are these differences of views. Mistakes have been made, as all can see and I admit, but it seems to me oftener in the selections made of the assistants appointed to aid in carrying out the various duties of administering the Government—in nearly every case selected without a personal acquaintance with the appointee, but upon recommendations of the representatives chosen directly by the people. It is impossible, where so many trusts are to be allotted, that the right parties should be chosen in every instance. History shows that no Administration from the time of Washington to the present has been free from these mistakes. But I leave comparisons to history, claiming only that I have acted in every instance from a conscientious desire to do what was right, constitutional, within the law, and for the very best interests of the whole people. Failures have been errors of judgment, not of intent.

PRESIDENT RUTHERFORD B. HAYES' DECISION TO REMOVE FEDERAL TROOPS FROM THE SOUTH, ENDING RECONSTRUCTION
22 April 1877

Rutherford Birchard Hayes gained the Presidency in the most disreputable election in American History. Only the exemplary character of this man—honest, pious, a war hero—shielded him from the venal circumstances of his ascendancy. Hayes' Democratic opponent, Samuel J. Tilden, of New York, won the popular vote, but both parties charged fraud in the returns from South Carolina, Louisiana and Florida. In each of those states, savage political battles over race separated the parties, with the Republicans clinging to office through occupying Federal military forces, which constituted the last vestiges of protection for people of color. Democrats represented the values of the Old South and the indefinite postponement of racial justice. In counting the presidential election returns, Republicans controlled the machinery and disqualified enough Democratic votes to retain the electoral edge for Hayes. Democrats rose in objection, calling the presence of Federal troops a Republican Party army of occupation. On 2 March 1877, two days before the scheduled inauguration in Washington, the Congressional special electoral commission appointed to resolve the dangerous situation decided all questions on the contested votes on the basis of 8–7 straight party line vote, and gave all the electoral votes to Hayes, who then became the new president. His supporters made the decision palatable to Democrats by pledges to withdraw the last Federal troops from the South, ending Reconstruction and restoring the Democrats' monopoly of power. Hayes, an optimist but not a hypocrite, clung to the belief that he could work with fair-minded Democrats and simultaneously re-build a Republican Party in the South, thereby gradually protecting and advancing the cause of freedmen without the presence of Federal bayonets. In April, a month after his inauguration, the President ordered the Federal troops to leave the South. Reconstruction finally ended and with it—for the next seventy-five years—the national commitment to racial equity.

We have got through with the South Carolina and Louisiana [problems]. At any rate, the troops are ordered away and I now hope for peace, and what is equally important, security and pros-perity for the colored people. The re-sult of my plans is to get from those States by their governors, legislators, press, and people pledges that the Thirteenth, Fourteenth, and Fifteenth Amendments shall be faithfully ob-served; that the colored people shall have equal rights to labor, education, and the privileges of citizenship. I am confident this is a good work, Time will tell.

PRESIDENT RUTHERFORD B. HAYES' REFLECTIONS ON THE GREAT RAILROAD STRIKES
5 August 1877

The transformation of the United States from the rural agricultural land of pre-Civil War days to the urban industrialized world power of 1900 produced unprecedented social tur-bulence, especially among farmers and day laborers. Traditional American values em-phasized individualism and self-reliance, but with the advent of an economy dominated by the factory-wage system controlled by financial and corporate capital increasing millions of ordinary Americans found themselves in perilous economic straits, often due to no fault of their own. In the spring of 1877, with the national economic depression continuing, four great trunk railroads, the New York Central, the Erie, the Pennsylvania, and the Balti-more & Ohio, secretly ended their long-standing rate war and agreed to fix rates. In ad-dition, they cut wages by 10 percent. On 14 July, when the B & O announced a further 10 percent wage cut, its workers went on strike, and the largest peacetime insurrection in American history brought the nation's economy to a halt. Railroad yards and roundhouses became battlefields, as state militias and troops deployed by the thousands to trouble spots all over the United States from the Atlantic to the Mississippi. Factory workers and min-ers left their jobs in sympathy, often taking up arms alongside the railroad union men. Forty thousand miners around Scranton went out, closing off the coal supply. Fifty people *were shot dead in Baltimore by undisciplined troops, nineteen in Chicago, dozens more along the rail lines everywhere. In Pittsburgh, the strikers become a ferocious mob, looting and burning up to $10,000,000 worth of equipment.*

President Hayes responded cautiously to requests from panicked governors for Federal troops, but agreed to dispatch military elements to the major trouble spots. The Hayes Administration helped to break the strike by designating all trains carrying U.S. mail to be exempt from labor interference. By 31 July the fury was spent and strikers began to straggle into the rail yards without gaining their objectives. On 5 August, Hayes reflected on the tumult, noting with regret that nothing more could have been done.

The strikes have been put down by *force*, but now for the *real* remedy. Cant [sic] something [be] done by education of the strikers, by judicious control of the capitalists, by wise general policy to end or diminish the evil? The R.R. strikers, as a rule are good men sober intelligent and industrious.

The mischiefs are

1. Strikers prevent men willing to work from doing so.
2. They sieze and hold the property of their employers.
3. The consequent excitement furnishes opportunity for the dangerous criminal classes to destroy life and property.

Now, "every man has a right if he sees fit to quarrel with his own bread and butter, but he has no right to quarrel with the bread and butter of other people." Every man has a right to determine for himself the value of his own labor, but he has no right to determine for other men the value of their labor. (not good).

Every man has a right to refuse to work if the wages dont [sic] suit him, but he has no right to prevent others from working if they are suited with the wages.

Every man has a right to refuse to work, but no man has a right to prevent others from working.

Every man has a right to decide for himself the question of wages, but no man has a right to decide that question for other men.

PRESIDENT JAMES A. GARFIELD'S REFLECTIONS ON POLITICAL PATRONAGE
6–13 June 1881

The life of James Abram Garfield is the epitome of the traditional American politician of yore. Born in a log cabin, a survivor of poverty, Garfield rose up by force of will and intellect. By the age of twenty-five he had graduated from Williams College as a student of the classics. Cited for bravery leading Ohio Volunteers in the Civil War, he later rose in Republican political circles. While a close observer of the sordid Republican inter-party wars of the Gilded Age, Garfield managed to retain his reputation for decency. When the 1880 Republican Convention split between its warring factions, Garfield emerged on the 36th ballot as a compromise candidate. The political brokering saddled him with a noted spoilsman as his vice-presidential running mate, Chester A. Arthur. Removed by President Hayes in 1879 as New York's Customs Collector, the urbane Arthur retained the support of the corrupt New York machine led by Senator Roscoe Conkling. Even after his victory in the 1880 election, Garfield found no relief from the venomous struggle for favors and appointments within the Republican Party. By tradition, the President himself made the personnel decisions even for minor offices like postmasters and surveyors. Thousands of place seekers advanced their cause in person, by letter and through political surrogates. In June, after just three months in the White House, the dutiful Garfield confessed himself to be overwhelmed by this unceasing and often angry process. Shortly thereafter, a deranged and disappointed office-seeker shot the President, who died in September from his wounds.

[On 6 June after three days absence from Washington], The stream of callers which was damned up by absence became a torrent and swept away my day. [8 June] My day in the office was very like its predecessors. Once or twice I felt like crying out in the agony of my soul against the greed for office and its consumption of my time. My services ought to be worth more to the government than to be spent thus. [13 June] I am feeling greatly dissatisfied for my lack of opportunity for study. My day is frittered away by the personal seeking of people, when it ought to be given to the great problem[s] which concern the whole country. Four years of this kind of intellectual dissipation may cripple me for the remainder of my life. What might not a vigorous thinker do, if he could be allowed to use the opportunities of a Presidential term in vital, useful activity! Some Civil Service Reform will come by necessity after the weariness of some years of wasted Presidents have paved the way for it.

PRESIDENT CHESTER A. ARTHUR CHAMPIONS CIVIL SERVICE REFORM
4 December 1882

Years of corruption during the 1880s produced a political stench so strong that even the professional politicians sought reform. Indeed President Chester Alan Arthur's own career prior to his unexpected ascension to the White House had partaken freely of the *spoils system. For a generation, Arthur's life revolved around the Grand Old Party and its intrigues. The factionalized Republicans were split three ways among reformers like Rutherford B. Hayes and James A. Garfield on one side, and on the other two rival machines called "Half Breeds" and "Stalwarts." Each bloc of "spoilsmen" sought whatever benefits might be found through political connivance. Arthur, a quintessential New York City "Stalwart" Republican, belonged to the corrupt organization of New York Senator Roscoe Conkling. On Conkling's advice, in 1871 President Grant had named Chester Arthur Collector of Customs for the Port of New York, where about 75 percent of the nation's customs receipts were collected. This $100,000,000-a-year "business" provided the greatest patronage source in the entire United States, and, through its arbitrary regulations, rewarded Collector Arthur with the highest salary in the Federal Government. One close associate who called Arthur "probably the ablest politician that has ever filled the collector's chair" surely meant it as a compliment. Successive investigations compelled President Hayes to force Arthur's resignation in 1879. In his defense, New York businessmen praised Arthur's efficiency in running the Customhouse, and claimed absence of evidence of pervasive corruption. Even so, he had accumulated a comfortable fortune, and following his removal returned to a part-time law practice and full-time involvement in party politics. In the near-riotous struggle for the Republican Presidential nomination for 1880, the Stalwarts and Half-Breeds remained deadlocked over thirty-five ballots before Senator Conkling agreed to throw his support to James A. Garfield of Ohio. The arrangement later resulted in presenting the second slot on the ticket to that trusted "Stalwart," Chester A. Arthur. President Garfield took office in March, was shot in July, and died in September. As President, Arthur attempted to imbue his short term with dignity, and accepted the popular call for civil service reform. With rich irony, this single action best represents his time as President.*

. . . The communication that I made to Congress at its first session, in December last, contained a somewhat full statement of my sentiments in relation to the principles and rules which ought to govern appointments to public service.

Referring to the various plans which had theretofore been the subject of discussion in the National Legislature (plans which in the main were modeled upon the system which obtains in Great Britain, but which lacked certain of the prominent features whereby that system is distinguished), I felt bound to intimate my doubts whether they, or any of them, would afford adequate remedy for the evils which they aimed to correct.

I declared, nevertheless, that if the proposed measures should prove acceptable to Congress they would receive the unhesitating support of the Executive.

Since these suggestions were submitted for your consideration there has been no legislation upon the subject to which they relate, but there has meanwhile been an increase in the public interest in that subject, and the people of the country, apparently without distinction of party, have in various ways and upon frequent occasions given expression to their earnest wish for prompt and definite action. In my judgment such action should no longer be postponed.

I may add that my own sense of its pressing importance has been quickened by observation of a practical phase of the matter, to which attention has more than once been called by my predecessors.

The civil list now comprises about 100,000 persons, far the larger part of whom must, under the terms of the Constitution, be selected by the President either directly or through his own appointees.

In the early years of the administration of the Government the personal direction of appointments to the civil service may not have been an irksome task for the Executive, but now that the burden has increased fully a hundredfold it has become greater than he ought to bear, and it necessarily diverts his time and attention from the proper discharge of other duties no less delicate and responsible, and which in the very nature of things can not be delegated to other hands.

In the judgment of not a few who have given study and reflection to this matter, the nation has outgrown the provisions which the Constitution has established for filling the minor offices in the public service.

But whatever may be thought of the wisdom or expediency of changing the fundamental law in this regard, it is certain that much relief may be afforded, not only to the President and to the heads of the Departments, but to Senators and Representatives in Congress, by discreet legislation. They would be protected in a great measure by the bill now pending before the Senate, or by any other which should embody its important features, from the pressure of personal importunity and from the labor of examining conflicting claims and pretensions of candidates.

I trust that before the close of the present session some decisive action may be taken for the correction of the evils which inhere in the present methods of appointment, and I assure you of my hearty cooperation in any measures which are likely to conduce to that end.

As to the most appropriate term and tenure of the official life of the subordinate employees of the Government, it seems to be generally agreed that, whatever their extent or character, the one should be definite and the other stable, and that neither should be regulated by zeal in the service of party or fidelity to the fortunes of an individual.

It matters little to the people at large what competent person is at the head of this department or of that bureau if they feel assured that the removal of one and the accession of another will not involve the retirement of honest and faithful subordinates whose duties are purely administrative and have no legitimate connection with the triumph of any political principles or the success of any political party or faction. It is to this latter class of officers that the Senate bill, to which I have already referred, exclusively applies.

While neither that bill nor any other prominent scheme for improving the civil service concerns the higher grade of officials, who are appointed by the President and confirmed by the Senate, I feel bound to correct a prevalent misapprehension as to the frequency with which the present Executive has displaced the incumbent of an office and appointed another in his stead.

It has been repeatedly alleged that he has in this particular signally departed from the course which has been pursued under recent Administrations of the Government. The facts are as follows:

The whole number of Executive appointments during the four years immediately preceding Mr. Garfield's accession to the Presidency was 2,696. Of this number 244, or 9 per cent, involved the removal of previous incumbents.

The ratio of removals to the whole number of appointments was much the same during each of those four years.

In the first year, with 790 appointments, there were 74 removals, or 9.3 per cent; in the second, with 917 appointments, there were 85 removals, or 8.5 per cent; in the third, with 480 appointments, there were 48 removals, or 10 per cent; in the fourth, with 429 appointments, there were 37 removals, or 8.6 per cent. In the four months of President Garfield's Administration there were 390 appointments and 89 removals, or 22.7 per cent. Precisely the same number of removals (89) has taken place in the fourteen months which have since elapsed, but they constitute only 7.8 per cent of the whole number of appointments (1,118) within that period and less than 2.6 of the entire list of officials (3,459), exclusive of the Army and Navy, which is filled by Presidential appointment.

I declare my approval of such legislation as may be found necessary for supplementing the existing provisions of law in relation to political assessments.

In July last I authorized a public announcement that employees of the Government should regard themselves as at liberty to exercise their pleasure in making or refusing to make political contributions, and that their action in that regard would in no manner affect their official status.

In this announcement I acted upon the view, which I had always maintained and still maintain, that a public officer should be as absolutely free as any other citizen to give or to withhold a contribution for the aid of the political party of his choice. It has, however, been urged, and doubtless not without foundation in fact, that by solicitation of official superiors and by other modes such contributions have at times been obtained from persons whose only motive for giving has been the fear of what might befall them if they refused. It goes without saying that such contributions are not voluntary, and in my judgment their collection should be prohibited by law. A bill which will effectually suppress them will receive my cordial approval. . . .

PRESIDENT GROVER CLEVELAND VETOES DISASTER RELIEF LEGISLATION
16 February 1887

President Grover Cleveland firmly believed in the adage that good Americans supported their government but the government supported no one in particular. Hence as Mayor of Buffalo and Governor of New York, he sought to prevent rather than promote government activity. For him, the primary role of any Executive—Mayor, Governor, or President—was to receive and dispose of the proposals of the Legislature. Since proper functions of government were so limited, Cleveland regularly disapproved of Congressional initiatives. Both of his presidential terms produced a flood of vetoes, two of every three bills reaching his desk being rejected. By the end of his presidency, Cleveland's vetoes numbered three times more than all his predecessors combined. However politically hazardous this austere approach, Cleveland nonetheless stuck to his principles and conveyed an integrity which clearly distinguished him from the lax ethics and addiction to spoils that characterized the times. No item seemed too insignificant for the President's attention, no good cause or obvious need too commanding to avoid the veto pen. In 1887, natural disasters devastated crops in the Texas Panhandle and Congress appropriated $10,000 so that desperate farmers could purchase seed grain. The President strongly objected in his veto message.

I return without my approval House bill No. 10203, entitled "An act to enable the Commissioner of Agriculture to make a special distribution of seeds in the drought-stricken counties of Texas, and making an appropriation therefor."

It is represented that a long-continued and extensive drought has existed in certain portions of the State of Texas, resulting in a failure of crops and consequent distress and destitution.

Though there has been some difference in statements concerning the extent of the people's needs in the localities thus affected, there seems to be no doubt that there has existed a condition calling for relief; and I am willing to believe that, notwithstanding the aid already furnished, a donation of seed grain to the farmers located in this region, to enable them to put in new crops, would serve to avert a continuance or return of an unfortunate blight.

And yet I feel obliged to withhold my approval of the plan, as propposed by this bill, to indulge a benevolent and charitable sentiment through the appropriation of public funds for that purpose.

I can find no warrant for such an appropriation in the Constitution, and I do not believe that the power and duty of the General Government ought to be extended to the relief of individual suffering which is in no manner properly related to the public service or benefit. A prevalent tendency to disregard the limited mission of this power and duty should, I think, be steadfastly resisted, to the end that the lesson should be constantly enforced that though the people support the Government the Government should not support the people.

The friendliness and charity of our countrymen can always be relied upon to relieve their fellow-citizens in misfortune. This has been repeatedly and quite lately demonstrated. Federal aid in such cases encourages the expectation of paternal care on the part of the Government and weakens the sturdiness of our national character, while it prevents the indulgence among our people of that kindly sentiment and conduct which strengthens the bonds of a common brotherhood.

It is within my personal knowledge that individual aid has to some extent already been extended to the sufferers mentioned in this bill. The failure of the proposed appropriation of $10,000 additional to meet their remaining wants will not necessarily result in continued distress if the emergency is fully made known to the people of the country.

It is here suggested that the Commissioner of Agriculture is annually directed to expend a large sum of money for the purchase, propagation, and distribution of seeds and other things of this description, two-thirds of which are, upon the request of Senators, Representatives, and Delegates in Congress, supplied to them for distribution among their constituents.

The appropriation of the current year for this purpose is $100,000, and it will probably be no less in the appropriation for the ensuing year. I understand that a large quantity of grain is furnished for such distribution, and it is supposed that this free apportionment among their neighbors is a privilege which may be waived by our Senators and Representatives.

If sufficient of them should request the Commissioner of Agriculture to send their shares of the grain thus allowed them to the suffering farmers of Texas, they might be enabled to sow their crops, the constituents for whom in theory this grain is intended could well bear the temporary deprivation, and the donors would experience the satisfaction attending deeds of charity.

PRESIDENT GROVER CLEVELAND ATTACKS
HIGH PROTECTIVE TARIFFS
3 December 1888

For years the Republican Party proclaimed tariff protection to be the secret of America's economic success. Indeed the appealing idea of imposing taxes on incoming foreign goods reached back to the founding of the Republic, when legislative bodies responded to pleas from newborn American businesses for protection against the more sophisticated enterprises of Europe. By the 1880s, the Republican Party proudly and emphatically equated the protective tariff with American prosperity. For President Grover Cleveland, however, existing tariff rates represented a fraud on the electorate and a shameful use of government power. Not only did tariff legislation bring government interference to benefit the most powerful manufacturing interests, Cleveland believed, but rates artificially raised prices on all commodities. The President understood that a frontal attack on the tariff entailed great political risks for himself and his party, he being the first Democrat to be elected since James Buchanan in 1856. With characteristic bluntness, nonetheless, Cleveland took on the nation's majority party and denounced its most popular issue. "What is the use in being elected," he noted, "if you don't stand for something." Breaking precedent, he devoted his entire Annual Message of December 1887 to the one issue. Cleveland summoned his considerable force of conviction to make a political and public case for fundamental change in America's economic operations—and failed. Subsequent legislation designed to lower tariffs languished in the Republican-controlled Senate, and his political opponents had an excellent issue against him in the election of 1888.

As you assemble for the discharge of the duties you have assumed as the representatives of a free and generous people, your meeting is marked by an interesting and impressive incident. With the expiration of the present session of the Congress the first century of our constitutional existence as a nation will be completed.

Our survival for one hundred years is not sufficient to assure us that we no longer have dangers to fear in the maintenance, with all its promised blessings, of a government founded upon the freedom of the people. The time rather admonishes us to soberly inquire whether in the past we have always closely kept in the course of safety, and whether we have before us a way plain and clear which leads to happiness and perpetuity. . . .

A century has passed. Our cities are the abiding places of wealth and luxury; our manufactories yield fortunes never dreamed of by the fathers of the Republic; our business men are madly striving in the race for riches, and immense aggregations of capital outrun the imagination in the magnitude of their undertakings.

We view with pride and satisfaction this bright picture of our country's growth and prosperity, while only a closer scrutiny develops a somber shading. Upon more careful inspection we find the wealth and luxury of our cities mingled with poverty and wretchedness and unremunerative toil. A crowded and constantly increasing urban population suggests the impoverishment of rural sections and discontent with agricultural pursuits. The farmer's son, not satisfied with his father's simple and laborious life, joins the eager chase for easily acquired wealth.

We discover that the fortunes realized by our manufacturers are no longer solely the reward of sturdy industry and enlightened foresight, but that they result from the discriminating favor of the Government and are largely built upon undue exactions from the masses of our people. The gulf between employers and the employed is constantly widening, and classes are rapidly forming, one comprising the very rich and powerful, while in another are found the toiling poor.

As we view the achievements of aggregated capital, we discover the existence of trusts, combinations, and monopolies, while the citizen is struggling far in the rear or is trampled to death beneath an iron heel. Corporations, which should be the carefully restrained creatures of the law and the servants of the people, are fast becoming the people's masters.

Still congratulating ourselves upon the wealth and prosperity of our country and complacently contemplating every incident of change inseparable from these conditions, it is our duty as patriotic citizens to inquire at the present stage of our progress how the bond of the Government made with the people has been kept and performed.

Instead of limiting the tribute drawn from our citizens to the necessities of its economical administration, the Government persists in exacting from the substance of the people millions which, unapplied and useless, lie dormant in its Treasury. This flagrant injustice and this breach of faith and obligation add to extortion the danger attending the diversion of the currency of the country from the legitimate channels of business.

Under the same laws by which these results are produced the Government permits many millions more to be added to the cost of the living of our people and to be taken from our consumers, which unreasonably swell the profits of a small but powerful minority.

The people must still be taxed for the support of the Government under the operation of tariff laws. But to the extent that the mass of our citizens are inordinately burdened beyond any useful public purpose and for the benefit of a favored few, the Government, under pretext of an exercise of its taxing power, enters gratuitously into partnership with these favorites, to their advantage and to the injury of a vast majority of our people.

This is not equality before the law.

The existing situation is injurious to the health of our entire body politic. It stifles in those for whose benefit it is permitted all patriotic love of country, and substitutes in its place selfish greed and grasping avarice. Devotion to American citizenship for its own sake and for what it should accomplish as a motive to our nation's advancement and the happiness of all our people is displaced by the assumption that the Government, instead of being the embodiment of equality, is but an instrumentality through which especial and individual advantages are to be gained.

The arrogance of this assumption is unconcealed. It appears in the sordid disregard of all but personal interests, in the refusal to abate for the benefit of others one iota of selfish advantage, and in combinations to perpetuate such advantages through efforts to control legislation and improperly influence the suffrages of the people.

The grievances of those not included within the circle of these beneficiaries, when fully realized, will surely arouse irritation and discontent. Our farmers, long suffering and patient, struggling in the race of life with the hardest and most unremitting toil, will not fail to see, in spite of misrepresentations and misleading fallacies, that they are obliged to accept such prices for their products as are fixed in foreign markets where they compete with the farmers of the world; that their lands are declining in value while their debts increase, and

that without compensating favor they are forced by the action of the Government to pay for the benefit of others such enhanced prices for the things they need that the scanty returns of their labor fail to furnish their support or leave no margin for accumulation.

Our workingmen, enfranchised from all delusions and no longer frightened by the cry that their wages are endangered by a just revision of our tariff laws, will reasonably demand through such revision steadier employment, cheaper means of living in their homes, freedom for themselves and their children from the doom of perpetual servitude, and an open door to their advancement beyond the limits of a laboring class. Others of our citizens, whose comforts and expenditures are measured by moderate salaries and fixed incomes, will insist upon the fairness and justice of cheapening the cost of necessaries for themselves and their families.

When to the selfishness of the beneficiaries of unjust discrimination under our laws there shall be added the discontent of those who suffer from such discrimination, we will realize the fact that the beneficent purposes of our Government, dependent upon the patriotism and contentment of our people, are endangered.

Communism is a hateful thing and a menace to peace and organized government; but the communism of combined wealth and capital, the outgrowth of overweening cupidity and selfishness, which insidiously undermines the justice and integrity of free institutions, is not less dangerous than the communism of oppressed poverty and toil, which, exasperated by injustice and discontent, attacks with wild disorder the citadel of rule.

He mocks the people who proposes that the Government shall protect the rich and that they in turn will care for the laboring poor. Any intermediary between the people and their Government or the least delegation of the care and protection the Government owes to the humblest citizen in the land makes the boast of free institutions a glittering delusion and the pretended boon of American citizenship a shameless imposition.

A just and sensible revision of our tariff laws should be made for the relief of those of our countrymen who suffer under present conditions. Such a revision should receive the support of all who love that justice and equality due to American citizenship; of all who realize that in this justice and equality our Government finds its strength and its power to protect the citizen and his property; of all who believe that the contented competence and comfort of many accord better with the spirit of our institutions than colossal fortunes unfairly gathered in the hands of a few; of all who appreciate that the forbearance and fraternity among our people, which recognize the value of every American interest, are the surest guaranty of our

national progress, and of all who desire to see the products of American skill and ingenuity in every market of the world, with a resulting restoration of American commerce.

The necessity of the reduction of our revenues is so apparent as to be generally conceded, but the means by which this end shall be accomplished and the sum of direct benefit which shall result to our citizens present a controversy of the utmost importance. There should be no scheme accepted as satisfactory by which the burdens of the people are only apparently removed. Extravagant appropriations of public money, with all their demoralizing consequences, should not be tolerated, either as a means of relieving the Treasury of its present surplus or as furnishing pretext for resisting a proper reduction in tariff rates. Existing evils and injustice should be honestly recognized, boldly met, and effectively remedied. There should be no cessation of the struggle until a plan is perfected, fair and conservative toward existing industries, but which will reduce the cost to consumers of the necessaries of life, while it provides for our manufacturers the advantage of freer raw materials and permits no injury to the interests of American labor.

The cause for which the battle is waged is comprised within lines clearly and distinctly defined. It should never be compromised. It is the people's cause. . . .

PRESIDENT BENJAMIN HARRISON RETRACES GEORGE WASHINGTON'S INAUGURAL ROUTE A CENTURY LATER
30 April 1889

A century after George Washington took the oath as the nation's first president, his successor, Benjamin Harrison, presided over a vivid celebration of the centennial. Accompanied by his cabinet and the members of the Supreme Court, the President traveled by overnight train on 28 April 1889, from Washington to Elizabeth, New Jersey. The next morning, Harrison began to follow the route taken by Washington on that first inaugural day. He lead a procession down to the Hudson River opposite Manhattan. Groups of young women in white dresses showered the Presidential party with roses and, like his illustrious predecessor of a century earlier, the bewiskered Harrison stopped under garlanded arches to thank the young women. Festooned ships of all descriptions filled New York's harbor when the presidential party boarded the U.S.S. Despatch. To the bridge went the President, accompanied by military dignitaries like General William Tecumseh Sherman. Canons roared and factory whistles squealed on both sides of the river while Harrison squinted through binoculars at an impressive array of ten newly commissioned warships. After two hours of review, the President landed at the Battery and began a day-long round of parades and receptions. At one point, at City Hall, he passed through an honor guard of girls armed with lilies of the valley and roses, once again being pleasantly covered with flowers. An open-air concert attracted thousands to Madison Square. Throughout the city neighborhoods were swathed in the stars-and-stripes. At day's end, President Harrison drove to the magnificent new Metropolitan Opera house, opened in 1883, to preside over a glittering Centennial banquet attended by eight hundred of America's best known citizens. Prior to the President's remarks, toasts were offered by ex-Presidents Rutherford B. Hayes and Grover Cleveland, and Chief Justice of the United States Melville W. Fuller. The President responded.

I should be unjust to myself, and, what is more serious, I should be unjust to you, if I did not at this first and last opportunity express to you the deep sense of obligation and thankfulness which I feel for these many personal and official courtesies which have been extended to me since I came to take part in this celebration. The official representatives of the State of New York and of this great city have attended me with the most courteous kindness, omitting no attention that could make my stay among you pleasant and gratifying. From you and at the hands of those who have thronged the streets of the city today I have received the most cordial expressions of good will. I would not, however, have you understand that these loud acclaims have been in any sense appropriated as a personal tribute to myself. I have realized that there was that in this occasion and all these interesting incidents which have made it so profoundly impressive to my mind which was above and greater than any living man. I have realized that the tribute of cordial interest which you have manifested was rendered to that great office which, by the favor of a greater people, I now exercise, rather than to me.

The occasion and all of its incidents will be memorable not only in the history of your own city, but in the history of our country. New York did not succeed in retaining the seat of national government here, although she made liberal provision for the assembling of the first Congress in the expectation that the Congress might find its permanent home here. But though you lost that which you coveted, I think the representatives here of all the States will agree that it was fortunate that the first inauguration of Washington took place in the State and the city of New York.

For where in our country could the centennial of the event be so worthily celebrated as here? What seaboard offered so magnificent a bay on which to display our merchant and naval marine? What city offered thoroughfares so magnificent, or a people so great, so generous, as New York has poured out today to celebrate that event?

I have received at the hands of the committee who have been charged with the details—onerous, exacting, and too

often unthankful—of this demonstration evidence of their confidence in my physical endurance. [Laughter.]

I must also acknowledge still one other obligation. The committee having in charge the exercises of this event have also given me another evidence of their confidence, which has been accompanied with some embarrassment. As I have noticed the progress of this banquet, it seemed to me that each of the speakers had been made acquainted with his theme before he took his seat at the banquet, and that I alone was left to make acquaintance with my theme when I sat down to the table. I prefer to substitute for the official title which is upon the programme the familiar and fireside expression, "Our Country."

I congratulate you today, as one of the instructive and interesting features of this occasion, that these great thoroughfares dedicated to trade have closed their doors and covered up the insignias of commerce; that your great exchanges have closed and your citizens given themselves up to the observance of the celebration in which we are participating.

I believe that patriotism has been intensified in many hearts by what we have witnessed today. I believe that patriotism has been placed in a higher and holier fane in many hearts. The bunting with which you have covered your walls, these patriotic inscriptions, must go down and the wage and trade be resumed again. Here may I not ask you to carry those inscriptions that now hang on the walls into your homes, into the schools of your city, into all of your great institutions where children are gathered, and teach them that the eye of the young and the old should look upon that flag as one of the familiar glories of every American? Have we not learned that no stocks and bonds, nor land, is our country? It is a spiritual thought that is in our minds—it is the flag and what it stands for; it is the fireside and the home; it is the thoughts that are in our hearts, born of the inspiration which comes with the story of the flag, of martyrs to liberty. It is the graveyard into which a common country has gathered the unconscious deeds of those who died that the thing might live which we love and call our country, rather than anything that can be touched or seen.

Let me add a thought due to our country's future. Perhaps never have we been so well equipped for war upon land as now, and we have never seen the time when our people were more smitten with the love of peace. To elevate the morals of our people; to hold up the law as that sacred thing which, like the ark of God of old, may not be touched by irreverent hands, but frowns upon any attempt to dethrone its supremacy; to unite our people in all that makes home comfortable, as well as to give our energies in the direction of material advancement, this service may we render. And out of this great demonstration let us draw lessons to inspire us to consecrate ourselves anew to this love and service of our country.

PRESIDENT BENJAMIN HARRISON ANNOUNCES THE CONSTRUCTION OF A GREAT NAVAL FLEET
6 December 1892

President Harrison's approach to foreign affairs differed significantly from the conventional isolationism of his predecessors. He appointed James G. Blaine, a popular if outspoken political veteran as Secretary of State. Blaine, with Harrison's encouragement, looked southward for an expansion of hemispheric contacts, which the Secretary familiarly called "pan-Americanism." This included such plans as a tariff-reducing customs union for the hemisphere, construction of a Central American canal and a court of arbitration. For one or another reason, all the initiatives failed. Yet the vision of the United States as a burgeoning imperial power seemed clear. To that end, President Harrison championed the construction of a modern navy. Under his plan, as executed by Secretary of the Navy Benjamin Franklin Tracy, the wooden ships of the old fleet were scuttled. Their replacements, reflecting the most modern designs of American naval architecture, immediately became the largest naval ships in the world. Within a decade, the United States would be permanently among the world's great powers.

. . . The report of the Secretary of the Navy exhibits great progress in the construction of our new Navy. When the present Secretary entered upon his duties, only 3 modern steel vessels were in commission. The vessels since put in commission and to be put in commission during the winter will make a total of 19 during his administration of the Department. During the current year 10 war vessels and 3 navy tugs have been launched, and during the four years 25 vessels will have been launched. Two other large ships and a torpedo boat are under contract and the work upon them well advanced, and the 4 monitors are awaiting only the arrival of their armor, which has been unexpectedly delayed, or they would have been before this in commission.

Contracts have been let during this Administration, under the appropriations for the increase of the Navy, including new vessels and their appurtenances, to the amount of $35,000,000, and there has been expended during the same period for labor at navy-yards upon similar work $8,000,000 without the smallest scandal or charge of fraud or partiality. The enthusiasm and interest of our naval officers, both of the staff and line, have been greatly kindled. They have responded magnificently to the confidence of Congress and have demonstrated to the world an unexcelled capacity in construction, in ordnance, and in everything involved in the building, equipping, and sailing of great war ships.

At the beginning of Secretary Tracy's administration several difficult problems remained to be grappled with and solved before the efficiency in action of our ships could be secured. It is believed that as the result of new processes in the construction of armor plate our later ships will be clothed with defensive plates of higher resisting power than are found on any war vessels afloat. We were without torpedoes. Tests have been made to ascertain the relative efficiency of different constructions, a torpedo has been adopted, and the work of construction is now being carried on successfully. We were without armor-piercing shells and without a shop instructed and equipped for the construction of them. We are now making what is believed to be a projectile superior to any before in use. A smokeless powder has been developed and a slow-burning powder for guns of large caliber. A high explosive capable of use in shells fired from service guns has been found, and the manufacture of gun cotton has been developed so that the question of supply is no longer in doubt.

The development of a naval militia, which has been organized in eight States and brought into cordial and co-operative relations with the Navy, is another important achievement. There are now enlisted in these organizations 1,800 men, and they are likely to be greatly extended. I recommend such legislation and appropriations as will encourage and develop this movement. The recommendations of the Secretary will, I do not doubt, receive the friendly consideration of Congress, for he has enjoyed, as he has deserved, the confidence of all those interested in the development of our Navy, without any division upon partisan lines. I earnestly express the hope that a work which has made such noble progress may not now be stayed. The wholesome influence for peace and the increased sense of security which our citizens domiciled in other lands feel when these magnificent ships under the American flag appear is already most gratefully apparent. The ships from our Navy which will appear in the great naval parade next April in the harbor of New York will be a convincing demonstration to the world that the United States is again a naval power.

President Grover Cleveland's Decision to Send Troops to Chicago to Counter the Pullman Strike
8 July 1894

The only President ever elected to two non-consecutive terms, Grover Cleveland returned to the White House in the year of one of the most severe economic collapses in American history, the "Panic of 1893." Despite this prolonged crisis, Cleveland's restrictive view of the proper role of government limited his response. He called for honesty, reductions in spending and taxes, and tariff reform. In this, Cleveland's fundamental beliefs generally matched other American Presidents throughout the nineteenth century. They regarded private property as inviolable and the involvement of government in the economic and social lives of American citizens as unconstitutional. Bad times, like natural disasters, were to be endured and survived. By the 1890s, however, unlike their ancestors, industrial workers in trouble no longer had the safety net of living off the land. In the second Cleveland administration, with the economy frozen and stocks at an all time low, the nation witnessed convulsions of protest. The bitter strike at the Homestead, Pennsylvania, steel mill of Andrew Carnegie raged from July to November 1892, involving 7,000 troops, violent confrontations between steelworkers and scabs, a score of deaths. Scabs who would work for less than union wages replaced strikers, while the militia patrolled the mill. Union militancy gradually attracted both sympathy and support through a rash of secondary strikes, but compelling power remained against them. The prevailing political *and judicial response to work stoppages included both the dispatch of troops to break the strike and the use of the courts to find strikes illegal. When workers at the Pullman Palace Car Company near Chicago struck on 11 May 1894, the American Railway Union ordered a sympathy strike of all railroad workers. The strikers, led by the charismatic Eugene V. Debs, met the unswerving opposition of the owners, who brought in strike-breakers and called for troops. Caught in the middle was Illinois Governor John Peter Altgeld, who kept contact with both sides and sought compromise without violence. President Cleveland's response was an injunction ordering Debs to end the strike. The President argued that interstate commerce and mail delivery were impeded. In Washington on 8 July, President Cleveland declared martial law and, over Altgeld's objection, Federal troops poured into Chicago. Death and general mayhem attended the struggle, Debs was indicted, and an estimated $80,000,000 in property and wages lost in the conflagration. Debs would soon be jailed for contempt, and Altgeld, who opposed the use of troops and the courts in a labor dispute, would soon forfeit his political career. Cleveland always found difficulty in understanding the positions of others, and in the Pullman affair believed that if it took the entire Army to deliver one post card, he would give the order.*

On the eighth day of July, in view of the apparently near approach of a crisis which the Government had attempted to avoid, the following Executive Proclamation was issued and at once extensively published in the city of Chicago:

Whereas, by reason of unlawful obstruction, combinations and assemblages of persons, it has become impracticable, in the judgment of the President, to enforce, by the ordinary course of judicial proceedings, the laws of the United States within the State of Illinois, and especially in the city of Chicago within said State; and

Whereas, for the purpose of enforcing the faithful execution of the laws of the United States and protecting its property and removing obstructions to the United States mails in the State and city aforesaid, the President has employed a part of the military forces of the United States:

Now, therefore, I, Grover Cleveland, President of the United States, do hereby admonish all good citizens, and all persons who may be or may come within the City and State aforesaid, against aiding, countenancing, encouraging, or taking any part in such unlawful obstructions, combinations, and assemblages; and I hereby warn all persons engaged in or in any way connected with such unlawful obstructions, combinations, and assemblages to disperse and retire peaceably to their respective abodes on or before twelve o'clock noon of the 9th day of July instant.

Those who disregard this warning and persist in taking part with a riotous mob in forcibly resisting and obstructing the execution of the laws of the United States, or interfering with the functions of the Government, or destroying or attempting to destroy the property belonging to the United States or under its protection, cannot be regarded otherwise than as public enemies.

Troops employed against such a riotous mob will act with all the moderation and forbearance consistent with the accomplishment of the desired end; but the stern necessities that confront them will not with certainty permit discrimination between guilty participants and those who are mingling with them from curiosity and without criminal intent. The only safe course, therefore, for those not actually participating, is to abide at their homes, or at least not to be found in the neighborhood of riotous assemblages.

While there will be no vacillation in the decisive treatment of the guilty, this warning is especially intended to protect and save the innocent.

PRESIDENT GROVER CLEVELAND'S DEFENSE OF THE GOLD STANDARD
28 January 1895

Turbulence in the second Cleveland administration spread from the factories to the farms. Farmers' actions ranged from simple violence to political organization. The Populist Party, representing farmer and labor demands for radical change in American life, quickly gained strength. In the 1892 election, Populists captured three state houses, and elected five United States Senators, ten Congressmen, and about fifteen hundred state legislators. In that election, while Grover Cleveland defeated the incumbent Republican President Benjamin Harrison, the Populist third party candidate James B. Weaver's showing promised a bright future for reform and radicalism. Weaver attracted more than one million votes, won electoral votes in six different states, and prevailed completely in Kansas, Nevada, Idaho, and Colorado. Populism came to the streets of the nation's capitol in the spring of 1894 when the futile but well-publicized "Coxey's Army" straggled into Washington to be met and harshly dealt with by an increasingly nervous Cleveland administration. Protesters had long demanded relief from the gold standard, which restricted the money supply and favored creditors over debtors. The Populists and their allies insisted that the Federal Government purchase and distribute silver as legal currency In 1890, Congress passed the Sherman Silver Purchase Act, which compelled the procurement of 4.5 million ounces of silver each month. Treasury notes became payable either in gold or silver. As the depression deepened, Cleveland's worst nightmare appeared. Runs on the Federal gold supply shrunk the nation's holdings and only *encouraged frightened investors to further runs. Hence in 1893 the President called a Special Session of Congress specifically to repeal the Sherman Silver Purchase Act. His success, which led one Populist to call Cleveland "Benedict Arnold," failed to end the run on the Treasury. So early in 1895, the President proposed an unusual deal with a group of Wall Street capitalists headed by the banker J. P. Morgan. The bankers would exchange 3.5 million ounces of gold for $62 million in U.S. Government bonds. The bonds would be resold by the bankers at a profit. The logic of Cleveland's defense of his plan notwithstanding, his scheme totally destroyed his political viability. The end of silver purchases contracted the nation's money supply and automatically alienated debtors and Western silver miners—and their political representatives in all political parties. With his own career in shambles, Cleveland created the furor over the gold standard that dominated the Election of 1896.*

In my last annual message I commended to the serious consideration of the Congress the condition of our national finances, and in connection with the subject indorsed a plan of currency legislation which at that time seemed to furnish protection against impending danger. This plan has not been approved by the Congress. In the meantime the situation has so changed and the emergency now appears so threatening that I deem it my duty to ask at the hands of the legislative branch of the Government such prompt and effective action as will restore confidence in our financial soundness and avert business disaster and universal distress among our people.

Whatever may be the merits of the plan outlined in my annual message as a remedy for ills then existing and as a safeguard against the depletion of the gold reserve then in the Treasury, I am now convinced that its reception by the Congress and our present advanced stage of financial perplexity necessitate additional or different legislation.

With natural resources unlimited in variety and productive strength and with a people whose activity and enterprise seek only a fair opportunity to achieve national success and greatness, our progress should not be checked by a false financial policy and a heedless disregard of sound monetary laws, nor should the timidity and fear which they engender stand in the way of our prosperity.

It is hardly disputed that this predicament confronts us today. Therefore no one in any degree responsible for the making and execution of our laws should fail to see a patriotic duty in honestly and sincerely attempting to relieve the situation. Manifestly this effort will not succeed unless it is made untrammeled by the prejudice of partisanship and with a steadfast determination to resist the temptation to accomplish party advantage. We may well remember that if we are threatened with financial difficulties all our people in every station of life are concerned; and surely those who suffer will not receive the promotion of party interests as an excuse for permitting our present troubles to advance to a disastrous conclusion. It is also of the utmost importance that we approach the study of the problems presented as free as possible from the tyranny of preconceived opinions, to the end that in a common danger we may be able to seek with unclouded vision a safe and reasonable protection.

The real trouble which confronts us consists in a lack of confidence, widespread and constantly increasing, in the continuing ability or disposition of the Government to pay its obligations in gold. This lack of confidence grows to some extent out of the palpable and apparent embarrassment attending the efforts of the Government under existing laws to procure gold and to a greater extent out of the impossibility of either keeping it in the Treasury or canceling obligations by its expenditure after it is obtained.

The only way left open to the Government for procuring gold is by the issue and sale of its bonds. The only bonds that can be so issued were authorized nearly twenty-five years ago and are not well calculated to meet our present needs. Among other disadvantages, they are made payable in coin instead of specifically in gold, which in existing conditions detracts largely and in an increasing ratio from their desirability as investments. It is by no means certain that bonds of this description can much longer be disposed of at a price creditable to the financial character of our Government.

The most dangerous and irritating feature of the situation, however, remains to be mentioned. It is found in the means by which the Treasury is despoiled of the gold thus obtained without canceling a single Government obligation and solely for the benefit of those who find profit in shipping it abroad or whose fears induce them to hoard it at home. We have outstanding about five hundred millions of currency notes of the Government for which gold may be demanded, and, curiously enough, the law requires that when presented and, in fact, redeemed and paid in gold they shall be reissued. Thus the same notes may do duty many times in drawing gold from the Treasury; nor can the process be arrested as long as private parties, for profit or otherwise, see an advantage in repeating the operation. More than $300,000,000 in these notes have already been redeemed in gold, and notwithstanding such redemption they are all still outstanding.

Since the 17th day of January 1894, our bonded interest-bearing debt has been increased $100,000,000 for the purpose of obtaining gold to replenish our coin reserve. Two issues were made amounting to fifty millions each, one in January and the other in November. As a result of the first issue there was realized something more than $58,000,000 in gold. Between that issue and the succeeding one in November, comprising a period of about ten months, nearly $103,000,000 in gold were drawn from the Treasury. This made the second issue necessary, and upon that more than fifty-eight millions in gold was again realized. Between the date of this second issue and the present time, covering a period of only about two months, more than $69,000,000 in gold have been drawn from the Treasury. These large sums of gold were expended without any cancellation of Government obligations or in any permanent way benefiting our people or improving our pecuniary situation. . . .

It will hardly do to say that a simple increase of revenue will cure our troubles. The apprehension now existing and constantly increasing as to our financial ability does not rest upon a calculation of our revenue. The time has passed when the eyes of investors abroad and our people at home were fixed upon the revenues of the Government. Changed conditions have attracted their attention to the gold of the Government. There need be no fear that we can not pay our current expenses with such money as we have. There is now in the Treasury a comfortable surplus of more than $63,000,000, but it is not in gold, and therefore does not meet our difficulty.

I can not see that differences of opinion concerning the extent to which silver ought to be coined or used in our currency should interfere with the counsels of those whose duty it is to rectify evils now apparent in our financial situation. They have to con-sider the question of national credit and the consequences that will follow from its collapse. Whatever ideas may be insisted upon as to silver or bimetallism, a proper solution of the question now pressing upon us only requires a recognition of gold as well as silver and a concession of its importance, rightfully or wrongfully acquired, as a basis of national credit, a necessity in the honorable discharge of our obligations payable in gold, and a badge of solvency. I do not understand that the real friends of silver desire a condition that might follow inaction or neglect to appreciate the meaning of the present exigency if it should result in the entire banishment of gold from our financial and currency arrangements.

Besides the Treasury notes, which certainly should be paid in gold, amounting to nearly $500,000,000, there will fall due in 1904 one hundred millions of bonds issued during the last year, for which we have received gold, and in 1907 nearly six hundred millions of 4 per cent bonds issued in 1877. Shall the payment of these obligations in gold be repudiated? If they are to be paid in such a manner as the preservation of our national honor and national solvency demands, we should not destroy or even imperil our ability to supply ourselves with gold for that purpose.

While I am not unfriendly to silver and while I desire to see it recognized to such an extent as is consistent with financial safety and the preservation of national honor and credit, I am not willing to see gold entirely banished from our currency and finances. To avert such a consequence I believe thorough and radical remedial legislation should be promptly passed. I therefore beg the Congress to give the subject immediate attention.

In my opinion the Secretary of the Treasury should be authorized to issue bonds of the Government for the purpose of procuring and maintaining a sufficient gold reserve and the redemption and cancellation of the United States legal-tender notes and the Treasury notes issued for the purchase of silver under the law of 14 July 1890. We should be relieved from the humiliating process of issuing bonds to procure gold to be immediately and repeatedly drawn out on these obligations for purposes not related to the benefit of our Government or our people. The principal and interest of these bonds should be payable on their face in gold, because they should be sold only for gold or its representative, and because there would now probably be difficulty in favorably disposing of bonds not containing this stipulation. I suggest that the bonds be issued in denominations of twenty and fifty dollars and their multiples and that they bear interest at a rate not exceeding 3 per cent per annum. I do not see why they should not be payable fifty years from their date. We of the present generation have large amounts to pay if we meet our obligations, and long bonds are most salable. The Secretary of the Treasury might well be permitted at his dis-

cretion to receive on the sale of bonds the legal-tender and Treasury notes to be retired, and of course when they are thus retired or redeemed in gold they should be canceled. . . .

As a constant means for the maintenance of a reasonable supply of gold in the Treasury, our duties on imports should be paid in gold, allowing all other dues to the Government to be paid in any other form of money.

I believe all the provisions I have suggested should be embodied in our laws if we are to enjoy a complete reinstatement of a sound financial condition. They need not interfere with any currency scheme providing for the increase of the circulating medium through the agency of national or State banks that may commend itself to the Congress, since they can easily be adjusted to such a scheme. Objection has been made to the issuance of interest-bearing obligations for the purpose of retiring the noninterest-bearing legal-tender notes. In point of fact, however, these notes have burdened us with a large load of interest, and it is still accumulating. The aggregate interest on the original issue of bonds, the proceeds of which in gold constituted the reserve for the payment of these notes, amounted to $70,326,250 on 1 January 1895, and the annual charge for interest on these bonds and those issued for the same purpose during the last year will be $9,145,000, dating from 1 January 1895.

While the cancellation of these notes would not relieve us from the obligations already incurred on their account, these figures are given by way of suggesting that their existence has not been free from interest charges and that the longer they are oustanding, judging from the experience of the last year, the more expensive they will become.

In conclusion I desire to frankly confess my reluctance to issuing more bonds in present circumstances and with no better results than have lately followed that course. I can not, however, refrain from adding to an assurance of my anxiety to cooperate with the present Congress in any reasonable measure of relief an expression of my determination to leave nothing undone which furnishes a hope for improving the situation or checking a suspicion of our disinclination or disability to meet with the strictest honor every national obligation.

PRESIDENT GROVER CLEVELAND'S THREAT OF WAR WITH ENGLAND
17 December 1895

In 1895, a quarrel about an obscure boundary line near the Orinoco River pitted the mighty British Empire against Venezuela, whose government amounted to a powerless and corrupt dependency of European imperial states. The dispute arose when Britain sought to expand the territory of British Guyana at Venezuela's expense. Naturally, they fully expected to prevail. On 20 July, the United States interjected itself into the quarrel in spectacular fashion. American Secretary of State Richard Olney wrote to Lord Salisbury, the Prime Minister and Foreign Secretary, that "Today the United States is practically sovereign on this continent, and its fiat is law upon the subjects to which it confines its interposition." This pronunciamento naturally angered Canada and all the states of Latin America, and Lord Salisbury merely ignored it by refusing to reply. In December, President Cleveland laid this correspondence before Congress, and demanded that the issue be arbitrated, threatening the British in the process. This incident constituted an unmistakable foreshadowing of the American imperial designs that would emerge during the administrations of Cleveland's immediate predecessors. The Orinoco crisis passed and the Anglo-American hostility wore off over the next few years. The rise of German power at the turn of the century pushed England into an informal alliance with the United States, thus recognizing American primacy in the New World.

In my annual message addressed to the Congress on the third instant I called attention to the pending boundary controversy between Great Britain and the Republic of Venezuela and recited the substance of a representation made by this Government to Her Britannic Majesty's Government suggesting reasons why such dispute should be submitted to arbitration for settlement, and inquiring whether it would be so submitted.

The answer of the British Government, which was then awaited, has since been received and, together with the dispatch to which it is a reply, is hereto appended.

Such reply is embodied in two communications addressed by the British Prime Minister to Sir Julian Pauncefote, the British Ambassador at this Capital. It will be seen that one of these communications is devoted exclusively to observations upon the Monroe doctrine, and claims that in the present instance a new and strange extension and development of this doctrine is insisted on by the United States, that the reasons justifying an appeal to the doctrine enunciated by President Monroe are generally inapplicable "to the state of things in which we live at the present day," and especially inapplicable to a controversy involving the boundary line between Great Britain and Venezuela.

Without attempting extended argument in reply to these positions, it may not be amiss to suggest that the doctrine upon which we stand is strong and sound because its enforcement is important to our peace and safety as a nation, and is essential to the integrity of our free institutions and the tranquil maintenance of our distinctive form of government. It was intended to apply to every stage of our national life, and can not become obsolete while our Republic endures. If the balance of power

is justly a cause for jealous anxiety among the governments of the old world, and a subject for our absolute noninterference, none the less is an observance of the Monroe doctrine of vital concern to our people and their Government.

Assuming, therefore, that we may properly insist upon this doctrine without regard to "the state of things in which we live," or any changed conditions here or elsewhere, it is not apparent why its application may not be invoked in the present controversy.

If a European power, by an extension of its boundaries, takes possession of the territory of one of our neighboring Republics against its will and in derogation of its rights, it is difficult to see why to that extent such European power does not thereby attempt to extend its system of government to that portion of this continent which is thus taken. This is the precise action which President Monroe declared to be "dangerous to our peace and safety," and it can make no difference whether the European system is extended by an advance of frontier or otherwise.

It is also suggested in the British reply that we should not seek to apply the Monroe doctrine to the pending dispute because it does not embody any principle of international law which "is founded on the general consent of nations," and that "no statesman, however eminent, and no nation, however powerful, are competent to insert into the code of international law a novel principle which was never recognized before, and which has not since been accepted by the Government of any other country."

Practically the principle for which we contend has peculiar if not exclusive relation to the United States. It may not have been admitted in so many words to the code of international law, but since in international councils every nation is entitled to the rights belonging to it, if the enforcement of the Monroe doctrine is something we may justly claim it has its place in the code of international law as certainly and as securely as if it were specifically mentioned, and where the United States is a suitor before the high tribunal that administers international law the question to be determined is whether or not we present claims which the justice of that code of law can find to be right and valid.

The Monroe doctrine finds its recognition in those principles of international law which are based upon the theory that every nation shall have its rights protected and its just claims enforced. . . .

In the belief that the doctrine for which we contend was clear and definite, that it was founded upon substantial considerations and involved our safety and welfare, that it was fully applicable to our present conditions and to the state of the world's progress and that it was directly related to the pending controversy and without any conviction as to the final merits of the dispute, but anxious to learn in a satisfactory and conclusive manner whether Great Britain sought, under a claim of boundary, to extend her possessions on this continent without right, or whether she merely sought possession of territory fairly included within her lines of ownership, this Government proposed to the Government of Great Britain a resort to arbitration as the proper means of settling the question to the end that a vexatious boundary dispute between the two contestants might be determined and our exact standing and relation in respect to the controversy might be made clear.

It will be seen from the correspondence herewith submitted that this proposition has been declined by the British Government, upon grounds which in the circumstances seem to me to be far from satisfactory. It is deeply disappointing that such an appeal actuated by the most friendly feelings towards both nations directly concerned, addressed to the sense of justice and to the magnanimity of one of the great powers of the world and touching its relations to one comparatively weak and small, should have produced no better results.

The course to be pursued by this Government in view of the present condition does not appear to admit of serious doubt. Having labored faithfully for many years to induce Great Britain to submit this dispute to impartial arbitration, and having been now finally apprized of her refusal to do so, nothing remains but to accept the situation, to recognize its plain requirements and deal with it accordingly.

Great Britain's present proposition has never thus far been regarded as admissible by Venezuela, though any adjustment of the boundary which that country may deem for her advantage and may enter into of her own free will cannot of course be objected to by the United States.

Assuming, however, that the attitude of Venezuela will remain unchanged, the dispute has reached such a stage as to make it now incumbent upon the United States to take measures to determine with sufficient certainty for its justification what is the true divisional line between the Republic of Venezuela and British Guiana. The inquiry to that end should of course be conducted carefully and judicially and due weight should be given to all available evidence records and facts in support of the claims of both parties.

In order that such an examination should be prosecuted in a thorough and satisfactory manner I suggest that the Congress make an adequate appropriation for the expenses of a Commission, to be appointed by the Executive, who shall make the necessary investigation and report upon the matter with the least possible delay. When such report is made and accepted it will in my opinion be the duty of the United States to resist by every means in its power as a willful aggression upon its rights and interests the appropriation by Great Britain of any lands or the exercise of governmental jurisdiction over any territory which after investigation we have determined of right belongs to Venezuela.

In making these recommendations I am fully alive to the responsibility incurred, and keenly realize all the consequences that may follow.

I am nevertheless firm in my conviction that while it is a grievous thing to contemplate the two great English-speaking peoples of the world as being otherwise than friendly competitors in the onward march of civilization, and strenuous and worthy rivals in all the arts of peace, there is no calamity which a great nation can invite which equals that which follows a supine submission to wrong and injustice and the consequent loss of national self respect and honor beneath which are shielded and defended a people's safety and greatness.

PRESIDENT WILLIAM McKINLEY'S DECISION TO WAGE WAR ON THE SPANISH EMPIRE
11 April 1898

On 15 February 1898, the shocking and mysterious explosion that destroyed the battleship U.S.S Maine in the harbor at Havana unleashed eager forces of war in the United States. As Assistant Navy Secretary Theodore Roosevelt put it, "The blood of the mur-

dered men of the Maine calls not for indemnity but for the full measure of atonement, which can only come by driving the Spaniard from the New World." Roosevelt spoke for political and military forces of a vigorous democracy coming of age as a world power at a time when the European empires had carved up the world among themselves. In Spain's empire, closest to the United States, oppression in Cuba had claimed the particular attention of the new sensationalist "Yellow Press," particularly Joseph Pulitzer's New York World *and William Randolph Hearst's* New York Journal. *In the daily glare of their headlines appeared lurid tales of despicable Spanish acts and brave Cuban responses, all supposedly observed by reporters in Cuba. This depravity, the press insisted, demanded an honorable response by the United States. When the Hearst-dispatched artist Frederick Remington reported back to New York that he could find no trouble, Hearst immediately cabled: "You furnish the pictures, I'll furnish the war." Both politicians and the press imagined the glory of a military exercise. Pulitzer predicted a bonanza for the* World's *circulation. Secretary Roosevelt thought it would be "a splendid thing" for the Navy. A week before the* Maine *went down a private letter written by a Spanish diplomat in Washington that characterized McKinley as "feebleminded" turned up in Hearst's* Journal. *In this atmosphere the* Maine *blew up, killing 266 crewmen. While the cause of the explosion has never been conclusively proven there has never been any doubt regarding the effect. Congress, unanimously, appropriated $50 million for the military. Roosevelt cabled Commodore George Dewey of the Asiatic Fleet to prepare to attack the Spanish Philippines. Diplomacy stood little chance, yet Spain, sensing the danger, sought any compromise short of national humiliation. For his part, McKinley feared losing his authority to warhawks in Congress. Spain's offer to negotiate Cuban independence arrived in Washington on 10 April, too late. On 11 April, McKinley requested intervention and Congress soon agreed with enthusiasm. McKinley, always popular, became America's hero. Spain severed diplomatic relations, and the "splendid little war" began. Ten weeks later it ended, with the United States in control of Cuba, and in possession of Puerto Rico, the Philippine Islands and Guam; Hawaii, Wake Island, and American Samoa soon joined the burgeoning empire.*

Obedient to that precept of the Constitution which commands the President to give from time to time to the Congress information of the state of the Union and to recommend to their consideration such measures as he shall judge necessary and expedient, it becomes my duty now to address your body with regard to the grave crisis that has arisen in the relations of the United States to Spain by reason of the warfare that for more than three years has raged in the neighboring island of Cuba.

I do so because of the intimate connection of the Cuban question with the state of our own Union and the grave relation the course which it is now incumbent upon the nation to adopt must needs bear to the traditional policy of our Government if it is to accord with the precepts laid down by the founders of the Republic and religiously observed by succeeding Administrations to the present day.

The present revolution is but the successor of other similar insurrections which have occurred in Cuba against the dominion of Spain, extending over a period of nearly half a century, each of which, during its progress, has subjected the United States to great effort and expense in enforcing its neutrality laws, caused enormous losses to American trade and commerce, caused irritation, annoyance, and disturbance among our citizens, and, by the exercise of cruel, barbarous, and uncivilized practices of warfare, shocked the sensibilities and offended the humane sympathies of our people.

Since the present revolution began, in February 1895, this country has seen the fertile domain at our threshold ravaged by fire and sword in the course of a struggle unequaled in the history of the island and rarely paralleled as to the numbers of the combatants and the bitterness of the contest by any revolution of modern times where a dependent people striving to be free have been opposed by the power of the sovereign state.

Our people have beheld a once prosperous community reduced to comparative want, its lucrative commerce virtually paralyzed, its exceptional productiveness diminished, its fields laid waste, its mills in ruins, and its people perishing by tens of thousands from hunger and destitution. We have found

ourselves constrained, in the observance of that strict neutrality which our laws enjoin, and which the law of nations commands, to police our own waters and watch our own seaports in prevention of any unlawful act in aid of the Cubans.

Our trade has suffered; the capital invested by our citizens in Cuba has been largely lost, and the temper and forbearance of our people have been so sorely tried as to beget a perilous unrest among our own citizens which has inevitably found its expression from time to time in the National Legislature, so that issues wholly external to our own body politic engross attention and stand in the way of that close devotion to domestic advancement that becomes a self-contained commonwealth whose primal maxim has been the avoidance of all foreign entanglements. All this must needs awaken, and has, indeed, aroused the utmost concern on the part of this Government, as well during my predecessor's term as in my own.

In April 1896, the evils from which our country suffered through the Cuban war became so onerous that my predecessor made an effort to bring about a peace through the mediation of this Government in any way that might tend to an honorable adjustment of the contest between Spain and her revolted colony, on the basis of some effective scheme of self-government for Cuba under the flag and sovereignty of Spain. It failed through the refusal of the Spanish Government then in power to consider any form of mediation or, indeed, any plan of settlement which did not begin with the actual submission of the insurgents to the mother country, and then only on such terms as Spain herself might see fit to grant. The war continued unabated. The resistance of the insurgents was in no wise diminished.

The efforts of Spain were increased, both by the dispatch of fresh levies to Cuba and by the addition to the horrors of the strife of a new and inhuman phase happily unprecedented in the modern history of civilized Christian peoples. The policy of devastation and concentration, inaugurated by the Captain-General's bando of 21 October 1896, in the Province of Pinar del Rio was thence extended to embrace all of the island to which the power of the Spanish arms was able to reach by occupation or by military operations. The peasantry, including all dwelling in the open agricultural interior, were driven into the garrison towns or isolated places held by the troops.

The raising and movement of provisions of all kinds were interdicted. The fields were laid waste, dwellings unroofed and fired, mills destroyed, and, in short, everything that could desolate the land and render it unfit for human habitation or support was commanded by one or the other of the contending parties and executed by all the powers at their disposal.

By the time the present administration took office a year ago, reconcentration—so called—had been made effective over the better part of the four central and western provinces, Santa Clara, Matanzas, Habana, and Pinar del Rio.

The agricultural population to the estimated number of 300,000 or more was herded within the towns and their immediate vicinage, deprived of the means of support, rendered destitute of shelter, left poorly clad, and exposed to the most unsanitary conditions. As the scarcity of food increased with the devastation of the depopulated areas of production, destitution and want became misery and starvation. Month by month the death rate increased in an alarming ratio. By March 1897, according to conservative estimates from official Spanish sources, the mortality among the reconcentrados from starvation and the diseases thereto incident exceeded 50 per centum of their total number.

No practical relief was accorded to the destitute. The overburdened towns, already suffering from the general dearth, could give no aid. So called "zones of cultivation" established within the immediate areas of effective military control about the cities and fortified camps proved illusory as a remedy for the suffering. The unfortunates, being for the most part women and children, with aged and helpless men, enfeebled by disease and hunger, could not have tilled the soil without tools, seed, or shelter for their own support or for the supply of the cities. Reconcentration, adopted avowedly as a war measure in order to cut off the resources of the insurgents, worked its predestined result. As I said in my message of last December, it was not civilized warfare; it was extermination. The only peace it could beget was that of the wilderness and the grave.

Meanwhile the military situation in the island had undergone a noticeable change. The extraordinary activity that characterized the second year of the war, when the insurgents invaded even the thitherto unharmed fields of Pinar del Rio and carried havoc and destruction up to the walls of the city of Havana itself, had relapsed into a dogged struggle in the central and eastern provinces. The Spanish arms regained a measure of control in Pinar del Rio and parts of Havana, but, under the existing conditions of the rural country, without immediate improvement of their productive situation. Even thus partially restricted, the revolutionists held their own, and their conquest and submission, put forward by Spain as the essential and sole basis of peace, seemed as far distant as at the outset.

In this state of affairs my Administration found itself confronted with the grave problem of its duty. My message of last December reviewed the situation and narrated the steps taken with a view to relieving its acuteness and opening the way to some form of honorable settlement. The assassination of the prime minister, Canovas, led to a change of government in Spain. The former administration, pledged to subjugation without concession, gave place to that of a more liberal party, committed long in advance to a policy of reform, involving the wider principle of home rule for Cuba and Puerto Rico.

The overtures of this Government, made through its new envoy, General Woodford, and looking to an immediate and effective amelioration of the condition of the island, although not accepted to the extent of admitted mediation in any shape, were met by assurances that home rule, in advanced phase, would be forthwith offered to Cuba, without waiting for the war to end, and that more humane methods should thenceforth prevail in the conduct of hostilities. Coincidentally with these declarations, the new Government of Spain continued and completed the policy already begun by its predecessor, of testifying friendly regard for this nation by releasing American citizens held under one charge or another connected with the insurrection, so that by the end of November not a single person entitled in any way to our national protection remained in a Spanish prison.

While these negotiations were in progress the increasing destitution of the unfortunate reconcentrados and the alarming mortality among them claimed earnest attention. The success which had attended the limited measure of relief extended to the suffering American citizens among them by the judicious expenditure through the consular agencies of the money appropriated expressly for their succor by the joint resolution approval 24 May 1897, prompted the humane extension of a similar scheme of aid to the great body of sufferers. A suggestion to this end was acquiesced in by the Spanish authorities. On the 24th of December last I caused to be issued an appeal to the American people, inviting contributions in money or in kind for the succor of the starving sufferers in Cuba, following this on the 8th of January by a similar public announcement of the formation of a central Cuban relief committee, with headquarters in New York City, composed of three members representing the American National Red Cross and the religious and business elements of the community.

The efforts of that committee have been untiring and have accomplished much. Arrangements for free transportation to Cuba have greatly aided the charitable work. The president of the American Red Cross and representatives of other contributory organizations have generously visited Cuba and cooperated with the consul-general and the local authorities to make effective distribution of the relief collected through the efforts of the central committee. Nearly $200,000 in money and supplies has already reached the sufferers and more is forthcoming. The supplies are admitted duty free, and transportation to the interior has been arranged so that the relief, at first necessarily confined to Havana and the larger cities, is now extended through most if not all of the towns where suffering exists.

Thousands of lives have already been saved. The necessity for a change

in the condition of the reconcentrados is recognized by the Spanish Government. Within a few days past the orders of General Weyler have been revoked; the reconcentrados, it is said, are to be permitted to return to their homes and aided to resume the self-supporting pursuits of peace. Public works have been ordered to give them employment, and a sum of $600,000 has been appropriated for their relief.

The war in Cuba is of such a nature that short of subjugation or extermination a final military victory for either side seems impracticable. The alternative lies in the physical exhaustion of the one or the other party, or perhaps of both—a condition which in effect ended the ten years' war by the truce of Zanjon. The prospect of such a protraction and conclusion of the present strife is a contingency hardly to be contemplated with equanimity by the civilized world, and least of all by the United States, affected and injured as we are, deeply and intimately, by its very existence.

Realizing this, it appeared to be my duty, in a spirit of true friendliness, no less to Spain than to the Cubans who have so much to lose by the prolongation of the struggle, to seek to bring about an immediate termination of the war. To this end I submitted, on the 27th ultimo, as a result of much representation and correspondence, through the United States minister at Madrid, propositions to the Spanish Government looking to an armistice until 1 October for the negotiation of peace with the good offices of the President.

In addition, I asked the immediate revocation of the order of reconcentration, so as to permit the people to return to their farms and the needy to be relieved with provisions and supplies from the United States, cooperating with the Spanish authorities, so as to afford full relief.

The reply of the Spanish cabinet was received on the night of the 31st ultimo. It offered, as the means to bring about peace in Cuba, to confide the preparation thereof to the insular parliament, inasmuch as the concurrence of that body would be necessary to reach a final result, it being, however, understood that the powers reserved by the constitution to the central Government are not lessened or diminished. As the Cuban parliament does not meet until the 4th of May next, the Spanish Government would not object, for its part, to accept at once a suspension of hostilities if asked for by the insurgents from the general in chief, to whom it would pertain, in such case, to determine the duration and conditions of the armistice.

The propositions submitted by General Woodford and the reply of the Spanish Government were both in the form of brief memoranda, the texts of which are before me, and are substantially in the language above given. The function of the Cuban parliament in the matter of "preparing" peace and the manner of its doing so are not expressed in the Spanish memorandum; but from General Woodford's explanatory reports of preliminary discussions preceding the final conference it is understood that the Spanish Government stands ready to give the insular congress full powers to settle the terms of peace with the insurgents—whether by direct negotiation or indirectly by means of legislation does not appear.

With this last overture in the direction of immediate peace, and its disappointing reception by Spain, the Executive is brought to the end of his effort.

In my annual message of December last I said:

Of the untried measures there remained only: Recognition of the insurgents as belligerents; recognition of the independence of Cuba; neutral intervention to end the war by imposing a rational compromise between the contestants, and, intervention in favor of one or the other party. I speak not of forcible annexation, for that can not be thought of. That, by our code of morality, would be criminal aggression.

Thereupon I reviewed these alternatives, in the light of President Grant's measured words, uttered in 1875, when after seven years of sanguinary, destructive, and cruel hostilities in Cuba he reached the conclusion that the recognition of the independence of Cuba was impracticable and indefensible, and that the recognition of belligerence was not warranted by the facts according to the tests of public law. I commented especially upon the latter aspect of the question, pointing out the inconveniences and positive dangers of a recognition of belligerence which, while adding to the already onerous burdens of neutrality within our own jurisdiction, could not in any way extend our influence or effective offices in the territory of hostilities.

Nothing has since occurred to change my view in this regard, and I recognize as fully now as then that the issuance of a proclamation of neutrality, by which process the so-called recognition of belligerents is published, could, of itself and unattended by other action, accomplish nothing toward the one end for which we labor—the instant pacification of Cuba and the cessation of the misery that afflicts the island. . . .

When it shall appear hereafter that there is within the island a government capable of performing the duties and discharging the functions of a separate nation, and having, as a matter of fact, the proper forms and attributes of nationality, such government can be promptly and readily recognized and the relations and interests of the United States with such nation adjusted.

There remain the alternative forms of intervention to end the war, either as an impartial neutral by imposing a rational compromise between the contestants, or as the active ally of the one party or the other.

As to the first it is not to be forgotten that during the last few months the relation of the United States has virtually been one of friendly intervention in many ways, each not of itself conclusive, but all tending to the exertion of a potential influence toward an ulti-

mate pacific result, just and honorable to all interests concerned. The spirit of all our acts hitherto has been an earnest, unselfish desire for peace and prosperity in Cuba, untarnished by differences between us and Spain, and unstained by the blood of American citizens.

The forcible intervention of the United States as a neutral to stop the war, according to the large dictates of humanity and following many historical precedents where neighboring States have interfered to check the hopeless sacrifices of life by internecine conflicts beyond their borders, is justifiable on rational grounds. It involves, however, hostile constraint upon both the parties to the contest as well to enforce a truce as to guide the eventual settlement.

The grounds for such intervention may be briefly summarized as follows:

First. In the cause of humanity and to put an end to the barbarities, bloodshed, starvation, and horrible miseries now existing there, and which the parties to the conflict are either unable or unwilling to stop or mitigate. It is no answer to say this is all in another country, belonging to another nation, and is therefore none of our business. It is specially our duty, for it is right at our door.

Second. We owe it to our citizens in Cuba to afford them that protection and indemnity for life and property which no government there can or will afford, and to that end to terminate the conditions that deprive them of legal protection.

Third. The right to intervene may be justified by the very serious injury to the commerce, trade, and business of our people, and by the wanton destruction of property and devastation of the island.

Fourth, and which is of the utmost importance. The present condition of affairs in Cuba is a constant menace to our peace, and entails upon this Government an enormous expense. With such a conflict waged for years in an island so near us and with which our people have such trade and business relations; when the lives and liberty of our citizens are in constant danger and their property destroyed and themselves ruined; where our trading vessels are liable to seizure and are seized at our very door by war ships of a foreign nation, the expeditions of filibustering that we are powerless to prevent altogether, and the irritating questions and entanglements thus arising—all these and others that I need not mention, with the resulting strained relations, are a constant menace to our peace, and compel us to keep on a semiwar footing with a nation with which we are at peace.

These elements of danger and disorder already pointed out have been strikingly illustrated by a tragic event which has deeply and justly moved the American people. I have already transmitted to Congress the report of the naval court of inquiry on the destruction of the battle ship *Maine* in the harbor of Havana during the night of the 15th of February. The destruction of that noble vessel has filled the national heart with inexpressible horror. Two hundred and fifty-eight brave sailors and marines and two officers of our Navy, reposing in the fancied security of a friendly harbor, have been hurled to death, grief and want brought to their homes, and sorrow to the nation.

The naval court of inquiry, which, it is needless to say, commands the unqualified confidence of the Government, was unanimous in its conclusion that the destruction of the *Maine* was caused by an exterior explosion, that of a submarine mine. It did not assume to place the responsibility. That remains to be fixed.

In any event the destruction of the *Maine,* by whatever exterior cause, is a patent and impressive proof of a state of things in Cuba that is intolerable. That condition is thus shown to be such that the Spanish Government can not assure safety and security to a vessel of the American Navy in the harbor of Havana on a mission of peace, and rightfully there.

Further referring in this connection to recent diplomatic correspondence, a dispatch from our minister to Spain, of the 26th ultimo, contained the statement that the Spanish minister for foreign affairs assured him positively that Spain will do all that the highest honor and justice require in the matter of the *Maine.* . . .

The long trial has proved that the object for which Spain has waged the war can not be attained. The fire of insurrection may flame or may smolder with varying seasons, but it has not been and it is plain that it can not be extinguished by present methods. The only hope of relief and repose from a condition which can no longer be endured is the enforced pacification of Cuba. In the name of humanity, in the name of civilization, in behalf of endangered American interests which give us the right and the duty to speak and to act, the war in Cuba must stop.

In view of these facts and of these considerations, I ask the Congress to authorize and empower the President to take measures to secure a full and final termination of hostilities between the Government of Spain and the people of Cuba, and to secure in the island the establishment of a stable government, capable of maintaining order and observing its international obligations, insuring peace and tranquillity and the security of its citizens as well as our own, and to use the military and naval forces of the United States as may be necessary for these purposes.

And in the interest of humanity and to aid in preserving the lives of the starving people of the island I recommend that the distribution of food and supplies be continued, and that an appropriation be made out of the public Treasury to supplement the charity of our citizens.

The issue is now with the Congress. It is a solemn responsibility. I have exhausted every effort to relieve the intolerable condition of affairs which is at our doors. Prepared to execute every obligation imposed upon me by the Constitution and the law, I await your action.

Yesterday, and since the preparation of the foregoing message, official information was received by me that the latest decree of the Queen Regent of Spain directs General Blanco, in order to prepare and facilitate peace, to proclaim a suspension of hostilities, the duration and details of which have not yet been communicated to me.

This fact with every other pertinent consideration will, I am sure, have your just and careful attention in the solemn deliberations upon which you are about to enter. If this measure attains a successful result, then our aspirations as a Christian, peace-loving people will be realized. If it fails, it will be only another justification for our contemplated action.

PRESIDENT WILLIAM MCKINLEY'S EXPLANATION OF THE ACQUISITION OF THE PHILIPPINE ISLANDS
21 November 1899

It is ironic that international affairs define William McKinley's standing in American history, since domestic concerns dominated his long and successful career in politics and government. From his 1869 election to local office in Ohio, he spent the rest of his life representing the Republican Party as Governor, Congressman, and President. Modest, honest and enormously likable, by the 1890s McKinley's attractive political skills commanded national attention. He was most closely associated with the protective tariff, the Republican Party's most fundamental policy. In 1890, the highest protective tariff ever passed by Congress took the name of its chief proponent as the "McKinley Tariff." He ran for President in 1896 with the slogan "Bill McKinley and the McKinley Bill." Although the coming of the Spanish-American War seemed to overwhelm him, McKinley derived great prestige from its quick and eventful resolution. In the aftermath, America faced the vexing question of the disposition of its war booty. "Imperialists" and "anti-Imperialists" debated the question of the new island acquisitions from the Caribbean to the far Pacific. The President concentrated on the problem of the Philippines, where a nationalist movement led by Emilio Aguinaldo had proclaimed an independent Philippine Republic. Besides the geopolitical fears that the Islands would be snatched by another Great Power, McKinley wrestled with the difficult ideological proposition: Could the United States remain true to its heritage and still prevent another people from exercising their own independence? His answer impressed a group of chuchmen who were visiting the President in the White House. Afterward, the United States put down the Philippine nationalists in a bloody war that cost 5,000 American and 200,000 Filipino lives. The Philippines remained a protectorate of the United States until 1944.

Hold a moment longer! Not quite yet, gentlemen! Before you go I would like to say just a word about the Philippine business. I have been criticized a good deal about the Philippines, but don't deserve it. The truth is I didn't want the Philippines, and when they came to us, as a gift from the gods, I did not know what to do with them. When the Spanish War broke out, Dewey was at Hongkong, and I ordered him to go to Manila and to capture or destroy the Spanish fleet, and he had to; because, if defeated, he had no place to refit on that side of the globe, and if the Dons were victorious, they would likely cross the Pacific and ravage our Oregon and California coasts. And so he had to destroy the Spanish fleet, and did it! But that was as far as I thought then.

When next I realized that the Philippines had dropped into our laps I confess I did not know what to do with them. I sought counsel from all sides—Democrats as well as Republicans—but got little help. I thought first we would take only Manila; then Luzon; then other islands, perhaps, also. I walked the floor of the White House night after night until midnight; and I am not ashamed to tell you, gentlemen, that I went down on my knees and prayed Almighty God for light and guidance more than one night. And one night late it came to me this way—I don't know how it was, but it came: (1) That we could not give them back to Spain—that would be cowardly and dishonorable; (2) that we could not turn them over to France or Germany—our commercial rivals in the Orient—that would be bad business and discreditable; (3) that we could not leave them to themselves—they were unfit for self-government—and they would soon have anarchy and misrule over there worse than Spain's was; and (4) that there was nothing left for us to do but to take them all, and to educate the Filipinos, and uplift and civilize and Christianize them, and by God's grace do the very best we could by them, as our fellow-men for whom Christ also died. And then I went to bed, and went to sleep, and slept soundly, and the next morning I sent for the chief engineer of the War Department (our map-maker), and I told him to put the Philippines on the map of the United States [pointing to a large map on the wall of his office], and there they are, and there they will stay while I am President!

PRESIDENT THEODORE ROOSEVELT'S DENUNCIATION OF "BAD" TRUSTS
3 December 1901

Even the passage of one hundred years cannot dim the extraordinary American phenomenon who was President Theodore Roosevelt. By the age of forty, his biography identified him as soldier and scholar, Dakota rancher and Washington power broker, Police Commissioner of New York City, intimate in Boston of the Cabots and Lodges and Heavyweight Champion John L. Sullivan, naturalist, sportsman, at home at Harvard or on the Frontier. One cartoonist depicted Roosevelt astride a flaring horse, prominent teeth glistening, going off in all four directions at once. Part instigator and full hero of the Spanish-American War, the charismatic and tireless Roosevelt rode his celebrity into the New York Governor's Mansion in 1898, thereby posing a serious problem for the conservative masters of the Republican Party. He was too popular and restless to be ignored, yet too volatile to be controlled. The solution? A tried and true formula: Roosevelt was assigned to the obscurity of the vice-presidency on the McKinley ticket of 1900. It seemed a safe route. Excepting presidential death in office, no sitting Vice President had been able to move up since Martin Van Buren in 1836. President William McKinley certainly looked hale and hardy at age fifty-eight. Six weeks into his new term, McKinley fell to an assassin's bullet and, in the memorable words of Senator Mark Hanna, "that damned cowboy is President of the United States." At forty-two the youngest President in history, Roosevelt wasted no time in imposing himself. He took office in September and in December dispatched his first Annual Message, the core of which addressed the central issue of American life—the power of corporate and financial monopoly. On one flank of his approach, Roosevelt tacitly acknowledged the valid-

ity of protests from farms and cities against "the trusts" that had been accumulating over for two decades. His major theme, however, held that great corporate fortunes resulted from "natural causes in the business world." In tones mirroring the Darwinian thinking so common to that age, the new young President argued that laws aimed at destroying trusts per se were unnatural. Roosevelt sought to focus public attention rather on corrupt concentrations of or those alien to the public interest. In these cases, he argued, National Government would use its powers against "bad trusts." Henceforth, in Roosevelt's formulation, the government would assume powers to examine, regulate and, in some cases, outlaw business practices. No occupant of the White House before him had dared such a vision.

The tremendous and highly complex industrial development which went on with ever accelerated rapidity during the latter half of the nineteenth century brings us face to face, at the beginning of the twentieth, with very serious social problems. The old laws, and the old customs which had almost the binding force of law, were once quite sufficient to regulate the accumulation and distribution of wealth. Since the industrial changes which have so enormously increased the productive power of mankind, they are no longer sufficient.

The growth of cities has gone on beyond comparison faster than the growth of the country, and the upbuilding of the great industrial centers has meant a startling increase, not merely in the aggregate of wealth, but in the number of very large individual, and especially of very large corporate, fortunes. The creation of these great corporate fortunes has not been due to the tariff nor to any other governmental action, but to natural causes in the business world, operating in other countries as they operate in our own.

The process has aroused much antagonism, a great part of which is wholly without warrant. It is not true that as the rich have grown richer the poor have grown poorer. On the contrary, never before has the average man, the wage-worker, the farmer, the small trader, been so well off as in this country and at the present time. There have been abuses connected with the accumulation of wealth; yet it remains true that a fortune accumulated in legitimate business can be accumulated by the person specially benefited only on condition of conferring immense incidental benefits upon others. Successful enterprise, of the type which benefits all mankind, can only exist if the conditions are such as to offer great prizes as the rewards of success.

The captains of industry who have driven the railway systems across this continent, who have built up our commerce, who have developed our manufactures, have on the whole done great good to our people. Without them the material development of which we are so justly proud could never have taken place. Moreover, we should recognize the immense importance of this material development of leaving as unhampered as is compatible with the public good the strong and forceful men upon whom the success of business operations inevitably rests. The slightest study of business conditions will satisfy anyone capable of forming a judgment that the personal equation is the most important factor in a business operation; that the business ability of the man at the head of any business concern, big or little, is usually the factor which fixes the gulf between striking success and hopeless failure.

An additional reason for caution in dealing with corporations is to be found in the international commercial conditions of today. The same business conditions which have produced the great aggregations of corporate and individual wealth have made them very potent factors in international commercial competition. Business concerns which have the largest means at their disposal and are managed by the ablest men are naturally those which take the lead in the strife for commercial supremacy among the nations of the world. America has only just begun to assume that commanding position in the international business world which we believe will more and more be hers. It is of the utmost importance that this position be not jeoparded, especially at a time when the overflowing abundance of our own natural resources and the skill, business energy, and mechan-

ical aptitude of our people make foreign markets essential. Under such conditions it would be most unwise to cramp or to fetter the youthful strength of our Nation.

Moreover, it cannot too often be pointed out that to strike with ignorant violence at the interests of one set of men almost inevitably endangers the interests of all. The fundamental rule in our national life—the rule which underlies all others—is that, on the whole, and in the long run, we shall go up or down together. There are exceptions; and in times of prosperity some will prosper far more, and in times of adversity, some will suffer far more, than others; but speaking generally, a period of good times means that all share more or less in them, and in a period of hard times all feel the stress to a greater or less degree. It surely ought not to be necessary to enter into any proof of this statement; the memory of the lean years which began in 1893 is still vivid, and we can contrast them with the conditions in this very year which is now closing. Disaster to great business enterprises can never have its effects limited to the men at the top. It spreads throughout, and while it is bad for everybody, it is worst for those farthest down. The capitalist may be shorn of his luxuries; but the wage-worker may be deprived of even bare necessities.

The mechanism of modern business is so delicate that extreme care must be taken not to interfere with it in a spirit of rashness or ignorance. Many of those who have made it their vocation to denounce the great industrial combinations which are popularly, although with technical inaccuracy, known as "trusts," appeal especially to hatred and fear. These are precisely the two emotions, particularly when combined with ignorance, which unfit men for the exercise of cool and steady judgment. In facing new industrial conditions, the whole history of the world shows that legislation will generally be both unwise and ineffective unless undertaken after calm inquiry and with sober self-restraint. Much of the legislation directed at the trusts would have been exceedingly mischievous had it not also been entirely ineffective. In accordance with a well-known sociological law, the ignorant or reckless agitator has been the really effective friend of the evils which he has been nominally opposing. In dealing with business interests, for the Government to undertake by crude and ill-considered legislation to do what may turn out to be bad, would be to incur the risk of such far-reaching national disaster that it would be preferable to undertake nothing at all. The men who demand the impossible or the undesirable serve as the allies of the forces with which they are nominally at war, for they hamper those who would endeavor to find out in rational fashion what the wrongs really are and to what extent and in what manner it is practicable to apply remedies.

All this is true; and yet it is also true that there are real and grave evils, one of the chief being over-capitalization because of its many baleful consequences; and a resolute and practical effort must be made to correct these evils.

There is a widespread conviction in the minds of the American people that the great corporations known as trusts are in certain of their features and tendencies hurtful to the general welfare. This springs from no spirit of envy or uncharitableness, nor lack of pride in the great industrial achievements that have placed this country at the head of the nations struggling for commercial supremacy. It does not rest upon a lack of intelligent appreciation of the necessity of meeting changing and changed conditions of trade with new methods, nor upon ignorance of the fact that combination of capital in the effort to accomplish great things is necessary when the world's progress demands that great things be done. It is based upon sincere conviction that combination and concentration should be, not prohibited, but supervised and within reasonable limits controlled; and in my judgment this conviction is right.

It is no limitation upon property rights or freedom of contract to require that when men receive from Government the privilege of doing business under corporate form, which frees them from individual responsibility, and enables them to call into their enterprises the capital of the public, they shall do so upon absolutely truthful representations as to the value of the property in which the capital is to be invested. Corporations engaged in interstate commerce should be regulated if they are found to exercise a license working to the public injury. It should be as much the aim of those who seek for social betterment to rid the business world of crimes of cunning as to rid the entire body politic of crimes of violence. Great corporations exist only because they are created and safeguarded by our institutions; and it is therefore our right and our duty to see that they work in harmony with these institutions.

The first essential in determining how to deal with the great industrial combinations is knowledge of the facts—publicity. In the interest of the public, the Government should have the right to inspect and examine the workings of the great corporations engaged in interstate business. Publicity is the only sure remedy which we can now invoke. What further remedies are needed in the way of governmental regulation, or taxation, can only be determined after publicity has been obtained, by process of law, and in the course of administration. The first requisite is knowledge, full and complete—knowledge which may be made public to the world.

Artificial bodies, such as corporations and joint stock or other associations, depending upon any statutory law for their existence or privileges, should be subject to proper governmental supervision, and full and accurate information as to their operations should be made public regularly at reasonable intervals.

The large corporations, commonly called trusts, though organized in one State, always do business in many States, often doing very little business in the State where they are incorporated. There is utter lack of uniformity in the State laws about them; and as no State has any exclusive interest in or power over their acts, it has in practice proved impossible to get adequate regulation through State action. Therefore, in the interest of the whole people, the Nation should, without interfering with the power of the States in the matter itself, also assume power of supervision and regulation over all corporations doing an interstate business. This is especially true where the corporation derives a portion of its wealth from the existence of some monopolistic element or tendency in its business. There would be no hardship in such supervision; banks are subject to it, and in their case it is now accepted as a simple matter of course. Indeed, it is probable that supervision of corporations by the National Government need not go so far as is now the case with the supervision exercised over them by so conservative a State as Massachusetts, in order to produce excellent results.

When the Constitution was adopted, at the end of the eighteenth century, no human wisdom could foretell the sweeping changes, alike in industrial and political conditions, which were to take place by the beginning of the twentieth century. At that time it was accepted as a matter of course that the several States were the proper authorities to regulate, so far as was then necessary, the comparatively insignificant and strictly localized corporate bodies of the day. The conditions are now wholly different and wholly different action is called for. I believe that a law can be framed which will enable the National Government to exercise control along the lines above indicated; profiting by the experience gained through the passage and administration of the Interstate-Commerce Act. If, however, the judgment of the Congress is that it lacks the constitutional power to pass such an act, then a constitutional amendment should be submitted to confer the power.

There should be created a Cabinet officer, to be known as Secretary of Commerce and Industries, as provided in the bill introduced at the last session of the Congress. It should be his province to deal with commerce in its broadest sense; including among many other things whatever concerns labor and all matters affecting the great business corporations and our merchant marine.

The course proposed is one phase of what should be a comprehensive and far-reaching scheme of constructive statesmanship for the purpose of broadening our markets, securing our business interests on a safe basis, and making firm our new position in the international industrial world; while scrupulously safeguarding the rights of wage-worker and capitalist, of investor and private citizen, so as to secure equity as between man and man in this Republic. . . .

PRESIDENT THEODORE ROOSEVELT'S DECISION TO INVOKE FEDERAL LEGAL POWER AGAINST FINANCIER J. P. MORGAN
5 September 1903

Scarcely three months after President Theodore Roosevelt's announcement of the Federal Government's intention to judge and regulate the nation's major corporations, his administration invoked the Sherman Anti-Trust Act against the Northern Securities Company. Organized by John Pierpont Morgan, the most powerful figure in American finance, Northern Securities exercised monopolistic control over the great national railroad lines, fulcrum of the American economy. Just a year earlier, in forming the United States Steel Corporation, Morgan had assumed dominance over steel. Indeed for decades, Morgan and a few other Wall St. venture capitalists had shaped the economic configuration of American business, buying, merging, and organizing vertically and horizontally the basic industries. In 1896, Morgan had restored the nation's gold re-

serves in an agreement with President Grover Cleveland. Accustomed to dealing with Presidents of the United States simply as other representatives of authority, he responded to Theodore Roosevelt's Northern Securities suit typically: "If we have done anything wrong, send your man to my man and they can fix it up." Roosevelt sought both more and less than Morgan and the other corporate titans realized. Though prosecuting Northern Securities, the President stayed away from U.S. Steel, despite its monopolistic reach. The President saw distinctions and was never a simple "trust buster." He believed that in business and commerce, size and concentrated power was both inevitable and desirable. What Roosevelt sought was the role for the United States Government as arbiter and surrogate, representing "the public interest." The Executive branch and Congress would judge the corporations and trusts, defining "good" and "bad" combinations, dissolving some, regulating others. In this fundamental sense, Roosevelt first established the government as the countervailing force to corporate power, which it has since remained. He explained the Northern Securities case within this context in a letter to Lyman Abbott, editor of Outlook *and a prominent supporter of the President. References are to Attorney-General Philander Knox, former Secretary of the Navy William C. Whitney, financier J. P. Morgan and industrialist James J. Hill and politician David B. Hill.*

M*y dear Dr. Abbott:* I have read your editorial with greatest interest. . . .

The *Sun* and the *Harper's Weekly,* who seem at present to be the recognized exponents of that portion of the capitalistic class which objects to any kind of supervision or control, no matter how limited, over the great corporations and great controllers of corporations, have entered upon a systematic campaign, not merely against me, which is not important, but against the principles for which I stand. Both those papers, and in addition to those, papers like the *Times* and Brooklyn *Eagle,* so far as their financial columns go, have been endeavoring, sometimes by open statements, sometimes by insinuation, to persuade the public that my action in the Northern Securities suit, and in addition, my action in securing the passage of the law creating a Department of Commerce, with in it a Bureau of Corporations to secure publicity, has been mainly responsible for the financial stringency in Wall Street. Of course this is a preposterous falsehood. A promoters', speculators' and overcapitalizers' panic—it is this which we have seen. But any disturbance in the business world, no matter how purely due to the excesses of speculators, is sure to effect great numbers of other people, and when these feel the pinch it is invariably a relief to them to have somebody or something concrete on which to lay the blame; and there are plenty of businessmen, wealthy, venturous and unscrupulous, men of whom the archetype is William C. Whitney, who find it for their advantage to encourage this feeling, as what they most wish is absolute and unfettered freedom to act without regard to law. Such being the case I think it is well to recall that on this labor and capital question the following are the important steps I have taken:

On the advice of Knox I directed the bringing of the Northern Securities case. The court of first resort was unanimously, by a vote of four judges, declared in favor of the Government. The position of the *Sun* and the *Harper's Weekly* in this matter is then baldly that although the law may be clear, yet it must not be invoked against Mr. Pierpont Morgan and Mr. Hill; that is against any people whose financial interests are sufficiently vast. To my view this position is not only profoundly immoral, but quite as profoundly foolish, from the standpoint of property itself. Nothing would so jeopardize the rights of wealthy men in this country as the acceptance by the public of the belief that the laws could not touch these men if they offended against it.

Securing the enactment of the law in reference to a bureau of corporations. This was the law against which the Standard Oil Company so bitterly fought. The creation of this bureau is undoubtedly a very important thing from the standpoint of these big corporations doing an interstate business; for from it can be developed by experiment and trial, an effective method of regulation and supervision over them. But

avowedly, in its present form, what is to be done is of tentative character; our first object being merely to get at and publish the facts that ought properly to be made public. The peculiar venom the passage of this law has caused among corporations like the Standard Oil is sufficient to show its need; and moreover, emphasizes how much more may be accomplished by resolute but moderate and practical action than by anything revolutionary. The Standard Oil and similar corporations have never really been frightened by any of the demagogic assaults upon them; they do not mind David B. Hill's empty threats about nationalizing them; and they laugh at the populists and professional labor agitators; but they have been aroused to intense hostility by having put upon the statute books a measure which does mean that a practical step in advance has been taken in reference to their supervision and regulation. . . .

When the miners' strike in Arizona became a riot and the Acting Governor telegraphed that the territorial authorities could not deal with it and could not restore order, I sent thither instantly some regular troops. At their coming resistance to the civil authority ceased at once, peace was restored and I was able to withdraw them. This was simply putting into practice what I had said over and over again as to putting down of crimes of violence, just as the Northern Securities suit was enforcing what I had said about putting down crimes of greed and cunning. . . .

PRESIDENT THEODORE ROOSEVELT ANNOUNCES THE "ROOSEVELT COROLLARY" TO THE MONROE DOCTRINE
6 December 1904

Like no other President before him, Theodore Roosevelt welcomed the responsibilities of world power. American industrial and financial maturity and the rapid building of the U.S. Navy in the 1890s provided his administration with unprecedented possibilities for major involvement in a world then dominated by the Europeans and their far-flung empires. In 1899 and 1900, the State Department had issued "Open Door Notes" to the several powers with commercial and financial interests in China "requesting" that American business be given equal opportunities there. Latin America, when Roosevelt entered the White House, represented a troublesome situation where dictatorship, corruption and miserable living conditions prevailed, often producing international complications. Seventy-five years earlier, President James Monroe had issued his unilateral "Monroe Doctrine," which declared the Western Hemisphere closed to European colonization and political interference. Although several European states violated the Monroe Doctrine during the nineteenth century when the United States lacked sufficient military power to restrain them, such was no longer the case after 1900. Ironically, Roosevelt arrived at the conviction that hemispheric law and order depended solely on the judgments and actions of the United States inadvertently. Early in his term, the sitting Venezuelan dictator refused to pay debts to Germany and Great Britain. With American connivance, the Europeans sent naval forces to launch attacks sufficient to collect the debt, and Roosevelt announced that if a Latin American nation "misbehaved," he would "let [a] European country spank it." Surprisingly, his approach provoked substantial public outcry, not because of its paternalism but because Americans no longer wanted European forces in "our back yard." Roosevelt then formulated his "corollary" to the Monroe Doctrine. Monroe had warned against interference from outside the Hemisphere. Roosevelt affirmed Monroe and argued that whereas the Europeans were forbidden to interfere, intervention by the United States was justified. In short order, political, financial, and military involvement, already established in Panama, soon followed, first in the Dominican Republic, Haiti, and Nicaragua, later elsewhere in the hemisphere. The pattern continued through the ensuing decades.

In treating of our foreign policy and of the attitude that this great Nation should assume in the world at large, it is absolutely necessary to consider the Army and the Navy, and the Congress, through which the thought of the Nation finds its expression, should keep ever vividly in mind the fundamental fact that it is impossible to treat our foreign policy, whether this policy takes shape in the effort to secure justice for others or justice for ourselves, save as conditioned upon the attitude we are willing to take toward our Army, and especially toward our Navy. It is not merely unwise, it is contemptible, for a nation, as for an individual, to use high-sounding language to proclaim its purposes, or to take positions which are ridiculous if unsupported by potential force, and then to refuse to provide this force. If there is no intention of providing and of keeping the force necessary to back up a strong attitude, then it is far better not to assume such an attitude. . . .

Until some method is devised by which there shall be a degree of international control over offending nations, it would be a wicked thing for the most civilized powers, for those with most sense of international obligations and with keenest and most generous appreciation of the difference between right and wrong, to disarm. If the great civilized nations of the present day should completely disarm, the result would mean an immediate recrudescence of barbarism in one form or another. Under any circumstances a sufficient armament would have to be kept up to serve the purposes of international police; and until international cohesion and the sense of international duties and rights are far more advanced than at present, a nation desirous both of securing respect for itself and of doing good to others must have a force adequate for the work which it feels is allotted to it as its part of the general world duty. Therefore it follows that a self-respecting, just, and far-seeing nation should on the one hand endeavor by every means to aid in the development of the various movements which tend to provide substitutes for war, which tend to render nations in their actions toward one another, and indeed toward their own peoples, more responsive to the general sentiment of humane and civilized mankind; and on the other hand that it should keep prepared, while scrupulously avoiding wrongdoing itself, to repel any wrong, and in exceptional cases to take action which in a more advanced stage of international relations would come under the head of the exercise of the international police. A great free people owes it to itself and to all mankind not to sink into helplessness before the powers of evil.

We are in every way endeavoring to help on, with cordial good will, every movement which will tend to bring us into more friendly relations with the rest of mankind. In pursuance of this policy I shall shortly lay before the Senate treaties of arbitration with all powers which are willing to enter into these treaties with us. It is not possible at this period of the world's development to agree to arbitrate all matters, but there are many matters of possible difference between us and other nations which can be thus arbitrated. Furthermore, at the request of the Interparliamentary Union, an eminent body composed of practical statesmen from all countries, I have asked the

Powers to join with this Government in a second Hague conference, at which it is hoped that the work already so happily begun at The Hague may be carried some steps further toward completion. This carries out the desire expressed by the first Hague conference itself.

It is not true that the United States feels any land hunger or entertains any projects as regards the other nations of the Western Hemisphere save such as are for their welfare. All that this country desires is to see the neighboring countries stable, orderly, and prosperous. Any country whose people conduct themselves well can count upon our hearty friendship. If a nation shows that it knows how to act with reasonable efficiency and decency in social and political matters, if it keeps order and pays its obligations, it need fear no interference from the United States. Chronic wrongdoing, or an impotence which results in a general loosening of the ties of civilized society, may in America, as elsewhere, ultimately require intervention by some civilized nation, and in the Western Hemisphere the adherence of the United States to the Monroe Doctrine may force the United States, however reluctantly, in flagrant cases of such wrongdoing or impotence, to the exercise of an international police power. If every country washed by the Caribbean Sea would show the progress in stable and just civilization which with the aid of the Platt amendment Cuba has shown since our troops left the island, and which so

many of the republics in both Americas are constantly and brilliantly showing, all question of interference by this Nation with their affairs would be at an end. Our interests and those of our southern neighbors are in reality identical. They have great natural riches, and if within their borders the reign of law and justice obtains, prosperity is sure to come to them. While they thus obey the primary laws of civilized society they may rest assured that they will be treated by us in a spirit of cordial and helpful sympathy. We would interfere with them only in the last resort, and then only if it became evident that their inability or unwillingness to do justice at home and abroad had violated the rights of the United States or had invited foreign aggression to the detriment of the entire body of American nations. It is a mere truism to say that every nation, whether in America or anywhere else, which desires to maintain its freedom, its independence, must ultimately realize that the right of such independence can not be separated from the responsibility of making good use of it.

In asserting the Monroe Doctrine, in taking such steps as we have taken in regard to Cuba, Venezuela, and Panama, and in endeavoring to circumscribe the theater of war in the Far East, and to secure the open door in China, we have acted in our own interest as well as in the interest of humanity at large. There are, however, cases in which, while our own interests are not greatly involved, strong appeal is made to our sympathies. Ordinarily it is very much wiser and more useful for us to concern ourselves with striving for our own moral and material betterment here at home than to concern ourselves with trying to better the condition of things in other nations. We have plenty of sins of our own to war against, and under ordinary circumstances we can do more for the general uplifting of humanity by striving with heart and soul to put a stop to civic corruption, to brutal lawlessness and violent race prejudices here at home than by passing resolutions about wrongdoing elsewhere. Nevertheless there are occasional crimes committed on so vast a scale and of such peculiar horror as to make us doubt whether it is not our manifest duty to endeavor at least to show our disapproval of the deed and our sympathy with those who have suffered by it. The cases must be extreme in which such a course is justifiable. There must be no effort made to remove the mote from our brother's eye if we refuse to remove the beam from our own. But in extreme cases action may be justifiable and proper. What form the action shall take must depend upon the circumstances of the case; that is, upon the degree of the atrocity and upon our power to remedy it. . . .

PRESIDENT THEODORE ROOSEVELT ANNOUNCES THE ACQUISITION OF THE PANAMA CANAL ZONE
7 December 1903

The opening of the Suez Canal in 1869 secured England's imperial lifeline, the wealth and power of its globe-girdling empire protected and promoted by the mighty British fleet. A generation later, a similar scenario appealed to America's expansionists. By the turn of the century, great power competition for spheres of interest and world markets characterized international relations. The newly modernizing United States joined the imperial contest, having acquired Caribbean and Pacific territories in the Spanish-American War. There remained the task of bisecting the continent with an isthmian canal. American naval strategists learned a valuable lesson on the eve of the Spanish-American war in 1898, when the battleship U.S.S. Oregon *took sixty-seven days to steam from San Francisco to the Caribbean by way of Cape Horn. A canal across Central America, besides facilitating Asian trade, would at once create a two-ocean navy. The most logical site lay in the northernmost part of Columbia, across the isthmus of Panama. Theodore Roosevelt imaginatively conceived of a bold plan to overcome the major diplomatic, financial, and technological obstacles to building this Panama Canal. Long-standing agreements with Great Britain that any isthmian canal would be a joint enterprise by the two countries*

70

were quietly modified. Columbia's sovereignty over the territory constituted another problem, exacerbated by the Colombian Senate's refusal to accept $10 million to cede rights, plus $250,000 annual rental. Roosevelt refused to permit "inefficient bandits" and "contemptible little creatures" in Bogota to thwart his plans. Speculators soon arranged for a "rebellion" in the province of Panama, and American troops were present to support it. The United States immediately recognized the "independence" of Panama, and signed a treaty through which the Panamanian agents agreed to the construction of the Canal in return for the exact amounts offered earlier to Columbia. The signatory for Panama was a Frenchman, Philippe Bunau-Varilla, a major agent in the uprising, and a man who held extensive interests in the Canal project. The vast construction job, begun in 1904, opened in 1914, and immediately changed the patterns and volume of world trade. In 1922, the American Congress paid $25 million to Columbia, generally understood as "conscience money." As President, Theodore Roosevelt initially denied any culpability, responding to congressional critics that "no one connected with this Government had any part in preparing, inciting, or encouraging the late revolution." A few years out of office, he told a different story: "I took the Canal Zone and let Congress debate; and while the debate goes on the Canal does also." At the time, however, Roosevelt explained the great incident to Congress by justifying American power and moral superiority, both acting in the interest of "civilization."

For four hundred years, ever since shortly after the discovery of this hemisphere, the canal across the Isthmus has been planned. For two score years it has been worked at. When made it is to last for the ages. It is to alter the geography of a continent and the trade routes of the world. We have shown by every treaty we have negotiated or attempted to negotiate with the peoples in control of the Isthmus and with foreign nations in reference thereto our consistent good faith in observing our obligations; on the one hand to the peoples of the Isthmus, and on the other hand to the civilized world whose commercial rights we are safeguarding and guaranteeing by our action. We have done our duty to others in letter and in spirit, and we have shown the utmost forbearance in exacting our own rights.

Last spring, under the act above referred to, a treaty concluded between the representatives of the Republic of Colombia and of our Government was ratified by the Senate. This treaty was entered into at the urgent solicitation of the people of Colombia and after a body of experts appointed by our Government especially to go into the matter of the routes across the Isthmus had pronounced unanimously in favor of the Panama route. In drawing up this treaty every concession was made to the people and to the Government of Colombia. We were more than just in dealing with them. Our generosity was such as to make it a serious question whether we had not gone too far in their interest at the expense of our own; for in our scrupulous desire to pay all possible heed, not merely to the real but even to the fancied rights of our weaker neighbor, who already owed so much to our protection and forbearance, we yielded in all possible ways to her desires in drawing up the treaty. Nevertheless the Government of Colombia not merely repudiated the treaty, but repudiated it in such manner as to make it evident by the time the Colombian Congress adjourned that not the scantiest hope remained of ever getting a satisfactory treaty from them. The Government of Colombia made the treaty, and yet when the Colombian Congress was called to ratify it the vote against ratification was unanimous. It does not appear that the Government made any real effort to secure ratification.

Immediately after the adjournment of the Congress a revolution broke out in Panama. The people of Panama had long been discontented with the Republic of Colombia, and they had been kept quiet only by the prospect of the conclusion of the treaty, which was to them a matter of vital concern. When it became evident that the treaty was hopelessly lost, the people of Panama rose literally as one man. Not a shot was fired by a single man on the Isthmus in the interest of the Colombian Government. Not a life was lost in the accomplishment of the revolution. The Colombian troops stationed on the Isthmus, who had

long been unpaid, made common cause with the people of Panama, and with astonishing unanimity the new Republic was started. The duty of the United States in the premises was clear. . . . the United States gave notice that it would permit the landing of no expeditionary force, the arrival of which would mean chaos and destruction along the line of the railroad and of the proposed canal, and an interruption of transit as an inevitable consequence. The de facto Government of Panama was recognized in the following telegram to Mr. Ehrman:

"The people of Panama have, by apparently unanimous movement, dissolved their political connection with the Republic of Colombia and resumed their independence. When you are satisfied that a de facto government, republican in form and without substantial opposition from its own people, has been established in the State of Panama, you will enter into relations with it as the responsible government of the territory and look to it for all due action to protect the persons and property of citizens of the United states and to keep open the isthmian transit, in accordance with the obligations of existing treaties governing the relations of the United States to that Territory."

The Government of Colombia was notified of our action by the following telegram to Mr. Beaupre:

"The people of Panama having, by an apparently unanimous movement, dissolved their political connection with the Republic of Colombia and resumed their independence, and having adopted a Government of their own, republican in form, with which the Government of the United States of America has entered into relations, the President of the United States, in accordance with the ties of friendship which have so long and so happily existed between the respective nations, most earnestly commends to the Governments of Colombia and of Panama the peaceful and equitable settlement of all questions at issue between them. He holds that he is bound not merely by treaty obligations, but by the interests of civilization, to see that the peaceful traffic of the world across the Isthmus of Panama shall not longer be disturbed by a constant succession of unnecessary and wasteful civil wars.". . .

The control, in the interest of the commerce and traffic of the whole civilized world, of the means of undisturbed transit across the Isthmus of Panama has become of transcendent importance to the United States.

The above recital of facts establishes beyond question: First, that the United States has for over half a century patiently and in good faith carried out its obligations under the treaty of 1846; second, that when for the first time it became possible for Colombia to do anything in requital of the services thus repeatedly rendered to it for fifty-seven years by the United States, the Colombian Government peremptorily and offensively refused thus to do its

part, even though to do so would have been to its advantage and immeasurably to the advantage of the State of Panama, at that time under its jurisdiction; third, that throughout this period revolutions, riots, and factional disturbances of every kind have occurred one after the other in almost uninterrupted succession, some of them lasting for months and even for years, while the central government was unable to put them down or to make peace with the rebels; fourth, that these disturbances instead of showing any sign of abating have tended to grow more numerous and more serious in the immediate past; fifth, that the control of Colombia over the Isthmus of Panama could not be maintained without the armed intervention and assistance of the United States. In other words, the Government of Colombia, though wholly unable to maintain order on the Isthmus, has nevertheless declined to ratify a treaty the conclusion of which opened the only chance to secure its own stability and to guarantee permanent peace on, and the construction of a canal across, the Isthmus.

Under such circumstances the Government of the United States would have been guilty of folly and weakness, amounting in their sum to a crime against the Nation, had it acted otherwise than it did when the revolution of 3 November last took place in Panama. This great enterprise of building the interoceanic canal can not be held up to gratify the whims, or out of respect to the governmental impotence, or to the even more sinister and evil political peculiarities, of people who, though they dwell afar off, yet, against the wish of the actual dwellers on the Isthmus, assert an unreal supremacy over the territory. The possession of a territory fraught with such peculiar capacities as the Isthmus in question carries with it obligations to mankind. The course of events has shown that this canal can not be built by private enterprise, or by any other nation than our own; therefore it must be built by the United States.

Every effort has been made by the Government of the United States to persuade Colombia to follow a course which was essentially not only to our interest and to the interests of the world, but to the interests of Columbia itself. These efforts have failed; and Colombia, by her persistence in repulsing the advances that have been made, has forced us, for the sake of our own honor, and of the interest and well-being, not merely of our own people, but of the people of the Isthmus of Panama and the people of the civilized countries of the world, to take decisive steps to bring to an end a condition of affairs which had become intolerable. The new Republic of Panama immediately offered to negotiate a treaty with us. This treaty I herewith submit. By it our interests are better safeguarded than in the treaty with Colombia which was ratified by the Senate at its last session. It is better in its terms than the treaties offered to us by the Republics of Nicaragua and Costa Rica. At last the

right to begin this great undertaking is made available. Panama has done her part. All that remains is for the American Congress to do its part, and forthwith this Republic will enter upon the execution of a project colossal in its size and of well-nigh incalculable possibilities for the good of this country and the nations of mankind.

By the provisions of the treaty the United States guarantees and will maintain the independence of the Republic of Panama. There is granted to the United States in perpetuity the use, occupation, and control of a strip ten miles wide and extending three nautical miles into the sea at either terminal, with all lands lying outside of the zone necessary for the construction of the canal or for its auxiliary works, and with the islands in the Bay of Panama. The cities of Panama and Colon are not embraced in the canal zone, but the United States assumes their sanitation and, in case of need, the maintenance of order therein; the United States enjoys within the granted limits all the rights, power, and authority which it would possess were it the sovereign of the territory to the exclusion of the exercise of sovereign rights by the Republic. All railway and canal property rights belonging to Panama and needed for the canal pass to the United States, including any property of the respective companies in the cities of Panama and Colon; the works, property, and personnel of the canal and railways are exempted from taxation as well in the cities of Panama and Colon as in the canal zone and its dependencies. Free immigration of the personnel and importation of supplies for the construction and operation of the canal are granted. Provision is made for the use of military force and the building of fortifications by the United States for the protection of the transit. In other details, particularly as to the acquisition of the interests of the New Panama Canal Company and the Panama Rail- way by the United States and the condemnation of private property for the uses of the canal, the stipulations of the Hay-Herran treaty are closely followed, while the compensation to be given for these enlarged grants remains the same, being ten millions of dollars payable on exchange of ratifications; and, beginning nine years from that date, an annual payment of $250,000 during the life of the convention.

PRESIDENT THEODORE ROOSEVELT ON THE IMPORTANCE OF CONSERVATION
11 November 1907

Theodore Roosevelt eagerly took on the perennial challenge posed by America's natural bounty—that is, to use how much of it? and to save how much? Throughout the nineteenth century, natural resources fit perfectly into the opportunities presented to pioneers and private enterprise. Countless new fortunes and general economic growth resulted from vigorous use of the landscape, its rich soil and precious ores, its timber and water and grasslands. Development and profit seemed almost a natural right in an era of economic expansion without government regulation. During the Roosevelt administration, contrary arguments gained momentum. Conservationists assumed an obligation to future generations to preserve finite resources, to ensure that scenic lands and wildlife habitats survived. Characteristically, Roosevelt sought to balance the objectives of the competing forces. Thus, when possible, he devised procedures preserving natural resources and avoiding direct confrontations with the Congress and Supreme Court, each of which, resolutely pro-business, favored free reign for developers. The resulting Roosevelt conservation program instituted controls on private uses of public lands, and the establishment of a Forest Service with broad authority. This underlying question of the utilization of natural resources and the preservation of the environment, first faced under Theodore Roosevelt, has remained a staple issue in American political life. In May of 1907, he called the nation's governors to the White House to discuss the issue. The letter below is addressed to Braxton Bragg Comer, Democratic Governor of Alabama.

The natural resources of the territory of the United States were, at the time of settlement, richer, more varied, and more available than those of any other equal area on the surface of the earth. The development of these resources has given us, for more than a century, a rate of increase in population and wealth undreamed of by the men who founded our Government and without parallel in history. It is obvious that the prosperity which we now enjoy rests directly upon these resources. It is equally obvious that the vigor and success which we desire and foresee for this Nation in the future must have this as its ultimate material basis.

In view of these evident facts it seems to me time for the country to take account of its natural resources, and to inquire how long they are likely to last. We are prosperous now; we should not forget that it will be just as important to our descendants to be prosperous in their time as it is to us to be prosperous in our time.

Recently I expressed the opinion that there is no other question now before the Nation of equal gravity with the question of the conservation of our natural resources; and I added that it is the plain duty of those of us who, for the moment, are responsible, to make inventory of the natural resources which have been handed down to us, to forecast as well as we may the needs of the future, and so to handle the great sources of our prosperity as not to destroy in advance all hope of the prosperity of our descendants.

It is evident that the abundant natural resources on which the welfare of this Nation rests are becoming depleted and in not a few cases are already exhausted. This is true of all portions of the United States; it is especially true of the longer-settled communities of the East. The gravity of the situation must, I believe, appeal with special force to the Governors of the States because of their close relations to the people and their responsibility for the welfare of their communities. I have therefore decided, in accordance with the suggestion of the Inland Waterways Commission, to ask the Governors of the States and Territories to meet at the White House on 13, 14 and 15 May to confer with the President and with each other upon the conservation of natural resources.

It gives me great pleasure to invite you to take part in this conference. I should be glad to have you select three citizens to accompany you and to attend the conference as your assistants or advisors. I shall also invite the Senators and Representatives of the Sixtieth Congress to be present at the sessions so far as their duties will permit.

The matters to be considered at this conference are not confined to any region or group of States, but are of vital concern to the Nation as a whole and to all the people. These subjects include the use and conservation of the mineral resources, the resources of the land, and the resources of the waters, in every part of our territory.

In order to open discussion I shall invite a few recognized authorities to present brief descriptions of actual facts and conditions, without argument, leaving the conference to deal with each topic as it may elect. The members of the Inland Waterways Commission will be present in order to share with me the benefit of information and suggestion, and, if desired, to set forth their provisional plans and conclusions.

Facts, which I cannot gainsay, force me to believe that the conservation of our natural resources is the most weighty question now before the people of the United States. If this is so, the proposed conference, which is the first of its kind, will be among the most important gatherings in our history in its effects upon the welfare of all our people.

I earnestly hope, my dear Governor, that you will find it possible to be present.

President William Howard Taft's Denunciation of Fellow Republican Theodore Roosevelt
10 November 1912

Early in 1909 Theodore Roosevelt left the White House to his hand-picked successor, William Howard Taft, and went off on a long safari in Africa. While Taft considered T. R. his close friend, and had loyally served Roosevelt in several important capacities, Roosevelt regarded Taft as a reliable junior partner who was expected to carry out established policies. Remarkably soon, the two men became personal and political enemies, with notable consequences for public policy and American politics. Part of the unique Roosevelt-Taft rupture resided in the startling differences between the two men. In contrast to Roosevelt's bravura and casual regard for legal and constitutional procedures was Taft—cautious, devoted to legal procedure, and, as well, corpulent, phlegmatic, anti-social and awkward in public among the voters. Indeed as President, Taft emphasized precedent, precise analysis and Congressional prerogatives. From their quite different conceptions of the role of President naturally flowed policy distinctions. Of the several issues raised by the Taft administration, which enraged Roosevelt, nothing surpassed the question of conservation. Taft used carefully-drawn legislation to replace the Executive Orders through which Roosevelt imposed his environmental vision. Taft favored state as opposed to Federal authority, and substituted his own men for key environmentalists appointed by Roosevelt. The differences escalated into a celebrated duel between Taft's Secretary of the Interior, Richard A. Ballinger, and the Roosevelt appointee Gifford Pinchot, head of the Forestry Service. These surrogates fought a nasty public battle over the whole issue of economic development versus preservation, with each attack widening the rift between their sponsors, and shortening the stay of Presi-

dent Taft in the White House. Despite Taft's incumbency and desire for a second term, ex-President Roosevelt broke with political tradition by seeking to regain the office at the expense of his own erstwhile friend and their common party. He only succeeded in splitting the party. Taft won the Republican nomination, driving Roosevelt into a third-party campaign. As candidate of the Progressive (or "Bull-Moose") Party, the former President took with him Republican reformers and progressives. Taft may have carried the banner of the nation's majority party, but he still attracted only a quotient of its memebers, mostly conservatives, and finished third in the race. The Republican split of 1912 presented the Presidency to Democrat Woodrow Wilson, who drew but 41.8% of the vote. Taft, sorry to leave office to a Democrat, nonetheless felt he had saved the country from Roosevelt.

I am becoming convinced . . . that the number of Republicans who voted for Wilson, in order to escape the danger of Roosevelt, reaches into the hundreds of thousands, and I must think, therefore, that Roosevelt drew a great many Democratic votes from Wilson of the labor, socialistic, discontented, ragtag and bobtail variety. Roosevelt had in addition the votes of the faddists, the radical progressives, the people with isms, the emotional clergymen and women, in states where women voted, and all the factional sore-heads in the Republican party. . . . What I got was the irreducible minimum of the Republican party that was left after Roosevelt got through with it and after Wilson drew from it the votes of those Republicans who feared Roosevelt. Roosevelt polled a much larger vote than I thought was possible.

PRESIDENT WILLIAM HOWARD TAFT'S ESPOUSAL OF "DOLLAR DIPLOMACY"
3 December 1912

The foreign policy objectives that President William Howard Taft inherited from Theodore Roosevelt stressed the conviction that America had global stakes to promote and protect. As Taft assured the Congress in 1912, "now American interests in every quarter of the globe are being cultivated with equal assiduity." But whereas Roosevelt had emphasized the intricacies of diplomacy and geopolitics, Taft relied on commerce and capital. The idea behind "dollar diplomacy" was familiar, that in the world as in the United States, investment and trade produced middle-class self-interest, and thus created stability. The Taft Administration worked closely with business interests and ven-

ture capitalists who staked out projects in Latin America and in China. The State Department advised the entrepreneurs and provided technical and diplomatic support for investments ranging from Cuban sugar production to railroads in Manchuria. Behind these ventures stood the power of the American military should problems arise.

The foreign relations of the United States actually and potentially affect the state of the Union to a degree not widely realized and hardly surpassed by any other factor in the welfare of the whole Nation. The position of the United States in the moral, intellectual, and material relations of the family of nations should be a matter of vital interest to every patriotic citizen. The national prosperity and power impose upon us duties which we can not shirk if we are to be true to our ideals. The tremendous growth of the export trade of the United States has already made that trade a very real factor in the industrial and commercial prosperity of the country. With the development of our industries the foreign commerce of the United States must rapidly become a still more essential factor in its economic welfare. Whether we have a farseeing and wise diplomacy and are not recklessly plunged into unnecessary wars, and whether our foreign policies are based upon an intelligent grasp of present-day world conditions and a clear view of the potentialities of the future, or are governed by a temporary and timid expediency or by narrow views befitting an infant nation, are questions in the alternative consideration of which must convince any thoughtful citizen that no department of national polity offers greater opportunity for promoting the interests of the whole people on the one hand, or greater chance on the other of permanent national injury, than that which deals with the foreign relations of the United States.

The fundamental foreign policies of the United States should be raised high above the conflict of partisanship and wholly dissociated from differences as to domestic policy. In its foreign affairs the United States should present to the world a united front. The intellectual, financial, and industrial interests of the country and the publicist, the wage earner, the farmer, and citizen of whatever occupation must cooperate in a spirit of high patriotism to promote that national solidarity which is indispensable to national efficiency and to the attainment of national ideals.

The relations of the United States with all foreign powers remain upon a sound basis of peace, harmony, and friendship. A greater insistence upon justice to American citizens or interests wherever it may have been denied and a stronger emphasis of the need of mutuality in commercial and other relations have only served to strengthen our friendships with foreign countries by placing those friendships upon a firm foundation of realities as well as aspirations.

Before briefly reviewing the more important events of the last year in our foreign relations, which it is my duty to do as charged with their conduct and because diplomatic affairs are not of a nature to make it appropriate that the Secretary of State make a formal annual report, I desire to touch upon some of the essentials to the safe management of the foreign relations of the United States and to endeavor, also, to define clearly certain concrete policies which are the logical modern corollaries of the undisputed and traditional fundamentals of the foreign policy of the United States. . . .

DIPLOMACY A HAND MAID OF COMMERCIAL INTERCOURSE AND PEACE

The diplomacy of the present administration has sought to respond to modern ideas of commercial intercourse. This policy has been characterized as substituting dollars for bullets. It is one that appeals alike to idealistic humanitarian sentiments, to the dictates of sound policy and strategy, and to legitimate commercial aims. It is an effort frankly directed to the increase of American trade upon the axiomatic principle that the Government of the United States shall extend all proper support to every legitimate and beneficial American enterprise abroad. How great have been the results of this diplomacy, coupled with the maximum and minimum provision of the tariff law, will be seen by some consideration of the wonderful increase in the export

trade of the United States. Because modern diplomacy is commercial, there has been a disposition in some quarters to attribute to it none but materialistic aims. How strikingly erroneous is such an impression may be seen from a study of the results by which the diplomacy of the United States can be judged. . . .

CHINA

In China the policy of encouraging financial investment to enable that country to help itself has had the result of giving new life and practical application to the open-door policy. The consistent purpose of the present administration has been to encourage the use of American capital in the development of China by the promotion of those essential reforms to which China is pledged by treaties with the United States and other powers. The hypothecation to foreign bankers in connection with certain industrial enterprises, such as the Hukuang railways, of the national revenues upon which these reforms depended, led the Department of State early in the administration to demand for American citizens participation in such enterprises, in order that the United States might have equal rights and an equal voice in all questions pertaining to the disposition of the public revenues concerned. The same policy of promoting international accord among the powers having similar treaty rights as ourselves in the matters of reform, which could not be put into practical effect without the common consent of all, was likewise adopted in the case of the loan desired by China for the reform of its currency. The principle of international cooperation in matters of common interest upon which our policy had already been based in all of the above instances has admittedly been a great factor in that concert of the powers which has been so happily conspicuous during the perilous period of transition through which the great Chinese nation has been passing.

CENTRAL AMERICA NEEDS OUR HELP IN DEBT ADJUSTMENT

In Central America the aim has been to help such countries as Nicaragua and Honduras to help themselves. They are the immediate beneficiaries. The national benefit to the United States is two-fold. First, it is obvious that the Monroe doctrine is more vital in the neighborhood of the Panama Canal and the zone of the Caribbean than anywhere else. There, too, the maintenance of that doctrine falls most heavily upon the United States. It is therefore essential that the countries within that sphere shall be removed from the jeopardy involved by heavy foreign debt and chaotic national finances and from the ever-present danger of international complications due to disorder at home. Hence the United States has been glad to encourage and support American bankers who were willing to lend a helping hand to the financial rehabilitation of such countries because this financial rehabilitation and the protection of their customhouses from being the prey of would be dictators would remove at one stroke the menace of foreign creditors and the menace of revolutionary disorder.

The second advantage of the United States is one affecting chiefly all the southern and Gulf ports and the business and industry of the South. The Republics of Central America and the Caribbean possess great natural wealth. They need only a measure of stability and the means of financial regeneration to enter upon an era of peace and prosperity, bringing profit and happiness to themselves and at the same time creating conditions sure to lead to a flourishing interchange of trade with this country. . . .

PRESIDENT WOODROW WILSON INAUGURATES THE PRESIDENTIAL PRESS CONFERENCE
22 March 1913

On 22 March 1913, President Woodrow Wilson presided over the first-ever presidential press conference. Part of Wilson's calculated decision to communicate directly with the general public, the press conference would serve as a means of advancing and controlling the flow of news about the presidency thus serving to shape public opinion. Simultaneously, the administration began to issue for public consumption a variety of state papers, addresses, and statements. Wilson came to the White House as the only president who had devoted scholarly attention to the office. His classic book Constitutional Government in the United States, *published in 1908, constructed a blueprint for the presidency that combined aspects of the British parliamentary system with American tradition. In Wilson's view, the President should remove the customary division between executive and legislative branches. He determined that he would be, openly and vigorously, also the leader of his party, working with the Democratic leadership to shape and pass a legislative package. This model would focus American public life on the President as the one political and moral leader of the entire people. Thoroughly planned in his years as a scholar, especially at Princeton, Wilson inaugurated his strategy in the earliest days of his presidency by calling in the press, not to respond to their questions, but to instruct them on their responsibility.*

I feel that this gathering has a degree of formality which I wish it might not have. If there were any other room in which we could have met, it would have been more pleasing to me. I asked Mr. Tumulty to ask you gentlemen to come together this afternoon, because the other day when I saw you, just after the fatigue of the morning, I did not feel that I had anything more to say; and if it is agreeable to you, I would be obliged if you would regard what I say this afternoon as just between ourselves. Because I want an opportunity to open some part of my mind to you, so that you may know my point of view a little better than perhaps you have had an opportunity to know it so far.

I feel that a large part of the success of public affairs depends on the newspaper men—not so much on the editorial writers, because we can live down what they say, as upon the news writers, because the news is the atmosphere of public affairs. Unless you get the right setting to affairs—disperse the right impression—things go wrong. Now, the United States is just now at a very critical turning point in respect to public opinion, not in respect to parties, for that is not the part that is most interesting. They may go to pieces or they may hold together. So far as the United States is concerned, it does not make much difference whether they do or not, because a party hasn't any vitality whatever unless it is an embodiment of something real in the way of public opinion and public purpose. I am not interested in a party that is not an embodied program based upon a set of principles; and our present job is to get the people who believe in principles to stand shoulder to shoulder to do things from one side of this continent to the other.

Now, that being the case, I can illustrate one of the bad things that the newspapers may do in order to speak of the good things they may do. If you play up every morning differences of opinion and predict difficulties, and say there are going to be so many factions of this and so many groups of that, and things are going to pull at such and such cross purposes, you are not so much doing an injury to an individual or to any one of the groups of individuals you are talking about as impeding the public business. Our present business is to get together, not to get divided, and to draw a line and say, "Now, you fellows who do not believe that genuine public government will work, please stand on that side," (I choose the left because it is scriptural) "and you fellows who do believe that it will work, get on that side. And all the fellows who get on this side, then get together and just put these fellows to rout in such fashion that they will not stop until Doomsday."

Now, in order to do that you have got to have a lot of fellows who in the news try to interpret the times and to get the momentum in things without which they will not go. I do not mean in the least to imply that any of you gentlemen are interested in making trouble. That is not the point. I would be a mighty proud man if I could get it into your imaginations that you can oblige people, almost, to get together by the atmosphere with which you surround them in the daily news. And the atmosphere has got to come, not from Washington, but from the country. You have got to write from the country in and not from Washington out. The only way I can succeed is by not having my mind live in Washington. My body has got to live there, but my mind has got to live in the United States, or else I will fail. Now, you fellows can help me and help everybody else by just swathing my mind and other people's minds in the atmosphere of the thought of the United States. The great advantage that you enjoy is that you represent papers all over the country, and therefore you can import the opinion and the impulse of the country into Washington and import them after a fashion that nobody else can employ. A congressman has to import opinion according to the repairing of his fences—or, at least, he thinks he has; I do not think so but he thinks he has. Now, you have not got any fences to repair or to keep in order. Your interest is simply to see that the thinking of the people comes pressing in all the time on Washington. It would help me immensely, and it would help every man in public life immensely, should you do that.

So the thought I have in dealing with you fellows is this, that you, more than any other persons, can lubricate—quicken—the processes by which you are going to do what? Serve the people of the United States. If we do not serve them (the "we" now applies to politicians), if we do not serve them, then we will go out of business; and we ought to go out of business. We will go out of business with the applause of the world; because if we do not serve the people of the United States, there is going to be so radical a change of venue—and it will be an entirely new kind of trial for public men. So that I do not feel that I am engaged in a partisan enterprise or a party enterprise, or in anything except interpreting what you men ought to make it your business to bring to them—the country. I have got to understand the country, or I will not understand my job. Therefore, I have brought you here to say to you this very simple thing: "Please do not tell the country what Washington is thinking, for that does not make any difference. Tell Washington what the country is thinking; and then we will get things with a move on, we will get them so refreshed, so shot through with airs from every wholesome part of the country, that they cannot go stale, they cannot go rotten, and men will stand up and take notice, and know that they have got to vote according to the purposes of the country and the needs of the country, and the interpreted general interests of the country, and in no other way.

I sent for you, therefore, to ask that you go into partnership with me, that you lend me your assistance as nobody else can and then, after you have brought this precious freight of opinion into Washington, let us try and make true gold here that will go out from Washington. Because nothing better will go out than comes in. It is the old law of compensation, the law of equivalence. In proportion that Washington is enriched, so will the fruition in Washington itself be rich. Now, all this is obvious enough to you gentlemen. I am not telling you anything that you did not know before, but I did want you to feel that I was depending upon you, and from what I can learn of you, I think I have reason to depend with confidence on you to do this thing, not for me, but for the United States, for the people of the United States, and so bring about a day which will be a little better than the days that have gone before us. I think we can cooperate with enthusiasm along that line, and if you agree with me, I shall be very happy.

President Woodrow Wilson on the Establishment of the Federal Reserve System
23 June 1913

By the early twentieth century the booming economy of industrial America had outgrown its banking system. Its financial nucleus remained firmly in the hands of the great financial barons of the northeast, which created political protest as well as setting limits for growth. The old populist objections from the west and south continued to target Wall

Street as the major cause of economic distresses. Ironically, America's manufacturing and corporate sectors provided similar criticism. The established world of banking constituted a small and interlocked collection of private bankers who were quite free to enforce fiscal and monetary rules designed to achieve their own self interest. Consequently, they controlled the volume of money in circulation and the rate of interest, thus determining the availability of credit. Although the nation's economy steadily expanded the amount of money in circulation remained static. Furthermore, without a central bank there was no mechanism to prevent sharp fluctuations nationally or regionally. President Woodrow Wilson regarded this archaic system as unfair and harmful to American economic development, and moved vigorously toward a total reconfiguration of the banking system. Thus emerged the Federal Reserve System. The importance of this issue attained symbolic distinction on 23 June 1913, when Wilson for the second time in two months appeared personally before the Congress (the first president to do so since John Adams over a century before). Strong passions accompanied the ensuing Congressional debates and public discussions. On 23 December 1913, the Federal Reserve System assumed its place in the center of American finance and banking.

It is under the compulsion of what seems to me a clear and imperative duty that I have a second time this session sought the privilege of addressing you in person. I know, of course, that the heated season of the year is upon us, that work in these chambers and in the committee rooms is likely to become a burden as the season lengthens, and that every consideration of personal convenience and personal comfort, perhaps, in the cases of some of us, considerations of personal health even, dictate an early conclusion of the deliberations of the session; but there are occasions of public duty when these things which touch us privately seem very small; when the work to be done is so pressing and so fraught with big consequence that we know that we are not at liberty to weigh against it any point of personal sacrifice. We are now in the presence of such an occasion. It is absolutely, imperative that we should give the business men of this country a banking and currency system by means of which they can make use of the freedom of enterprise and of individual initiative which we are about to bestow upon them.

We are about to set them free; we must not leave them without the tools of action when they are free. We are about to set them free by removing the trammels of the protective tariff. Ever since the Civil War they have waited for this emancipation and for the free opportunities it will bring with it. It has been reserved for us to give it to them. Some fell in love, indeed, with the slothful security of their dependence upon the Government; some took advantage of the shelter of the nursery to set up a mimic mastery of their own within its walls. Now both the tonic and the discipline of liberty and maturity are to ensue. There will be some readjustments of purpose and point of view. There will follow a period of expansion and new enterprise, freshly conceived. It is for us to determine now whether it shall be rapid and facile and of easy accomplishment. This it can not be unless the resourceful business men who are to deal with the new circumstances are to have at hand and ready for use the instrumentalities and conveniences of free enterprise which independent men need when acting on their own initiative.

It is not enough to strike the shackles from business. The duty of statesmanship is not negative merely. It is constructive also. We must show that we understand what business needs and that we know how to supply it. No man, however casual and superficial his observation of the conditions now prevailing in the country, can fail to see that one of the chief things business needs now, and will need increasingly as it gains in scope and vigor in the years immediately ahead of us, is the proper means by which readily to vitalize its credit, corporate and individual, and its originative brains. What will it profit us to be free if we are not to have the best and most accessible instrumentalities of commerce and enterprise? What will it profit us to be quit of one kind of monopoly if we are to remain in the grip of another and

more effective kind? How are we to gain and keep the confidence of the business community unless we show that we know how both to aid and to protect it? What shall we say if we make fresh enterprise necessary and also make it very difficult by leaving all else except the tariff just as we found it? The tyrannies of business, big and little, lie within the field of credit. We know that. Shall we not act upon the knowledge? Do we not know how to act upon it? If a man can not make his assets available at pleasure, his assets of capacity and character and resource, what satisfaction is it to him to see opportunity beckoning to him on every hand, when others have the keys of credit in their pockets and treat them as all but their own private possession? It is perfectly clear that it is our duty to supply the new banking and currency system the country needs, and it will need it immediately more than it has ever needed it before.

The only question is, When shall we supply it—now, or later, after the demands shall have become reproaches that we were so dull and so slow? Shall we hasten to change the tariff laws and then be laggards about making it possible and easy for the country to take advantage of the change? There can be only one answer to that question. We must act now, at whatever sacrifice to ourselves. It is a duty which the circumstances forbid us to postpone. I should be recreant to my deepest convictions of public obligation did I not press it upon you with solemn and urgent insistence.

The principles upon which we should act are also clear. The country has sought and seen its path in this matter within the last few years—sees it more clearly now than it ever saw it before—much more clearly than when the last legislative proposals on the subject were made. We must have a currency, not rigid as now, but readily, elastically responsive to sound credit, the expanding and contracting credits of everyday transactions, the normal ebb and flow of personal and corporate dealings. Our banking laws must mobilize reserves; must not permit the concentration anywhere in a few hands of the monetary resources of the country or their use for speculative purposes in such volume as to hinder or impede or stand in the way of other more legitimate, more fruitful uses. And the control of the system of banking and of issue which our new laws are to set up must be public, not private, must be vested in the Government itself, so that the banks may be the instruments, not the masters, of business and of individual enterprise and initiative.

The committees of the Congress to which legislation of this character is referred have devoted careful and dispassionate study to the means of accomplishing these objects. They have honored me by consulting me. They are ready to suggest action. I have come to you, as the head of the Government and the responsible leader of the party in power, to urge action now, while there is time to serve the country deliberately and as we should, in a clear air of common counsel. I appeal to you with a deep conviction of duty. I believe that you share this conviction. I therefore appeal to you with confidence. I am at your service without reserve to play my part in any way you may call upon me to play it in this great enterprise of exigent reform which it will dignify and distinguish us to perform and discredit us to neglect.

PRESIDENT WOODROW WILSON'S AGREEMENT TO THE RE-SEGREGATION OF THE FEDERAL GOVERNMENT
23 July 1913, 29 July 1913, 8 September 1913

Woodrow Wilson, the first Democrat elected since Grover Cleveland in 1892, re-segregated the Federal Government. Although he had welcomed "Negro" support in the 1912 campaign by alluding vaguely to the need for improved race relations, Wilson, born in Virginia and raised in the South, reflected traditional Southern views on race. While not associating with primitive Democrats whose public race-baiting had become the stock in trade of most Southern Democrats, the President nonetheless adopted the posture that separation served the interests of both races. He came to the presidency at a time of vigorous public debate on "the race question." The national debate featured two giants of the early black struggle, Booker T. Washington and W. E. B. Du Bois. The former advocated compromise and tokenism, a gradualist approach toward making incremental advances, which assumed that white racial hostility would permit no more than that. Du Bois, fiery intellectual and political radical, took the opposing view that emphasized militancy and action to achieve social equity and constitutional privileges. In 1909, he founded the major organization fighting for civil rights, the National Association for the Advancement of Colored People, which attracted support from prominent white liberals as well. From the NAACP and its supporters came heavy objection to Wilson's policy of separating the races in Federal facilities. Yet the new President persisted, as he explained in letters to interested parties.

I do not think you know what is going on down here. We are handling the force of colored people who are now in the departments in just the way in which they ought to be handled. We are trying—and by degrees succeeding—a plan of concentration which will put them all together and will not in any one bureau mix the two races . . .

It would not be right for me to look at this matter in any other way than as the leader of a great national party. I am trying to handle these matters with the best judgment but in the spirit of the whole country, though with entire comprehension of the considerations which certainly do not need to be pointed out to me . . .

It is true that the segregation of the colored employees in the several departments was begun upon the initiative and at the suggestion of several of the heads of departments, but as much in the interest of the negroes as for any

other reason, with the approval of some of the most influential negroes I know, and with the idea that the friction, or rather the discontent and uneasiness, which had prevailed in many of the departments would thereby be removed. It is as far as possible from being a movement *against* the negroes. I sincerely believe it to be in their interest. And what distresses me about your letter is to find that you look at it in so different a light.

I am sorry that those who interest themselves most in the welfare of the negroes should misjudge this action on the part of the departments, for they are seriously misjudging it. My own feeling is, by putting certain bureaus and sections of the service in the charge of negroes we are rendering them more safe in their possession of office and less likely to be discriminated against . . .

In reply to your kind letter of September fourth, I would say that I do approve of the segregation that is being attempted in several of the departments. I have not always approved of the way in which the thing was done and have tried to change that in some instances for the better, but I think if you were here on the ground you would see, as I seem to see, that it is distinctly to the advantage of the colored people themselves that they should be organized, so far as possible and convenient, in distinct bureaux where they will center their work. Some of the most thoughtful colored men I have conversed with have themselves approved of this policy. I certainly would not myself have approved of it if I had not thought it to their advantage and likely to remove many of the difficulties which have surrounded the appointment and advancement of colored men and women . . .

PRESIDENT WOODROW WILSON ORDERS THE INVASION OF MEXICO
20 April 1914

In the spring of 1914, President Woodrow Wilson's moral sense came to bear on the unseemly world of Mexican politics. Three years earlier, the twenty-five year dictatorship of Porfirio Diaz had come to an end amidst revolutionary violence. European and American support for Diaz had rested upon his protection of profitable foreign investments. As President Taft noted during the 1911 uprising, " we have two billions American capital in Mexico that will be greatly endangered if Diaz had come to die." Fall Diaz did, to be replaced briefly by Francisco Madero, who was assassinated by reactionary forces in February 1913. European support easily transferred to General Victoriano Huerta, strongman protector of the great landowners and ruthless foe of the exploited landless peons. American business interests and State Department officials also favored working with Huerta, but Wilson refused to recognize the new Mexican dictator. As he declared on 24 November 1913, "If General Huerta does not retire by force of circumstances, it will become the duty of the United States to use less peaceful means to put him out." A convenient pretext materialized on 9 April 1914, when crew members from the U.S.S. Dolphin, ashore in Tampico for supplies, were briefly detained by Huerta's police. American Admiral Henry Mayo issued an ultimatum difficult for any sovereign nation to accept: an official apology, and a 21-gun salute to the American flag. Huerta refused and on 11 April, broke diplomatic relations with the United States. Diplomats and business interests quailed. Revolutionary rumblings already redounded across Mexico from growing private armies led by Venustiano Carranza, Francisco (Pancho) Villa, and Emiliano Zapata. Anarchy spread, as the American President extended the pressure. On 21 April, the President ordered the United States Navy to occupy Vera Cruz.

Gentlemen of the Congress: It is my duty to call your attention to a situation which has arisen in our dealings with General Victoriano Huerta at Mexico City which calls for action, and to ask your advice and cooperation in acting upon it. On the ninth of April a paymaster of the U.S.S. *Dolphin* landed at the Iturbide Bridge landing at Tampico with a whaleboat and boat's crew to take off certain supplies needed by his ship, and while engaged in loading the boat was arrested by an officer and squad of men of the army of General Huerta. Neither the paymaster nor anyone of the boat's crew was armed. Two of the men were in the boat when the arrest took place and were obliged to leave it and submit to be taken into custody, notwithstanding the fact that the boat carried, both at her bow and at her stern, the flag of the United States. The officer who made the arrest was proceeding up one of the streets of the town with his prisoners when met by an officer of higher authority, who ordered him to return to the landing and await orders; and within an hour and a half from the time of the arrest orders were received from the commander of the Huertista forces at Tampico for the release of the paymaster and his men. The release was followed by apologies from the commander and later by an expression of regret by General Huerta himself. General Huerta urged that martial law obtained at the time at Tampico; that orders had been issued that no one should be allowed to land at the Iturbide Bridge; and that our

sailors had no right to land there. Our naval commanders at the port had not been notified of any such prohibition; and, even if they had been, the only justifiable course open to the local authorities would have been to request the paymaster and his crew to withdraw and to lodge a protest with the commanding officer of the fleet. Admiral Mayo regarded the arrest as so serious an affront that he was not satisfied with the apologies offered but demanded that the flag of the United States be saluted with special ceremony by the military commander of the port.

The incident cannot be regarded as a trivial one, especially as two of the men arrested were taken from the boat itself,—that is to say, from the territory of the United States; but had it stood by itself it might have been attributed to the ignorance or arrogance of a single officer. Unfortunately, it was not an isolated case. A series of incidents have recently occurred which cannot but create the impression that the representatives of General Huerta were willing to go out of their way to show disregard for the dignity and rights of this government and felt perfectly safe in doing what they pleased, making free to show in many ways their irritation and contempt. A few days after the incident at Tampico an orderly from the U.S.S. *Minnesota* was arrested at Vera Cruz while ashore in uniform to obtain the ship's mail and was for a time thrown into jail. An official dispatch from this government to its embassy at Mexico City was withheld by the authorities of the tele-graphic service until peremptorily de-manded by our Chargé d'Affaires in person. So far as I can learn, such wrongs and annoyances have been suffered to occur only against repre-sentatives of the United States. I have heard of no complaints from other governments of similar treatment. Sub-sequent explanations and formal apol-ogies did not and could not alter the popular impression, which it is pos-sible it had been the object of the Huertista authorities to create, that the Government of the United States was being singled out, and might be sin-gled out with impunity, for slights and affronts in retaliation for its refusal to recognize the pretensions of General Huerta to be regarded as the consti-tutional provisional President of the Republic of Mexico.

The manifest danger of such a situa-tion was that such offences might grow from bad to worse until something hap-pened of so gross and intolerable a sort as to lead directly and inevitably to armed conflict. It was necessary that the apologies of General Huerta and his representatives should go much further, that they should be such as to attract the attention of the whole pop-ulation to their significance, and such as to impress upon General Huerta himself the necessity of seeing to it that no further occasion for explanations and professed regrets should arise. I, therefore, felt it my duty to sustain Ad-miral Mayo in the whole of his demand and to insist that the flag of the United States should be saluted in such a way as to indicate a new spirit and attitude on the part of the Huertistas.

Such a salute General Huerta has refused, and I have come to ask your approval and support in the course I now purpose to pursue.

This Government can, I earnestly hope, in no circumstances be forced into war with the people of Mexico. Mexico is torn by civil strife. If we are to accept the tests of its own constitu-tion, it has no government. General Huerta has set his power up in the City of Mexico, such as it is, without right and by methods for which there can be no justification. Only part of the coun-try is under his control. If armed con-flict should unhappily come as a result of his attitude of personal resentment towards this government, we should be fighting only General Huerta and those who adhere to him and give him their support, and our object would be only to restore to the people of the dis-tracted republic the opportunity to set up again their own laws and their own government.

But I earnestly hope that war is not now in question. I believe that I speak for the American people when I say that we do not desire to control in any degree the affairs of our sister republic. Our feeling for the people of Mexico is one of deep and genuine friendship, and everything that we have so far done or refrained from doing has proceeded from our desire to help them, not to hinder or embarrass them. We would not wish even to exercise the good offices of friendship without their welcome and consent. The people of Mexico are entitled to settle their own domestic affairs in their own way, and we sincerely desire to respect their right. The present situation need have none of the grave implications of interference if we deal with it promptly, firmly, and wisely.

No doubt I could do what is necessary in the circumstances to enforce respect for our government without recourse to the Congress, and yet not exceed my constitutional powers as President; but I do not wish to act in a matter possibly of so grave consequence except in close conference and cooperation with both the Senate and House.

I, therefore, come to ask your approval that I should use the armed forces of the United States in such ways and to such an extent as may be necessary to obtain from General Huerta and his adherents the fullest recognition of the rights and dignity of the United States, even amidst the distressing conditions now unhappily obtaining in Mexico.

There can in what we do be no thought of aggression or of selfish aggrandizement. We seek to maintain the dignity and authority of the United States only because we wish always to keep our great influence unimpaired for the uses of liberty, both in the United States and wherever else it may be employed for the benefit of mankind.

PRESIDENT WOODROW WILSON'S MESSAGE OF WAR AGAINST GERMANY
2 April 1917

In August of 1914 the assassination of the Austrian Crown Prince in the remote Balkan town of Sarajevo instantly unfolded into a continental war of savagery that changed the course of history. At the time, however, few Americans noticed the killing or the attendant political threats. Just another European squabble, Europeans threatening to fight again, certainly no concern on this side of the wonderfully broad Atlantic. President Wilson reflected this instinctive stance of neutrality. He encouraged the sides to settle peacefully as he began to try to protect American lives and trade on the high seas. Though the sympathies of the President were pro-English, he attempted to broker a peace without involving the United States. As both England and Germany sought control of the ocean, however, the United States was drawn into the conflict. Britain's superior naval forces set up naval blockades to deny the Germans arms and food. Germany retaliated with a weapon of dreadful prospect—the submarine. On 7 May 1915, a German U-boat sunk the great English luxury liner Luisitania *off the Irish coast, killing 1,198 passengers, including 128 Americans. The resulting furor in the United States persuaded Berlin to suspend unre-*

stricted submarine warfare, although some civilian and merchant vessels continued to be victimized. Meanwhile, in the 1916 presidential election, Wilson, running on the slogan "he kept us out of war," won reelection. Soon after, in the beginning of 1917, German strategic thinking returned to unrestricted submarine warfare as the key to victory, notwithstanding the likely entry of the Americans into the war. Consequently, on 31 January 1917, Germany announced its intention to use U-Boats against transatlantic shipping, stunning the Wilson Administration, which promptly broke diplomatic relations. The final factor in the decision to intervene came three weeks later with the interception of a secret despatch from the German Foreign Minister Arthur Zimmerman to his Embassy in Mexico City. The "Zimmerman Telegram" instructed German diplomats to approach the Mexican Government with a simple proposal of extraordinary scope: if Mexico joined Germany in war against the United States, the Germans would aid Mexico in recovering Texas, Arizona, and New Mexico. On 2 April, President Wilson went to Congress and demanded war with Germany.

Gentlemen of the Congress: I have called the Congress into extraordinary session because there are serious, very serious, choices of policy to be made, and made immediately, which it was neither right nor constitutionally permissible that I should assume the responsibility of making.

On the third of February last I officially laid before you the extraordinary announcement of the Imperial German Government that on and after the first day of February it was its purpose to put aside all restraints of law or of humanity and use its submarines to sink every vessel that sought to approach either the ports of Great Britain and Ireland or the western coasts of Europe or any of the ports controlled by the enemies of Germany within the Mediterranean. That had seemed to be the object of the German submarine warfare earlier in the war, but since April of last year the Imperial Government had somewhat restrained the commanders of its undersea craft in conformity with its promise then given to us that passenger boats should not be sunk and that due warning would be given to all other vessels which its submarines might seek to destroy, when no resistance was offered or escape attempted, and care taken that their crews were given at least a fair chance to save their lives in their open boats. The precautions taken were meagre and haphazard enough, as was proved in distressing instance after instance in the progress of the cruel and unmanly business, but a certain degree of restraint was observed. The new policy has swept every restriction aside. Vessels of every kind, whatever their flag, their character, their cargo, their destination, their errand, have been ruthlessly sent to the bottom without warning and without thought of help or mercy for those on board, the vessels of friendly neutrals along with those of belligerents. Even hospital ships and ships carrying relief to the sorely bereaved and stricken people of Belgium, though the latter were provided with safe conduct through the proscribed areas by the German Government itself and were distinguished by unmistakable marks of identity, have been sunk with the same reckless lack of compassion or of principle.

I was for a little while unable to believe that such things would in fact be done by any government that had hitherto subscribed to the humane practices of civilized nations. International law had its origin in the attempt to set up some law which would be respected and observed upon the seas, where no nation had right of dominion and where lay the free highways of the world. By painful stage after stage has that law been built up, with meagre enough results, indeed, after all was accomplished that could be accomplished, but always with a clear view, at least, of what the heart and conscience of mankind demanded. This minimum of right the German Government has swept aside under the plea of retaliation and necessity and because it had no weapons which it could use at sea except these which it is impossible to employ as it is employing them without throwing to the winds all scruples of humanity or of respect for the understandings that were supposed to underlie the intercourse of the world. I am not now thinking of the loss of property involved, immense and serious as that is,

but only of the wanton and wholesale destruction of the lives of non-combatants, men, women, and children, engaged in pursuits which have always, even in the darkest periods of modern history, been deemed innocent and legitimate. Property can be paid for; the lives of peaceful and innocent people cannot be. The present German submarine warfare against commerce is a warfare against mankind.

It is a war against all nations. American ships have been sunk, American lives taken, in ways which it has stirred us very deeply to learn of, but the ships and people of other neutral and friendly nations have been sunk and overwhelmed in the waters in the same way. There has been no discrimination. The challenge is to all mankind. Each nation must decide for itself how it will meet it. The choice we make for ourselves must be made with a moderation of counsel and a temperateness of judgment befitting our character and our motives as a nation. We must put excited feeling away. Our motive will not be revenge or the victorious assertion of the physical might of the nation, but only the vindication of right, of human right, of which we are only a single champion.

When I addressed the Congress on the twenty-sixth of February last I thought that it would suffice to assert our neutral rights with arms, our right to use the seas against unlawful interference, our right to keep our people safe against unlawful violence. But armed neutrality, it now appears, is impracticable. Because submarines are in effect outlaws when used as the German submarines have been used against merchant shipping, it is impossible to defend ships against their attacks as the law of nations has assumed that merchantmen would defend themselves against privateers or cruisers, visible craft giving chase upon the open sea. It is common prudence in such circumstances, grim necessity, indeed, to endeavour to destroy them before they have shown their own intention. They must be dealt with upon sight, if dealt with at all. The German Government denies the right of neutrals to use arms at all within the areas of the sea which it has proscribed, even in the defense of rights which no modern publicist has ever before questioned their right to defend. The intimation is conveyed that the armed guards which we have placed on our merchant ships will be treated as beyond the pale of law and subject to be dealt with as pirates would be. Armed neutrality is ineffectual enough at best; in such circumstances and in the face of such pretensions it is worse than ineffectual: it is likely only to produce what it was meant to prevent; it is practically certain to draw us into the war without either the rights or the effectiveness of belligerents. There is one choice we cannot make, we are incapable of making: we will not choose the path of submission and suffer the most sacred rights of our nation and our people to be ignored or violated. The wrongs against which we now array ourselves are no common wrongs; they cut to the very roots of human life.

With a profound sense of the solemn and even tragical character of the step I am taking and of the grave responsibilities which it involves, but in unhesitating obedience to what I deem my constitutional duty, I advise that the Congress declare the recent course of the Imperial German Government to be in fact nothing less than war against the government and people of the United States; that it formally accept the status of belligerent which has thus been thrust upon it; and that it take immediate steps not only to put the country in a more thorough state of defense but also to exert all its power and employ all its resources to bring the Government of the German Empire to terms and end the war.

What this will involve is clear. It will involve the utmost practicable cooperation in counsel and action with the governments now at war with Germany, and, as incident to that, the extension to those governments of the most liberal financial credits, in order that our resources may so far as possible be added to theirs. It will involve the organization and mobilization of all the material resources of the country to supply the materials of war and serve the incidental needs of the nation in the most abundant and yet the most economical and efficient way possible. It will involve the immediate full equipment of the navy in all respects but particularly in supplying it with the best means of dealing with the enemy's submarines. It will involve the immediate addition to the armed forces of the United States already provided for by law in case of war at least five hundred thousand men, who should, in my opinion, be chosen upon the principle of universal liability to service, and also the authorization of subsequent additional increments of equal force so soon as they may be needed and can be handled in training. It will involve also, of course, the granting of adequate credits to the Government, sustained, I hope, so far as they can equitably be sustained by the present generation, by well conceived taxation.

I say sustained so far as may be equitable by taxation because it seems to me that it would be most unwise to base the credits which will now be necessary entirely on money borrowed. It is our duty, I most respectfully urge, to protect our people so far as we may against the very serious hardships and evils which would be likely to arise out of the inflation which would be produced by vast loans.

In carrying out the measures by which these things are to be accomplished we should keep constantly in mind the wisdom of interfering as little as possible in our own preparation and in the equipment of our own military forces with the duty,—for it will be a very practical duty,—of supplying the nations already at war with Germany with the materials which they can obtain only from us or by our assistance. They are in the field and we should help them in every way to be effective there. . . .

While we do these things, these deeply momentous things, let us be very clear, and make very clear to all the world what our motives and our objects are. My own thought has not been driven from its habitual and normal course by the unhappy events of the last two months, and I do not believe that the thought of the nation has been altered or clouded by them. I have exactly the same things in mind now that I had in mind when I addressed the Senate on the twenty-second of January last; the same that I had in mind when I addressed the Congress on the third of February and on the twenty-sixth of February. Our object now, as then, is to vindicate the principles of peace and justice in the life of the world as against selfish and autocratic power and to set up amongst the really free and self-governed peoples of the world such a concert of purpose and of action as will henceforth ensure the observance of those principles. Neutrality is no longer feasible or desirable where the peace of the world is involved and the freedom of its peoples, and the menace to that peace and freedom lies in the existence of autocratic governments backed by organized force which is controlled wholly by their will, not by the will of their people. We have seen the last of neutrality in such circumstances. We are at the beginning of an age in which it will be insisted that the same standards of conduct and of responsibility for wrong done shall be observed among nations and their governments that are observed among the individual citizens of civilized states.

We have no quarrel with the German people. We have no feeling towards them but one of sympathy and friendship. It was not upon their impulse that their government acted in entering this war. It was not with their previous knowledge or approval. It was a war determined upon as wars used to be determined upon in the old, unhappy days when peoples were nowhere consulted by their rulers and wars were provoked and waged in the interest of dynasties or of little groups of ambitious men who were accustomed to use their fellow men as pawns and tools. Self-governed nations do not fill their neighbour states with spies or set the course of intrigue to bring about some critical posture of affairs which will give them an opportunity to strike and make conquest. Such designs can be successfully worked out only under cover and where no one has the right to ask questions. Cunningly contrived plans of deception or aggression, carried, it may be, from generation to generation, can be worked out and kept from the light only within the privacy of courts or behind the carefully guarded confidences of a narrow and privileged class. They are happily impossible where public opinion commands and insists upon full information concerning all the nation's affairs.

A steadfast concert for peace can never be maintained except by a partnership of democratic nations. No au-tocratic government could be trusted to keep faith within it or observe its covenants. It must be a league of honour, a partnership of opinion. Intrigue would eat its vitals away; the plottings of inner circles who could plan what they would and render account to no one would be a corruption seated at its very heart. Only free peoples can hold their purpose and their honour steady to a common end and prefer the interests of mankind to any narrow interest of their own.

Does not every American feel that assurance has been added to our hope for the future peace of the world by the wonderful and heartening things that have been happening within the last few weeks in Russia? Russia was known by those who knew it best to have been always in fact democratic at heart, in all the vital habits of her thought, in all the intimate relationships of her people that spoke their natural instinct, their habitual attitude towards life. The autocracy that crowned the summit of her political structure, long as it had stood and terrible as was the reality of its power, was not in fact Russian in origin, character, or purpose; and now it has been shaken off and the great, generous Russian people have been added in all their naive majesty and might to the forces that are fighting for freedom in the world, for justice, and for peace. Here is a fit partner for a League of Honour.

One of the things that has served to convince us that the Prussian autocracy was not and could never be our friend is that from the very outset of the present war it has filled our unsuspecting communities and even our offices of government with spies and set criminal intrigues everywhere afoot against our national unity of counsel, our peace within and without, our industries and our commerce. Indeed it is now evident that its spies were here even before the war began; and it is unhappily not a matter of conjecture but a fact proved in our courts of justice that the intrigues which have more than once come perilously near to disturbing the peace and dislocating the industries of the country have been carried on at the instigation, with the support, and even under the personal direction of official agents of the Imperial Government accredited to the Government of the United States. Even in checking these things and trying to extirpate them we have sought to put the most generous interpretation possible upon them because we knew that their source lay, not in any hostile feeling or purpose of the German people towards us (who were, no doubt as ignorant of them as we ourselves were), but only in the selfish designs of a Government that did what it pleased and told its people nothing. But they have played their part in serving to convince us at last that that Government entertains no real friendship for us and means to act against our peace and security at its convenience. That it means to stir up enemies against us at our very doors the intercepted note to the German

Minister at Mexico City is eloquent evidence.

We are accepting this challenge of hostile purpose because we know that in such a government, following such methods, we can never have a friend; and that in the presence of its organized power, always lying in wait to accomplish we know not what purpose, there can be no assured security for the democratic governments of the world. We are now about to accept gauge of battle with this natural foe to liberty and shall, if necessary, spend the whole force of the nation to check and nullify its pretensions and its power. We are glad, now that we see the facts with no veil of false pretense about them, to fight thus for the ultimate peace of the world and for the liberation of its peoples, the German peoples included: for the rights of nations great and small and the privilege of men everywhere to choose their way of life and of obedience. The world must be made safe for democracy. Its peace must be planted upon the tested foundations of political liberty. We have no selfish ends to serve. We desire no conquest, no dominion. We seek no indemnities for ourselves, no material compensation for the sacrifices we shall freely make. We are but one of the champions of the rights of mankind. We shall be satisfied when those rights have been made as secure as the faith and the freedom of nations can make them.

Just because we fight without rancour and without selfish object, seeking nothing for ourselves but what we shall wish to share with all free peoples, we shall, I feel confident, conduct our operations as belligerents without passion and ourselves observe with proud punctilio the principles of right and of fair play we profess to be fighting for.

I have said nothing of the governments allied with the Imperial Government of Germany because they have not made war upon us or challenged us to defend our right and our honour. The Austro-Hungarian Government has, indeed, avowed its unqualified endorsement and acceptance of the reckless and lawless submarine warfare adopted now without disguise by the Imperial German Government, and it has therefore not been possible for this Government to receive Count Tarnowski, the Ambassador recently accredited to this Government by the Imperial and Royal Government of Austria-Hungary; but that Government has not actually engaged in warfare against citizens of the United States on the seas, and I take the liberty, for the present at least, of postponing a discussion of our relations with the authorities at Vienna. We enter this war only where we are clearly forced into it because there are no other means of defending our rights.

It will be all the easier for us to conduct ourselves as belligerents in a high spirit of right and fairness because we act without animus, not in enmity towards a people or with the desire to bring any injury or disadvantage upon them, but only in armed opposition to an irresponsible government which has thrown aside all considerations of humanity and of right and is running amuck. We are, let me say again, the sincere friends of the German people, and shall desire nothing so much as the early re-establishment of intimate relations of mutual advantage between us,—however hard it may be for them, for the time being, to believe that this is spoken from our hearts. We have borne with their present government through all these bitter months because of that friendship,—exercising a patience and forbearance which would otherwise have been impossible. We shall, happily, still have an opportunity to prove that friendship in our daily attitude and actions towards the millions of men and women of German birth and native sympathy who live amongst us and share our life, and we shall be proud to prove it towards all who are in fact loyal to their neighbours and to the Government in the hour of test. They are, most of them, as true and loyal Americans as if they had never known any other fealty or allegiance. They will be prompt to stand with us in rebuking and restraining the few who may be of a different mind and purpose. If there should be disloyalty, it will be dealt with with a firm hand of stern repression; but, if it lifts its head at all, it will lift it only here and there and without countenance except from a lawless and malignant few.

It is a distressing and oppressive duty, Gentlemen of the Congress, which I have performed in thus addressing you. There are, it may be, many months of fiery trial and sacrifice ahead of us. It is a fearful thing to lead this great peaceful people into war, into the most terrible and disastrous of all wars, civilization itself seeming to be in the balance. But the right is more precious than peace, and we shall fight for the things which we have always carried nearest our hearts,—for democracy, for the right of those who submit to authority to have a voice in their own governments, for the rights and liberties of small nations, for a universal dominion of right by such a concert of free peoples as shall bring peace and safety to all nations and make the world itself at last free. To such a task we can dedicate our lives and our fortunes, everything that we are and everything that we have, with the pride of those who know that the day has come when America is privileged to spend her blood and her might for the principles that gave her birth and happiness and the peace which she has treasured. God helping her, she can do no other.

President Woodrow Wilson's "Fourteen Points" Plan for Ending the War
8 January 1918

Throughout the nineteen months of American military involvement in the so-called Great War, President Wilson regularly spoke of achieving "peace without victory." He considered United States' war objectives to be distinct from those of its principal allies, Great Britain and France. Wilson even insisted that United States forces be designated as an "associated power" rather than a member of the alliance. To Wilson, this distinction was crucial. He believed the world to be approaching an epic historical crossroads, with the power and diplomatic strategy of the United States capable of shaping a global future based on American beliefs and institutions. The alternatives, both unacceptable to Wilson, were two opposing systems. On the left, radical socialism had seized control of Russia and promised world revolution. On his right was the old imperialism of the British, French, and Italians, to whom he was temporarily tied in the struggle against Germany. Indeed his partners in the war were determined to seek the spoils of victory to atone for their cost in blood. The British would lose 1 million, the core of their young manhood. Fully half of those Frenchmen between the ages of twenty and thirty-two in 1914 were dead before 1919. Both nations were eager for the spoils of war. In 1915, they signed secret treaties carving up among themselves German colonies around the world. Wilson's vision appalled them, and only the irrepressible military and economic power of the United States kept the coalition intact. From revolutionary Moscow came the pledge of V. I. Lenin to promote upheavals against liberalism and capitalism every-

where, alarming all the Western nations. In this context of war and revolution, President Wilson went before the Congress on 8 January 1918 to advocate the establishment of a new world order with "a general association of nations" to oversee it.

Gentlemen of the Congress: Once more, as repeatedly before, the spokesmen of the Central Empires have indicated their desire to discuss the objects of the war and the possible bases of a general peace. Parleys have been in progress at Brest-Litovsk between representatives of the Central Powers, to which the attention of all the belligerents has been invited for the purpose of ascertaining whether it may be possible to extend these parleys into a general conference with regard to terms of peace and settlement. The Russian representatives presented not only a perfectly definite statement of the principles upon which they would be willing to conclude peace, but also an equally definite programme of the concrete application of those principles. The representatives of the Central Powers, on their part, presented an outline of settlement which, if much less definite, seemed susceptible of liberal interpretation until their specific programme of practical terms was added. That programme proposed no concessions at all either to the sovereignty of Russia or to the preferences of the populations with whose fortunes it dealt, but meant, in a word, that the Central Empires were to keep every foot of territory their armed forces had occupied,—every province, every city, every point of vantage,—as a permanent addition to their territories

and their power. It is a reasonable conjecture that the general principles of settlement which they at first suggested originated with the more liberal statesmen of Germany and Austria, the men who have begun to feel the force of their own peoples' thought and purpose, while the concrete terms of actual settlement came from the military leaders who have no thought but to keep what they have got. The negotiations have been broken off. The Russian representatives were sincere and in earnest. They cannot entertain such proposals of conquest and domination.

The whole incident is full of significance. It is also full of perplexity. With whom are the Russian representatives dealing? For whom are the representatives of the Central Empires speaking? Are they speaking for the majorities of their respective parliaments or for the minority parties, that military and imperialistic minority which has so far dominated their whole policy and controlled the affairs of Turkey and of the Balkan states which have felt obliged to become their associates in this war? The Russian representatives have insisted, very justly, very wisely, and in the true spirit of modern democracy, that the conferences they have been holding with the Teutonic and Turkish statesmen should be held within open, not closed doors, and all the world has been audience, as was desired. To whom have we been listening, then? To those who speak the spirit and intention of the Resolutions of the German Reichstag of the ninth of July last, the spirit and intention of the liberal leaders and parties of Germany, or to those who resist and defy that spirit and intention and insist upon conquest and subjugation? Or are we listening, in fact, to both, unreconciled and in open and hopeless contradiction? These are very serious and pregnant questions. Upon the answer to them depends the peace of the world.

But, whatever the results of the parleys at Brest-Litovsk, whatever the confusions of counsel and of purpose in the utterances of the spokesmen of the Central Empires, they have again attempted to acquaint the world with their objects in the war and have again challenged their adversaries to say what their objects are and what sort of settlement they would deem just and satisfactory. There is no good reason why that challenge should not be responded to, and responded to with the utmost candor. We did not wait for it. Not once, but again and again, we have laid our whole thought and purpose before the world, not in general terms only, but each time with sufficient definition to make it clear what sort of definitive terms of settlement must necessarily spring out of them. Within the last week Mr. Lloyd George has spoken with admirable candor and in admirable spirit for the people and Government of Great Britain. There is

no confusion of counsel among the adversaries of the Central Powers, no uncertainty of principle, no vagueness of detail. The only secrecy of counsel, the only lack of fearless frankness, the only failure to make definite statement of the objects of the war, lies with Germany and her Allies. The issues of life and death hang upon these definitions. No statesman who has the least conception of his responsibility ought for a moment to permit himself to continue this tragical and appalling outpouring of blood and treasure unless he is sure beyond a peradventure that the objects of the vital sacrifice are part and parcel of the very life of Society and that the people for whom he speaks think them right and imperative as he does.

There is, moreover, a voice calling for these definitions of principle and of purpose which is, it seems to me, more thrilling and more compelling than any of the many moving voices with which the troubled air of the world is filled. It is the voice of the Russian people. They are prostrate and all but helpless, it would seem, before the grim power of Germany, which has hitherto known no relenting and no pity. Their power, apparently, is shattered. And yet their soul is not subservient. They will not yield either in principle or in action. Their conception of what is right, of what is humane and honorable for them to accept, has been stated with a frankness, a largeness of view, a generosity of spirit, and a universal human sympathy which must challenge the admiration of every friend of mankind; and they have refused to compound their ideals or desert others that they themselves may be safe. They call to us to say what it is that we desire, in what, if in anything, our purpose and our spirit differ from theirs; and I believe that the people of the United States would wish me to respond, with utter simplicity and frankness. Whether their present leaders believe it or not, it is our heartfelt desire and hope that some way may be opened whereby we may be privileged to assist the people of Russia to attain their utmost hope of liberty and ordered peace.

It will be our wish and purpose that the processes of peace, when they are begun, shall be absolutely open and that they shall involve and permit henceforth no secret understandings of any kind. The day of conquest and aggrandizement is gone by; so is also the day of secret covenants entered into in the interest of particular governments and likely at some unlooked-for moment to upset the peace of the world. It is this happy fact, now clear to the view of every public man whose thoughts do not still linger in an age that is dead and gone, which makes it possible for every nation whose purposes are consistent with justice and the peace of the world to avow now or at any other time the objects it has in view.

We entered this war because violations of right had occurred which touched us to the quick and made the life of our own people impossible unless they were corrected and the world secured once for all against their recurrence. What we demand in this war, therefore, is nothing peculiar to ourselves. It is that the world be made fit and safe to live in; and particularly that it be made safe for every peace-loving nation which, like our own, wishes to live its own life, determine its own institutions, be assured of justice and fair dealing by the other peoples of the world as against force and selfish aggression. All the peoples of the world are in effect partners in this interest, and for our own part we see very clearly that unless justice be done to others it will not be done to us. The programme of the world's peace, therefore, is our programme; and that programme, the only possible programme, as we see it, is this:

I. Open covenants of peace, openly arrived at, after which there shall be no private international understandings of any kind but diplomacy shall proceed always frankly and in the public view.

II. Absolute freedom of navigation upon the seas, outside territorial waters, alike in peace and in war, except as the seas may be closed in whole or in part by international action for the enforcement of international covenants.

III. The removal, so far as possible, of all economic barriers and the establishment of an equality of trade conditions among all the nations consenting to the peace and associating themselves for its maintenance.

IV. Adequate guarantees given and taken that national armaments will be reduced to the lowest point consistent with domestic safety.

V. A free, open-minded, and absolutely impartial adjustment of all colonial claims, based upon a strict observance of the principle that in determining all such questions of sovereignty the interests of the populations concerned must have equal weight with the equitable claims of the government whose title is to be determined.

VI. The evacuation of all Russian territory and such a settlement of all questions affecting Russia as will secure the best and freest cooperation of the other nations of the world in obtaining for her an unhampered and unembarrassed opportunity for the independent determination of her own political development and national policy and assure her of a sincere welcome into the society of free nations under institutions of her own choosing; and, more than a welcome, assistance also of every kind that she may need and may herself desire. The treatment accorded Russia by her sister nations in the months to come will be the acid test of their good will, of their comprehension of her needs as distinguished from their own interests, and of their intelligent and unselfish sympathy.

VII. Belgium, the whole world will agree, must be evacuated and restored, without any attempt to limit the sovereignty which she enjoys in common with all other free nations. No other single act will serve as this will serve to restore confidence among the nations

in the laws which they have themselves set and determined for the government of their relations with one another. Without this healing act the whole structure and validity of international law is forever impaired.

VIII. All French territory should be freed and the invaded portions restored, and the wrong done to France by Prussia in 1871 in the matter of Alsace-Lorraine, which has unsettled the peace of the world for nearly fifty years, should be righted, in order that peace may once more be made secure in the interests of all.

IX. A readjustment of the frontiers of Italy should be effected along clearly recognizable lines of nationality.

X. The peoples of Austria-Hungary, whose place among the nations we wish to see safeguarded and assured, should be accorded the freest opportunity of autonomous development.

XI. Rumania, Serbia, and Montenegro should be evacuated; occupied territories restored; Serbia accorded free and secure access to the sea; and the relations of the several Balkan states to one another determined by friendly counsel along historically established lines of allegiance and nationality; and international guarantees of the political and economic independence and territorial integrity of the several Balkan states should be entered into.

XII. The Turkish portions of the present Ottoman Empire should be assured a secure sovereignty, but the other nationalities which are now under Turkish rule should be assured an undoubted security of life and an absolutely unmolested opportunity of autonomous development, and the Dardanelles should be permanently opened as a free passage to the ships and commerce of all nations under international guarantees.

XIII. An independent Polish state should be erected which should include the territories inhabited by indisputably Polish populations, which should be assured a free and secure access to the sea, and whose political and economic independence and territorial integrity should be guaranteed by international covenant.

XIV. A general association of nations must be formed under specific covenants for the purpose of affording mutual guarantees of political independence and territorial integrity to great and small states alike.

In regard to these essential rectifications of wrong and assertions of right we feel ourselves to be intimate partners of all the governments and peoples associated together against the Imperialists. We cannot be separated in interest or divided in purpose. We stand together until the end.

For such arrangements and covenants we are willing to fight and to continue to fight until they are achieved; but only because we wish the right to prevail and desire a just and stable peace such as can be secured only by removing the chief provocations to war, which this programme does remove. We have no jealousy of German greatness, and there is nothing in this programme that impairs it. We grudge her no achievement or distinction of learning or of pacific enterprise such as have made her record very bright and very enviable. We do not wish to injure her or to block in any way her legitimate influence or power. We do not wish to fight her either with arms or with hostile arrangements of trade if she is willing to associate herself with us and the other peace-loving nations of the world in covenants of justice and law and fair dealing. We wish her only to accept a place of equality among the peoples of the world,—the new world in which we now live,—instead of a place of mastery.

Neither do we presume to suggest to her any alteration or modification of her institutions. But it is necessary, we must frankly say, and necessary as a preliminary to any intelligent dealings with her on our part, that we should know whom her spokesmen speak for when they speak to us, whether for the Reichstag majority or for the military party and the men whose creed is imperial domination.

We have spoken now, surely, in terms too concrete to admit of any further doubt or question. An evident principle runs through the whole programme I have outlined. It is the principle of justice to all peoples and nationalities, and their right to live on equal terms of liberty and safety with one another, whether they be strong or weak. Unless this principle be made its foundation no part of the structure of international justice can stand. The people of the United States could act upon no other principle; and to the vindication of this principle they are ready to devote their lives, their honor, and everything that they possess. The moral climax of this the culminating and final war for human liberty has come, and they are ready to put their own strength, their own highest purpose, their own integrity and devotion to the test.

PRESIDENT WARREN G. HARDING'S FIRST ANNUAL MESSAGE
6 December 1921

President Warren G. Harding's style of oratory quickly attracted the scorn of critics. This wounded Harding, who prided himself on speeches that relied on warm conventional homilies. Audiences bathed in the presence of a famous man about whom, it was repeatedly said, "looked like a President." Harding revealed his style in his first State of the Union address.

It is a very gratifying privilege to come to the Congress with the Republic at peace with all the nations of the world. More, it is equally gratifying to report that our country is not only free from every impending menace of war, but there are growing assurances of the permanency of the peace which we so deeply cherish.

For approximately ten years we have dwelt amid menaces of war or as participants in war's actualities, and the inevitable aftermath, with its disordered conditions, has added to the difficulties of government which adequately can not be appraised except by those who are in immediate contact and know the responsibilities. Our tasks would be less difficult if we had only ourselves to consider, but so much of the world was involved, the disordered conditions are so well-nigh universal, even among nations not engaged in actual warfare, that no permanent readjustments can be effected without consideration of our inescapable relationship to world affairs in finance and trade. Indeed, we should be unworthy of our best traditions if we were unmindful of social, moral, and political conditions which are not of direct concern to us, but which do appeal to the human sympathies and the very becoming interest of a people blest with our national good fortune.

It is not my purpose to bring to you a program of world restoration. In the main such a program must be worked out by the nations more directly concerned. They must themselves turn to the heroic remedies for the menacing conditions under which they are struggling, then we can help, and we mean to help. We shall do so unselfishly because there is compensation in the consciousness of assisting, selfishly because the commerce and international exchanges in trade, which marked our high tide of fortunate advancement, are possible only when the nations of all continents are restored to stable order and normal relationship.

In the main the contribution of this Republic to restored normalcy in the world must come through the initiative of the executive branch of the Government, but the best of intentions and most carefully considered purposes would fail utterly if the sanction and the cooperation of Congress were not cheerfully accorded. . . .

Encroachment upon the functions of Congress or attempted dictation of its policy are not to be thought of, much less attempted, but there is an insistent call for harmony of purpose and concord of action to speed the solution of the difficult problems confronting both the legislative and executive branches of the Government. . . .

There is vastly greater security, immensely more of the national viewpoint, much larger and prompter accomplishment where our divisions are along party lines, in the broader and loftier sense, than to divide geographically, or according to pursuits, or personal following. For a century and a third, parties have been charged with responsibility and held to strict accounting. When they fail, they are relieved of authority; and the system has brought us to a national eminence no less than a world example. . . .

PRESIDENT WARREN G. HARDING'S
CONFESSION OF INCOMPETENCE
May 1922

Scandals and sordid allegations have soiled the historical reputation of President Warren G. Harding, probably permanently. Yet during the days of his prominence in the early 1920s, public opinion unblushingly paired Harding with Abraham Lincoln as the two great Republicans. His popularity surely benefitted when Harding's genial personality, so seemingly friendly and engaging, was contrasted with that of his predecessor, the stern and intellectual Woodrow Wilson. Wilson fought a great war, toured Europe in triumph, and dreamed of reshaping the world. Then the Congress rejected his League of Nations, post-war Europe remained chaotic, Wilson fell gravely ill, and the nation welcomed Harding. No Wilsonian visions obscured the uncomplicated politics of

Warren Harding, and the public approved. His small-town Ohio manners featured compromise and harmony, no sharp edges, poker games, and golf dates, and unswerving loyalty to friends. He ran a soothing but competent campaign in 1920, and overwhelmed his Democratic opponent by seven million votes. His administration achieved a record of modest domestic and foreign policy accomplishment during its brief tenure, a legacy soon engulfed by public disgrace. At the time of his death on 2 August 1923, President Harding knew of some of the scandals perpetrated by his political cronies, stories of corruption that would be spread out before the public for years after he was gone. Moreover, Harding had been physically and spiritually weakened by the burdens of the office itself, which, he sometimes confessed, were beyond him. Most presidents feel trapped at times in the splendid isolation of the office, but by the summer of 1922 Warren G. Harding longed to return to Main Street in Marion, Ohio. One evening, as Harding insisted on personally answering a huge stack of mail, much of it eccentric in nature, a visitor gently suggested that the President of the United States was wasting his time in such mundane activity.

[Nicholas Murray Butler, President of Columbia University]: Oh, come on, Mr. President, this is ridiculous. Even in my office they do not burden me with reading or answering letters like these.

President Harding: I suppose so, but I am not fit for this office and should never have been here.

PRESIDENT CALVIN COOLIDGE'S "SECRET" PRESS CONFERENCE
22 April 1927

Calvin Coolidge spent most of his public life safely disguised behind an effective stereotype of his own creation. While he certainly did reflect the standard elements of the familiar image of Vermonters, Coolidge's well-honed political skills tend to be overlooked. "Silent Cal" memorialized himself with his response to a loquacious woman who told the President of her bet that she could get more than two words out of him: "You lose," he supposedly replied. Terse and private, Coolidge's demeanor did suggest the simple rectitude, shrewdness, and practicality of rural New England. He had come to national prominence in 1919 as Governor of Massachusetts during a strike by the Boston Police. Not only did he decisively end the walkout, but Governor Coolidge won great acclaim by refusing to allow the strikers to return to their jobs. "There is no right to strike against the public safety by anybody, anywhere, any time," he declared. The resulting celebrity boosted him onto the Republican ticket in 1920 and into the White House when President Warren G. Harding died in 1923. Coolidge moved effectively to dispose of the scandals he inherited, and won an overwhelming victory in the 1924 election. Belying his pose of passive indifference, Coolidge sought to illuminate his presidency through the means of twice-weekly press conferences, which had unprecedented rules. None of the dozen-or-so regularly attending newsmen could quote the President directly—he once even threatened to evict a reporter using shorthand. But the substance of the President's paraphrased comments to questions submitted in advance would be attributed to a "spokesman." Within these confines, and with greater regularity than any other President, Calvin Coolidge managed to present his views and advance his policies to a mass audience throughout America by way of the great newspapers and wire services.

I have had called to my attention lately the fact that some of the press are beginning to get a little careless about quoting the President as the result of these conferences. It seems that it is necessary to have eternal vigilance to keep that from being done, and to caution the members of the conference against that. Of course, it is a violation of the understanding to say that the spokesman said so and so, and put in quotations on that. I think, by the way, that it would be a good plan to drop that reference to these conferences. It was never authorized in any way that I could determine by the President. It has been used from time to time, but it has been used so long and there has been so much reference to it that one might as well say that the President said so and so, or the White House spokesman or the official spokesman said so and so.

PRESS: Mr. President, do we understand that the term spokesman is not permissible?

PRESIDENT: It has never been authorized and has been used in a way that it is perfectly apparent that when the word is used it means the President. Now, that need not have been done, but it has been done, and having been done I think it would be better to drop that. . . . What I said about quoting the President in relation to the use of the term as spokesman wasn't said for publication. It was just said for the information of the conference. That part of the conference we will consider carried on in executive session.

PRESS: Have you any formula to suggest?

PRESIDENT: I think your ingenuity will provide you with one. The only thing I am suggesting is that you observe the rule of not quoting the President.

President Herbert Hoover's Vision of Prosperity
4 March 1929

Within six months of his inauguration President Herbert Hoover would face the Great Stock Market Crash of October 1929. The dreadful era of the Depression then began, ending Hoover's political career and leaving a legacy so negative that Democrats ran against his specter for decades thereafter. Back on 4 March 1929, however, Hoover began his presidency with the kind of enormous confidence felt by a man whose entire career had been marked by notable achievements. By the end of the 1920s, Herbert Clark Hoover was recognized as one of the most talented and successful men in the world. Born poor and orphaned at a young age, Hoover persevered, graduated from Stanford University and soon gained fame and fortune as a mining engineer in China and Australia. His Quaker beliefs taught public service, and in the Great War his relief efforts fed millions of hapless Europeans. Joining the Harding Cabinet in 1920 as Secretary of Commerce, Hoover spent the decade as one of the capitol's most powerful men. His landslide victory in the election of 1928 seemed to presage a brilliant administration.

This occasion is not alone the administration of the most sacred oath which can be assumed by an American citizen. It is a dedication and consecration under God to the highest office in service of our people. I assume this trust in the humility of knowledge that only through the guidance of Almighty Providence can I hope to discharge its ever-increasing burdens.

It is in keeping with tradition throughout our history that I should express simply and directly the opinions which I hold concerning some of the matters of present importance.

Our Progress

If we survey the situation of our Nation both at home and abroad, we find many satisfactions; we find some causes for concern. We have emerged from the losses of the Great War and the re-construction following it with increased virility and strength. From this strength we have contributed to the recovery and progress of the world. What America has done has given renewed hope and courage to all who have faith in government by the people. In the large view, we have reached a higher degree of comfort and security than ever existed before in the history of the world. Through liberation from widespread poverty we have reached a higher degree of individual freedom than ever before. The devotion to and concern for our institutions are deep and sincere. We are steadily building a new race—a new civilization great in its own attainments. The influence and high purposes of our Nation are respected among the peoples of the world. We aspire to distinction in the world, but to a distinction based upon confidence in our sense of justice as well as our accomplishments within our own borders and in our own lives. For wise guidance in this great period of recovery the Nation is deeply indebted to Calvin Coolidge. . . .

The election has again confirmed the determination of the American people that regulation of private enterprise and not Government ownership or operation is the course rightly to be pursued in our relation to business. In recent years we have established a differentiation in the whole method of business regulation between the industries which produce and distribute commodities on the one hand and public utilities on the other. In the former, our laws insist upon effective competition; in the latter, because we substantially confer a monopoly by limiting competition, we must regulate their services and rates. The rigid enforcement of the laws applicable to both groups is the very base of equal opportunity and freedom from domination for all our people, and it is just as essential for the stability and prosperity of business itself as for the protection of the public at large. Such regulation should be extended by the Federal Government within the limitations of the Constitution and only when the individual States are without power to protect their citizens through their own authority. . . .

Ours is a land rich in resources, stimulating in its glorious beauty, filled with millions of happy homes, blessed with comfort and opportunity. In no nation are the institutions of progress more advanced. In no nation are the fruits of accomplishment more secure. In no nation is the government more worthy of respect. No country is more loved by its people. I have an abiding faith in their capacity, integrity, and high purpose. I have no fears for the future of our country. It is bright with hope. . . .

PRESIDENT HERBERT HOOVER'S COMMENTS ON THE STOCK MARKET CRASH
5 November 1929

In the third week of October 1929, the Stock Exchanges began to rumble like a volcano emitting early warnings. On 24 October, prices collapsed. Five days later, on "Black Tuesday," the most catastrophic day in the history of the New York Stock Exchange, billions of dollars were lost in the value of stocks. The Crash plunged the new President into unprecedented circumstances. He had inherited the feverish stock speculation on Wall Street yet lacked Federal regulatory powers to control private banks and brokerages and their financial practices. Moreover, Hoover's bedrock philosophy of individual responsibility opposed government subsidies or relief measures. In bad times, he believed, the sprit of volunteerism would rally the citizenry to the aid of those temporarily disadvantaged. Moreover, the President felt that the turbulence on Wall St. would have little effect on basically healthy market forces already at work.

I thought perhaps you might like that I discuss the business situation with you just a little, but not from the point of view of publication at all—simply for your own information. I see no particular reasons for making any public statements about it, either directly or indirectly.

The question is one somewhat of analysis. We have had a period of overspeculation that has been extremely widespread, one of those waves of speculation that are more or less uncontrollable, as evidenced by the efforts of the Federal Reserve Board, and that ultimately results in a crash due to its own weight. That crash was perhaps a little expedited by the foreign situation, in that one result of this whole phenomenon has been the congestion of capital in the loan market in New York in the driving up of money rates all over the world.

The foreign central banks having determined that they would bring the crisis to an end, at least so far as their own countries were concerned, advanced money rates very rapidly in practically every European country in order to attract capital that had drifted from Europe into New York, back into their own industry and commerce. Incidentally, the effect of increasing discount rates in Europe is much greater on their

business structure than it is with us. Our business structure is not so sensitive to interest rates as theirs is. So their sharp advancement of discount rates tended to affect this market, and probably expedited or even started this movement. But once the movement has taken place we have a number of phenomena that rapidly develop. The first is that the domestic banks in the interior of the United States, and corporations, withdraw their money from the call market.

There has been a very great movement out of New York into the interior of the United States, as well as some movement out of New York into foreign countries. The incidental result of that is to create a difficult situation in New York, but also to increase the available capital in the interior. In the interior there has been, in consequence, a tendency for interest rates to fall at once because of the unemployed capital brought back into interior points.

Perhaps the situation might be clearer on account of its parallel with the last very great crisis, 1907–1908. In that crash the same drain of money immediately took place into the interior. In that case there was no Federal Reserve System. There was no way to acquaint of capital movement over the country, and the interest rates ran up to 300 percent. The result was to bring about a monetary panic in the entire country.

Here with the Federal Reserve System and the activity of the Board, and the ability with which the situation has been handled, there has been a complete isolation of the stock market phenomenon from the rest of the business phenomena in the country. The Board, in cooperation with the banks in New York, has made ample capital available for the call market in substitution of the withdrawals. This has resulted in a general fall of interest rates, not only in the interior, but also in New York, as witness the reduction of the discount rate. So that instead of having a panic rise in interest rates with monetary rise following it, we have exactly the reverse phenomenon—we have a fallen interest rate. That is the normal thing to happen when capital is withdrawn from the call market through diminution in values.

The ultimate result of it is a complete isolation of the stock market phenomenon from the general business phenomenon. In other words, the financial world is functioning entirely normal and rather more easily today than it was 2 weeks ago, because interest rates are less and there is more capital available.

The effect on production is purely psychological. So far there might be said to be from such a shock some tendency on the part of people through alarm to decrease their activities, but there has been no cancellation of any orders whatsoever. There has been some lessening of buying in some of the luxury contracts, but that is not a phenomenon itself.

The ultimate result of the normal course of things would be that with a large release of capital from the speculative market there will be more capital available for the bond and mortgage market. That market has been practically starved for the last 4 or 5 months. There has been practically no—or very little at least—of mortgage or bond money available, practically no bond issues of any consequence. One result has been to create considerable reserves of business. A number of States have not been able to place their bonds for construction; a number of municipalities with bond issues have been held up because of the inability to put them out at what they considered fair rates. There are a great number of business concerns that would proceed with their activities in expansion through mortgage and bond money which have had to delay. All of which comprises a very substantial reserve in the country at the present time. The normal result will be for the mortgage and bond market to spring up again and those reserves to come in with increased activities.

The sum of it is, therefore, that we have gone through a crisis in the stock market, but for the first time in history the crisis has been isolated to the stock market itself. It has not extended into either the production activities of the country or the financial fabric of the country, and for that I think we may give the major credit to the constitution of the Federal Reserve System.

And that is about a summary of the whole situation as it stands at this moment.

PRESIDENT HERBERT HOOVER'S VETO OF A BILL FOR PUBLIC POWER AUTHORITY IN THE TENNESSEE VALLEY
3 March 1931

Philosophical opposition to Government competition with private enterprise formed the cornerstone of Herbert Hoover's personal and political beliefs. Even as the Depression deepened in the winter of 1930–1931, Hoover resisted the politically popular demands that he engage the government in schemes designed to stimulate the dormant economy. One such plan envisioned a huge public works program to harness the water power of the Tennessee Valley, creating thousands of jobs in the process of providing affordable electricity to millions of Americans. This scheme, inspired by progressive Republican Senator George Norris of Nebraska, had been vetoed by President Coolidge in 1928. It would be signed, as the Tennessee Valley Authority Bill, by President Franklin D. Roosevelt in 1933. President Hoover's 1931 veto message thus marks a significant dividing line between two fundamentally different concepts of the proper role of the Federal Government.

I am firmly opposed to the government entering into any business, the major purpose of which is competition with our citizens. There are national emergencies which require that the government should temporarily enter the field of business, but these must be emergency actions and in matters where the cost of the project is secondary to much higher considerations. There are many localities where the Federal Government is justified in the construction of great dams and reservoirs, where navigation, flood control, reclamation, or stream regulation are of dominant importance, and where they are beyond the capacity of purpose of private or local government capital to construct. In these cases power is often a by-product and should be disposed of by contract or lease. But for the Federal Government deliberately to go out to build up and expand such an occasion to the major purpose of a power and manufacturing business is to break down the initiative and enterprise of the American people; it is destruction of equality of opportunity amongst our people; it is the negation of the ideals upon which our civilization is based.

This bill raises one of the important issues confronting our people. That is squarely the issue of Federal Government ownership and operation of power and manufacturing business not as a minor by-product but as a major purpose. Involved in this question is the agitation against the conduct of the power industry. The power problem is not to be solved by the Federal Government going into the power business, nor is it to be solved by the project in this bill. The remedy for abuses in the conduct of that industry lies in regulation and not by the Federal Government entering upon the business itself. I have recommended to the Congress on various occasions that action should be taken to establish Federal regulation of interstate power in cooperation with State authorities. This bill would launch the Federal Government upon a policy of ownership and operation of power utilities upon a basis of competition instead of by the proper government function of regulation for the protection of all the people. I hesitate to contemplate the future of our institutions, of our government, and of our country if the preoccupation of its officials is to be no longer the promotion of justice and equal opportunity, but is to be devoted to barter in the markets. That is not liberalism, that is degeneration.

I sympathize greatly with the desire of the people of Tennessee and Alabama to see this great asset turned to practical use. It can be so turned and to their benefit. I am loath to leave a subject of this character without a sug-

gestion for solution. Congress has been thwarted for ten years in finding solution, by rivalry of private interests and by the determination of certain groups to commit the Federal Government to government ownership and operation of power.

The real development of the resources and the industries of the Tennessee Valley can be only accomplished by the people in that valley themselves. Muscle Shoals can only be administered by the people upon the ground, responsible to their own communities, directing them solely for the benefit of their communities and not for purposes of pursuit of social theories or natural politics. Any other course deprives them of liberty.

I would therefore suggest that the States of Alabama and Tennessee, who are the ones primarily concerned, should set up a commission of their own representatives, together with a representative from the national farm organization and the corps of army engineers; that there be vested in that commission full authority to lease the plants at Muscle Shoals in the interest of the local community and agriculture generally. . . .

The Federal Government should, as in the case of Boulder Canyon, construct Cove Creek Dam as a regulatory measure for the flood protection of the Tennessee Valley and the development of its water resources, but on the same bases as those imposed at Boulder Canyon—that is, that construction should be undertaken at such time as the proposed commission is able to secure contracts for use of the increased water supply to power uses, or the lease of the power produced as a by-product from such a dam on terms that will return to the government interest upon its outlay with amortization. On this basis the Federal Government will have cooperated to place the question into the hands of the people primarily concerned. They can lease as their wisdom dictates, and for the industries that they deem best in their own interest. It would get a war relic out of politics and into the realm of service.

PRESIDENT HERBERT HOOVER'S PRESCRIPTION FOR COMBATING THE DEPRESSION
31 May 1932

President Hoover's dogged commitment to fixed principles of government persisted to the end of his term, even as the Depression deepened and the American social fabric threatened to unravel. With the challenges of re-election just weeks away, Hoover made a dramatic personal appearance before the United States Senate on 31 May 1932. He declared that "An emergency has developed in the last few days which it is my duty to lay before the Senate." Seemingly alarmed, the President acknowledged that conditions continued to worsen. He brought the formula for recovery, he told the Senate, and proceeded to lay out a legislative initiative that would drastically reduce the fiscal and monetary scope of government involvement in the economic cycle. In other words, Hoover proposed that the Federal Government do less rather than more.

An emergency has developed in the last few days which it is my duty to lay before the Senate.

The continued downward movement in the economic life of the country has been particularly accelerated during the past few days, and it relates in part definitely to the financial program of the Government. There can be no doubt that superimposed upon other causes the long-continued delays in the passage of legislation providing for such reduction in expenses and such addition to revenues as would balance the budget, together with proposals of projects which would greatly increase governmental expenditures, have given rise to doubt and anxiety as to the ability of our Government to meet its responsibilities. These fears and doubts have been foolishly exaggerated in foreign countries. They know from bitter experience that the course of unbalanced budgets is the road of ruin. They do not realize that slow as our processes may be we are determined and have the resources to place the finances of the United States on an unassailable basis.

The immediate result has been to create an entirely unjustified run upon the American dollar from foreign countries and within the past few days despite our national wealth and resources and our unparalleled gold reserves our dollar stands at a serious discount in the markets of the world for the first time in half a century. This can be and must be immediately corrected or the reaction upon our economic situation will be such as to cause great losses to our people and will still further retard recovery. Nor is the confusion in public mind and the rising feeling of doubt and fear confined to foreign countries. It reflects itself directly in diminished economic activity and increased unemployment within our own borders and among our own citizens. There is thus further stress upon already diminished and strained economic life of the country.

No one has a more sympathetic realization than I of the difficulties and complexities of the problem with which the Congress is confronted. The decrease in revenues due to the depression by upwards of $1,700 million and the consequent necessity to reduce Government expenditures, the sacrifice such reduction calls for from many groups and sections, the further sacrifice called for in the distribution of the remaining burden by the imposition of new taxes, all constitute a problem which naturally arouses wide divergence of sectional interest and individual views. Yet if we are to secure a just distribution of these sacrifices in such fashion as to establish confidence in the integrity of the Government we must secure an adjustment of these views to quick and prompt national action, directed at one sole purpose, that is to unfetter the rehabilitation of industry, agriculture, and unemployment. The time has come when we must all make sacrifice of some parts of our particular views and bring these dangers and degenerations to halt by expeditious action.

In the stress of this emergency I have conferred with members of both parties of the Senate as to methods by which the strains and stresses could be overcome and the gigantic resources and energies of our people released from the fetters in which they are held. I have felt in the stress of this emergency a grave responsibility rests upon me not only to present the situation to the Senate but to make suggestions as to the basis of adjustment between these views which I hope will lead to early action. And I am addressing myself to the Senate on this occasion as the major questions under consideration are now before this body.

We have three major duties in legislation in order to accomplish our fundamental purposes.

1. Drastic reduction of expenditures.
2. Passage of adequate revenue legislation, the combination of which with reductions will unquestionably beyond all manner of doubt declare to the world the balancing of the Federal

budget and the stabilizing of the American dollar.
3. Passage of adequate relief legislation to assure the country against distress and to aid in employment pending the next session of Congress. . . .

The sharp degeneration has its many reflexes in distress and hardship upon our people. I hold that the maintenance of the sense of individual and personal responsibility of men to their neighbors and the proper separation of functions of the Federal and local governments requires the maintenance of the fundamental principle that the obligation of distress rests upon the individuals, upon the communities and upon the States. In order, however, that there may be no failure on the part of any State to meets its obligation in this direction I have, after consultation with some of the party leaders on both sides, favored authorization to the Reconstruction Finance Corporation to loan up to $300 million to State governments where they are unable to finance themselves in provision of relief to distress. Such loans should be made by purchase of State bonds by the Corporation but where States are unable to issue bonds then loans should be made upon application of State authorities, and if they are not regularized by the issuance of bonds within a period of 12 to 18 months, they should become a charge upon the Federal aid funds to which such States may be entitled. . . .

I have not been able to favor the expansion of public works beyond the program already proposed in the budget. I have for many years advocated speeding up of public works as relief to unemployment in times of depression. Since the beginning of this depression, in consonance with this view, the Federal Government will have expended in excess of $1,500 million in construction and maintenance of one kind or another as against a normal program of perhaps $650 million for a similar period. The budget for next year calls for over $550 million or double our usual outlay. If we shall now increase these programs we shall need instantly to increase taxes still further. . . .

The natural wealth of this country is unimpaired, and the inherent abilities of our people to meet their problems are being restrained by failure of the Government to act. Time is of the essence. Every day's delay makes new wounds and extends them. I come before you in sympathy with the difficulties which the problem presents and in a sincere spirit of helpfulness. I ask of you to accept such a basis of practical adjustment essential to the welfare of our people. In your hands at this moment is the answer to the question whether democracy has the capacity to act speedily enough to save itself in emergency. The Nation urgently needs unity. It needs solidarity before the world in demonstrating that America has the courage to look its difficulties in the face and the capacity and resolution to meet them.

President Herbert Hoover's Comments on the Veteran's "Bonus Army"
28 July 1932

The low point of the Hoover Administration occurred in mid-1932 when about 15,000 World War veterans assembled in Washington to demand immediate payment of a World War I bonus not scheduled for redemption until 1945. The economically-depressed and tattered assemblage found little encouragement in the nation's capitol. The Senate rejected the bonus payment, 62–18, and nearly all members of Congress took extravagant measures to avoid contact with the veterans. The ugly atmosphere exploded into rage and violence late in July producing a riot and the intervention of the U.S. Army. Acting under the President's orders, Army troops commanded by General Douglas MacArthur used horse cavalry, drawn swords and tear gas to drive the veterans out of the District of Columbia. Hoover later accused MacArthur of exceeding his instructions, and both men later alleged that communists and criminals had infiltrated the Bonus Army.

For some days police authorities and Treasury officials have been endeavoring to persuade the so-called bonus marchers to evacuate certain buildings which they were occupying without permission. These buildings are on sites where government construction is in progress and their demolition was necessary in order to extend employment in the district and to carry forward the government's construction program.

This morning the occupants of these buildings were notified to evacuate and at the request of the police did evacuate the buildings concerned. Thereafter, however, several thousand men from different camps marched in and attacked the police with brickbats and otherwise injuring several policemen, one probably fatally.

I have received the attached letter from the commissioners of the District of Columbia stating that they can no longer preserve law and order in the District.

In order to put an end to this rioting and defiance of civil authority, I have asked the army to assist the district authorities to restore order. . . .

Congress made provision for the return home of the so-called bonus marchers who have for many weeks been given every opportunity of free assembly, free speech and free petition to the Congress. Some 5,000 took advantage of this arrangement and have returned to their homes. An examination of a large number of names discloses the fact that a considerable part of those remaining are not veterans; many are Communists and persons with criminal records.

The veterans amongst these numbers are no doubt unaware of the character of their companions and are being led into violence which no government can tolerate.

I have asked the Attorney-General to investigate the whole incident and to cooperate with the District civil authorities in such measures against leaders and rioters as may be necessary.

PRESIDENT HERBERT HOOVER DEFENDS HIS POLITICAL PRINCIPLES
12 October 1932

As Herbert Hoover neared Election Day of 1932 and the end of his Presidency he stoutly affirmed his political principles, even in the face of economic disaster and his own political ruin. At the annual convention of the American Bar Association in Washington three weeks before his loss to Franklin Delano Roosevelt, the President warned against deviation from fixed principles.

... Today, perhaps as never before, our very form of government is on trial in the eyes of millions of our citizens. Economic stresses of unparalleled magnitude have wracked our people, and in their distress some are tempted to lay the blame for their troubles upon the system of government under which they live. It is a not unnatural instinct however mistaken it may be. It can be a dangerous thing, if wise and trusted men fail to explain to the people how often in history the people's interests have been betrayed by false prophets of a millenium, promised through seductive but unworkable and disastrous theories of government. The menace is doubled by the fact that these vain allurements are today being offered to our harassed people by men of public

reputation in economics and even by men in public life. No man can foretell to what lengths the pressure of public clamor may at any time be brought to bear upon those charged with the processes of government to yield to changes which you know, before they are tried, would destroy personal liberty and sweep away the security of savings and wages built up by centuries of experience. All progress and growth is a matter of change, but change must be growth within our social and governmental concepts if it should not destroy them.

You have your duty in this area to expound the history of the painful past through which rights and liberties have been won, to warn of repetitions of old and fatal experiments under new and glamorous names, to defend our system of government against reckless assaults of designing persons. It is your task to prove again what none knows better than you, that the very citadel of the rights of the poor against the oppression of rulers and against the extortions of the rapacious is the judicial system of the country, and that the impregnable apex of that system is the Supreme Court of the United States. It is impregnable because its membership in successive generations down to this moment has comprised the highest character of our land who, preserving its great traditions, have armored it with the moral support of the people, and thus, without physical power or the need of it, is able to stand equal and alone against legislative encroachment upon the people's rights or executive usurpation of them, and, more precious than either, against private injustice and the enactment of public laws in violation of the fundamental protections of the Constitution.

These deviations from steadfast constitutional limitations, which I have last named, are of paramount significance in these times of growth and change. The last 50 years have witnessed a progress in expansion of business and industry unmatched in any five centuries of previous history. The United States has been in the forefront of this progress. Inventions in transportation, communications, and factory production have multiplied the conveniences of life and have widened the fields of human intercourse immeasurably. Economic forces have spread business across State lines and have brought new strains upon our Federal system in its relationships with the State sovereignties. Laws that once were adequate to control private operations affecting the public interest proved unequal to these new conditions. Regulation and control were more than ever necessary. In the readjustment of Federal laws to State laws required by this situation, the Supreme Court has played a part of incalculable practical value. Without its prestige, without its independence, without its wisdom and power, these delicate alterations could not have been effected except at tremendous costs of injury to our people and of excessive disturbance of political equilibrium. But for the success with which this transition to large Federal regulation over interstate commerce was accomplished, the development of our great system of economic production would have been delayed, individual rights would have been trampled down, and our system of State authorities within the Union of Federal Government could scarcely have survived with all its values of local control of local issues.

We have long recognized that certain functions in our economic life are affected with public interest, which requires that their activities shall be in some measure controlled by government, either State or Federal, in protection of the citizens. In that situation we have sought to find a bridge between these controls and the maintenance of that initiative and enterprise which assures the conduct and expansion and perfection of these functions.

One of the great good fortunes of our form of government is that in the 48 States we have 48 laboratories of social and economic experimentation. But, as I have said, many of these activities—particularly those of banking and finance, of transportation, communications, and power—have expanded beyond State borders. It has become necessary during these years to develop gradually increasing burden of Federal control. With growth and experience, these regulatory functions require constant revision: On the one hand that we may prevent wrongdoing and give justice and equality of opportunity to our people, and on the other that we should not stifle these vital functions and services through the extinction of that enterprise and initiative which must dominate a growing organism.

And here lies also one of the most delicate relations of our Republic. We must maintain on the one hand a sense of responsibility in the States. It is the local communities that can best safeguard their liberties. We must therefore impose upon the States the maximum responsibility in these regulatory powers over economic functions. It may be even necessary in the long view of the Republic that the people of some States whose governments are negligent of the interests of their own people should be inadequately protected rather than destroy the initiative and responsibility of local communities and of all States and un-dermine the very foundations of local government. On the other hand, we must be courageous in providing for extension of these regulatory powers when they run beyond the capacity of the States to protect their citizens.

In the ebb and flow of economic life our people in times of prosperity and ease naturally tend to neglect the vigilance over their rights. Moreover, wrongdoing is obscured by apparent success in enterprise. Then insidious diseases and wrongdoings grow apace. But we have in the past seen that in times of distress and difficulty wrongdoing and weakness comes to the surface and our people, in their endeavors to correct these wrongs, are tempted to extremes which may destroy rather than build.

In the separation of responsibilities between the Federal and State Governments on matters outside of the economic field we have constantly to resist the well-meaning reformer who, witnessing the failure of local communities to discharge responsibilities of government, to extinguish crime, and to set up agencies of government free of corruption, to move apace with the thousand social and other advances which the country sorely needs, constantly advocates and agitates that the powers of the Federal Government be applied, that we may have a rigid uniformity of reform throughout the Nation. Yet even here it is better that we should witness some instances of failure of municipal and State governments to discharge responsibilities in protection and government of their people rather than that we should drive this Republic to a centralization which will mean the deadening of its great mainspring of progress which is the discovery and experimentation and advancement by the local community.

Diversity within unity is the essence of government and progress in our country. If we are to preserve the foundations of liberty in the community and the State, just as is true in the case of the individual, we must have room for self-creation and self-development, for it is the sum of these accomplishments which make the progress of the Nation. We must not believe that by guaranteeing the medium of perfection to all individuals, to all communities, to all municipalities and all States, through the deadening hand of centralization, we will secure progress. . . .

PRESIDENT FRANKLIN D. ROOSEVELT'S FIRST INAUGURAL ADDRESS
4 March 1933

When the Democratic Convention assembled in Chicago at the end of June 1932, winning the Presidential nomination seemed to promise the White House. The Republicans had already renominated President Hoover even as the historic economic decline continued to drive the nation toward social instability. Hoover's insistence that individual will, private enterprise and local institutions would solve the agony felt by most Americans had only increased his political unpopularity as the Depression deepened. Stocks had collapsed, over 1,500 banks failed, unemployment soared from three to four to five million, the Smoot-Hawley Tariff Bill—championed by the President—soon dried up international trade. In Chicago the strongly-contested Democratic nomination went to the fourth ballot before choosing the Governor of New York, Franklin Delano Roosevelt. This fifty-year-old Hudson River Valley aristocrat, a familiar figure in state and national Democratic affairs since 1910, had suffered a crippling attack of polio in 1921. Although he would never walk unaided again, few Americans realized the extent of his disability, in large part because his public personality emitted confidence and caring and good humor. The buoyant nominee immediately broke precedent by flying to Chicago to accept in person, declaring to the roaring Democrats, "I pledge you, I pledge myself, a 'new deal' for the American people." Whatever that meant, in November Roosevelt won in a landslide while sweeping Congress for the Democrats. In the long four-month interregnum between election and inauguration, terrible economic news became much worse. Unemployment topped thirteen million as industry functioned at less than half capacity of just four years previously. All banks had closed and most financial transactions had ceased. Helplessness infected the American spirit. The nation, the world, paused for the new President's official entrance.

I am certain that my fellow Americans expect that on my induction into the Presidency I will address them with a candor and a decision which the present situation of our Nation impels. This is preeminently the time to speak the truth, the whole truth, frankly and boldly. Nor need we shrink from honestly facing conditions in our country today. This great Nation will endure as it has endured, will revive and will prosper. So, first of all, let me assert my firm belief that the only thing we have to fear is fear itself—nameless, unreasoning, unjustified terror which paralyzes needed efforts to convert retreat into advance. In every dark hour of our national life a leadership of frankness and vigor has met with that understanding and support of the people themselves which is essential to victory. I am convinced that you will again give that support to leadership in these critical days.

In such a spirit on my part and on yours we face our common difficulties. They concern, thank God, only material things. Values have shrunken to fantastic levels; taxes have risen; our ability to pay has fallen; government of all kinds is faced by serious curtailment of income; the means of exchange are frozen in the currents of trade; the withered leaves of industrial enterprise lie on every side; farmers find no markets for their produce; the savings of many years in thousands of families are gone.

More important, a host of unemployed citizens face the grim problem of existence, and an equally great number toil with little return. Only a foolish optimist can deny the dark realities of the moment.

Yet our distress comes from no failure of substance. We are stricken by no plague of locusts. Compared with the perils which our forefathers conquered because they believed and were not afraid, we have still much to be thankful for. Nature still offers her bounty and human efforts have multiplied it. Plenty is at our doorstep, but a generous use of it languishes in the very sight of the supply. Primarily this is because rulers of the exchange of mankind's goods have failed through their own stubbornness and their own incompetence, have admitted their failure, and have abdicated. Practices of the unscrupulous money changers stand indicted in the court of public opinion, rejected by the hearts and minds of men.

True they have tried, but their efforts have been cast in the pattern of an outworn tradition. Faced by failure of credit they have proposed only the lending of more money. Stripped of the lure of profit by which to induce our people to follow their false leadership, they have resorted to exhortations, pleading tearfully for restored confidence. They know only the rules of a generation of self-seekers. They have no vision, and when there is no vision the people perish.

The money changers have fled from their high seats in the temple of our civilization. We may now restore that temple to the ancient truths. The measure of the restoration lies in the extent to which we apply social values more noble than mere monetary profit.

Happiness lies not in the mere possession of money; it lies in the joy of achievement, in the thrill of creative effort. The joy and moral stimulation of work no longer must be forgotten in the mad chase of evanescent profits. These dark days will be worth all they cost us if they teach us that our true destiny is not to be ministered unto but to minister to ourselves and to our fellow men.

Recognition of the falsity of material wealth as the standard of success goes hand in hand with the abandonment of the false belief that public office and high political position are to be valued only by the standards of pride of place and personal profit; and there must be an end to a conduct in banking and in business which too often has given to a sacred trust the likeness of callous and selfish wrongdoing. Small wonder that confidence languishes, for it thrives only on honesty, on honor, on the sacredness of obligations, on faithful protection, on unselfish performance; without them it cannot live.

Restoration calls, however, not for changes in ethics alone. This Nation asks for action, and action now.

Our greatest primary task is to put people to work. This is no unsolvable problem if we face it wisely and courageously. It can be accomplished in part by direct recruiting by the Government itself, treating the task as we would treat the emergency of a war, but at the same time, through this employment, accomplishing greatly needed projects to stimulate and reorganize the use of our natural resources.

Hand in hand with this we must frankly recognize the overbalance of population in our industrial centers and, by engaging on a national scale in a redistribution, endeavor to provide a better use of the land for those best fitted for the land. The task can be helped by definite efforts to raise the values of agricultural products and with this the power to purchase the output of our cities. It can be helped by preventing realistically the tragedy of the growing loss through foreclosure of our small homes and our farms. It can be helped by insistence that the Federal, State, and local governments act forthwith on the demand that their cost be drastically reduced. It can be helped by the unifying of relief activities which today are often scattered, uneconomical, and unequal. It can be helped by national planning for and supervision of all forms of transportation and of communications and other utilities which have a definitely public character. There are many ways in which it can be helped, but it can never be helped merely by talking about it. We must act and act quickly.

Finally, in our progress toward a resumption of work we require two safeguards against a return of the evils of the old order: there must be a strict supervision of all banking and credits and investments, so that there will be an end to speculation with other people's money; and there must be provision for an adequate but sound currency.

These are the lines of attack. I shall presently urge upon a new Congress, in special session, detailed measures for their fulfillment, and I shall seek the immediate assistance of the several States.

Through this program of action we address ourselves to putting our own national house in order and making income balance outgo. Our international trade relations, though vastly important, are in point of time and necessity secondary to the establishment of a sound national economy. I favor as a practical policy the putting of first things first. I shall spare no effort to restore world trade by international economic readjustment, but the emergency at home cannot wait on that accomplishment.

The basic thought that guides these specific means of national recovery is not narrowly nationalistic. It is the insistence, as a first consideration, upon the interdependence of the various elements in and parts of the United States—a recognition of the old and permanently important manifestation of the American spirit of the pioneer. It is the way to recovery. It is the immediate way. It is the

strongest assurance that the recovery will endure.

In the field of world policy I would dedicate this Nation to the policy of the good neighbor—the neighbor who resolutely respects himself and, because he does so, respects the rights of others—the neighbor who respects his obligations and respects the sanctity of his agreements in and with a world of neighbors.

If I read the temper of our people correctly, we now realize as we have never realized before our interdependence on each other; that we cannot merely take but we must give as well; that if we are to go forward, we must move as a trained and loyal army willing to sacrifice for the good of a common discipline, because without such discipline no progress is made, no leadership becomes effective. We are, I know, ready and willing to submit our lives and property to such discipline, because it makes possible a leadership which aims at a larger good. This I propose to offer, pledging that the larger purposes will bind upon us all as a sacred obligation with a unity of duty hitherto evoked only in time of armed strife.

With this pledge taken, I assume unhesitatingly the leadership of this great army of our people dedicated to a disciplined attack upon our common problems.

Action in this image and to this end is feasible under the form of government which we have inherited from our ancestors. Our Constitution is so simple and practical that it is possible always to meet extraordinary needs by changes in emphasis and arrangement without loss of essential form. That is why our constitutional system has proved itself the most superbly enduring political mechanism the modern world has produced. It has met every stress of vast expansion of territory, of foreign wars, of bitter internal strife, of world relations.

It is to be hoped that the normal balance of Executive and legislative authority may be wholly adequate to meet the unprecedented task before us. But it may be that an unprecedented demand and need for undelayed action may call for temporary departure from that normal balance of public procedure.

I am prepared under my constitutional duty to recommend the measures that a stricken Nation in the midst of a stricken world may require. These measures, or such other measures as the Congress may build out of its experience and wisdom, I shall seek, within my constitutional authority, to bring to speedy adoption.

But in the event that the Congress shall fail to take one of these two courses, and in the event that the national emergency is still critical, I shall not evade the clear course of duty that will then confront me. I shall ask the Congress for the one remaining instrument to meet the crisis—broad Executive power to wage a war against the emergency, as great as the power that would be given to me if we were in fact invaded by a foreign foe.

For the trust reposed in me I will return the courage and the devotion that befit the time. I can do no less.

We face the arduous days that lie before us in the warm courage of national unity; with the clear consciousness of seeking old and precious moral values; with the clean satisfaction that comes from the stern performance of duty by old and young alike. We aim at the assurance of a rounded and permanent national life.

We do not distrust the future of essential democracy. The people of the United States have not failed. In their need they have registered a mandate that they want direct, vigorous action. They have asked for discipline and direction under leadership. They have made me the present instrument of their wishes. In the spirit of the gift I take it.

In this dedication of a Nation we humbly ask the blessing of God. May He protect each and every one of us. May He guide me in the days to come.

PRESIDENT FRANKLIN D. ROOSEVELT'S FIRST "FIRESIDE CHAT"
12 March 1933

On Sunday evening, 12 March 1933, just eight days after his inauguration, President Roosevelt spoke to a national radio audience estimated at sixty million listeners. National radio hookups emerged in the 1920s, but had hardly been used by Roosevelt's predecessors.

This first "fireside chat" identified the new President as a master of radio communication. His resonant and comforting tone of voice, use of the familiar "my friends," and manner of confidence made this mass public event somehow seem personal and intimate. All across the nation, in homes and shops and schools and taverns, the great audience listened carefully to the President's assurances. His principal theme was the banking system and the national panic produced by bank failures. President Roosevelt assured the American people that banks were now safe. The very next morning, as reported by newspapers from around the nation, long lines formed at re-opened banks, with people again depositing their money.

I want to talk for a few minutes with the people of the United States about banking—with the comparatively few who understand the mechanics of banking but more particularly with the overwhelming majority who use banks for the making of deposits and the drawing of checks. I want to tell you what has been done in the last few days, why it was done, and what the next steps are going to be. I recognize that the many proclamations from State capitols and from Washington, the legislation, the Treasury regulations, etc., couched for the most part in banking and legal terms, should be explained for the benefit of the average citizen. I owe this in particular because of the fortitude and good temper with which everybody has accepted the inconvenience and hardships of the banking holiday. I know that when you understand what we in Washington have been about I shall continue to have your cooperation as fully as I have had your sympathy and help during the past week.

First of all, let me state the simple fact that when you deposit money in a bank the bank does not put the money into a safe deposit vault. It invests your money in many different forms of credit—bonds, commercial paper, mortgages and many other kinds of loans. In other words, the bank puts your money to work to keep the wheels of industry and of agriculture turning around. A comparatively small part of the money you put into the bank is kept in currency—an amount which in normal times is wholly sufficient to cover the cash needs of the average citizen. In other words, the total amount of all the currency in the country is only a small fraction of the total deposits in all of the banks.

What, then, happened during the last few days of February and the first few days of March? Because of undermined confidence on the part of the public, there was a general rush by a large portion of our population to turn bank deposits into currency or gold—a rush so great that the soundest banks could not get enough currency to meet the demand. The reason for this was that on the spur of the moment it was, of course, impossible to sell perfectly sound assets of a bank and convert them into cash except at panic prices far below their real value.

By the afternoon of 3d March scarcely a bank in the country was open to do business. Proclamations temporarily closing them in whole or in part had been issued by the Governors in almost all the States.

It was then that I issued the proclamation providing for the nationwide bank holiday, and this was the first step in the Government's reconstruction of our financial and economic fabric.

The second step was the legislation promptly and patriotically passed by the Congress confirming my proclamation and broadening my powers so that it became possible in view of the requirement of time to extend the holiday and lift the ban of that holiday gradually. This law also gave authority to develop a program of rehabilitation of our banking facilities. I want to tell our citizens in every part of the Nation that the national Congress—Republicans and Democrats alike—showed by this action a devotion to public welfare and a realization of the emergency and the necessity for speed that it is difficult to match in our history.

The third stage has been the series of regulations permitting the banks to continue their functions to take care of the distribution of food and household necessities and the payment of payrolls.

This bank holiday, while resulting in many cases in great inconvenience, is affording us the opportunity to supply the currency necessary to meet the situation. No sound bank is a dollar worse off than it was when it closed its doors last Monday. Neither is any bank which may turn out not to be in a position for immediate opening. The new law allows the twelve Federal Reserve Banks to issue additional currency on good assets and thus the banks which reopen will be able to meet every legitimate call. The new currency is being sent out by the Bureau of Engraving and Printing in large volume to every part of the country. It is sound currency because it is backed by actual, good assets.

A question you will ask is this: why are all the banks not to be reopened at the same time? The answer is simple. Your Government does not intend that the history of the past few years shall be repeated. We do not want and will not have another epidemic of bank failures.

As a result, we start tomorrow, Monday, with the opening of banks in the twelve Federal Reserve Bank cities—those banks which on first examination by the Treasury have already been found to be all right. This will be followed on Tuesday by the resumption of all their functions by banks already found to be sound in cities where there are recognized clearing houses. That means about 250 cities of the United States.

On Wednesday and succeeding days banks in smaller places all through the country will resume business, subject, of course, to the Government's physical ability to complete its survey. It is necessary that the reopening of banks be extended over a period in order to permit the banks to make applications for necessary loans, to obtain currency needed to meet their requirements and to enable the Government to make common sense checkups.

Let me make it clear to you that if your bank does not open the first day you are by no means justified in believing that it will not open. A bank that opens on one of the subsequent days is in exactly the same status as the bank that opens tomorrow.

I know that many people are worrying about State banks not members of the Federal Reserve System. These banks can and will receive assistance from member banks and from the Reconstruction Finance Corporation. These State banks are following the same course as the National banks except that they get their licenses to resume business from the State authorities, and these authorities have been asked by the Secretary of the Treasury to permit their good banks to open up on the same schedule as the national banks. I am confident that the State Banking Departments will be as careful as the national Government in the policy relating to the opening of banks and will follow the same broad policy.

It is possible that when the banks resume a very few people who have not recovered from their fear may again begin withdrawals. Let me make it clear that the banks will take care of all needs—and it is my belief that

hoarding during the past week has become an exceedingly unfashionable pastime. It needs no prophet to tell you that when the people find that they can get their money—that they can get it when they want it for all legitimate purposes—the phantom of fear will soon be laid. People will again be glad to have their money where it will be safely taken care of and where they can use it conveniently at any time. I can assure you that it is safer to keep your money in a reopened bank than under the mattress.

The success of our whole great national program depends, of course, upon the cooperation of the public—on its intelligent support and use of a reliable system.

Remember that the essential accomplishment of the new legislation is that it makes it possible for banks more readily to convert their assets into cash than was the case before. More liberal provision has been made for banks to borrow on these assets at the Reserve Banks and more liberal provision has also been made for issuing currency on the security of these good assets. This currency is not fiat currency. It is issued only on adequate security, and every good bank has an abundance of such security.

One more point before I close. There will be, of course, some banks unable to reopen without being reorganized. The new law allows the Government to assist in making these reorganizations quickly and effectively and even allows the Government to subscribe to at least a part of new capital which may be required.

I hope you can see from this elemental recital of what your Government is doing that there is nothing complex, or radical, in the process.

We had a bad banking situation. Some of our bankers had shown themselves either incompetent or dishonest in their handling of the people's funds. They had used the money entrusted to them in speculations and unwise loans. This was, of course, not true in the vast majority of our banks, but it was true in enough of them to shock the people for a time into a sense of insecurity and to put them into a frame of mind where they did not differentiate, but seemed to assume that the acts of a comparative few had tainted them all. It was the Government's job to straighten out this situation and do it as quickly as possible. And the job is being performed.

I do not promise you that every bank will be reopened or that individual losses will not be suffered, but there will be no losses that possibly could be avoided; and there would have been more and greater losses had we continued to drift. I can even promise you salvation for some at least of the sorely pressed banks. We shall be engaged not merely in reopening sound banks but in the creation of sound banks through reorganization.

It has been wonderful to me to catch the note of confidence from all over the country. I can never be sufficiently grateful to the people for the loyal support they have given me in their acceptance of the judgment that has dictated our course, even though all our processes may not have seemed clear to them.

After all, there is an element in the readjustment of our financial system more important than currency, more important than gold, and that is the confidence of the people. Confidence and courage are the essentials of success in carrying out our plan. You people must have faith; you must not be stampeded by rumors or guesses. Let us unite in banishing fear. We have provided the machinery to restore our financial system; it is up to you to support and make it work.

It is your problem no less than it is mine. Together we cannot fail.

PRESIDENT FRANKLIN D. ROOSEVELT INTRODUCES THE "GOOD NEIGHBOR POLICY"
12 April 1933

Relationships among the nations of the New World changed fundamentally when the United States became a world power around 1900. Although President James Monroe's famous Doctrine of 1823 told the world that Europe could neither establish new colonies nor interfere in the affairs of the New World, the United States lacked the ability to enforce its primacy until seven decades later. In the interim, American diplomacy relied on a general identity of interests in the hemisphere with Britain, and its powerful Navy. By the 1890s, however, the American Secretary of State would bluntly inform his counterpart in London that "Today the United States is practically sovereign on this continent. . . ." In 1904, President Theodore Roosevelt proclaimed his "corollary" to the Monroe Doctrine: while intervention by the European in the affairs of the Americas was forbidden, it was justified when undertaken by the United States. Within a generation, the economic, political, and military might of the United States controlled much of the Caribbean and Central America. The economic base of areas under American control featured agricultural products destined for U.S. markets, with both production and price established by major American corporations. Sugar, citrus products, tobacco, and coffee were particularly valuable. Opposition to U.S. interests in Central America and the Caribbean frequently produced the dispatch of American military units; by the 1920s, American troops patrolled Cuba, the Dominican Republic, Haiti, Nicaragua and Panama—all important for its U.S.-controlled Canal. With the rise of aggressive dictatorships in the 1930s, critics of "American imperialism" grew more persuasive. To distinguish itself, the administration of Franklin D. Roosevelt unveiled a "Good Neighbor" policy toward nations to the South. Roosevelt never lost sight of maintaining full control of hemispheric affairs, but now sought to present the situation in attractive terms. With some exceptions, the United States would henceforth rely less on military intervention and economic strong-arm tactics. Instead, pliable and usually corrupt hemispheric dictators would be supported, they would grow rich, their military and police were trained to confront non-cooperative nationalists, leftists and other troublemakers. American military intervention remained as a last option. With considerable economic profit at stake, The Export-Import Bank, created in 1934, capitalized and regulated hemispheric trade from Washington. While the Monroe Doctrine, the Roosevelt Corollary and the Good Neighbor Policy struck very different tones and relied on varied tactics, the determination of the United States to pursue its economic and strategic objectives throughout the hemisphere remained constant. President Roosevelt took the occasion of "Pan-American Day" to greet representatives of the Pan American Union Washington soon after his Inauguration.

I rejoice in this opportunity to participate in the celebration of "Pan-American Day" and to extend on behalf of the people of the United States a fraternal greeting to our sister American Republics. The celebration of "Pan-American Day" in this building, dedicated to international good-will and cooperation, exemplifies a unity of thought and purpose among the peoples of this hemisphere. It is a manifestation of the common ideal of mutual helpfulness, sympathetic understanding and spiritual solidarity.

There is inspiration in the thought that on this day the attention of the citizens of the twenty-one Republics of America is focused on the common ties—historical, cultural, economic, and social—which bind them to one another. Common ideals and a community of interest, together with a spirit of cooperation, have led to the realization that the well-being of one Nation depends in large measure upon the well-being of its neighbors. It is upon these foundations that Pan Americanism has been built.

This celebration commemorates a movement based upon the policy of fraternal cooperation. In my Inaugural Address I stated that I would "dedicate this Nation to the policy of the good neighbor—the neighbor who resolutely respects himself and, because he does so, respects the rights of others—the neighbor who respects his obligations and respects the sanctity of his agreements in and with a world of neighbors." Never before has the significance of the words "good neighbor" been so manifest in international relations. Never have the need and benefit of neighborly cooperation in every form of human activity been so evident as they are today.

Friendship among Nations, as among individuals, calls for constructive efforts to muster the forces of humanity in order that an atmosphere of close understanding and cooperation may be cultivated. It involves mutual obligations and responsibilities, for it is only by sympathetic respect for the rights of others and a scrupulous fulfillment of the corresponding obligations by each member of the community that a true fraternity can be maintained.

The essential qualities of a true Pan Americanism must be the same as those which constitute a good neighbor, namely, mutual understanding, and, through such understanding, a sympathetic appreciation of the other's point of view. It is only in this manner that we can hope to build up a system of which confidence, friendship and good-will are the cornerstones.

In this spirit the people of every Republic on our continent are coming to a deep understanding of the fact that the Monroe Doctrine, of which so much has been written and spoken for more than a century, was and is directed at the maintenance of independence by the peoples of the continent. It was aimed and is aimed against the acquisition in any manner of the control of additional territory in this hemisphere by any non-American power.

Hand in hand with this Pan-American doctrine of continental self-defense, the peoples of the American Republics understand more clearly, with the passing years, that the independence of each Republic must recognize the independence of every other Republic. Each one of us must grow by an advancement of civilization and social well-being and not by the acquisition of territory at the expense of any neighbor.

In this spirit of mutual understanding and of cooperation on this continent you and I cannot fail to be disturbed by any armed strife between neighbors. I do not hesitate to say to you, the distinguished members of the Governing Board of the Pan-American Union, that I regard existing conflicts between four of our sister Republics as a backward step.

Your Americanism and mine must be a structure built of confidence, cemented by a sympathy which recognizes only equality and fraternity. It finds its source and being in the hearts of men and dwells in the temple of the intellect.

We all of us have peculiar problems, and, to speak frankly, the interest of our own citizens must, in each instance, come first. But it is equally true that it is of vital importance to every Nation of this Continent that the American Governments, individually, take, without further delay, such action as may be possible to abolish all unnecessary and artificial barriers and restrictions which now hamper the healthy flow of trade between the peoples of the American Republics.

I am glad to deliver this message to you, Gentlemen of the Governing Board of the Pan-American Union, for I look upon the Union as the outward expression of the spiritual unity of the Americas. It is to this unity which must be courageous and vital in its element that humanity must look for one of the great stabilizing influences in world affairs. . . .

PRESIDENT FRANKLIN D. ROOSEVELT SUPPORTS THE PRINCIPLE OF COLLECTIVE BARGAINING
5 July 1935

For decades after the beginning of American industrialization in the late nineteenth century the Federal Government's attitude toward organized labor ranged from indifference to hostility. Employers reigned supreme, setting wages and conditions of work as they pleased. Strikes often meant unrestricted violence, from company "goon squads" or government troops. Attempts at organizing were often frustrated by the judiciary, which welcomed injunctions to forestall union activity. As late as the 1930s, in the Great Depression's darkest period, labor remained powerless, workers avoiding unions out of fear of losing whatever jobs remained. In 1935, President Roosevelt threw his support behind a bill authored by Senator Robert F. Wagner (D-NY), the passage of which permanently altered the terms of contention between business and labor. The Wagner Act created the National Labor Relations Board (NLRB), which provided for the right of union organization and, most importantly, compelled a business to bargain collectively with the union that represented the majority of its workers. Quickly, millions of American workers poured into the unions, creating a new and powerful permanent force in American life.

This Act defines, as a part of our substantive law, the right of self-organization of employees in industry for the purpose of collective bargaining, and provides methods by which the Government can safeguard that legal right. It establishes a National Labor Relations Board to hear and determine cases in which it is charged that this legal right is abridged or denied, and to hold fair elections to ascertain who are the chosen representatives of employees.

A better relationship between labor and management is the high purpose of this Act. By assuring the employees the right of collective bargaining it fosters the development of the employment contract on a sound and equitable basis. By providing an orderly procedure for determining who is entitled to represent the employees, it aims to remove one of the chief causes of wasteful economic strife. By preventing practices which tend to destroy the independence of labor, it seeks, for every worker within its scope, that freedom of choice and action which is justly his.

The National Labor Relations Board will be an independent quasi-judicial body. It should be clearly understood that it will not act as mediator or conciliator in labor disputes. The function of mediation remains, under this Act, the duty of the Secretary of Labor and of the Conciliation Service of the Department of Labor. It is important that the judicial function and the mediation function should not be confused. Compromise, the essence of mediation, has no place in the interpretation and enforcement of the law.

This Act, defining rights, the enforcement of which is recognized by the Congress to be necessary as an act of both common justice and economic advance, must not be misinterpreted. It may eventually eliminate one major cause of labor disputes, but it will not stop all labor disputes. It does not cover all industry and labor, but is applicable only when violation of the legal right of independent self-organization would burden or obstruct interstate commerce. Accepted by management, labor and the public with a sense of sober responsibility and of willing cooperation, however, it should serve as an important step toward the achievement of just and peaceful labor relations in industry.

PRESIDENT FRANKLIN D. ROOSEVELT ADVOCATES SOCIAL SECURITY
14 August 1935

Perhaps the cruelest victims of the Depression were the aged poor. In the 1930s there were few established provisions for the countless men and women in their fifties and sixties whose working days ended so abruptly with the economic collapse. This genera-

tion of Americans had gone to work at the turn of the century, when care in old age remained exclusively a family concern. Earlier generations of rural Americans would conventionally retire to their children's homes, the family providing for its own. Now, in a new America where over half the population relied on wages and lived in cities, sustenance depended on a payroll check. Meager local relief resources, like space in "poorhouses," scarcely met the new conditions of mass poverty. Radical notions arose to address the social calamity. One came from Dr. Francis E. Townsend's Old Age Revolving Pensions plan. Each month, Townsend preached, the government would pay all citizens over the age of sixty $200, providing that they spent it immediately. The next month, another $200, another collective surge of purchasing power to revive the dormant economy. By early 1935, Townsend claimed 3.5 million adherents. In Louisiana, the remarkable Governor Huey P. Long launched his "Share Our Wealth Society," with lavish promises to support all poor people through taxing the rich. With seven or eight million supporters and national recognition, Long, with his sights set on the 1936 Presidential election, fell to an assassin's bullet in 1935. At the same time, other popular schemes competed for attention, raising the hopes of the poor and terrifying the rich. President Franklin D. Roosevelt's New Deal, attacked by both extremes, sought in The Social Security Act of 1935 to build a consensus to include business and labor. The legislation signed by President Roosevelt on 15 August 1935, depended upon moneys raised by taxing both employers and employees to create a fund to support a number of purposes. Social Security included pensions for aged, joint federal-state programs of unemployment insurance, provisions for dependent poor children and for the physically handicapped. The coverage assumed responsibility for citizens over the age of sixty-five not otherwise provided for. Critics favoring more generous and comprehensive coverage easily pointed out the weakness of Roosevelt's approach. Benefits, to begin in 1942, were relatively slight (ranging from $10 to $85 monthly), many categories of workers were not covered, and the taxes imposed were both regressive and deflationary. Critics from the opposite direction cited the traditional American reliance on personal responsibility and decried the entire idea. But Roosevelt correctly assumed that Social Security would grow in size and proceeds over time. One of the permanent achievements of the New Deal, Social Security represented a fundamental shift in the American concept of government in the assumption of responsibility for individual welfare.

Today a hope of many years' standing is in large part fulfilled. The civilization of the past hundred years, with its startling industrial changes, has tended more and more to make life insecure. Young people have come to wonder what would be their lot when they came to old age. The man with a job has wondered how long the job would last.

This social security measure gives at least some protection to thirty millions of our citizens who will reap direct benefits through unemployment compensation, through old-age pensions and through increased services for the protection of children and the prevention of ill health.

We can never insure one hundred percent of the population against one hundred percent of the hazards and vicissitudes of life, but we have tried to frame a law which will give some measure of protection to the average citizen and to his family against the loss of a job and against poverty-ridden old age.

This law, too, represents a cornerstone in a structure which is being built but is by no means complete. It is a structure intended to lessen the force of possible future depressions. It will act as a protection to future Administrations against the necessity of going deeply into debt to furnish relief to the needy. The law will flatten out the peaks and valleys of deflation and of inflation. It is, in short, a law that will take care of human needs and at the same time provide for the United States an economic structure of vastly greater soundness.

I congratulate all of you ladies and gentlemen, all of you in the Congress, in the executive departments and all of you who come from private life, and I thank you for your splendid efforts in behalf of this sound, needed and patriotic legislation.

If the Senate and the House of Representatives in this long and arduous session had done nothing more than pass this Bill, the session would be regarded as historic for all time.

PRESIDENT FRANKLIN D. ROOSEVELT'S ATTEMPT TO "REFORM" THE SUPREME COURT
5 February 1937

Emboldened by his landslide re-election in 1936, Franklin Delano Roosevelt soon committed the worst political blunder of his distinguished career. He had demolished Republican Alf Landon, Governor of Kansas, by 523–8 in the Electoral College, carried every state but two, won over 60 percent of the popular vote. His victory produced a 76 to 16 Democratic margin in the Senate, and a Democratic House by 331–89. With power and prestige soaring, the President quickly moved against the most formidable opponent of New Deal legislation, the Supreme Court of the United States. During his first term, the Court's majority adopted a narrow interpretation regarding the Federal Government's power to regulate interstate commerce. Already, nine major New Deal initiatives had been declared unconstitutional, and the Court's narrowness threw into doubt the legality of both the National Labor Relations Board (and collective bargaining), and the Social Security Act. The President acted on 5 February 1937 by announcing his plan to "reform" the Court, all nine of whose members had been appointed by his predecessors. He said he sought to ease the heavy workload of the six justices who were over seventy by appointing a new man to the Court for each of them. As other sitting justices reached their seventieth birthday, another would be appointed to join the Court, up to a total maximum of fifteen members. This radical trial balloon never left the ground, political and popular reaction stunning Roosevelt. Conservative politicians from both parties, constitutional scholars, newspapers from across the country—all were unanimous in their revulsion at tinkering with this basic American institution. Anti-Roosevelt partisans, so recently trounced in the presidential election, emerged in full roar against "that man in the White House." The debate in Congress, however heavily controlled by his own party, soon convinced the President to give up on an obviously lost cause. The defeat proved costly. Roosevelt's legislative program stagnated through the second term, and he would not regain his political preeminence until the valiant days of World War II. While the "Court Packing" debate went on, however, the Justices affirmed both the National Labor Relations Board (and collective bargaining) and the Social Security Act. Ironically, through his longest-ever Presidency, Roosevelt would reshape the Court by appointing eight Justices, the most of any President.

I have recently called the attention of the Congress to the clear need for a comprehensive program to reorganize the administrative machinery of the Executive Branch of our Government. I now make a similar recommendation to the Congress in regard to the Judicial Branch of the Government, in order that it also may function in accord with modern necessities.

The Constitution provides that the President "shall from time to time give to the Congress information of the State of the Union, and recommend to their consideration such measures as he shall judge necessary and expedient." No one else is given a similar mandate. It is therefore the duty of the President to advise the Congress in regard to the Judiciary whenever he deems such information or recommendation necessary.

I address you for the further reason that the Constitution vests in the Congress direct responsibility in the creation of courts and judicial offices and in the formulation of rules of practice and procedure. It is, therefore, one of the definite duties of the Congress constantly to maintain the effective functioning of the Federal Judiciary.

The Judiciary has often found itself handicapped by insufficient personnel with which to meet a growing and more complex business. It is true that the physical facilities of conducting the business of the courts have been greatly improved, in recent years, through the erection of suitable quarters, the provision of adequate libraries and the addition of subordinate court officers. But in many ways these are merely the trappings of judicial office. They play a minor part in the processes of justice. . . .

The simple fact is that today a new need for legislative action arises because the personnel of the Federal Judiciary is insufficient to meet the business before them. A growing body of our citizens complain of the complexities, the delays, and the expense of litigation in United States Courts. . . .

The attainment of speedier justice in the courts below will enlarge the task of the Supreme Court itself. And still more work would be added by the recommendation which I make later in this message for the quicker determination of constitutional questions by the highest court.

Even at the present time the Supreme Court is laboring under a heavy burden. Its difficulties in this respect were superficially lightened some years ago by authorizing the court, in its discretion, to refuse to hear appeals in many classes of cases. This discretion was so freely exercised that in the last fiscal year, although 867 petitions for review were presented to the Supreme Court, it declined to hear 717 cases. If petitions in behalf of the Government are excluded, it appears that the court permitted private litigants to prosecute appeals in only 108 cases out of 803 applications. Many of the refusals were doubtless warranted. But can it be said that full justice is achieved when a court is forced by the sheer necessity of keeping up with its business to decline, without even an explanation, to hear 87 percent of the cases presented to it by private litigants?

It seems clear, therefore, that the necessity of relieving present congestion extends to the enlargement of the capacity of all the federal courts.

A part of the problem of obtaining a sufficient number of judges to dispose of cases is the capacity of the judges themselves. This brings forward the question of aged or infirm judges—a subject of delicacy and yet one which requires frank discussion.

In the federal courts there are in all 237 life tenure permanent judgeships. Twenty-five of them are now held by judges over seventy years of age and eligible to leave the bench on full pay. Originally no pension or retirement allowance was provided by the Congress. When after eighty years of our national history the Congress made provision for pensions, it found a well-entrenched tradition among judges to cling to their posts, in many instances far beyond their years of physical or mental capacity. Their salaries were small. As with other men, responsibilities and obligations accumulated. No alternative had been open to them except to attempt to perform the duties of their offices to the very edge of the grave.

In exceptional cases, of course, judges, like other men, retain to an advanced age full mental and physical vigor. Those not so fortunate are often unable to perceive their own infirmities. . . .

With the opening of the twentieth century, and the great increase of population and commerce, and the growth of a more complex type of litigation, similar proposals were introduced in the Congress. To meet the situation, in 1913, 1914, 1915 and 1916, the Attorneys General then in office recommended to the Congress that when a district or a circuit judge failed to retire at the age of seventy, an additional judge be appointed in order that the affairs of the court might be promptly and adequately discharged.

In 1919 a law was finally passed providing that the President "may" appoint additional district and circuit judges, but only upon a finding that the incumbent judge over seventy "is unable to discharge efficiently all the duties of his office by reason of mental or physical disability of permanent character." The discretionary and indefinite nature of this legislation has rendered it ineffective. No President should be asked to determine the ability or disability of any particular judge.

The duty of a judge involves more than presiding or listening to testimony or arguments. It is well to remember that the mass of details involved in the average of law cases today is vastly greater and more complicated than even twenty years ago. Records and briefs must be read; statutes, decisions, and extensive material of a technical, scientific, statistical and economic nature must be searched and studied; opinions must be formulated and written. The modern tasks of judges call for the use of full energies.

Modern complexities call also for a constant infusion of new blood in the courts, just as it is needed in executive functions of the Government and in private business. A lowered mental or physical vigor leads men to avoid an examination of complicated and changed conditions. Little by little, new facts become blurred through old glasses fitted, as it were, for the needs of another generation; older men, assuming that the scene is the same as it was in the past, cease to explore or inquire into the present or the future.

We have recognized this truth in the civil service of the nation and of many states by compelling retirement on pay at the age of seventy. We have recognized it in the Army and Navy by retiring officers at the age of sixty-four. A number of states have recognized it by providing in their constitutions for compulsory retirement of aged judges.

Life tenure of judges, assured by the Constitution, was designed to place the courts beyond temptations or influences which might impair their judgments: it was not intended to create a static judiciary. A constant and systematic addition of younger blood will vitalize the courts and better equip them to recognize and apply the essential concepts of justice in the light of the needs and the facts of an ever-changing world.

It is obvious, therefore, from both reason and experience, that some provision must be adopted, which will operate automatically to supplement the work of older judges and accelerate the work of the court.

I, therefore, earnestly recommend that the necessity of an increase in the number of judges be supplied by legislation providing for the appointment of additional judges in all federal courts, without exception, where there are incumbent judges of retirement age who do not choose to retire or to resign. If an elder judge is not in fact incapacitated, only good can come from the presence of an additional judge in the crowded state of the dockets; if the capacity of an elder judge is in fact impaired, the appointment of an additional judge is indispensable. This seems to be a truth which cannot be contradicted.

I also recommend that the Congress provide machinery for taking care of sudden or long-standing congestion in the lower courts. The Supreme Court should be given power to appoint an administrative assistant who may be called a Proctor. He would be charged with the duty of watching the calendars and the business of all the courts in the federal system. The Chief Justice thereupon should be authorized to make a temporary assignment of any circuit or district judge hereafter appointed in order that he may serve as long as needed in any circuit or district where the courts are in arrears.

I attach a carefully considered draft of a proposed bill, which, if enacted, would, I am confident, afford substantial relief. The proposed measure also contains a limit on the total number of judges who might thus be appointed and also a limit on the potential size of any one of our federal courts.

These proposals do not raise any issue of constitutional law. They do not suggest any form of compulsory retirement for incumbent judges. Indeed, those who have reached the retirement age, but desire to continue their judicial work, would be able to do so under less physical and mental strain and would be able to play a useful part in relieving the growing congestion in the business of our courts. Among them are men of eminence and great ability whose services the Government would be loath to lose. If, on the other hand, any judge eligible for retirement should feel that his court would suffer because of an increase in its membership, he may retire or resign under already existing provisions of law if he wishes so to do. In this connection let me say that the pending proposal to extend to the Justices of the Supreme Court the same retirement privileges now available to other federal judges, has my entire approval.

One further matter requires immediate attention. We have witnessed the spectacle of conflicting decisions in both trial and appellate courts on the constitutionality of every form of important legislation. Such a welter of uncomposed differences of judicial opinion has brought the law, the courts, and, indeed, the entire administration of justice dangerously near to disrepute.

A federal statute is held legal by one judge in one district; it is simultaneously held illegal by another judge in another district. An act valid in one judicial circuit is invalid in another judicial circuit. Thus rights fully accorded to one group of citizens may be denied to others. As a practical matter this means that for periods running as long as one year or two years or three years—until final determination can be made by the Supreme Court—the law loses its most indispensable element—equality.

Moreover, during the long processes of preliminary motions, original trials, petitions for rehearings, appeals, reversals on technical grounds requiring re-trials, motions before the Supreme Court and the final hearing by the highest tribunal—during all this time labor, industry, agriculture, commerce and the Government itself go through an unconscionable period of uncertainty and embarrassment. And it is well to remember that during these long processes the normal operations of society and government are handicapped in many cases by differing and divided opinions in the lower courts and by the lack of any clear guide for the dispatch of business. Thereby our legal system is fast losing another essential of justice—certainty.

Finally, we find the processes of government itself brought to a complete stop from time to time by injunctions issued almost automatically, sometimes even without notice to the Government, and not infrequently in clear violation of the principle of equity that injunctions should be granted only in those rare cases of manifest illegality and irreparable damage against which the ordinary course of the law offers no protection. Statutes which the Congress enacts are set aside or suspended for long periods of time, even in cases to which the Government is not a party.

In the uncertain state of the law, it is not difficult for the ingenious to devise novel reasons for attacking the validity of new legislation or its application. While these questions are laboriously brought to issue and debated through a series of courts, the Government must stand aside. It matters not that the Congress has enacted the law, that the Executive has signed it and that the administrative machinery is waiting to function. Government by injunction lays a heavy hand upon normal processes; and no important statute can take effect—against any individual or organization with the means to employ lawyers and engage in wide-flung litigation—until it has passed through the whole hierarchy of the courts. Thus the judiciary, by postponing the effective date of Acts of the Congress, is assuming an additional function and is coming more and more to constitute a scattered, loosely organized and slowly operating third house of the National Legislature.

This state of affairs has come upon the nation gradually over a period of decades. In my annual message to this Congress I expressed some views and some hopes.

Now, as an immediate step, I recommend that the Congress provide that no decision, injunction, judgment or decree on any constitutional question be promulgated by any federal court without previous and ample notice to the Attorney General and an opportunity for the United States to present evidence and be heard. This is to prevent court action on the constitutionality of Acts of the Congress in suits between private individuals, where the Government is not a party to the suit, without giving opportunity to the Government of the United States to defend the law of the land.

I also earnestly recommend that in cases in which any court of first instance determines a question of constitutionality, the Congress provide that there shall be a direct and immediate appeal to the Supreme Court, and that such cases take precedence over all other matters pending in that court. Such legislation will, I am convinced, go far to alleviate the in-equality, uncertainty and delay in the disposition of vital questions of constitutionality arising under our fundamental law.

My desire is to strengthen the administration of justice and to make it a more effective servant of public need. In the American ideal of government the courts find an essential and constitutional place. In striving to fulfill that ideal, not only the judges but the Congress and the Executive as well, must do all in their power to bring the judicial organization and personnel to the high standards of usefulness which sound and efficient government and modem conditions require. . . .

PRESIDENT FRANKLIN D. ROOSEVELT ANNOUNCES THE "LEND-LEASE" PLAN TO AID GREAT BRITAIN
10 June 1941

On 3 September 1939, two days after Germany's invasion of Poland began World War II, President Franklin D. Roosevelt spoke to the American people. "This nation will remain a neutral nation," he assured Americans, "but I cannot ask that every American remain neutral in thought as well." Both friend and foe understood perfectly well that the President supported Great Britain and the other enemies of Nazi Germany. Beginning with his 4 January 1939, State of the Union message, Roosevelt had sought to warn Americans of the mounting danger to democracy itself. Through the months immediately preceding war, he worked toward balancing power. Thus in the summer of 1939, the President won modification of the prevailing ban on American arms sales, and abrogated a longstanding trade agreement with Japan. Yet when World War II began on 1 September, Germany and Japan enjoyed huge military advantages. In the twenty-six months which remained before the Japanese attack on Pearl Harbor brought the United States officially into the war, and despite substantial political obstacles, the clever and imaginative Roosevelt found means just short of war to assist the beleaguered British. The President faced considerable domestic opposition. Isolationist conviction had developed from the bleakness of the Depression as well as through a popular conviction that entering World War I had been a great mistake. Furthermore, Roosevelt had decided to run for an unprecedented third term, and could not afford to move too dramatically. Yet through 1940 and 1941, the association of the United States with the British became evident. "Cash-and-Carry" and "Lend-Lease" entered the American vocabulary. Secretly, the plans discussed by Roosevelt with British Prime Minister Winston S. Churchill, and the increasingly frequent contacts between their military staffs, made the United States a virtual ally of Britain. The Lend-Lease arrangement, one memorable element of Roosevelt's maneuvering through this crisis, presented the Congress with an unlikely scenario in the beguiling rhetoric of Roosevelt at his dramatic best. In March 1941, the Senate approved, 60–31; and the House of Representatives, 260–165. President Roosevelt reported on its results.

. . . We have supplied, and we will supply, planes, guns, ammunition, and other defense articles in ever-increasing quantities to Britain, China, and other democracies resisting aggression.

Wars are not won by guns alone, but wars are not won without guns. We all know this full well now. Beginning with the outbreak of the war the American public began to realize that it was in our own national interest and security to help Britain, China, and other democratic Nations.

Beginning with the outbreak of the war British and French orders began to be placed. But dollars could not be immediately turned into airplanes and ships and guns and ammunition.

In those dark days when France was falling, it was clear that this Government, to carry out the will of the people, had to render aid over and above the matériel coming off the assembly line. This Government, therefore, made available all that it possibly could out of its surplus stocks of munitions.

In June of 1940, the British Government received from our surplus stocks rifles, machine guns, field artillery, ammunition, and aircraft in a value of more than 43 million dollars. This was equipment that would have taken months and months to produce and which, with the exception of the aircraft, cost about 300 million dollars to produce during the World War period. Most of this matériel would not have been usable if we had kept it much longer. This equipment arrived in Britain after the retreat from Dunkirk, where the British had lost great quantities of guns and other military supplies. No one can appraise what effect the delivery of these supplies had upon the successful British resistance in the summer and fall of 1940 when they were fighting against such terrific odds.

Since June 1940, this Government has continued to supply war matériel from its surplus stocks, in addition to the matériel produced by private manufacturers. The fifty over-age destroyers which Britain received in exchange for the defense bases were a part of the aid supplied by the Government.

By the turn of the year 1941, the British commitments in this country for defense articles had reached the limit of their future dollar resources. Their striking power required the assurance that their munitions and equipment would steadily and certainly be augmented, not curtailed.

The will of our people, as expressed through the Congress, was to meet this problem, not only by the passage of the Lend-Lease Act but by the appropriation of 7 billion dollars made on 27 March of this year to carry out this task.

In the ninety days since the Lend-Lease Act was passed, and in the seventy-four days since the funds were appropriated, we have started in motion the vast supply program which is essential to the defeat of the Axis powers.

In these seventy-four days, more than 4 1/4 billion dollars out of the 7 billion dollars have been allocated to the War, Navy, Agriculture, and Treasury Departments and to the Maritime Commission to procure the aid authorized. Contracts have been let for long-range bombers, ships, tanks, and the other sinews of war that will be needed for the defense of the democracies. The balance of less than 2 3/4 billion is being rapidly allocated.

To be effective, the aid rendered by us must be many sided. Ships are necessary to carry the munitions and the food. We are immediately making available to Britain 2 million gross tons of cargo ships and oil tankers.

But this is not enough. Adequate shipping for every day to come must be reasonably assured. Since the Appropriation Act was passed, 550 million dollars has been allocated for the construction of new ships under the Lend-Lease Act. Contracts have been let and the new ways required to build these ships are now nearing completion. Allied ships are being repaired by us. Allied ships are being equipped by us to protect them from mines, and are being armed by us to protect them as much as possible against raiders. Naval vessels of Britain are being repaired by us so that they can return quickly to their naval tasks.

The training program of 7,000 British pilots in our schools in this country is under way. Valuable information is being communicated, and other material assistance is being rendered in a mounting benefit to the democracies.

Millions of pounds of food are being and will be sent. Iron and steel, machine tools and the other essentials to maintain and increase the production of war materials in Britain are being sent and received in larger quantities day by day.

Since September 1939, the war goods sent to Britain have risen steadily. The over-all total exports to the British Empire have greatly increased in 1941 over 1940. What is more important, the increase of those things which are necessary for fighting have increased far beyond our other exports. In the first five months of this year we have sent more than twelve times as many airplanes to Britain as we did in the first five months of 1940. For the first four months of this year the dollar value of explosives sent to the British Empire was about seventeen times as much as for the first four months of 1940. Ninety times as much in dollar value of firearms and ammunition was sent to Britain during the first four months of this year as for the first four months of 1940.

With our national resources, our productive capacity, and the genius of our people for mass production we will help Britain to outstrip the Axis powers in munitions of war, and we will see to it that these munitions get to the places where they can be effectively used to weaken and defeat the aggressors. . . .

PRESIDENT FRANKLIN D. ROOSEVELT'S MESSAGE OF WAR AGAINST JAPAN
8 December 1941

On 25 July 1941, in response to the Japanese seizure of French Indochina, President Franklin D. Roosevelt froze all Japanese assets in the United States, halting trade and denying to Japan strategic materials necessary to her industrial base. While Japanese diplomats pledged to seek a peaceful resolution to the intensifying hostility between the two nations, the Japanese Imperial Government concentrated on war plans. Early in November, the American Embassy in Tokyo reported on plans for a sneak attack on undetermined American military bases. Realizing that only American naval power stood in the way of its own great imperial plans, Japan struck. On Sunday morning 7 December 1941, just before 8 A.M., an aircraft-based armada of Japanese planes surprised the U.S. fleet assembled at Pearl Harbor on the Hawaiian island of Oahu. Nineteen ships (including six battleships) were sunk or disabled, 150 planes destroyed, and 2,403 soldiers, sailors and civilians killed. The next day, Roosevelt came to Congress asking for war. The Senate approved, 82–0, and the House of Representatives, 388–1. The sole dissenter, Rep. Jeannette Rankin of Montana, the first woman ever to sit in the House, had also voted against the war declaration in 1917. The President convinced everyone else.

Yesterday, 7 December 7 1941—a date which will live in infamy—the United States of America was suddenly and deliberately attacked by naval and air forces of the Empire of Japan.

The United States was at peace with that Nation and, at the solicitation of Japan, was still in conversation with its Government and its Emperor looking toward the maintenance of peace in the

Pacific. Indeed, one hour after Japanese air squadrons had commenced bombing in the American Island of Oahu, the Japanese Ambassador to the United States and his colleague delivered to our Secretary of State a formal reply to a recent American message. And while this reply stated that it seemed useless to continue the existing diplomatic negotiations, it contained no threat or hint of war or of armed attack.

It will be recorded that the distance of Hawaii from Japan makes it obvious that the attack was deliberately planned many days or even weeks ago. During the intervening time the Japanese Government has deliberately sought to deceive the United States by false statements and expressions of hope for continued peace.

The attack yesterday on the Hawaiian Islands has caused severe damage to American naval and military forces. I regret to tell you that very many American lives have been lost. In addition American ships have been reported torpedoed on the high seas between San Francisco and Honolulu.

Yesterday the Japanese Government also launched an attack against Malaya.

Last night Japanese forces attacked Hong Kong.

Last night Japanese forces attacked Guam.

Last night Japanese forces attacked the Philippine Islands.

Last night the Japanese attacked Wake Island.

And this morning the Japanese attacked Midway Island.

Japan has, therefore, undertaken a surprise offensive extending throughout the Pacific area. The facts of yesterday and today speak for themselves. The people of the United States have already formed their opinions and well understand the implications to the very life and safety of our Nation.

As Commander in Chief of the Army and Navy I have directed that all measures be taken for our defense.

But always will our whole Nation remember the character of the onslaught against us.

No matter how long it may take us to overcome this premeditated invasion, the American people in their righteous might will win through to absolute victory.

I believe that I interpret the will of the Congress and of the people when I assert that we will not only defend ourselves to the uttermost but will make it very certain that this form of treachery shall never again endanger us.

Hostilities exist. There is no blinking at the fact that our people, our territory, and our interests are in grave danger.

With confidence in our armed forces—with the unbounding determination of our people—we will gain the inevitable triumph—so help us God.

I ask that the Congress declare that since the unprovoked and dastardly attack by Japan on Sunday, 7 December 1941, a state of war has existed between the United States and the Japanese Empire.

PRESIDENT HARRY S. TRUMAN ANNOUNCES THE DROPPING OF AN ATOMIC BOMB ON JAPAN
6 August 1945

6 August 1945, began with President Harry S. Truman aboard the U.S.S. Augusta as it neared the North American coast south of Newfoundland. He was returning home from the Potsdam Conference meeting with the British and Soviet Russian heads of state which had been held amid the rubble of destroyed and defeated Berlin. Only four months before, Harry Truman had first appeared on the world stage as America recoiled at the death of his legendary predecessor, Franklin Delano Roosevelt. Truman immediately established himself as a very different kind of man, plain-spoken, sometimes bluntly aggressive. By August President Truman had already overseen the inauguration of the United Nations, announced the death of Hitler and defeat of Nazism, and assumed command of the still-brutal war against Japan. He spent three weeks in Potsdam, joining Winston Churchill and his successor as Prime Minister Clement Atlee in vigorous negotiation with Joseph Stalin. On the negotiating table lay the fate of Germany and all of Eastern Europe. Yet for Truman the crucial issue remained Japan, still-powerful and recalcitrant, and obtaining Stalin's military assistance in its defeat. At Potsdam the President was told the astonishing details about the testing of a nuclear device in the New Mexico desert. He tried to imagine a "huge ball of fire . . . a lighting effect within a radius of 20 miles, equal to several suns in midday." Truman weighed the use of atomic power against his advisors assurance that an invasion of Japan would cost 250,000 American casualties. He ordered the bomb dropped. Three weeks later, on 6 August at about 8 A.M. three Army Air Force B-29s appeared over Hiroshima, a city of about 340,000 people. The lead plane, the Enola Gay released the first atomic bomb from 31,600 feet. An intense flash of light momentarily blinded the fliers. The plane trembled in the shock, as the men saw the huge mushroom-shaped cloud of debris rise 40,000 feet into the atmosphere. Below, an eruption of suffocating heat covered the city. Four of every five buildings were blown apart, and 130,000 people died in a flash. Surrender would soon follow. No American lives would be spent invading Japan. Truman knew this, and the martial mood on the ship buoyed his spirits as he joined the crew and listened to the radio broadcast of a statement just issued in his name at the White House.

A short time ago an American airplane dropped one bomb on Hiroshima and destroyed its usefulness to the enemy. That bomb has more power than 20,000 tons of T.N.T.

The Japanese began the war from the air at Pearl Harbor. They have been repaid many fold. And the end is not yet. With this bomb we have now added a new and revolutionary increase in destruction to supplement the growing power of our armed forces. In their present form these bombs are now in production and even more powerful forms are in development.

It is an atomic bomb. It is a harnessing of the basic power of the universe. The force from which the sun draws its power has been loosed against those who brought war to the Far East.

We have spent more than two billion dollars on the greatest scientific gamble in history—and we have won.

But the greatest marvel is not the size of the enterprise, its secrecy, or its cost, but the achievement of scientific brains in making it work. And hardly less marvellous has been the capacity of industry to design, and of labor to operate, the machines and methods to do things never done before. Both science and industry worked under the direction of the United States Army, which achieved a unique success in an amazingly short time. It is doubtful if such another combination could be got together in the world. What has been done is the greatest achievement of organized science in history.

We are now prepared to obliterate more rapidly and completely every productive enterprise the Japanese have in any city. We shall destroy their docks, their factories, and their communications. Let there be no mistake; we shall completely destroy Japan's power to make war.

It was to spare the Japanese people from utter destruction that the ultimatum of 26 July was issued at Potsdam. Their leaders promptly rejected that ultimatum. If they do not now accept our terms they may expect a rain of ruin from the air, the like of which has never been seen on this earth. Behind this air attack will follow sea and land forces in such numbers and power as they have not yet seen and with the fighting skill of which they are already well aware.

PRESIDENT HARRY S. TRUMAN ANNOUNCES THE "TRUMAN DOCTRINE" TO COUNTER THE SOVIET UNION
12 March 1947

From the end of World War II in August 1945 until the fateful spring of 1947, the Soviet Union and the United States confirmed each other's worst fears. For Stalin, personally paranoid but historically conscious about the advance of invaders toward Russia, the Americans interest in spreading trade networks and democratic institutions into his Eastern European sphere of influence seemed an obvious imperialist plan. From Washington, the revolutionary rhetoric and military might of the USSR appeared to imperil the people and wealth of Europe. Many American observers took the Soviet Union's Marxist-Leninist rhetoric literally and concluded that world conquest was indeed Stalin's objective, with control of Eastern Europe the first step. In March 1946, Winston Churchill described an Iron Curtain sealing off Eastern Europe's Soviet-allied "police governments." Acrimonious meetings between representatives of the two superpowers reflected tension and suspicion. American nuclear testing continued. All across Europe, the war torn lands of both victors and vanquished teemed with the hopeless and hungry. Even proud Britain, long a dominant world power and the bulwark against Hitler, had paid too large a price in resources. The terrible winter of 1946–47 froze the continent, hitting England hardest. In February, London secretly notified Washington that it would be compelled to abandon its traditional political and economic role in southeastern Europe. This meant withdrawing from Greece just at the moment when a royalist government struggled against a leftist uprising. The Soviets claimed that the Greek civil war remained exclusively an internal matter between Greek factions. The Americans did not believe them. The resulting Truman Doctrine broke historic American tradition, for the United States had always avoided foreign commitments in peacetime. While Truman referred specifically to helping Greece and Turkey, his speech appeared open-ended, a pledge to support all friendly nations against subversion from within and aggression from without. To win over the traditionally isolationist American public, Truman took one senator's advice to "scare hell out of the people."

Mr. President, Mr. Speaker, Members of the Congress of the United States:

The gravity of the situation which confronts the world today necessitates my appearance before a joint session of the Congress.

The foreign policy and the national security of this country are involved.

One aspect of the present situation, which I present to you at this time for your consideration and decision, concerns Greece and Turkey.

The United States has received from the Greek Government an urgent appeal for financial and economic assistance. Preliminary reports from the American Economic Mission now in Greece and reports from the American Ambassador in Greece corroborate the statement of the Greek Government that assistance is imperative if Greece is to survive as a free nation.

I do not believe that the American people and the Congress wish to turn a deaf ear to the appeal of the Greek Government.

Greece is not a rich country. Lack of sufficient natural resources has always forced the Greek people to work hard to make both ends meet. Since 1940, this industrious, peace loving country has suffered invasion, four years of cruel enemy occupation, and bitter internal strife.

When forces of liberation entered Greece they found that the retreating Germans had destroyed virtually all the railways, roads, port facilities, communications, and merchant marine. More than a thousand villages had been burned. Eighty-five percent of the children were tubercular. Livestock, poultry, and draft animals had almost disappeared. Inflation had wiped out practically all savings.

As a result of these tragic conditions, a militant minority, exploiting human want and misery, was able to create political chaos which, until now, has made economic recovery impossible.

Greece is today without funds to finance the importation of those goods which are essential to bare subsistence. Under these circumstances the people of Greece cannot make progress in solving their problems of reconstruction. Greece is in desperate need of financial and economic assistance to enable it to resume purchases of food, clothing, fuel and seeds. These are indispensable for the subsistence of its people and are obtainable only from abroad. Greece must have help to import the goods necessary to restore internal order and security so essential for economic and political recovery.

The Greek Government has also asked for the assistance of experienced American administrators, economists and technicians to insure that the financial and other aid given to Greece shall be used effectively in creating a stable and self-sustaining economy and in improving its public administration.

The very existence of the Greek state is today threatened by the terrorist activities of several thousand armed men, led by Communists, who defy the government's authority at a number of points, particularly along the northern boundaries. A Commission appointed by the United Nations Security Council is at present investigating disturbed conditions in northern Greece and alleged border violations along the frontier between Greece on the one hand and Albania, Bulgaria, and Yugoslavia on the other.

Meanwhile, the Greek Government is unable to cope with the situation. The Greek army is small and poorly equip-ped. It needs supplies and equipment if it is to restore authority to the government throughout Greek territory.

Greece must have assistance if it is to become a self-supporting and self-respecting democracy.

The United States must supply this assistance. We have already extended to Greece certain types of relief and economic aid but these are inadequate.

There is no other country to which democratic Greece can turn.

No other nation is willing and able to provide the necessary support for a democratic Greek government.

The British Government, which has been helping Greece, can give no further financial or economic aid after 31 March. Great Britain finds itself under the necessity of reducing or liquidating its commitments in several parts of the world, including Greece.

We have considered how the United Nations might assist in this crisis. But the situation is an urgent one requiring immediate action, and the United

Nations and its related organizations are not in a position to extend help of the kind that is required. . . .

The Greek Government has been operating in an atmosphere of chaos and extremism. It has made mistakes. The extension of aid by this country does not mean that the United States condones everything that the Greek Government has done or will do. We have condemned in the past, and we condemn now, extremist measures of the right or the left. We have in the past advised tolerance, and we advise tolerance now.

Greece's neighbor, Turkey, also deserves our attention.

The future of Turkey as an independent and economically sound state is clearly no less important to the freedom-loving peoples of the world than the future of Greece. The circumstances in which Turkey finds itself today are considerably different from those of Greece. Turkey has been spared the disasters that have beset Greece. And during the war, the United States and Great Britain furnished Turkey with material aid.

Nevertheless, Turkey now needs our support.

Since the war Turkey has sought additional financial assistance from Great Britain and the United States for the purpose of effecting that modernization necessary for the maintenance of its national integrity.

That integrity is essential to the preservation of order in the Middle East.

The British Government has informed us that, owing to its own difficulties, it can no longer extend financial or economic aid to Turkey.

As in the case of Greece, if Turkey is to have the assistance it needs, the United States must supply it. We are the only country able to provide that help.

I am fully aware of the broad implications involved if the United States extends assistance to Greece and Turkey, and I shall discuss these implications with you at this time.

One of the primary objectives of the foreign policy of the United States is the creation of conditions in which we and other nations will be able to work out a way of life free from coercion. This was a fundamental issue in the war with Germany and Japan. Our victory was won over countries which sought to impose their will, and their way of life, upon other nations.

To ensure the peaceful development of nations, free from coercion, the United States has taken a leading part in establishing the United Nations. The United Nations is designed to make possible lasting freedom and independence for all its members. We shall not realize our objectives, however, unless we are willing to help free peoples to maintain their free institutions and their national integrity against aggressive movements that seek to impose upon them totalitarian regimes. This is no more than a frank recognition that totalitarian regimes imposed upon free peoples, by direct or indirect aggression, undermine the foundations of international peace and hence the security of the United States.

The peoples of a number of countries of the world have recently had totalitarian regimes forced upon them against their will. The Government of the United States has made frequent protests against coercion and intimidation, in violation of the Yalta agreement, in Poland, Rumania, and Bulgaria. I must also state that in a number of other countries there have been similar developments.

At the present moment in world history nearly every nation must choose between alternative ways of life. The choice is too often not a free one.

One way of life is based upon the will of the majority, and is distinguished by free institutions, representative government, free elections, guarantees of individual liberty, freedom of speech and religion, and freedom from political oppression.

The second way of life is based upon the will of a minority forcibly imposed upon the majority. It relies upon terror and oppression, a controlled press and radio, fixed elections, and the suppression of personal freedoms.

I believe that it must be the policy of the United States to support free peoples who are resisting attempted subjugation by armed minorities or by outside pressures.

I believe that we must assist free peoples to work out their own destinies in their own way.

I believe that our help should be primarily through economic and financial aid which is essential to economic stability and orderly political processes.

The world is not static, and the *status quo* is not sacred. But we cannot allow changes in the *status quo* in violation of the Charter of the United Nations by such methods as coercion, or by such subterfuges as political infiltration. In helping free and independent nations to maintain their freedom, the United States will be giving effect to the principles of the Charter of the United Nations.

It is necessary only to glance at a map to realize that the survival and integrity of the Greek nation are of grave importance in a much wider situation. If Greece should fall under the control of an armed minority, the effect upon its neighbor, Turkey, would be immediate and serious. Confusion and disorder might well spread throughout the entire Middle East.

Moreover, the disappearance of Greece as an independent state would have a profound effect upon those countries in Europe whose peoples are struggling against great difficulties to maintain their freedoms and their independence while they repair the damages of war.

It would be an unspeakable tragedy if these countries, which have struggled so long against overwhelming odds, should lose that victory for which they sacrificed so much. Collapse of free institutions and loss of independence would be disastrous not only for them but for the world. Discouragement and possibly failure would quickly be the lot of neighboring peoples striving to maintain their freedom and independence.

Should we fail to aid Greece and Turkey in this fateful hour, the effect will be far reaching to the West as well as to the East.

We must take immediate and resolute action.

I therefore ask the Congress to provide authority for assistance to Greece and Turkey in the amount of $400,000,000 for the period ending 30 June 1948. In requesting these funds, I have taken into consideration the maximum amount of relief assistance which would be furnished to Greece out of the $350,000,000 which I recently requested that the Congress authorize for the prevention of starvation and suffering in countries devastated by the war.

In addition to funds, I ask the Congress to authorize the detail of American civilian and military personnel to Greece and Turkey, at the request of those countries, to assist in the tasks of reconstruction, and for the purpose of supervising the use of such financial and material assistance as may be furnished. I recommend that authority also be provided for the instruction and training of selected Greek and Turkish personnel.

Finally, I ask that the Congress provide authority which will permit the speediest and most effective use, in terms of needed commodities, supplies, and equipment, of such funds as may be authorized.

If further funds, or further authority, should be needed for the purposes indicated in this message, I shall not hesitate to bring the situation before the Congress. On this subject the Executive and Legislative branches of the Government must work together.

This is a serious course upon which we embark.

I would not recommend it except that the alternative is much more serious.

The United States contributed $341,000,000,000 toward winning World War II. This is an investment in world freedom and world peace.

The assistance that I am recommending for Greece and Turkey amounts to little more than $1/10$ of 1 percent of this investment. It is only common sense that we should safeguard this investment and make sure that it was not in vain.

The seeds of totalitarian regimes are nurtured by misery and want. They spread and grow in the evil soil of poverty and strife. They reach their full growth when the hope of a people for a better life has died.

We must keep that hope alive.

The free peoples of the world look to us for support in maintaining their freedoms.

If we falter in our leadership, we may endanger the peace of the world—and we shall surely endanger the welfare of this Nation.

Great responsibilities have been placed upon us by the swift movement of events.

I am confident that the Congress will face these responsibilities squarely.

PRESIDENT HARRY S. TRUMAN ANNOUNCES DIPLOMATIC RECOGNITION OF THE STATE OF ISRAEL
14 May 1948

The spring of 1948 was the worst of times for Harry S. Truman as the world's politics seemed to career toward catastrophe. On 17 March, he went before a joint session of Congress to call for immediate passage of the Marshall Plan and reinstatement of the draft, expensive and troubling measures—especially in an election year. The President justified himself by citing Soviet provocation. In February, a Moscow-inspired coup in Czechoslovakia created a satellite state there, rudely echoing Hitler's seizure of Czechoslovakia a decade earlier. Ominous intelligence reports centered on Berlin, where American and Allied occupation sectors were isolated inside the Soviet military zone. Despite all of these concerns, the most emotionally volatile issue before Truman lay in the Middle East, where determined Jews insisted that a homeland be carved out of Palestine. This objective of modern Zionism arose late in the 19th century but met decades of opposition, ridicule and delay. Palestine, for centuries part of the Ottoman Empire, had passed to British control in World War I. In 1917, the so-called Balfour Declaration issued in London committed the British to the creation, sometime, of a Jewish state. After World War II, Britain's diminished world role produced the announcement that in May 1948, it would withdraw its 50,000 troops from Palestine. Zionists around the world demanded the partition of Palestine, part to be Arab, part a new Jewish state. Implacable Arab opposition promised to "push the Jews into the sea." As the date for British withdrawal neared, moral, political, and strategic pressures on Truman grew nearly intolerable. The President freely acknowledged the effects of unimaginable Holocaust suffering, and the need for the refuge of a homeland after all the centuries of Diaspora prejudice. Yet his Joint Chiefs and State Department stood determinedly against recognition. Postpone, they demanded, throw the problem to the UN, do not jeopardize relations with the Arab states, lose their oil, and drive them toward the Soviet Union. Two days before the deadline the debate continued to rage inside the White House, opposition to recognition led by Secretary of State George C. Marshall, whom Truman respected more than any man in Washington. The moment arrived at 6 P.M. on 14 May 1948. Eleven minutes later, President Truman, signed it.

This government has been informed that a Jewish state has been proclaimed in Palestine, and recognition has been requested by the provisional government thereof.

The United States recognizes the provisional government as the de facto authority of the new State of Israel.

PRESIDENT HARRY S. TRUMAN'S "WHISTLESTOP" CAMPAIGN FOR REELECTION
11 October 1948

The bipartisan support enjoyed by President Harry S. Truman during the early Cold War years did not translate to his domestic programs. These times of complex and difficult transition from a wartime to peacetime economy, produced a political nightmare for Truman. At one point, automobiles, razor blades, nylon stockings, electrical appliances and cigarettes—even meat—were either unavailable or in such short supply that pent-up savings drove prices skyward, producing a dangerous increase in inflation. Industrialists chafed under government controls, workers demanded the end of wages frozen during the war. A rash of angry, sometimes violent strikes affected basic industries. Truman was pounded from all sides, nastily lampooned by political cartoonists as a little man far out of his depth. As one measure of protest, the Republicans swept the 1946 midterm elections, gaining control of both Houses of Congress for the first time since the days of Herbert Hoover in 1930. With Truman's popular approval rating around 30 percent, the GOP eagerly awaited the 1948 election. They nominated a ticket of two popular and progressive governors, Thomas E. Dewey of New York, and Earl Warren of California, men who represented states with seventy-two electoral votes. Meanwhile, the Republican 80th Congress had stymied Truman's legislative program. More seriously, the Democratic party began to fragment. Southern conservatives objected to Truman's views on civil rights, coalesced behind South Carolina Governor Strom Thurmond, and threatened to leave the party (which they soon did). The progressive left-wing Democrats objected to the President's strong measures against Soviet Russia, and looked for leadership from former Secretary of Commerce Henry A. Wallace, whom Truman had fired for his views on foreign policy. The Progressives also deserted the Democrats. With the Republicans controlling the political landscape and his own party disintegrating, Truman never flinched. He accepted nomination in Philadelphia in July with a blistering attack on Congress, then recalled them into special session ten days later and dared them to approve his social and economic programs. When the Congress achieved nothing, Truman had his campaign theme, the "do-nothing, good-for-nothing 80th Congress." Governor Dewey ran a confident almost smug campaign, assuming victory. Governor Thurmond stayed in the Deep South, promising the continuation of segregation. Henry Wallace found only isolated support for his pleas for disarmament and reconciliation with the Soviets. Meanwhile, President Truman alone thundered across the political stage, relentlessly attacking the Republicans, defending his foreign and domestic policy. The highlight of the underdog campaign was Truman's 30,000-mile "whistle-stop" campaign aboard a special train, as he delivered scores of speeches in cities, towns and crossroads hamlets wherever he could find voters. On 11 October, one characteristic speech from the back end of his train occurred in the rail-

road town of Willard, Ohio, most of whose 4,000 people listened to the President. Three weeks later, after election night, when the Republican Chicago Tribune headlined "Dewey Defeats Truman," the President awoke to the greatest political upset in American history.

WILLARD, OHIO (Rear platform, 4:55 P.M.)

I have had a most wonderful reception in Ohio today. It has been just like this all across the State of Ohio. We started in Cincinnati and came up the western border of the State, and now we are headed for Akron, and it seems as if everybody in the neighborhood and in every city has turned out, because they are interested in what is taking place in the country today and in the world.

It is good to be here in Willard this afternoon, even for a short stop. You people here in Willard have a great tradition, a tradition set by Dan Willard many years ago when he was President of the Baltimore and Ohio Railroad. I think it is significant that the name of Dan Willard is loved and respected all over the country, because he was the man who believed in the common people of the Nation. He liked and respected the people who worked for him, and he recognized their right to join a union and bargain collectively.

Now, Dan Willard did not sneer at the "whistlestops" of our country. He trusted people, and people trusted him. I think that is a good principle. It is a good way to run a railroad, and it is a good way to run a country. That is the way I have tried to run the country, but the Republican Congress would not cooperate, this 80th Congress.

Now, that is the way, with your help, we are going to run the country for the next 4 years.

The Republican candidate and the Republican Congress do not trust the people. They just work along at their old problem of trying to fool the people into voting for the interests of the few. They try to do it without telling you what they think. I have been out among the people now for nearly a month. I believe you have got a right to know what I think, and I have been telling you what I think.

Tonight, in Akron, I am going to talk over the radio about the Republican Taft-Hartley law. I am really going to tear the mask off the Republican Congress and the Republican candidate.

In Cincinnati this morning, at a splendid meeting, I talked about housing. I told the people there how your President had tried for 3 years to get a decent housing bill passed. At other places we stopped at in Ohio, I talked about prices. I told the people how your President had twice called Congress into special session in an effort to get something done about inflation that is picking your pockets.

Since I have been in the White House, there has not been a moment of doubt about where I stood on issues which are of concern to the people of America today. I have always spoken out and I have taken a stand on every issue as it has come up. I don't wait for any polls to tell me what to think. That is a statement some of the Republican candidates cannot make.

You know, since I started this campaign, I have talked to over 3 million people in various communities. They have come down to the train, just as you did this afternoon, because they were interested in this election. They know that the peace of the Nation and the peace of the world depend, to a large extent, on this election. They know that the continued prosperity of our Nation depends upon this election, and they want to know where the candidates stand on the issues. And that is what I have been telling you as simply and as plainly as I know how.

There is not a single, solitary man or woman in the United States today who can't find out in two minutes where I stand on the important matters like foreign policy, labor, agriculture, social security, housing, high prices, and all the other problems we as a nation have to face.

But there is not a single, solitary man or woman in the United States who has been able, within the last 2 months, to find out where the Re-publican candidate stands on these issues.

I think he is going to get a shock on the second of November. He is going to get the results of one big poll that counts—that is the voice of the American people speaking at the ballot box.

And he is going to find out that the people have had enough of such fellows as the one from this district who has been helping the 80th Congress to turn the clock back. And I think you are going to elect Dwight Blackmore to Congress in his place. And I think you are going to elect Frank Lausche Governor of Ohio.

If you do that, you will be voting in your own interests, and when you vote in your own interests on the second of November, you cannot do anything else but vote the straight Democratic ticket, and I won't be troubled with the housing problem. I will live in the White House 4 more years.

Now, that will be entirely to your interests. You will have a Congress who believes in the people, and you will have a President who has shown you right along that he believes in the welfare of the country as a whole, and not in the welfare of just a few at the top.

President Harry S. Truman Fires General Douglas MacArthur
11 April 1951

On 25 June 1950, communist forces of North Korea crossed the demarcation line established by the United Nations and invaded South Korea. President Harry S. Truman mobilized the United Nations against the aggression, committing American military power as the basis for U.N. action. For the first ten weeks, the battle raged near the southern end of the peninsula, where United Nations forces faced military defeat. In September the battle turned following the landing of American and allied troops behind enemy lines at the port of Inchon, a brilliant strategic maneuver planned and executed by the U.N. commander, General Douglas MacArthur. His forces pressed vigorously to the far northern border-lands of China, and full victory seemed possible. On 26 November, China entered the war in a massive counter-offensive, which again moved the front toward the 38th parallel line, the original demarcation line. At this point in Washington, President Truman and his ad-visors agreed to enter negotiations with enemy forces on the basis of achieving the status quo ante bellum. Truman's thinking reflected a global strategy that placed emphasis on the defense and unity of Europe and the status quo in Asia. To the President, Korea merely re-flected a Soviet and Chinese attempt to divert American policy from Europe by causing in-stability throughout Asia. Consequently, on 20 March 1951, the White House released a carefully worded offer to negotiate with the Chinese and North Koreans on the basis of the boundary line that existed before the war. MacArthur stunned the President a few days later when he issued a statement that simultaneously identified, threatened, and de-meaned "Red China," America's "real enemy." At the same time, the General wrote to Congressman Joseph W. Martin, the Republican leader of the House, that the great world battle between freedom and communism had begun in Asia, and "there is no substitute for victory." Even before receiving the unanimous support of his political and military advi-sors, President Truman made up his mind, as he wrote in his Memoirs.

. . . I realized that I would have no other choice myself than to relieve the nation's top field commander.

If there is one basic element in our Constitution, it is civilian control of the military. Policies are to be made by the elected political officials, not by gener-als or admirals. Yet time and again General MacArthur had shown that he was unwilling to accept the policies of the administration. By his repeated public statements he was not only con-fusing our allies as to the true course of our policies but, in fact, was also setting his policy against the President's.

I have always had, and I have to this day, the greatest respect for General MacArthur, the soldier. Nothing I could do, I knew, could change his stature as one of the outstanding mili-tary figures of our time—and I had no desire to diminish his stature. I had hoped, and I had tried to convince him, that the policy he was asked to follow was right. He had disagreed. He had been openly critical. Now, at last, his actions had frustrated a political course decided upon, in conjunction with its allies, by the government he was sworn to serve. If I allowed him to defy the civil authorities in this man-ner, I myself would be violating my oath to uphold and defend the Consti-tution. . . .

The reporters were handed a series of papers, the first being my announcement of General MacArthur's relief.

"With deep regret," this announcement read, "I have concluded that General of the Army Douglas MacArthur is unable to give his whole-hearted support to the policies of the United States Government and of the United Nations in matters pertaining to his official duties. In view of the specific responsibilities imposed upon me by the Constitution of the United States and the added responsibility which has been entrusted to me by the United Nations, I have decided that I must make a change of command in the Far East. I have, therefore, relieved General MacArthur of his commands and have designated Lieutenant General Matthew B. Ridgway as his successor.

"Full and vigorous debate on matters of national policy is a vital element in the constitutional system of our free democracy. It is fundamental, however, that military commanders must be governed by the policies and directives issued to them in the manner provided by our laws and Constitution. In time of crisis, the consideration is particularly compelling.

"General MacArthur's place in history as one of our greatest commanders is fully established. The Nation owes him a debt of gratitude for the distinguished and exceptional service which he has rendered his country in posts of great responsibility. For that reason I repeat my regret at the necessity for the action I feel compelled to take in his case."

The second document was the actual order of relief. It notified General MacArthur that he was relieved of his several commands and instructed him to turn over his authority to General Ridgway. There was a further document instructing General Ridgway to assume the functions formerly held by General MacArthur and informing him that Lieutenant General Van Fleet was on his way to Korea to take Ridgway's post as Eighth Army commander.

A number of background documents were also released. These included my order of December 6 concerning the clearance of public statements, the notification to MacArthur of the proposed presidential statement, his own counterpronouncement, the reminder that followed it of the clearance-of-statements requirements, the letter to Congressman Martin, the message of the JCS to MacArthur on 4 January asking for his advice on the arming of additional ROK Army units, and his reply of 6 January.

The last two papers were included because of a new statement of MacArthur's that had just come to light. A periodical that had always been critical of administration policy had sent a series of questions to MacArthur. One of them had been aimed at the arming of South Koreans. The magazine said it had heard that South Koreans were eager to defend themselves but that "Washington" had refused them arms.

The principal reason, of course, that the Republic of Korea's request for additional arms had been denied was that General MacArthur had recommended against it in his message of 6 January. But he had told this periodical that the matter was one that involved issues beyond his authority—implying that if it had been up to him the ROK's would have received the additional arms!

As far as I was concerned, these papers stated the case. The American people were still faced with Communist aggression in Korea; the Communist conspiracy was still threatening the West in Europe and in Asia. I went on the air on the evening of April 11 to restate the government's policy to the American people. I explained why we were in Korea and why we could not allow the Korean affair to become a general all-out war. I proclaimed our desire to arrive at a settlement along the lines of the statement that had been drafted in March and then not used. I explained why it had become necessary to relieve General MacArthur.

"The free nations," I told the radio audience, "have united their strength in an effort to prevent a third world war.

"That war can come if the Communist leaders want it to come. But this nation and its allies will not be responsible for its coming."

PRESIDENT DWIGHT D. EISENHOWER CALLS FOR THE INTERSTATE HIGHWAY SYSTEM
22 February 1955

Dwight David Eisenhower entered to the White House on the strength of a remarkable military career in which he combined strategic wisdom and personal charisma to lead Allied forces to victory in Europe. At the same time, his political beliefs remained shrouded in platitudes and abstract musings. In general, his two terms in the White House were concentrated on the containment of communism abroad and the preservation of the status quo in the world. The first Republican elected since 1928, Eisenhower pursued moderate policies, which revealed little intention of reversing the New Deal. While budget constraints prevented significant expansion of most social programs, the Eisenhower Administration actually increased the scope of government, particularly in massive public works projects. The St. Lawrence Seaway, a joint venture with Canada that permitted ocean shipping to penetrate to the western extent of the Great Lakes, opened in 1959. Even more consequential for American society, the Federal Highway Act of 1956 authorized the construction of 42,500 miles of limited-access interstate highways, with Federal funds committed to up to 90 percent of cost. Gradually, this Interstate Highway System laid down a grid of concrete linking every section of the nation, coast to coast and border to border, as never before. Commerce expanded, automobile use for business and pleasure compounded, and economic and social dependence on the internal combustion engine became a permanent feature of the American way of life. At the same time, cities and mass transportation, particularly the railroad, suffered. The huge road systems cut through urban residential neighborhoods of workers and minorities, particularly in New York, Philadelphia, Chicago, and Miami, precipitating "white flight" to the suburbs and leaving poor and disfigured black ghettos in most major cities. To the great majority of 1950s Americans, the social consequences seemed a reasonable price to pay for the American love affair with the automobile and the economic advantages of interstate highway travel. The Interstate Highway System immediately became one of the Eisenhower Administration's most enduring legacies.

Our unity as a nation is sustained by free communication of thought and by easy transportation of people and goods. The ceaseless flow of information throughout the Republic is matched by individual and commercial movement over a vast system of interconnected highways criss-crossing the Country and joining at our national borders with friendly neighbors to the north and south.

Together, the uniting forces of our communication and transportation systems are dynamic elements in the very name we bear—United States. Without them, we would be a mere alliance of many separate parts.

The Nation's highway system is a gigantic enterprise, one of our largest items of capital investment. Generations have gone into its building. Three million, three hundred and sixty-six thousand miles of road, travelled by 58 million motor vehicles, comprise it. The replacement cost of its drainage and bridge and tunnel works is incalculable. One in every seven Americans gains his livelihood and supports his family out of it. But, in large part, the network is inadequate for the nation's growing needs.

In recognition of this, the Governors in July of last year at my request began a study of both the problem and methods by which the Federal Government might assist the States in its solution. I appointed in September the President's Advisory Committee on a National Highway Program, headed by Lucius D. Clay, to work with the Governors and to propose a plan of action for submission to the Congress. At the same time, a committee representing departments and agencies of the national Government was organized to conduct studies coordinated with the other two groups.

All three were confronted with inescapable evidence that action, comprehensive and quick and forward-looking, is needed.

First: Each year, more than 36 thousand people are killed and more than a million injured on the highways. To the home where the tragic aftermath of an accident on an unsafe road is a gap in the family circle, the monetary worth of preventing that death cannot be reckoned. But reliable estimates place the measurable economic cost of the highway accident toll to the Nation at more than $4.3 billion a year.

Second: The physical condition of the present road net increases the cost of vehicle operation, according to many estimates, by as much as one cent per mile of vehicle travel. At the present rate of travel, this totals more than $5 billion a year. The cost is not borne by the individual vehicle operator alone. It pyramids into higher expense of doing the nation's business. Increased highway transportation costs, passed on through each step in the distribution of goods, are paid ultimately by the individual consumer.

Third: In case of an atomic attack on our key cities, the road net must permit quick evacuation of target areas, mobilization of defense forces and maintenance of every essential economic function. But the present system in critical areas would be the breeder of a deadly congestion within hours of an attack.

Fourth: Our Gross National Product, about $357 billion in 1954, is estimated to reach over $500 billion in 1965 when our population will exceed 180 million and, according to other estimates, will travel in 81 million vehicles 814 billion vehicle miles that year. Unless the present rate of highway improvement and development is increased, existing traffic jams only faintly foreshadow those of ten years hence.

To correct these deficiencies is an obligation of Government at every level. The highway system is a public enterprise. As the owner and operator, the various levels of Government have a responsibility for management that promotes the economy of the nation and properly serves the individual user. In the case of the Federal Government, moreover, expenditures on a highway program are a return to the highway user of the taxes which he pays in connection with his use of the highways. . . .

Of all these, the Interstate System must be given top priority in construction planning. But at the current rate of development, the Interstate network would not reach even a reasonable level of extent and efficiency in half a century. State highway departments cannot effectively meet the need. Adequate right-of-way to assure control of access; grade separation structures; relocation and realignment of present highways; all these, done on the necessary scale within an integrated system, exceed their collective capacity.

If we have a congested and unsafe and inadequate system, how then can we improve it so that ten years from now it will be fitted to the nation's requirements?

A realistic answer must be based on a study of all phases of highway financing, including a study of the costs of completing the several systems of highways, made by the Bureau of Public Roads in cooperation with the State highway departments and local units of government. This study, made at the direction of the 83rd Congress in the 1954 Federal-aid Highway Act, is the most comprehensive of its kind ever undertaken.

Its estimates of need show that a 10-year construction program to modernize all our roads and streets will require expenditure of $101 billion by all levels of Government.

A sound Federal highway program, I believe, can and should stand on its own feet, with highway users providing the total dollars necessary for improvement and new construction. Financing of interstate and Federal-aid systems should be based on the planned use of increasing revenues from present gas and diesel oil taxes, augmented in limited instances with tolls.

I am inclined to the view that it is sounder to finance this program by special bond issues, to be paid off by the above-mentioned revenues which will be collected during the useful life of the roads and pledged to this purpose, rather than by an increase in general revenue obligations. . . .

President Dwight D. Eisenhower Calls for "Open Skies" to End the Cold War
21 July 1955

Ten years passed between the unsuccessful conference at Potsdam at the end of World War II and the summit meeting of 1955, which attempted to repair the relations among the erstwhile allies. In Geneva, Switzerland, President Eisenhower joined Prime Minister Anthony Eden of Great Britain, French Premier Edgar Faure and the nominal leader of the Soviet Union, Premier Nikolai Bulganin. For a change, the international situation showed signs of détente. The recently concluded Austrian Peace Treaty demonstrated the willingness of the Soviets to settle that problem, allowing Austria to be transformed from an occupied state to an independent nation. The aftereffects of Josef Stalin's death two years earlier remained uncertain, persuading the United States and its allies to meet the new Soviet leadership face to face to take its pulse. Premier Bulganin came to Geneva accompanied by the First Secretary of the Communist Party, Nikolai Khrushchev, whose ascension to power soon afterward did not surprise the Americans who encountered him at Geneva. Eisenhower had determined to use the conference as a pulpit to issue dramatic appeals for the transformation of international relations from its decade of political hostility and militarization to a new era of conciliation. His opening address to the Conference on 18 July 1955, struck these themes. Three days later, he shocked the world (and certainly the Soviet delegation) with a proposal to exchange military secrets and provide facilities and open access for Russian pilots on American air bases, requesting only reciprocal arrangements for the American military in the Soviet Union. Although the plan met quick rejection by the suspicious Soviets, the "spirit of Geneva" did provide an extended period of reduced Cold War tensions.

Disarmament is one of the most important subjects on our agenda. It is also extremely difficult. In recent years the scientists have discovered methods of making weapons many, many times more destructive of opposing armed forces—but also of homes, and industries and lives—than ever known or even imagined before. These same scientific discoveries have made much more complex the problems of limitation and control and reduction of armament.

After our victory as Allies in World War II, my country rapidly disarmed. Within a few years our armament was at a very low level. Then events occurred beyond our borders which caused us to realize that we had disarmed too much. For our own security and to safeguard peace we needed greater strength. Therefore we proceeded to rearm and to associate with others in a partnership for peace and for mutual security.

The American people are determined to maintain and if necessary increase this armed strength for as long a period as is necessary to safeguard peace and to maintain our security.

But we know that a mutually dependable system for less armament on the part of all nations would be a better way to safeguard peace and to maintain our security.

It would ease the fears of war in the anxious hearts of people everywhere. It would lighten the burdens upon the backs of the people. It would make it possible for every nation, great and small, developed and less developed, to advance the standards of living of its people, to attain better food, and clothing, and shelter, more of education and larger enjoyment of life.

Therefore the United States government is prepared to enter into a sound and reliable agreement making possible the reduction of armament. I have directed that an intensive and thorough study of this subject be made within our own government. From these studies, which are continuing, a very important principle is emerging to which I referred in my opening statement on Monday.

No sound and reliable agreement can be made unless it is completely covered by an inspection and reporting system adequate to support every portion of the agreement.

The lessons of history teach us that disarmament agreements without adequate reciprocal inspection increase the dangers of war and do not brighten the prospects of peace.

Thus it is my view that the priority attention of our combined study of disarmament should be upon the subject of inspection and reporting.

Questions suggest themselves.

How effective an inspection system can be designed which would be mutually and reciprocally acceptable within our countries and the other nations of the world? How would such system operate? What could it accomplish?

Is certainty against surprise aggression attainable by inspection? Could violations be discovered promptly and effectively counteracted?

We have not as yet been able to discover any scientific or other inspection method which would make certain of the elimination of nuclear weapons. So far as we are aware no other nation has made such a discovery. Our study of this problem is continuing. We have not as yet been able to discover any accounting or other inspection method of being certain of the true budgetary facts of total expenditures for armament. Our study of this problem is continuing. We by no means exclude the possibility of finding useful checks in these fields.

As you can see from these statements, it is our impression that many past proposals of disarmament are more sweeping than can be insured by effective inspection.

Gentlemen, since I have been working on this memorandum to present to this Conference, I have been searching my heart and mind for something that I could say here that could convince everyone of the great sincerity of the United States in approaching this problem of disarmament.

I should address myself for a moment principally to the Delegates from the Soviet Union, because our two great countries admittedly possess new and terrible weapons in quantities which do give rise in other parts of the world, or reciprocally, to the fears and dangers of surprise attack.

I propose, therefore, that we take a practical step, that we begin an arrangement, very quickly, as between ourselves—immediately. These steps would include:

To give to each other a complete blueprint of our military establishments, from beginning to end, from one end of our countries to the other; lay out the establishments and provide the blue prints to each other.

Next, to provide within our countries facilities for aerial photography to the other country—we to provide you the facilities within our country, ample facilities for aerial reconnaissance, where you can make all the pictures you choose and take them to your own country to study, you to provide exactly the same facilities for us and we to make these examinations, and by this step to convince the world that we are providing as between ourselves against the possibility of great surprise attack, thus lessening danger and relaxing tension. Likewise we will make more easily attainable a comprehensive and effective system of inspection and disarmament, because what I propose, I assure you, would be but a beginning.

Now from my statements I believe you will anticipate my suggestion. It is that we instruct our representatives in the Subcommittee on Disarmament in discharge of their mandate from the United Nations to give priority effort to the study of inspection and reporting. Such a study could well include a step by step testing of inspection and reporting methods.

The United States is ready to proceed in the study and testing of a reliable system of inspections and reporting, and when that system is proved, then to reduce armaments with all others to the extent that the system will provide assured results.

The successful working out of such a system would do much to develop the mutual confidence which will open wide the avenues of progress for all our peoples.

The quest for peace is the statesman's most exacting duty. Security of the nation entrusted to his care is his greatest responsibility. Practical progress to lasting peace is his fondest hope. Yet in pursuit of his hope he must not betray the trust placed in him as guardian of the people's security. A sound peace—with security, justice, wellbeing, and freedom for the people of the world—*can* be achieved, but only by patiently and thoughtfully following a hard and sure and tested road.

PRESIDENT DWIGHT D. EISENHOWER'S DECISION TO SEND FEDERAL TROOPS TO INTEGRATE LITTLE ROCK HIGH SCHOOL
24 September 1957

On 17 May 1954, Chief Justice Earl Warren read the unanimous decision of the Supreme Court in the case Brown v. School Board of Topeka: *"We conclude that in the field of public education the doctrine of 'separate but equal' has no place. Separate educational facilities are inherently unequal." This removal of legal justification for segregation in public schools was unpopular with many Americans who were quite comfortable with the long practice of separation of the races. It positively enraged the vast majority of Southern whites from every social class. Black Americans, however, drew encouragement from the Court. On 1 December 1955, in Montgomery, Alabama a middle-aged black seamstress named Rosa Parks boarded a public bus to go home after work. Tired, she refused to yield her seat to a white passenger, as custom and local law required. So began a year of boycotts and organizing, the emergence of a charismatic young minister, Rev. Martin Luther King, Jr., and the seeds of a civil rights revolution. At every stage, the South resisted. The absence of legality after* Brown *was offset by hostile political power, social customs, and, not infrequently, mob violence. Southern Democratic politicians, the most powerful bloc in Congress,*

issued a "Southern Manifesto" in 1956 decrying the Court's decision and vowing re-
sistance. Most of the region's politicians proudly proclaimed, in the words of one, "seg-
regation today, segregation tomorrow, segregation forever." Firebombed black homes
and street violence involving police and protesters became a staple on the evening
news. In this context, in August 1957, the Eisenhower Administration pushed through
Congress the first Civil Rights legislation in eight decades. This moderate bill reflected
President Dwight D. Eisenhower's careful approach to the subject. In July, responding
to a question at a news conference on enforcing school integration orders, the Presi-
dent had said that "I can't imagine any set of circumstances that would ever induce
me to send Federal troops into . . . any area to enforce the orders of a Federal
court. . . ." At the same time, Eisenhower deeply respected the rule of law. He told
one prominent Southern leader that "customs were established in certain sections of
our country which were repudiated and declared illegal by the Supreme Court ruling
of 1954." Still the South resisted. In September 1957, Governor Orville Faubus of
Arkansas defied a court order and mobilized the National Guard to prevent black stu-
dents from entering Central High School in Little Rock. Faced with this direct threat,
President Eisenhower addressed the nation.

For a few minutes I want to speak to you about the serious situation that has arisen in Little Rock. For this talk I have come to the President's office in the White House . . . I felt that, in speaking from the house of Lincoln, of Jackson and of Wilson, my words would more clearly convey both the sadness I feel in the action I was compelled today to take and the firmness with which I intend to pursue this course until the orders of the Federal Court at Little Rock can be executed without unlawful interference.

In that city, under the leadership of demagogic extremists, disorderly mobs have deliberately prevented the carrying out of proper orders from a Federal Court. Local authorities have not eliminated that violent opposition and, under the law, I yesterday issued a Proclamation calling upon the mob to disperse.

This morning the mob again gathered in front of the Central High School of Little Rock, obviously for the purpose of again preventing the carrying out of the Court's order relating to the admission of Negro children to the school.

Whenever normal agencies prove inadequate to the task and it becomes necessary for the Executive Branch of the Federal Government to use its powers and authority to uphold Federal Courts, the President's responsibility is inescapable.

In accordance with that responsibility, I have today issued an Executive Order directing the use of troops under Federal authority to aid in the execution of Federal law at Little Rock, Arkansas. This became necessary when my Proclamation of yesterday was not observed, and the obstruction of justice still continues.

It is important that the reasons for my action be understood by all citizens.

As you know, the Supreme Court of the United States has decided that separate public educational facilities for the races are inherently unequal and therefore compulsory school segregation laws are unconstitutional.

Our personal opinions about the decision have no bearing on the matter of enforcement; the responsibility and authority of the Supreme Court to interpret the Constitution are clear. Local Federal Courts were instructed by the Supreme Court to issue such orders and decrees as might be necessary to achieve admission to public schools without regard to race—and with all deliberate speed.

During the past several years, many communities in our Southern States have instituted public school plans for gradual progress in the enrollment and attendance of school children of all races in order to bring themselves into compliance with the law of the land.

They thus demonstrated to the world that we are a nation in which laws, not men, are supreme.

I regret to say that this truth—the cornerstone of our liberties—was not observed in this instance.

It was my hope that this localized situation would be brought under control by city and State authorities. If the use of local police powers had been sufficient, our traditional method of leaving the problem in those hands would have been pursued. But when large gatherings of obstructionists made it impossible for the decrees of the Court to be carried out, both the law and the national interest demanded that the President take action.

Here is the sequence of events in the development of the Little Rock school case.

In May of 1955, the Little Rock School Board approved a moderate plan for the gradual desegregation of the public schools in that city. It provided that a start toward integration would be made at the present term in the high school, and that the plan would be in full operation by 1963. This plan was challenged in the courts by some who believed that the period of time as proposed was too long.

The United States Court at Little Rock, which has supervisory responsibility under the law for the plan of desegregation in the public schools, dismissed the challenge, thus approving a gradual rather than an abrupt change from the existing system. It found that the school board had acted in good faith in planning for a public school system free from racial discrimination.

Since that time, the court has on three separate occasions issued orders directing that the plan be carried out. All persons were instructed to refrain from interfering with the efforts of the school board to comply with the law.

Proper and sensible observance of the law then demanded the respectful obedience which the nation has a right to expect from all the people. This, unfortunately, has not been the case at Little Rock. Certain misguided persons, many of them imported into Little Rock by agitators, have insisted upon defying the law and have sought to bring it into disrepute. The orders of the court have thus been frustrated.

The very basis of our individual rights and freedoms is the certainty that the President and the Executive Branch of Government will support and insure the carrying out of the decisions of the Federal Courts, even, when necessary with all the means at the President's command.

Unless the President did so, anarchy would result.

There would be no security for any except that which each one of us could provide for himself.

The interest of the nation in the proper fulfillment of the law's requirements cannot yield to opposition and demonstrations by some few persons.

Mob rule cannot be allowed to override the decisions of the courts.

Let me make it very clear that Federal troops are not being used to relieve local and state authorities of their primary duty to preserve the peace and order of the community. Nor are the troops there for the purpose of taking over the responsibility of the School Board and the other responsible local officials in running Central High School. In the present case the troops are there, pursuant to law, solely for the purpose of preventing interference with the orders of the Court.

The proper use of the powers of the Executive Branch to enforce the orders of a Federal Court is limited to extraordinary and compelling circumstances. Manifestly, such an extreme situation has been created in Little Rock. This challenge must be met with such measures as will preserve to the people as a whole their lawfully-protected rights in a climate permitting their free and fair exercise.

The overwhelming majority of our people in every section of the country are united in their respect for observance of the law—even in those cases where they may disagree with that law.

They deplore the call of extremists to violence.

The decision of the Supreme Court concerning school integration affects the South more seriously than it does other sections of the country. In that region I have many warm friends, some of them in the city of Little Rock. I have deemed it a great personal privilege to spend in our Southland tours of duty while in the military service and enjoyable recreational periods since that time.

So from intimate personal knowledge, I know that the overwhelming majority of the people in the South— including those of Arkansas and of Little Rock—are of good will, united in their efforts to preserve and respect the law even when they disagree with it.

They do not sympathize with mob rule. They, like the rest of the nation, have proved in two great wars their readiness to sacrifice for America.

A foundation of our American way of life is our national respect for law.

In the South, as elsewhere, citizens are keenly aware of the tremendous disservice that has been done to the people of Arkansas in the eyes of the nation, and that has been done to the nation in the eyes of the world.

At a time when we face a grave situation abroad because of the hatred that Communism bears toward a system of government based on human rights, it would be difficult to exaggerate the harm that is being done to the prestige and influence, and indeed to the safety, of our nation and the world.

Our enemies are gloating over this incident and using it everywhere to misrepresent our nation. We are portrayed as a violator of those standards of conduct which the peoples of the world united to proclaim in the Charter of the United Nations. There they affirmed "faith in fundamental human rights and in the dignity of the human person" and did so "without distinction as to race, sex, language or religion."

And so, with confidence, I call upon citizens of the State of Arkansas to assist in bringing to an immediate end all interference with the law and its processes. If resistance to the Federal Court orders ceases at once, the further presence of Federal troops will be unnecessary and the City of Little Rock will return to its normal habits of peace and order and a blot upon the fair name and high honor of our nation in the world will be removed.

Thus will be restored the image of America and of all its parts as one nation, indivisible, with liberty and justice for all.

President Dwight D. Eisenhower's Comments on the "Military-Industrial Complex"
17 January 1961

By the time President Eisenhower prepared to leave office in January 1961, journalists and other pundits had already begun to characterize his time in office as bland and inconsequential, "the time of the great postponement," as one critic observed. Comparisons between the avuncular Eisenhower and youthful and dynamic President-elect John F. Kennedy added to the sense of outdated convention. Retrospect treats Eisenhower differently, however. He understood, particularly in foreign policy, the limited capacity of the United States to achieve the end of the Cold War. Hence, American power responded in low-risk situations as the President sought détente and deescalation of the arms race. Eisenhower's Farewell Address, on 17 January 1961, sought to leave with his "fellow citizens" the sense of how his wisdom and experience interpreted the nation's problems, including the dangers of "the military-industrial complex."

My fellow Americans:

Three days from now, after half a century in the service of our country, I shall lay down the responsibilities of office as, in traditional and solemn ceremony, the authority of the Presidency is vested in my successor.

This evening I come to you with a message of leave-taking and farewell, and to share a few final thoughts with you, my countrymen.

Like every other citizen, I wish the new President, and all who will labor with him, Godspeed. I pray that the coming years will be blessed with peace and prosperity for all. . . .

We now stand ten years past the midpoint of a century that has witnessed four major wars among great nations. Three of these involved our own country. Despite these holocausts America is today the strongest, the most influential and most productive nation in the world. Understandably proud of this pre-eminence, we yet realize that America's leadership and prestige depend, not merely upon our unmatched material progress, riches and military strength, but on how we use our power in the interests of world peace and human betterment. . . .

Crises there will continue to be. In meeting them, whether foreign or domestic, great or small, there is a recurring temptation to feel that some spectacular and costly action could become the miraculous solution to all current difficulties. A huge increase in newer elements of our defense; development of unrealistic programs to cure every ill in agriculture; a dramatic expansion in basic and applied research—these and many other possibilities, each possibly promising in itself, may be suggested as the only way to the road we wish to travel.

But each proposal must be weighed in the light of a broader consideration: the need to maintain balance in and among national programs—balance between the private and the public economy, balance between cost and hoped for advantage—balance between the clearly necessary and the comfortably desirable; balance between our essential requirements as a nation and the duties imposed by the nation upon the individual; balance between actions of the moment and the national welfare of the future. Good judgment seeks balance and progress; lack of it eventually finds imbalance and frustration.

The record of many decades stands as proof that our people and their government have, in the main, understood these truths and have responded to them well, in the face of stress and threat. But threats, new in kind or degree, constantly arise. I mention two only.

A vital element in keeping the peace is our military establishment. Our arms must be mighty, ready for instant action, so that no potential aggressor may be tempted to risk his own destruction.

Our military organization today bears little relation to that known by any of my predecessors in peacetime, or indeed by the fighting men of World War II or Korea.

Until the latest of our world conflicts, the United States had no armaments industry. American makers of plowshares could, with time and as required, make swords as well. But now we can no longer risk emergency improvisation of national defense; we have been compelled to create a permanent armaments industry of vast proportions. Added to this, three and a half million men and women are directly engaged in the defense establishment. We annually spend on military security more than the net income of all United States corporations.

This conjunction of an immense military establishment and a large arms industry is new in the American experience. The total influence—economic, political, even spiritual—is felt in every city, every State house, every office of the Federal government. We recognize the imperative need for this development. Yet we must not fail to comprehend its grave implications. Our toil, resources and livelihood are all involved; so is the very structure of our society.

In the councils of government, we must guard against the acquisition of unwarranted influence, whether sought or unsought, by the military-industrial complex. The potential for the disastrous rise of misplaced power exists and will persist.

We must never let the weight of this combination endanger our liberties or democratic processes. We should take nothing for granted. Only an alert and knowledgeable citizenry can compel the proper meshing of the huge industrial and military machinery of defense with our peaceful methods and goals, so that security and liberty may prosper together.

Akin to, and largely responsible for the sweeping changes in our industrial-military posture, has been the technological revolution during recent decades.

In this revolution, research has become central; it also becomes more formalized, complex, and costly. A steadily increasing share is conducted for, by, or at the direction of, the Federal government.

Today, the solitary inventor, tinkering in his shop, has been overshadowed by task forces of scientists in laboratories and testing fields. In the same fashion, the free university, historically the fountainhead of free ideas and scientific discovery, has experienced a revolution in the conduct of research. Partly because of the huge costs involved, a government contract becomes virtually a substitute for intellectual curiosity. For every old blackboard there are now hundreds of new electronic computers.

The prospect of domination of the nation's scholars by Federal employment, project allocations, and the power of money is ever present—and is gravely to be regarded.

Yet, in holding scientific research and discovery in respect, as we should, we must also be alert to the equal and opposite danger that public policy could itself become the captive of a scientific-technological elite.

It is the task of statesmanship to mold, to balance, and to integrate these and other forces, new and old, within the principles of our democratic system—ever aiming toward the supreme goals of our free society.

Another factor in maintaining balance involves the element of time. As we peer into society's future, we—you and I, and our government—must avoid the impulse to live only for today, plundering, for our own ease and convenience, the precious resources of tomorrow. We cannot mortgage the material assets of our grandchildren without risking the loss also of their political and spiritual heritage. We want democracy to survive for all generations to come, not to become the insolvent phantom of tomorrow.

Down the long lane of the history yet to be written America knows that this world of ours, ever growing smaller, must avoid becoming a community of dreadful fear and hate, and be, instead, a proud confederation of mutual trust and respect.

Such a confederation must be one of equals. The weakest must come to the conference table with the same confidence as do we, protected as we are by our moral, economic, and military strength. That table, though scarred by many past frustrations, cannot be abandoned for the certain agony of the battlefield.

Disarmament, with mutual honor and confidence, is a continuing imperative. Together we must learn how to compose differences, not with arms, but with intellect and decent purpose. Because this need is so sharp and apparent I confess that I lay down my official responsibilities in this field with a definite sense of disappointment. As one who has witnessed the horror and the lingering sadness of war—as one who knows that another war could utterly destroy this civilization which has been so slowly and painfully built over thousands of years—I wish I could say tonight that a lasting peace is in sight.

Happily, I can say that war has been avoided. Steady progress toward our ultimate goal has been made. But, so much remains to be done. As a private citizen, I shall never cease to do what little I can to help the world advance along that road.

So—in this my last good night to you as your President—I thank you for the many opportunities you have given me for public service in war and peace. I trust that in that service you find some things worthy; as for the rest of it, I know you will find ways to improve performance in the future.

You and I—my fellow citizens—need to be strong in our faith that all nations, under God, will reach the goal of peace with justice. May we be ever unswerving in devotion to principle, confident but humble with power, diligent in pursuit of the Nation's great goals.

To all the peoples of the world, I once more give expression to America's prayerful and continuing aspiration:

We pray that peoples of all faiths, all races, all nations, may have their great human needs satisfied; that those now denied opportunity shall come to enjoy it to the full; that all who yearn for freedom may experience its spiritual blessings; that those who have freedom will understand, also, its heavy responsibilities; that all who are insensitive to the needs of others will learn charity; that the scourges of poverty, disease and ignorance will be made to disappear from the earth, and that, in the goodness of time, all peoples will come to live together in a peace guaranteed by the binding force of mutual respect and love.

PRESIDENT JOHN F. KENNEDY'S INAUGURAL ADDRESS
20 January 1961

As he appeared at the rostrum to be inaugurated on a frigid January day in 1961, John Fitzgerald Kennedy so clearly personified a dramatic change in American politics. Near Kennedy sat his two immediate predecessors, both old men. Harry Truman had served in World War I, and Dwight Eisenhower had directed the European phase of World War II during which Kennedy served as a junior naval officer. Truman and Eisenhower were grandfathers, while the new President had a three-year-old and an infant just born. Handsome and athletic despite war injuries, he projected both grace and passion. Television now enveloped America and Kennedy used the revolutionary new medium like no other politician before him. His self-deprecating wit, delivered in the odd inflection common to the Boston Irish but unfamiliar to the rest of America, charmed voters, particularly the young. To his own generation, Kennedy's exploits and near-death in the South Pacific created the lore of an authentic war hero. As he took the rostrum, the youngest man ever elected President looked out from the steps of the Capitol on a sharp frozen day and delivered an inaugural address remarkable for its power and poetry.

We observe today not a victory of party but a celebration of freedom, symbolizing an end as well as a beginning, signifying renewal as well as change. For I have sworn before you and Almighty God the same solemn oath our forebears prescribed nearly a century and three-quarters ago.

The world is very different now. For man holds in his mortal hands the power to abolish all forms of human poverty and all forms of human life. And yet the same revolutionary belief for which our forebears fought is still at issue around the globe, the belief that the rights of man come not from the generosity of the state but from the hand of God.

We dare not forget today that we are the heirs of that first revolution. Let the word go forth from this time and place, to friend and foe alike, that the torch has been passed to a new generation of Americans, born in this century, tempered by war, disciplined by a hard and bitter peace, proud of our ancient heritage, and unwilling to witness or permit the slow undoing of those human rights to which this nation has always been committed, and to which we are committed today at home and around the world.

Let every nation know, whether it wishes us well or ill, that we shall pay any price, bear any burden, meet any hardship, support any friend, oppose any foe to assure the survival and the success of liberty.

This much we pledge—and more.

To those old allies whose cultural and spiritual origins we share, we pledge the loyalty of faithful friends. United, there is little we cannot do in a host of co-operative ventures. Divided, there is little we can do, for we dare not meet a powerful challenge at odds and split asunder.

To those new states whom we welcome to the ranks of the free, we pledge our word that one form of colonial control shall not have passed away merely to be replaced by a far more iron tyranny. We shall not always expect to find them supporting our view. But we shall always hope to find them strongly supporting their own freedom, and to remember that, in the past, those who foolishly sought power by riding the back of the tiger ended up inside.

To those peoples in the huts and villages of half the globe struggling to break the bonds of mass misery, we pledge our best efforts to help them help themselves, for whatever period is required, not because the Communists may be doing it, not because we seek their votes, but because it is right. If a free society cannot help the many who are poor, it cannot save the few who are rich.

To our sister republics south of our border, we offer a special pledge: to convert our good words into good deeds, in a new alliance for progress, to assist free men and free governments in casting off the chains of poverty. But this peaceful revolution of hope cannot become the prey of hostile powers. Let all our neighbors know that we shall join with them to oppose agression or subversion anywhere in the Americas. And let every other power know that this hemisphere intends to remain the master of its own house.

To that world assembly of sovereign states, the United Nations, our last best hope in an age where the instruments of war have far outpaced the instruments of peace, we renew our pledge of support: to prevent it from becoming merely a forum for invective, to strengthen its shield of the new and the weak, and to enlarge the area in which its writ may run.

Finally, to those nations who would make themselves our adversary, we offer not a pledge but a request: that both sides begin anew the quest for peace, before the dark powers of destruction unleashed by science engulf all humanity in planned or accidental self-destruction.

We dare not tempt them with weakness. For only when our arms are sufficient beyond doubt can we be certain beyond doubt that they will never be employed.

But neither can two great and powerful groups of nations take comfort from our present course—both sides over-burdened by the cost of modern weapons, both rightly alarmed by the steady spread of the deadly atom, yet both racing to alter that uncertain balance of terror that stays the hand of mankind's final war.

So let us begin anew, remembering on both sides that civility is not a sign of weakness, and sincerity is always subject to proof. Let us never negotiate out of fear, but let us never fear to negotiate.

Let both sides explore what problems unite us instead of belaboring those problems which divide us.

Let both sides, for the first time, formulate serious and precise proposals for the inspection and control of arms, and bring the absolute power to destroy other nations under the absolute control of all nations.

Let both sides seek to invoke the wonders of science instead of its terrors. Together let us explore the stars, conquer the deserts, eradicate disease, tap the ocean depths and encourage the arts and commerce.

Let both sides unite to heed in all corners of the earth the command of Isaiah to "undo the heavy burdens . . . [and] let the oppressed go free."

And if a beachhead of co-operation may push back the jungle of suspicion, let both sides join in creating a new endeavor, not a new balance of power, but a new world of law, where the strong are just and the weak secure and the peace preserved.

All this will not be finished in the first one hundred days. Nor will it be finished in the first one thousand days, nor in the life of this Administration, nor even perhaps in our lifetime on this planet. But let us begin.

In your hands, my fellow citizens, more than mine, will rest the final success or failure of our course. Since this country was founded, each generation of Americans has been summoned to give testimony to its national loyalty. The graves of young Americans who answered the call to service surround the globe.

Now the trumpet summons us again—not as a call to bear arms, though arms we need; not as a call to battle, though embattled we are; but a call to bear the burden of a long twilight struggle, year in and year out, "rejoicing in hope, patient in tribulation," a struggle against the common enemies of man: tyranny, poverty, disease and war itself.

Can we forge against these enemies a grand and global alliance, North and South, East and West, that can assure a more fruitful life for all mankind? Will you join in that historic effort?

In the long history of the world, only a few generations have been granted the role of defending freedom in its hour of maximum danger. I do not shrink from this responsibility; I welcome it. I do not believe that any of us would exchange places with any other people or any other generation. The energy, the faith, the devotion which we bring to this endeavor will light our country and all who serve it, and the glow from that fire can truly light the world.

And so, my fellow Americans, ask not what your country can do for you; ask what you can do for your country.

My fellow citizens of the world, ask not what America will do for you, but what together we can do for the freedom of man.

Finally, whether you are citizens of America or citizens of the world, ask of us here the same high standards of strength and sacrifice which we ask of you. With a good conscience our only sure reward, with history the final judge of our deeds, let us go forth to lead the land we love, asking His blessing and His help, but knowing that here on earth God's work must truly be our own.

PRESIDENT JOHN F. KENNEDY INTRODUCES THE PEACE CORPS
1 March 1961

President Kennedy's vibrant style was reflected in the attitude of his administration in immediately addressing domestic and foreign problems. Ironically, his understanding of world affairs did not differ in any substantial way from his immediate predecessors, men born in the nineteenth century. Kennedy perceived a bipolar globe characterized by communist insurgencies directed from Moscow which provoked insurrection throughout the underdeveloped world. Events of 1961 and 1962, including the Bay of Pigs fiasco, the acrimonious Kennedy-Khrushchev Summit meeting in Vienna, and the Cuban Missile Crisis merely confirmed the President's world view. Of particular concern to the Kennedy Administration was Latin America, where the revolutionary regime of Fidel Castro in Cuba provided for American leadership a negative if vivid example of what might go wrong. Kennedy had attracted an impressive collection of intellectuals and strategic thinkers to Washington, and they laid comprehensive plans for the Third World which combined a vision of "modernization," (or "nation-building") with counter-insurgency. The latter would use intelligence and the newly-created Special Forces, or Green Berets, to thwart leftist operations. "Nation-building" included the creation of economic infrastructure, training of police and civil servants, and the promotion of democratic institutions. Perhaps the most striking part of this plan, the Peace Corps, came into existence in the earliest days of the Administration. On 1 March, President Kennedy signed an Executive Order creating the Corps, to be followed by Congressional action several months later. By 1963, 5,000 Americans had spread over the underdeveloped world planning irrigation schemes, purifying water, generating better crops, and combating illiteracy.

I recommend to the Congress the establishment of a permanent Peace Corps—a pool of trained American men and women sent overseas by the U.S. Government or through private organizations and institutions to help foreign countries meet their urgent needs for skilled manpower.

I have today signed an Executive Order establishing a Peace Corps on a temporary pilot basis.

The temporary Peace Corps will be a source of information and experience to aid us in formulating more effective plans for a permanent organization. In addition, by starting the Peace Corps now we will be able to begin training young men and women for overseas duty this summer with the objective of placing them in overseas positions by late fall. This temporary Peace Corps is being established under existing authority in the Mutual Security Act and will be located in the Department of State. Its initial expenses will be paid from appropriations currently available for our foreign aid program.

Throughout the world the people of the newly developing nations are struggling for economic and social progress which reflects their deepest desires. Our own freedom, and the future of freedom around the world, depend, in a very real sense, on their ability to build growing and independent nations where men can live in dignity, liberated from the bonds of hunger, ignorance and poverty.

One of the greatest obstacles to the achievement of this goal is the lack of trained men and women with the skill to teach the young and assist in the operation of development projects—men and women with the capacity to cope with the demands of swiftly evolving economies, and with the dedication to put that capacity to work in the villages, the mountains, the towns and the factories of dozens of struggling nations.

The vast task of economic development urgently requires skilled people to do the work of the society—to help teach in the schools, construct development projects, demonstrate modern methods of sanitation in the villages, and perform a hundred other tasks calling for training and advanced knowledge.

To meet this urgent need for skilled manpower we are proposing the establishment of a Peace Corps—an organization which will recruit and train American volunteers, sending them abroad to work with the people of other nations.

This organization will differ from existing assistance programs in that its members will supplement technical advisers by offering the specific skills needed by developing nations if they are to put technical advice to work. They will help provide the skilled manpower necessary to carry out the development projects planned by the host governments, acting at a working level and serving at great personal sacrifice. There is little doubt that the number of those who wish to serve will be far greater than our capacity to absorb them. . . .

Most heartening of all, the initial reaction to this proposal has been an enthusiastic response by student groups, professional organizations and private citizens everywhere—a convincing demonstration that we have in this country an immense reservoir of dedicated men and women willing to devote their energies and time and toil to the cause of world peace and human progress.

Among the specific programs to which Peace Corps members can contribute are: teaching in primary and secondary schools, especially as part of national English language teaching programs; participation in the worldwide program of malaria eradication; instruction and operation of public health and sanitation projects; aiding in village development through school construction and other programs; increasing rural agricultural productivity by assisting local farmers to use modern implements and techniques. The initial emphasis of these programs will be on teaching. Thus the Peace

Corps members will be an effective means of implementing the development programs of the host countries—programs which our technical assistance operations have helped to formulate.

The Peace Corps will not be limited to the young, or to college graduates. All Americans who are qualified will be welcome to join this effort. But undoubtedly the Corps will be made up primarily of young people as they complete their formal education. . . .

In all instances the men and women of the Peace Corps will go only to those countries where their services and skills are genuinely needed and desired. U.S. Operations Missions, supplemented where necessary by special Peace Corps teams, will consult with leaders in foreign countries in order to determine where Peace Corpsmen are needed, the types of job they can best fill, and the number of people who can be usefully employed. The Peace Corps will not supply personnel for marginal undertakings without a sound economic or social justification. In furnishing assistance through the Peace Corps careful regard will be given to the particular country's developmental priorities.

Membership in the Peace Corps will be open to all Americans, and applications will be available shortly. Where application is made directly to the Peace Corps—the vast majority of cases—they will be carefully screened to make sure that those who are selected can contribute to Peace Corps programs, and have the personal qualities which will enable them to represent the United States abroad with honor and dignity. In those cases where application is made directly to a private group, the same basic standards will be maintained. Each new recruit will receive a training and orientation period varying from six weeks to six months. This training will include courses in the culture and language of the country to which they are being sent and specialized training designed to increase the work skills of recruits. In some cases training will be conducted by participant agencies and universities in approved training programs. Other training programs will be conducted by the Peace Corps staff.

Length of service in the Corps will vary depending on the kind of project and the country, generally ranging from two to three years. Peace Corps members will often serve under conditions of physical hardship, living under primitive conditions among the people of developing nations. For every Peace Corps member service will mean a great financial sacrifice. They will receive no salary. Instead they will be given an allowance which will only be sufficient to meet their basic needs and maintain health. It is essential that Peace Corpsmen and women live simply and unostentatiously among the people they have come to assist. At the conclusion of their tours, members of the Peace Corps will receive a small sum in the form of severance pay based on length of service abroad, to assist them during their first weeks back in the United States. Service with the Peace Corps will not exempt volunteers from Selective Service.

The United States will assume responsibility for supplying medical services to Peace Corps members and ensuring supplies and drugs necessary to good health.

I have asked the temporary Peace Corps to begin plans and make arrangements for pilot programs. A minimum of several hundred volunteers could be selected, trained and at work abroad by the end of this calendar year. It is hoped that within a few years several thousand Peace Corps members will be working in foreign lands.

It is important to remember that this program must, in its early stages, be experimental in nature. This is a new dimension in our overseas program and only the most careful planning and negotiation can ensure its success.

The benefits of the Peace Corps will not be limited to the countries in which it serves. Our own young men and women will be enriched by the experience of living and working in foreign lands. They will have acquired new skills and experience which will aid them in their future careers and add to our own country's supply of trained personnel and teachers. They will return better able to assume the responsibilities of American citizenship and with greater understanding of our global responsibilities.

Although this is an American Peace Corps, the problem of world development is not just an American problem. Let us hope that other nations will mobilize the spirit and energies and skill of their people in some form of Peace Corps—making our own effort only one step in a major international effort to increase the welfare of all men and improve understanding among nations.

PRESIDENT JOHN F. KENNEDY CONFRONTS THE CUBAN MISSILE CRISIS
27 October 1962

From 16 October to 29 October 1962, a power struggle between the world's two great nuclear powers brought mankind to the moment of annihilation. Soviet missiles secretly established and deployed in Cuba fundamentally altered the world's strategic balance to the detriment of the United States by placing the lives of 100,000,000 Americans within easy range of sudden death and devastation. President John F. Kennedy immediately fixed as his principal objective the disarming and removal of the missiles from Cuban soil. How to achieve this goal engaged the highest level of American political, diplomatic, and military minds for thirteen frightening days. The Soviet missiles had been discovered on 15 October by a U-2 surveillance flight over Cuba. The next day, Kennedy convened a dozen or so advisors as the Special Executive Committee, or ExComm. In these meetings, the initial consensus emphasized a quick and overpowering military strike, either bombing the missile sites alone, or bombing all Cuban military installations. Some advisers advocated a full invasion of Cuba, and the replacement of the Castro government. As the entire military establishment went on highest alert, Kennedy ordered the callup of reserves. On 22 October the President addressed the nation on television, confirming the installation of missiles and demanding their removal. Rather than the military strikes advocated by most of his advisors, however, Kennedy announced a tactic designed to buy time for high-stakes diplomacy. The President announced that the U.S. Navy would establish a blockade to prevent all suspect shipping from reaching Cuba. In the tense days that followed, elements of the Soviet merchant and naval fleets steadily approached the Navy's line of ships in the Caribbean. Meanwhile, the two adversaries sent both threats and proposals through the United Nations to the world's diplomatic capitals. Top secret discussions within ExComm, which were covertly taped by President Kennedy and are now published, reveal both the resolve and the anguish of the nation's top leadership. At one point, the men around the President expected a Soviet invasion of West Berlin, or even a nuclear attack on the United States—with full knowledge that almost nothing could be done to avoid its consequences. On the evening of Friday, 26 October, a secret message arrived in Washington from Chairman Khrushchev which seemed to provide a

*way out for both parties. We will remove the missiles, the Soviet leader indicated, in re-
turn for a pledge by the United States not to invade Cuba. The next day, even as Ex-
Comm discussed this idea, Moscow Radio broadcast to the world another quite different
proposal from Khrushchev: missiles in Cuba would be removed only as the United States
removed its missiles from Turkey. President Kennedy immediately understood that to the
vast range of world public opinion the Soviet message would seem equitable. To the Turks
and other NATO allies, however, the bartering of allied security in the sole interests of the
United States threatened to destabilize Europe. The crisis had deepened when an American U-2 strayed over Soviet air space, and another U-2 was shot down over Cuba.
Soviet ships moved inexorably toward the American blockade fleet. President Kennedy
listened to hours of debate before gradually forming a unique response. At about 8 P.M.
on Saturday, 27 October, he released a public letter to Khrushchev that agreed to the initial secret Soviet proposal of 26 October, a no-invasion pledge in return for the removal
of the missiles in Cuba. In a top secret private message to the Soviet leader, Kennedy assured Khrushchev that in the near future, with the days of crisis past, the American missiles would be removed from Turkey (as they were). Khrushchev accepted, the Soviets removed their missiles, and the world avoided the greatest calamity in recorded history.*

Dear Mr. Chairman:

I am replying at once to your broadcast message of 28 October even though the official text has not yet reached me because of the great importance I attach to moving forward promptly to the settlement of the Cuban crisis. I think that you and I, with our heavy responsibilities for the maintenance of peace, were aware that developments were approaching a point where events could have become unmanageable. So I welcome this message and consider it an important contribution to peace.

The distinguished efforts of Acting Secretary General U Thant have greatly facilitated both our tasks. I consider my letter to you of 27th October and your reply of today as firm undertakings on the part of both our govern-

ments which should be promptly carried out. I hope that the necessary measures can at once be taken through the United Nations as your message says, so that the United States in turn can remove the quarantine measures now in effect. I have already made arrangements to report all these matters to the Organization of American States, whose members share a deep interest in a genuine peace in the Caribbean area.

You referred in your letter to a violation of your frontier by an American aircraft in the area of the Chukotsk Peninsula. I have learned that this plane, without arms or photographic equipment, was engaged in an air sampling mission in connection with your nuclear tests. Its course was direct from Eielson Air Force Base in Alaska to the North Pole and return. In turning south, the pilot made a serious navigational error which carried him over Soviet territory. He immediately made an emergency call on open radio for navigational assistance and was guided back to his home base by the most direct route. I regret this incident and will see to it that every precaution is taken to prevent recurrence.

Mr. Chairman, both of our countries have great unfinished tasks and I know that your people as well as those of the United States can ask for nothing better than to pursue them free from the fear of war. Modern science and technology have given us the possibility of making labor fruitful beyond anything that could have been dreamed of a few decades ago.

I agree with you that we must devote urgent attention to the problem of disarmament, as it relates to the whole world and also to critical areas. Perhaps now, as we step back from danger, we can together make real progress in this vital field. I think we should give priority to questions relating to the proliferation of nuclear weapons, on earth and in outer space, and to the great effort for a nuclear test ban. But we should also work hard to see if wider measures of disarmament can be agreed and put into operation at an early date. The United States government will be prepared to discuss these questions urgently, and in a constructive spirit, at Geneva or elsewhere.

John F. Kennedy

PRESIDENT JOHN F. KENNEDY ADDRESSES THE NATION ON CIVIL RIGHTS
11 June 1963

From the end of Reconstruction in 1877 to the early 1960s, an additional three generations of the descendants of former slaves were denied equality as citizens and justice before the law. The first two years of the Kennedy Administration were marked by a succession of violent clashes, some resulting in death, throughout the Old South. In the spring of 1963, Martin Luther King led massive demonstrations in Birmingham, Alabama, enlisting the large black community and some white supporters in a campaign of civil disobedience. The nation watched on the nightly television news programs as cops under the Police Commissioner, Eugene "Bull" Connor, used clubs and high-power fire hoses on the demonstrators, many of them young children. Kennedy attempted to work through the local business community to arrange some compromise, but with little success. Ku Klux Klan outrages continued. The fire-bombing of black homes led to riots and another cycle of violence. Meanwhile, Alabama Governor George Corley Wallace expanded his racist rhetoric. Promising "segregation today, segregation tomorrow, seg-

regation forever," he announced his refusal to allow the University of Alabama to admit its first two black students. As the confrontation approached on 11 June, the President called the State National Guard into Federal service, and ordered the students enrolled. Although the Governor backed down as the nation watched, he continued to pledge unremitting defiance. That evening, President Kennedy addressed the nation, speaking about race and civil rights more candidly than any of his predecessors in office.

This afternoon, following a series of threats and defiant statements, the presence of Alabama National Guardsmen was required on the University of Alabama to carry out the final and unequivocal order of the United States District Court of the Northern District of Alabama. That order called for the admission of two clearly qualified young Alabama residents who happened to have been born Negro.

That they were admitted peacefully on the campus is due in good measure to the conduct of the students of the University of Alabama, who met their responsibilities in a constructive way.

I hope that every American, regardless of where he lives, will stop and examine his conscience about this and other related incidents. This Nation was founded by men of many nations and backgrounds. It was founded on the principle that all men are created equal, and that the rights of every man are diminished when the rights of one man are threatened.

Today we are committed to a worldwide struggle to promote and protect the rights of all who wish to be free. And when Americans are sent to Viet-Nam or West Berlin, we do not ask for whites only. It ought to be possible, therefore, for American students of any color to attend any public institution they select without having to be backed up by troops.

It ought to be possible for American consumers of any color to receive equal service in places of public accommodation, such as hotels and restaurants and theaters and retail stores, without being forced to resort to demonstrations in the street, and it ought to be possible for American citizens of any color to register and to vote in a free election without interference or fear of reprisal.

It ought to be possible, in short, for every American to enjoy the privileges of being American without regard to his race or his color. In short, every American ought to have the right to be treated as he would wish to be treated, as one would wish his children to be treated. But this is not the case.

The Negro baby born in America today, regardless of the section of the Nation in which he is born, has about one-half as much chance of completing a high school as a white baby born in the same place on the same day, one-third as much chance of completing college, one-third as much chance of becoming a professional man, twice as much chance of becoming unemployed, about one-seventh as much chance of earning $10,000 a year, a life expectancy which is 7 years shorter, and the prospects of earning only half as much.

This is not a sectional issue. Difficulties over segregation and discrimination exist in every city, in every State of the Union, producing in many cities a rising tide of discontent that threatens the public safety. Nor is this a partisan issue. In a time of domestic crisis men of good will and generosity should be able to unite regardless of party or politics. This is not even a legal or legislative issue alone. It is better to settle these matters in the courts than on the streets, and new laws are needed at every level, but law alone cannot make men see right.

We are confronted primarily with a moral issue. It is as old as the scriptures and is as clear as the American Constitution.

The heart of the question is whether all Americans are to be afforded equal rights and equal opportunities, whether we are going to treat our fellow Americans as we want to be treated. If an American, because his skin is dark, cannot eat lunch in a restaurant open to the public, if he cannot send his children to the best public school available, if he cannot vote for the public officials who represent him, if, in short, he cannot enjoy the full and free life which all of us want, then who among us would be content to have the color of his skin changed and stand in his place? Who

among us would then be content with the counsels of patience and delay?

One hundred years of delay have passed since President Lincoln freed the slaves, yet their heirs, their grandsons, are not fully free. They are not yet freed from the bonds of injustice. They are not yet freed from social and economic oppression. And this Nation, for all its hopes and all its boasts, will not be fully free until all its citizens are free.

We preach freedom around the world, and we mean it, and we cherish our freedom here at home, but are we to say to the world, and much more importantly, to each other that this is a land of the free except for the Negroes; that we have no second-class citizens except Negroes; that we have no class or cast system, no ghettoes, no master race except with respect to Negroes?

Now the time has come for this Nation to fulfill its promise. The events in Birmingham and elsewhere have so increased the cries for equality that no city or State or legislative body can prudently choose to ignore them.

The fires of frustration and discord are burning in every city, North and South, where legal remedies are not at hand. Redress is sought in the streets, in demonstrations, parades, and protests which create tensions and threaten violence and threaten lives.

We face, therefore, a moral crisis as a country and as a people. It cannot be met by repressive police action. It cannot be left to increased demonstrations in the streets. It cannot be quieted by token moves or talk. It is a time to act in the Congress, in your State and local legislative body and, above all, in all of our daily lives.

It is not enough to pin the blame on others, to say this is a problem of one section of the country or another, or deplore the fact that we face. A great change is at hand, and our task, our obligation, is to make that revolution, that change, peaceful and constructive for all.

Those who do nothing are inviting shame as well as violence. Those who act boldly are recognizing right as well as reality.

Next week I shall ask the Congress of the United States to act, to make a commitment it has not fully made in this century to the proposition that race has no place in American life or law. The Federal judiciary has upheld that proposition in a series of forth-right cases. The executive branch has adopted that proposition in the conduct of its affairs, including the employment of Federal personnel, the use of Federal facilities, and the sale of federally financed housing.

But there are other necessary measures which only the Congress can provide, and they must be provided at this session. The old code of equity law under which we live commands for every wrong a remedy, but in too many communities, in too many parts of the country, wrongs are inflicted on Negro citizens and there are no remedies at law. Unless the Congress acts, their only remedy is in the street.

I am, therefore, asking the Congress to enact legislation giving all Americans the right to be served in facilities which are open to the public—hotels, restaurants, theaters, retail stores, and similar establishments.

This seems to me to be an elementary right. Its denial is an arbitrary indignity that no American in 1963 should have to endure, but many do.

I have recently met with scores of business leaders urging them to take voluntary action to end this discrimination and I have been encouraged by their response, and in the last 2 weeks over 75 cities have seen progress made in desegregating these kinds of facilities. But many are unwilling to act alone, and for this reason, nationwide legislation is needed if we are to move this problem from the streets to the courts.

I am also asking Congress to authorize the Federal Government to participate more fully in lawsuits designed to end segregation in public education. We have succeeded in persuading many districts to desegregate voluntarily. Dozens have admitted Negroes without violence. Today a Negro is attending a State-supported institution in every one of our 50 States, but the pace is very slow.

Too many Negro children entering segregated grade schools at the time of the Supreme Court's decision 9 years ago will enter segregated high schools this fall, having suffered a loss which can never be restored. The lack of an adequate education denies the Negro a chance to get a decent job.

The orderly implementation of the Supreme Court decision, therefore, can not be left solely to those who may not have the economic resources to carry the legal action or who may be subject to harassment.

Other features will be also requested, including greater protection for the right to vote. But legislation, I repeat, cannot solve this problem alone. It must be solved in the homes of every American in every community across our country.

In this respect, I want to pay tribute to those citizens North and South who have been working in their communities to make life better for all. They are acting not out of a sense of legal duty but out of a sense of human decency.

Like our soldiers and sailors in all parts of the world they are meeting freedom's challenge on the firing line, and I salute them for their honor and their courage.

My fellow Americans, this is a problem which faces us all—in every city of the North as well as the South. Today there are Negroes unemployed, two or three times as many compared to whites, inadequate in education, moving into the large cities, unable to find work, young people particularly out of work without hope, denied equal rights, denied the opportunity to eat at a restaurant or lunch counter or go to a movie theater, denied the right to a decent education, denied almost today the right to attend a State university even though qualified. It seems to me that these are matters which concern us all, not merely Presidents or Congressmen or Governors, but every citizen of the United States.

This is one country. It has become one country because all of us and all the people who came here had an equal chance to develop their talents.

We cannot say to 10 percent of the population that you can't have that right; that your children can't have the chance to develop whatever talents they have; that the only way that they are going to get their rights is to go into the streets and demonstrate. I think we owe them and we owe ourselves a better country than that.

Therefore, I am asking for your help in making it easier for us to move ahead and to provide the kind of equality of treatment which we would want ourselves; to give a chance for every child to be educated to the limit of his talents.

As I have said before, not every child has an equal talent or an equal ability or an equal motivation, but they should have the equal right to develop their talent and their ability and their motivation, to make something of themselves.

We have a right to expect that the Negro community will be responsible, will uphold the law, but they have a right to expect that the law will be fair, that the Constitution will be color blind, as Justice Harlan said at the turn of the century.

This is what we are talking about and this is a matter which concerns this country and what it stands for, and in meeting it I ask the support of all our citizens.

Thank you very much.

PRESIDENT JOHN F. KENNEDY SPEAKS
AT THE BERLIN WALL
26 June 1963

In June of 1963, John F. Kennedy encountered the celebrated "burdens of the Presidency" both at home and abroad. His 11 June speech to the nation on race relations preceded by one day the assassination of prominent civil rights leader Medgar Evers by a proud Klansman in Mississippi. The violent drama of the civil rights revolution continued. Simultaneously, the President undertook significant initiatives in the long and dangerous Cold War struggle with the Soviet Union. On 10 June, at The American University in Washington, Kennedy boldly proposed complete disarmament, beginning with the prohibition of atmospheric nuclear testing. Two months later, acting on this initiative, the Senate ratified the first-ever arms control agreement between Washington and Moscow, a modest but notable beginning toward détente. Two weeks after the American University speech the American President struck a more accustomed pose in Berlin, the divided city behind the Iron Curtain, long a flash point with the Soviets. Standing at the despised Wall before the most rapturous throng he had ever experienced, Kennedy pledged America's commitment, thundering "Today in the world of freedom, the proudest boast is 'Ich bin ein Berliner,' "I am a Berliner."

I am proud to come to this city as the guest of your distinguished Mayor, who has symbolized throughout the world the fighting spirit of West Berlin. And I am proud to visit the Federal Republic with your distinguished Chancellor who for so many years has committed Germany to democracy and freedom and progress, and to come here in the company of my fellow American, General Clay, who has been in this city during its great moments of crisis and will come again if ever needed.

Two thousand years ago the proudest boast was "*civis Romanus sum.*" Today, in the world of freedom, the proudest boast is "*Ich bin ein Berliner.*"

I appreciate my interpreter translating my German!

There are many people in the world who really don't understand, or say they don't, what is the great issue between the free world and the Communist world. Let them come to Berlin. There are some who say that communism is the wave of the future. Let them come to Berlin. And there are some who say in Europe and elsewhere we can work with the Communists. Let them come to Berlin. And there are even a few who say that it is true that communism is an evil system, but it permits us to make economic progress. *Lass' sie nach Berlin kommen.* Let them come to Berlin.

Freedom has many difficulties and democracy is not perfect, but we have never had to put a wall up to keep our people in, to prevent them from leaving us. I want to say, on behalf of my countrymen, who live many miles away on the other side of the Atlantic, who are far distant from you, that they take the greatest pride that they have been able to share with you, even from a distance, the story of the last 18 years. I know of no town, no city, that has been besieged for 18 years that still lives with the vitality and the force, and the hope and the determination of the city of West Berlin. While the wall is the most obvious and vivid demonstration of the failures of the Communist system, for all the world to see, we take no satisfaction in it, for it is, as your Mayor has said, an offense not only against history but an offense against humanity, separating families, dividing husbands and wives and brothers and sisters, and dividing a people who wish to be joined together.

What is true of this city is true of Germany—real, lasting peace in Europe can never be assured as long as one German out of four is denied the elementary right of free men, and that is to make a free choice. In 18 years of peace and good faith, this generation of Germans has earned the right to be free, including the right to unite their families and their nation in lasting peace, with good will to all people. You live in a defended island of freedom, but your life is part of the main. So let me ask you, as I close, to lift your eyes beyond the dangers of today, to the hopes of tomorrow, beyond the freedom merely of this city of Berlin, or your country of Germany, to the advance of freedom everywhere, beyond the wall to the day of peace with justice, beyond yourselves and ourselves to all mankind.

Freedom is indivisible, and when one man is enslaved, all are not free. When all are free, then we can look forward to that day when this city will be joined as one and this country and this great Continent of Europe in a peaceful and hopeful globe. When that day finally comes, as it will, the people of West Berlin can take sober satisfaction in the fact that they were in the front lines for almost two decades.

All free men, wherever they may live, are citizens of Berlin, and, therefore, as a free man, I take pride in the words *"Ich bin ein Berliner."*

President Lyndon B. Johnson's "Great Society" Plan
22 May 1964

Lyndon Baines Johnson was the eighth vice president to succeed to the presidency upon death or assassination. Despite the shocking and gruesome the events and memories of the shooting of President Kennedy on 22 November 1963, the new President from Texas took over confidently. He managed to find the proper balance between sorrow and hope in guiding a dazed nation. Johnson's first priority, he proclaimed, was to honor the memory of the assassinated President by enacting Kennedy's ambitious initiative in civil rights. Over his first few months in the White House, civil rights legislation remained his abiding priority. By the spring of 1964, with this legislative battle well in control, Johnson began to focus on his own popularity and historical legacy. This simply meant becoming the greatest of all presidents, even supplanting his hero, Franklin Delano Roosevelt. He struck out with passion and power to put his own mark on history. For the next two years, until the quicksand in Vietnam smothered American politics, the President presided over the remarkable accumulation of legislation identified as "the Great Society." Conceived in the New Deal tradition of social justice, Johnson's elaborate package of benefits and controls aimed to use the power of the Federal Government to provide opportunity and hope for the millions of Americans still denied the promise of American life by race or social class or gender or plain missed opportunities. The Equal Opportunity Act of August 1964, trumpeted as the first salvo in a "war against poverty," created Vista (the domestic version of Kennedy's Peace Corps), Head Start, and the Job Corps. Following Johnson's remarkable sweep of the 1964 Election (his 61.1 percent of the vote exceeded even FDR's greatest popular margin), Great Society bills flooded Congress. Two new Cabinet institutions appeared, the Department of Housing and Urban Development and the Department of Transportation. The landmark Medicare entitlement was signed by Johnson in Independence, Missouri, with ex-President Harry Truman alongside. To sign the Education Act of 1965, the President went to Texas to the one-room schoolhouse he had attended, accompanied by the aged woman who had been his first teacher. New legislation addressed immigration, voting rights and housing. The National Endowments, for the Arts and Humanities, came into being. The President seemed to hover over America, immersed in the great issues, energetic to a fault, dreaming a vision and bringing it to reality. Johnson spoke at the University of Michigan on 22 May 1964, about the America he foresaw.

... I have come today from the turmoil of your Capital to the tranquillity of your campus to speak about the future of your country.

The purpose of protecting the life of our Nation and preserving the liberty of our citizens is to pursue the happiness of our people. Our success in that pursuit is the test of our success as a Nation.

For a century we labored to settle and to subdue a continent. For half a century we called upon unbounded invention and untiring industry to create an order of plenty for all of our people.

The challenge of the next half century is whether we have the wisdom to use that wealth to enrich and elevate our national life, and to advance the quality of our American civilization.

Your imagination, your initiative, and your indignation will determine whether we build a society where progress is the servant of our needs, or a society where old values and new visions are buried under unbridled growth. For in your time we have the opportunity to move not only toward the rich society and the powerful society, but upward to the Great Society.

The Great Society rests on abundance and liberty for all. It demands an end to poverty and racial injustice, to which we are totally committed in our time. But that is just the beginning.

The Great Society is a place where every child can find knowledge to enrich his mind and to enlarge his talents. It is a place where leisure is a welcome chance to build and reflect, not a feared cause of boredom and restlessness. It is a place where the city of man serves not only the needs of the body and the demands of commerce but the desire for beauty and the hunger for community.

It is a place where man can renew contact with nature. It is a place which honors creation for its own sake and for what it adds to the understanding of the race. It is a place where men are more concerned with the quality of their goals than the quantity of their goods.

But most of all, the Great Society is not a safe harbor, a resting place, a final objective, a finished work. It is a challenge constantly renewed, beckoning us toward a destiny where the meaning of our lives matches the marvelous products of labor.

So I want to talk to you today about three places where we begin to build the Great Society—in our cities, in our countryside and in our classrooms.

Many of you will live to see the day, perhaps 50 years from now, when there will be 400 million Americans—four-fifths of them in urban areas. In the remainder of this century urban population will double, city land will double, and we will have to build homes, highways, and facilities equal to all those built since this country was first settled. So in the next 40 years we must rebuild the entire urban United States.

Aristotle said: "Men come together in cities in order to live, but they remain together in order to live the good life." It is harder and harder to live the good life in American cities today.

The catalog of ills is long: there is the decay of the centers and the despoiling of the suburbs. There is not enough housing for our people or transportation for our traffic. Open land is vanishing and old landmarks are violated.

Worst of all expansion is eroding the precious and time honored values of community with neighbors and communion with nature. The loss of these values breeds loneliness and boredom and indifference.

Our society will never be great until our cities are great. Today the frontier of imagination and innovation is inside those cities and not beyond their borders.

New experiments are already going on. It will be the task of your generation to make the American city a place where future generations will come, not only to live but to live the good life.

I understand that if I stayed here tonight I would see that Michigan students are really doing their best to live the good life.

This is the place where the Peace Corps was started. It is inspiring to see how all of you, while you are in this country, are trying so hard to live at the level of the people.

A second place where we begin to build the Great Society is in our countryside. We have always prided ourselves on being not only America the strong and America the free, but America the beautiful. Today that beauty is in danger. The water we drink, the food we eat, the very air that we breathe, are threatened with pollution. Our parks are overcrowded, our seashores overburdened. Green fields and dense forests are disappearing.

A few years ago we were greatly concerned about the "Ugly American." Today we must act to prevent an ugly America.

For once the battle is lost, once our natural splendor is destroyed, it can never be recaptured. And once man can no longer walk with beauty or wonder at nature his spirit will wither and his sustenance be wasted.

A third place to build the Great Society is in the classrooms of America. There your children's lives will be shaped. Our society will not be great until every young mind is set free to scan the farthest reaches of thought and imagination. We are still far from that goal.

Today, 8 million adult Americans, more than the entire population of Michigan, have not finished 5 years of school. Nearly 20 million have not finished 8 years of school. Nearly 54 million—more than one-quarter of all America—have not even finished high school.

Each year more than 100,000 high school graduates, with proved ability, do not enter college because they cannot afford it. And if we cannot educate today's youth, what will we do in 1970 when elementary school enrollment will be 5 million greater than 1960? And high school enrollment will rise by 5 million. College enrollment will increase by more than 3 million.

In many places, classrooms are overcrowded and curricula are outdated. Most of our qualified teachers are underpaid, and many of our paid teachers are unqualified. So we must give every child a place to sit and a teacher to learn from. Poverty must not be a bar to learning, and learning must offer an escape from poverty.

But more classrooms and more teachers are not enough. We must seek an educational system which grows in excellence as it grows in size. This means better training for our teachers. It means preparing youth to enjoy their hours of leisure as well as their hours of labor. It means exploring new techniques of teaching, to find new ways to stimulate the love of learning and the capacity for creation.

These are three of the central issues of the Great Society. While our Government has many programs directed at those issues, I do not pretend that we have the full answer to those problems.

But I do promise this: We are going to assemble the best thought and the broadest knowledge from all over the world to find those answers for America. I intend to establish working groups to prepare a series of White House conferences and meetings—on the cities, on natural beauty, on the quality of education, and on other emerging challenges. And from these meetings and from this inspiration and from these studies we will begin to set our course toward the Great Society. . . .

Within your lifetime powerful forces, already loosed, will take us toward a way of life beyond the realm of our experience, almost beyond the bounds of our imagination.

For better or for worse, your generation has been appointed by history to deal with those problems and to lead America toward a new age. You have the chance never before afforded to any people in any age. You can help build a society where the demands of morality, and the needs of the spirit, can be realized in the life of the Nation.

So, will you join in the battle to give every citizen the full equality which God enjoins and the law requires, whatever his belief, or race, or the color of his skin?

Will you join in the battle to give every citizen an escape from the crushing weight of poverty?

Will you join in the battle to make it possible for all nations to live in enduring peace—as neighbors and not as mortal enemies?

Will you join in the battle to build the Great Society, to prove that our material progress is only the foundation on which we will build a richer life of mind and spirit?

There are those timid souls who say this battle cannot be won; that we are condemned to a soulless wealth. I do not agree We have the power to shape the civilization that we want. But we need your will, your labor, your hearts, if we are to build that kind of society.

Those who came to this land sought to build more than just a new country. They sought a new world. So I have come here today to your campus to say that you can make their vision our reality. So let us from this moment begin our work so that in the future men will look back and say: It was then, after a long and weary way, that man turned the exploits of his genius to the full enrichment of his life.

President Lyndon B. Johnson Signs
the Civil Rights Bill of 1964
2 July 1964

In choosing to honor his martyred predecessor with landmark civil rights legislation President Johnson did not choose an easy task. The political consensus required to pass a law that would guarantee equal access to public accommodations amounted to a great politi-

cal war, in which the President would oppose old friends and cultivate unusual new ones. To all combatants, Johnson seemed an unusual leader in such a crusade. A traditional Southern politician of Johnson's age and time viewed black Americans, at best, with some combination of condescension and neglect. The antagonistic racial views of most Southern politicians—and many from other parts of the nation as well—were simply inherited from the Civil War. In the United States Senate, traditionally the graveyard for civil rights legislation, Johnson's nucleus of strength remained with the powerful Southern Democratic bloc, men of age and seniority who were accustomed to authority. Early in 1964 the President informed the Southern Democrats' leader, Senator Richard Russell of Georgia, of his intentions; the patriarchal Russell, Johnson's friend and one-time mentor, replied that he would lead the usual filibuster, and civil rights legislation would again die. Russell's assurance regarding the sure fate of comprehensive civil rights legislation rested on the fierce rejection of racial equality present throughout the southern states. While the landmark Brown v. Board of Education decision in 1954 had sparked a decade of protest, segregation remained a viable political position for southern politicians great and small. All of the fame and honor accorded Dr. Martin Luther King, Jr. did not prevent police riots and Ku Klux Klan-inspired terrorism from dominating the South's political climate, insuring the safety of segregationist southern politicians in Washington. Nonetheless, Johnson waged an uncompromising battle, enlisting notable black establishment leaders like Whitney Young and Roy Wilkins. He crossed the political divide to approach the Republican Senate Leader, Everett McKinley Dirksen of Illinois, with a mixture of appeals to vanity and promises of political favors and threats. Senator's Russell's filibuster was broken on 10 June. Almost as a cruel counterpoint, on 22 June, a Ku Klux Klan gang seized three young civil rights workers in rural Mississippi. On 2 July, President Johnson signed the Civil Rights Act of 1964. On 4 August, the three mutilated bodies were found in Mississippi; subsequently, twenty-one men, including a sheriff and his deputy, were arraigned. While Johnson's landmark legislative accomplishment could not immediately end racism and barbarity, the impenetrable legislative barrier to civil rights legislation would exist no more.

I am about to sign into law the Civil Rights Act of 1964. I want to take this occasion to talk to you about what that law means to every American.

One hundred and eighty-eight years ago this week a small band of valiant men began a long struggle for freedom. They pledged their lives, their fortunes, and their sacred honor not only to found a nation, but to forge an ideal of freedom—not only for political independence, but for personal liberty—not only to eliminate foreign rule, but to establish the rule of justice in the affairs of men.

That struggle was a turning point in our history. Today in far corners of distant continents, the ideals of those American patriots still shape the struggles of men who hunger for freedom.

This is a proud triumph. Yet those who founded our country knew that freedom would be secure only if each generation fought to renew and enlarge its meaning. From the minutemen at Concord to the soldiers in Viet-Nam, each generation has been equal to that trust.

Americans of every race and color have died in battle to protect our freedom. Americans of every race and color have worked to build a nation of widening opportunities. Now our generation of Americans has been called on to continue the unending search for justice within our own borders.

We believe that all men are created equal. Yet many are denied equal treatment.

We believe that all men have certain unalienable rights. Yet many Americans do not enjoy those rights.

We believe that all men are entitled to the blessings of liberty. Yet millions are being deprived of those blessings—not because of their own failures, but because of the color of their skin.

The reasons are deeply imbedded in history and tradition and the nature of man. We can understand—without rancor or hatred—how this all happened.

But it cannot continue. Our Constitution, the foundation of our Republic, forbids it. The principles of our freedom forbid it. Morality forbids it. And the law I will sign tonight forbids it.

That law is the product of months of the most careful debate and discussion. It was proposed more than one year ago by our late and beloved President John F. Kennedy. It received the bipartisan support of more than two-thirds of the Members of both the House and the Senate. An overwhelming majority of Republicans as well as Democrats voted for it.

It has received the thoughtful support of tens of thousands of civic and religious leaders in all parts of this Nation. And it is supported by the great majority of the American people.

The purpose of the law is simple.

It does not restrict the freedom of any American, so long as he respects the rights of others.

It does not give special treatment to any citizen.

It does say the only limit to a man's hope for happiness, and for the future of his children, shall be his own ability.

It does say that there are those who are equal before God shall now also be equal in the polling booths, in the classrooms, in the factories, and in hotels, restaurants, movie theaters, and other places that provide service to the public.

I am taking steps to implement the law under my constitutional obligation to "take care that the laws are faithfully executed. . . ."

We must not approach the observance and enforcement of this law in a vengeful spirit. Its purpose is not to punish. Its purpose is not to divide, but to end divisions—divisions which have all lasted too long. Its purpose is national, not regional.

Its purpose is to promote a more abiding commitment to freedom, a more constant pursuit of justice, and a deeper respect for human dignity.

We will achieve these goals because most Americans are law-abiding citizens who want to do what is right.

This is why the Civil Rights Act relies first on voluntary compliance, then on the efforts of local communities and States to secure the rights of citizens. It provides for the national authority to step in only when others cannot or will not do the job.

This Civil Rights Act is a challenge to all of us to go to work in our communities and our States, in our homes and in our hearts, to eliminate the last vestiges of injustice in our beloved country.

So tonight I urge every public official, every religious leader, every business and professional man, every workingman, every housewife—I urge every American—to join in this effort to bring justice and hope to all our people—and to bring peace to our land.

My fellow citizens, we have come now to a time of testing. We must not fail.

Let us close the springs of racial poison. Let us pray for wise and understanding hearts. Let us lay aside irrelevant differences and make our Nation whole. Let us hasten that day when our unmeasured strength and our unbounded spirit will be free to do the great works ordained for this Nation by the just and wise God who is the Father of us all.

PRESIDENT LYNDON B. JOHNSON'S EARLY FOREBODING ABOUT THE WAR IN VIETNAM
11 June 1964

Although President Johnson possessed minimal knowledge of (or interest in) international affairs, he managed a series of crises reasonably well in his first three years. The fractious relationships between the United States and Latin America produced challenges, particularly in Panama and in the Dominican Republic, where American Marines landed in the spring of 1965 to deny a popular leftist the Dominican Presidency. Elsewhere, relations with the Soviet Union were relatively satisfactory, particularly after a summit meeting with Premier Aleksey Kosygin in June 1967. By that time, however, the war in Vietnam, remote and inconsequential when Johnson took office, had become the inferno which would destroy his presidency and tarnish the historical legacy he held so dearly. At the time of President Kennedy's assassination there were approximately 16,000 American "advisors" in Vietnam seeking to develop the political stability and military effectiveness of the government in Saigon. This Vietnamese struggle reached back into the nineteenth century as nationalists rose up against France, the colonial master, and against those Vietnamese who supported the French. After France was driven out of Vietnam in 1954, the United States assumed the burden of preventing the absolute triumph of northern-based Vietnamese nationalist and leftist forces under the leadership of Ho Chi Minh. In the United States, Ho would soon come to represent the lightning rod for a generation of American war protesters and for their political and military leaders. To Johnson and nearly all of the influential members of his administration, Ho represented communism and subservience to the Soviets and Chinese, and defeating him became defined as a crucial moment in the Cold War. Military defeat for the United States, in common American fears, would endanger the stability of the entire Pacific Rim. For the growing company of dissenters, Ho represented Vietnamese nationalism and United States intervention—an unfortunate successor to French colonialism. By the later years of the Johnson Administration, this dramatic dispute began to flow into America's streets, particularly from colleges and universities across the nation. By 1967, with 500,000 troops committed (and more requested), Vietnam dominated American consciousness, freezing Johnson's ambitious plans. The Great Society was finished. Johnson put all of his potent energy into rallying the public and keeping prominent political figures in line. The size and ferocity of the anti-war movement notwithstanding, the President questioned the patriotism of protesters. Increasingly, he became a prisoner of the White House, as public appearances risked unseemly responses. In November 1967, Senator Eugene McCarthy of Minnesota shocked Washington with the announcement of his candidacy for the Democratic presidential nomination. Four months later, McCarthy attracted 42 percent of the votes in the New Hampshire primary. Four days after that, Johnson's worst political nightmare materialized when Robert Kennedy joined the race. On 31 March 1968, with his Gallup Poll favorable rating at 23 percent, Lyndon Baines Johnson announced his withdrawal from public life. Ironically, years earlier Johnson had clearly recognized the quicksand that Vietnam represented for him, but saw no way out. Recently published White House tapes, secretly controlled by President Johnson, reveal this apparently insoluble dilemma in a rumanative conversation between Johnson and his erstwhile mentor, Senator Richard Russell of Georgia.

THURSDAY, JUNE 11, 1964
RICHARD RUSSELL 12:26 P.M.

LBJ: I'm confronted. I don't believe the American people ever want me to run. If I lose it, I think that they'll say I've lost. I've pulled in. At the same time, I don't want to commit us to a war. And I'm in a hell of a shape.

RUSSELL: We're just like the damn cow over a fence out there in Vietnam.

LBJ: . . . I've got a study being made now by the experts . . . whether Malaysia will necessarily go and India'll go and how much it'll hurt our prestige if we just got out and let some conference fail or something. . . . A fellow like

A. W. Moursund said to me last night, "Goddamn, there's not anything that'll destroy you as quick as pulling out, pulling up stakes and running. America wants, by God, prestige and power." . . . I said, "Yeah, but I don't want to kill these folks." He said, "I don't give a damn. I didn't want to kill 'em in Korea, but if you don't stand up for America, there's nothing that a fellow in Johnson City"—or Georgia or any other place—"they'll forgive you for anything except being weak." Goldwater and all of 'em are raising hell about . . . hot pursuit and let's go in and bomb 'em. . . . You can't clean it up. That's the hell of it.

RUSSELL: . . . It'd take a half million men. They'd be bogged down in there for ten years. . . . We're right where we started, except for seventy thousand of 'em buried over there.

LBJ: Now Dick, you think, every time you can get your mind off of other things, think about some man. . . . My great weakness in this job is I just don't know these other people. The Kennedys—they know every damn fellow in the country or have got somebody that knows 'em. They're out at these universities and everyplace in the country—New York and Chicago.

. . . .

LBJ: We're just doing fine, except for this damned Vietnam thing. We're just doing wonderful. Every index. The businessmen are going wonderful. They're up 12, 14 percent investment over last year. The tax bill has just worked out wonderfully. There're

only 2.6 percent of the married people unemployed. . . . And 16 percent of these youngsters, and I'll have all them employed. . . . It's kids that are dropping out of school and then they go on a roll. But I'll take care of that with my poverty, just by organizing it all. We've got the money in these various departments—Labor and HEW and Justice. . . . I'm gonna put all of them in one and put one top administrator and really get some results. Go in and clear up these damn rolls. And I'll do it with only $300 million more than was in the budget anyway last year. . . . I was down in Kentucky the other day. We've got fifty kids there teaching beauty culture—how to fix Lynda's hair. And they're all going out and get jobs $50, $60 a week in another three months. . . . That's what we ought to do instead of paying out four billion a year on relief, for nothing, where you don't have to work. To hell with this unemployment compensation. It's relief. But I've got to find a man for Vietnam.

RUSSELL: I don't know what the hell to do. I didn't ever want to get messed up down there. I do not agree with those brain trusters who say that this thing has got tremendous strategic and economic value and that we'll lose everything in Southeast Asia if we lose Vietnam. . . . But as a practical matter, we're in there and I don't know how the hell you can tell the American people you're coming out. . . . They'll think that you've just been whipped, you've been ruined, you're scared. It'd be disastrous.

LBJ: I think that I've got to say that I didn't get you in here, but we're in here by treaty and our national honor's at stake. And if this treaty's no good, none of 'em are any good. Therefore we're there. And being there, we've got to conduct ourselves like men. That's number one. Number two, in our own revolution, we wanted freedom and we naturally look with sympathy with other people who want freedom and if you'll leave 'em alone and give 'em freedom, we'll get out tomorrow. . . . Third thing, we've got to try to find some proposal some way, like Eisenhower worked out in Korea. . . .

PRESIDENT RICHARD M. NIXON ANNOUNCES THE INVASION OF CAMBODIA
28 April 1970

In a nationally broadcast speech from the Oval Office on 30 April 1970, President Richard M. Nixon announced that American and allied military forces had invaded Cambodia, with land and air attacks continuing. In response, anti-war protests erupted across the nation. On college campuses as different as Kent State in Ohio and Jackson State in Mississippi, protesting students were killed by National Guard troops mobilized to control the national protests. Major cities swelled with protests, as they had in the same cause against President Lyndon B. Johnson. Nixon, shaken by the size and vehemence of protest, resolved to persevere, and was overheard referring to some protesters as "bums." His risky decision on Cambodia held the promise, he felt, of breaking a stalemate that had cost the United States such an enormous price in blood, money and prestige. He had entered office confident regarding his foreign policy expertise. "I'm not going to end up like LBJ," he bragged, "I'm going to stop that war. Fast." His "Vietnamization" concept promised to bolster the political stability and military competence of South Vietnam while simultaneously decreasing the American troop level by hundreds of thousands. Yet the corrupt and unpopular regime in Saigon proved incapable of reform. And the President's attempts to enlist the Soviet Union and China as agents in persuading Ho Chi Minh to accept United States terms of "peace with honor" failed. Left with an unpromising reliance on military means, Nixon found a potential prize in Cambodia in March 1970, when a pro-American general named Lon Nol successfully overthrew the neutralist regime of Prince Norodom Sihanouk. Cambodia abuts Vietnam, and its jungles had for years provided refuge for North Vietnamese storage and staging areas, a vital link in the "Ho Chi Trail," on which supplies and troops steadily flowed south. This dramatic invasion, taken by the President against the advice of most of his advisors, would actually cause more problems than it would solve, both in Indochina and at home. Nixon's presentation to the American people described a completely different scenario.

Ten days ago, in my report to the Nation on Vietnam, I announced a decision to withdraw an additional 150,000 Americans from Vietnam over the next year. I said then that I was making that decision despite our concern over increased enemy activity in Laos, in Cambodia, and in South Vietnam.

At that time, I warned that if I concluded that increased enemy activity in any of these areas endangered the lives of Americans remaining in Vietnam, I would not hesitate to take strong and effective measures to deal with that situation.

Despite that warning, North Vietnam has increased its military aggression in all these areas, and particularly in Cambodia.

After full consultation with the National Security Council, Ambassador Bunker, General Abrams, and my other advisers, I have concluded that the actions of the enemy in the last 10 days clearly endanger the lives of Americans who are in Vietnam now and would constitute an unacceptable risk to those who will be there after withdrawal of another 150,000.

To protect our men who are in Vietnam and to guarantee the continued success of our withdrawal and Vietnamization programs, I have concluded that the time has come for action.

Tonight, I shall describe the actions of the enemy, the actions I have ordered to deal with that situation, and the reasons for my decision.

Cambodia, a small country of 7 million people, has been a neutral nation since the Geneva agreement of 1954—an agreement, incidentally, which was signed by the Government of North Vietnam. . . .

North Vietnam, however, has not respected that neutrality.

For the past 5 years—as indicated on this map that you see here—North Vietnam has occupied military sanctuaries all along the Cambodian frontier with South Vietnam. Some of these extend up to 20 miles into Cambodia. The sanctuaries are in red and, as you note, they are on both sides of the border. They are used for hit and run attacks on American and South Vietnamese forces in South Vietnam.

These Communist occupied territories contain major base camps, training sites, logistics facilities, weapons and ammunition factories, airstrips, and prisoner-of-war compounds.

For 5 years, neither the United States nor South Vietnam has moved against these enemy sanctuaries because we did not wish to violate the territory of a neutral nation. Even after the Vietnamese Communists began to expand these sanctuaries 4 weeks ago, we counseled patience to our South Vietnamese allies and imposed restraints on our own commanders.

In contrast to our policy, the enemy in the past 2 weeks has stepped up his guerrilla actions and he is concentrating his main forces in these sanctuaries that you see on this map where they are building up to launch massive attacks on our forces and those of South Vietnam.

North Vietnam in the last 2 weeks has stripped away all pretense of respecting the sovereignty or the neutrality of Cambodia. Thousands of their soldiers are invading the country from the sanctuaries; they are encircling the capital of Phnom Penh. Coming from these sanctuaries, as you see here, they have moved into Cambodia and are encircling the capital.

Cambodia, as a result of this, has sent out a call to the United States, to a number of other nations, for assistance. Because if this enemy effort succeeds, Cambodia would become a vast enemy staging area and a springboard for attacks on South Vietnam along 600 miles of frontier—a refuge where enemy troops could return from combat without fear of retaliation.

North Vietnamese men and supplies could then be poured into that country, jeopardizing not only the lives of our own men but the people of South Vietnam as well.

Now confronted with this situation, we have three options.

First, we can do nothing. Well, the ultimate result of that course of action is

clear. Unless we indulge in wishful thinking, the lives of Americans remaining in Vietnam after our next withdrawal of 150,000 would be gravely threatened. . . .

Our second choice is to provide massive military assistance to Cambodia itself. Now unfortunately, while we deeply sympathize with the plight of 7 million Cambodians whose country is being invaded, massive amounts of military assistance could not be rapidly and effectively utilized by the small Cambodian Army against the immediate threat. With other nations, we shall do our best to provide the small arms and other equipment which the Cambodian Army of 40,000 needs and can use for its defense. But the aid we will provide will be limited to the purpose of enabling Cambodia to defend its neutrality and not for the purpose of making it an active belligerent on one side or the other.

Our third choice is to go to the heart of the trouble. That means cleaning out major North Vietnamese and Vietcong occupied territories—these sanctuaries which serve as bases for attacks on both Cambodia and American and South Vietnamese forces in South Vietnam. Some of these, incidentally, are as close to Saigon as Baltimore is to Washington. This one, for example [indicating], is called the Parrot's Beak. It is only 33 miles from Saigon.

Now faced with these three options, this is the decision I have made.

In cooperation with the armed forces of South Vietnam, attacks are being launched this week to clean out major enemy sanctuaries on the Cambodian-Vietnam border.

A major responsibility for the ground operations is being assumed by South Vietnamese forces. For example, the attacks in several areas, including the Parrot's Beak that I referred to a moment ago, are exclusively South Vietnamese ground operations under South Vietnamese command with the United States providing air and logistical support.

There is one area, however, immediately above Parrot's Beak, where I have concluded that a combined American and South Vietnamese operation is necessary.

Tonight, American and South Vietnamese units will attack the headquarters for the entire Communist military operation in South Vietnam. This key control center has been occupied by the North Vietnamese and Vietcong for 5 years in blatant violation of Cambodia's neutrality.

This is not an invasion of Cambodia. The areas in which these attacks will be launched are completely occupied and controlled by North Vietnamese forces. Our purpose is not to occupy the areas. Once enemy forces are driven out of these sanctuaries and once their military supplies are destroyed, we will withdraw.

These actions are in no way directed to the security interests of any nation. Any government that chooses to use these actions as a pretext for harming relations with the United States will be doing so on its own responsibility, and on its own initiative, and we will draw the appropriate conclusions.

Now let me give you the reasons for my decision.

A majority of the American people, a majority of you listening to me, are for the withdrawal of our forces from Vietnam. The action I have taken tonight is indispensable for the continuing success of that withdrawal program.

A majority of the American people want to end this war rather than to have it drag on interminably. The action I have taken tonight will serve that purpose.

A majority of the American people want to keep the casualties of our brave men in Vietnam at an absolute minimum. The action I take tonight is essential if we are to accomplish that goal.

We take this action not for the purpose of expanding the war into Cambodia but for the purpose of ending the war in Vietnam and winning the just peace we all desire. We have made—we will continue to make every possible effort to end this war through negotiation at the conference table rather than through more fighting on the battlefield.

Let us look again at the record. We have stopped the bombing of North Vietnam. We have cut air operations by over 20 percent. We have announced withdrawal of over 250,000 of our men. We have offered to withdraw all of our men if they will withdraw theirs. We have offered to negotiate all issues with only one condition—and that is that the future of South Vietnam be determined not by North Vietnam, and not by the United States, but by the people of South Vietnam themselves.

The answer of the enemy has been intransigence at the conference table, belligerence in Hanoi, massive military aggression in Laos and Cambodia, and stepped-up attacks in South Vietnam, designed to increase American casualties.

This attitude has become intolerable. We will not react to this threat to American lives merely by plaintive diplomatic protests. If we did, the credibility of the United States would be destroyed in every area of the world where only the power of the United States deters aggression.

Tonight, I again warn the North Vietnamese that if they continue to escalate the fighting when the United States is withdrawing its forces, I shall meet my responsibility as Commander in Chief of our Armed Forces to take the action I consider necessary to defend the security of our American men.

The action that I have announced tonight puts the leaders of North Vietnam on notice that we will be patient in working for peace; we will be conciliatory at the conference table, but we will not be humiliated. We will not be defeated. We will not allow American men by the thousands to be killed by an enemy from privileged sanctuaries.

The time came long ago to end this war through peaceful negotiations. We stand ready for those negotiations. We have made major efforts, many of which must remain secret. I say tonight: All the offers and approaches made previously remain on the conference table whenever Hanoi is ready to negotiate seriously.

But if the enemy response to our most conciliatory offers for peaceful negotiation continues to be to increase its attacks and humiliate and defeat us, we shall react accordingly.

My fellow Americans, we live in an age of anarchy, both abroad and at home. We see mindless attacks on all the great institutions which have been created by free civilizations in the last 500 years. Even here in the United States, great universities are being systematically destroyed. Small nations all over the world find themselves under attack from within and from without.

If, when the chips are down, the world's most powerful nation, the United States of America, acts like a pitiful, helpless giant, the forces of totalitarianism and anarchy will threaten free nations and free institutions throughout the world.

It is not our power but our will and character that is being tested tonight. The question all Americans must ask and answer tonight is this: Does the richest and strongest nation in the history of the world have the character to meet a direct challenge by a group which rejects every effort to win a just peace, ignores our warning, tramples on solemn agreements, violates the neutrality of an unarmed people, and uses our prisoners as hostages?

If we fail to meet this challenge, all other nations will be on notice that despite its overwhelming power the United States, when a real crisis comes, will be found wanting.

During my campaign for the Presidency, I pledged to bring Americans home from Vietnam. They are coming home.

I promised to end this war. I shall keep that promise.

I promised to win a just peace. I shall keep that promise.

We shall avoid a wider war. But we are also determined to put an end to this war. . . .

No one is more aware than I am of the political consequences of the action I have taken. It is tempting to take the easy political path: to blame this war on previous administrations and to bring all of our men home immediately, regardless of the consequences, even though that would mean defeat for the United States; to desert 18 million South Vietnamese people, who have put their trust in us and to expose them to the same slaughter and savagery which the leaders of North Vietnam inflicted on hundreds of thousands of North Vietnamese who chose freedom when the Communists took over North Vietnam in 1954; to get peace at any price now, even though I know that a peace of humiliation for the United States would lead to a bigger war or surrender later.

I have rejected all political considerations in making this decision.

Whether my party gains in November is nothing compared to the lives of 400,000 brave Americans fighting for our country and for the cause of peace and freedom in Vietnam. Whether I may be a one-term President is insignificant compared to whether by our failure to act in this crisis the United States proves itself to be unworthy to lead the forces of freedom in this critical period in world history. I would rather be a one-term President and do what I believe is right than to be a two-term President at the cost of seeing America become a second-rate power and to see this Nation accept the first defeat in its proud 190-year history.

I realize that in this war there are honest and deep differences in this country about whether we should have become involved, that there are differences as to how the war should have been conducted. But the decision I announce tonight transcends those differences.

For the lives of American men are involved. The opportunity for 150,000, Americans to come home in the next 12 months is involved. The future of 18 million people in South Vietnam and 7 million people in Cambodia is involved. The possibility of winning a just peace in Vietnam and in the Pacific is at stake.

It is customary to conclude a speech from the White House by asking support for the President of the United States. Tonight, I depart from that precedent. What I ask is far more important. I ask for your support for our brave men fighting tonight halfway around the world—not for territory—not for glory—but so that their younger brothers and their sons and your sons can have a chance to grow up in a world of peace and freedom and justice.

PRESIDENT RICHARD M. NIXON SPEAKS ON THE DESEGREGATION OF SOUTHERN SCHOOLS
25 May 1971

Richard M. Nixon's 1968 presidential campaign relied on a "Southern Strategy," which associated the Democrats with civil rights and black interests while inviting Southern whites into Republican ranks. This effective tactic began an historic switch in party allegiance, which soon took hold from courthouses to state houses to the Congress. The "solid South," for a century the base of Democratic power, soon eroded, replaced by Southern Republicans, of the party of the reviled Abraham Lincoln. Ironically, President Nixon discretely managed to advance civil rights without damaging his new political base. He entered office fifteen years after the Brown v. Board of Education *decision by the Supreme Court ruled school segregation unconstitutional, yet only 5.2 percent of Southern black children attended desegregated schools. As the protagonist and beneficiary of Southern Republican success, Nixon faced a legal impasse. Elected as a "law and order" president, he confronted a recalcitrant South determined to defy Federal court orders mandating desegregation. Nixon and his advisors opted to uphold the law in a series of delicate political maneuverings that followed the President's own public embrace of the virtue of the* Brown *decision. Within two years, desegregation of Southern public education exhibited dramatic change. Blacks in all-black schools declined from 68 percent to 18 percent. Blacks in schools more-than-half white increased from 18 percent to 38 percent. This variation, however incomplete, destroyed the historic barrier of school segregation and began a new era of incremental improvement in educational opportunity and race relations. The President referred to this historic change in a speech in Birmingham.*

. . . I spoke in Mobile of the fact that we have differences between regions, we have differences between races, we have differences between religions, we have differences between the generations today, and these differences have at times been very destructive. We must recognize that we will always have those differences. People of different races, different religions, from different backgrounds, and of different ages are not always going to agree.

The question is, can those differences be resolved peacefully, and second, can they be made creative rather than destructive? Must they be a drain upon us? Must they go so far that they destroy the confidence and faith of this great Nation in its destiny and its future? I do not believe that that is necessary.

Two specific points that I would like to mention. I would say this in the North if I were speaking there; I say it in the South. I know the difficult problems most of you in the Southern States have had on the school desegregation problem. I went to school in the South, and so, therefore, I am more familiar with how Southerners feel about that problem than others. Also, I went to school in the North, or the West I should say, and I have nothing but utter contempt for the double hypocritical standard of Northerners who look at the South and point the finger and say, "Why don't those Southerners do something about their race problem?"

Let's look at the facts. In the past year, 2 years, there has been a peaceful, relatively quiet, very significant revolution. Oh, it is not over, there are problems—there was one in Chattanooga, I understand, the last couple days; there will be more. But look what has happened in the South. Today 38 percent of all black children in the South go to majority white schools. Today only 28 percent of all black children in the North go to majority white schools. There has been no progress in the North in the past 2

years in that respect. There has been significant progress in the South.

How did it come about? It came about because farsighted leaders in the South, black and white, some of whom I am sure did not agree with the opinions handed down by the Supreme Court which were the law of the land, recognized as law-abiding citizens that they had the responsibility to meet that law of the land, and they had dealt with the problem—not completely, there is more yet to be done. The recent decision of the Supreme Court presents some more problems, but I am confident that over a period of time those problems will also be handled in a peaceful and orderly way for the most part.

But let's look at the deeper significance of this. As I speak today in what is called the Heart of Dixie, I realize that America at this time needs to become one country. Too long we have been divided. It has been North versus South versus West; Wall Street versus the country and the country versus the city and the rest. That does not mean we don't have differences and will not continue to have them, but those regional differences, it seems to me, must go. Presidents of the United States should come to Alabama and Mississippi and Georgia and Louisiana more than once, more often than every 50 years or every 100 years as the case might be, to some of the cities, and they should come because this is one nation, and we must speak as one nation, we must work as one nation. . . .

PRESIDENT RICHARD M. NIXON AND THE "OPENING" OF CHINA
27 February 1972

In the United States for more than two decades following the successful communist revolution in China in 1949, the Republican Party provided the foundation for political and emotional resistance to the Beijing regime. Richard M. Nixon first came to national political attention in the late 1940s as a California Congressman serving on the House Committee on un-American Activities, which conducted highly-publicized hearings on domestic subversion. A year later, Nixon became the principal Congressional actor when this Committee began to consider the celebrated Alger Hiss-Whittaker Chambers affair, an investigation of the role of communism in American political life at high levels. "Loyalty" or "disloyalty" became a passionate theme of American politics and society. Republican Senator Joseph McCarthy and his allies subsequently charged that the Democratic Party had "lost China" through subversion and stupidity. Through the years the mere public discussion of normalizing relations and diplomatic recognition remained out of the question. Meanwhile Nixon steadily rose in status and power until reaching the White House in 1968. In December of 1971, his Secretary of State Henry Kissinger made two secret trips to China to meet with Chairman Mao tse-Tung and Premier Chou en-Lai. Three months later, without prior announcement, President Richard M. Nixon arrived in Beijing, stunning the nation and the world. Nixon, erstwhile scourge of "Red China," now envisioned the "opening" of China as a major event in world history. "What we are doing now with China is so great, so historic, the word 'Vietnam' will be only a footnote when it is written in history," Kissinger confidently predicted. While this historical assertion remains dubious, the dramatic vision endures of Richard Nixon on the front pages of American newspapers sitting in the library of Mao tse-Tung, the world's most prominent revolutionary communist. The re-entry of China onto the world stage had begun.

This magnificent banquet marks the end of our stay in the People's Republic of China. We have been here a week. This was the week that changed the world.

As we look back over this week, we think of the boundless hospitality that has been extended to all of us by our Chinese friends.

We have, today, seen the progress of modern China. We have seen the matchless wonders of ancient China. We have seen also the beauty of the countryside, the vibrancy of a great city, Shanghai. All this we enjoyed enormously.

But most important was the fact that we had the opportunity to have talks with Chairman Mao, with Prime Minister Chou En-lai, with the Foreign Minister and other people in the government.

The joint communique which we have issued today summarizes the results of our talks. That communique will make headlines around the world tomorrow. But what we have said in that communique is not nearly as important as what we will do in the years ahead to build a bridge across 16,000 miles and 22 years of hostility which have divided us in the past.

What we have said today is that we shall build that bridge. And because the Chinese people and the American people, as the Prime Minister has said, are a great people, we can build that long bridge.

To do so requires more than the letters, the words of the communique. The letters and the words are a beginning, but the actions that follow must be in the spirit which characterized our talks.

With Chairman Mao, with the Prime Minister, and with others with whom we have met, our talks have been characterized by frankness, by honesty, by determination, and above all, by mutual respect.

Our communique indicates, as it should, some areas of difference. It also indicates some areas of agreement. To mention only one that is particularly appropriate here in Shanghai, is the fact that this great city, over the past, has on many occasions

been the victim of foreign aggression and foreign occupation. And we join the Chinese people, we the American people, in our dedication to this principle: That never again shall foreign domination, foreign occupation, be visited upon this city or any part of China or any independent country in this world.

Mr. Prime Minister, our two peoples tonight hold the future of the world in our hands. As we think of that future, we are dedicated to the principle that we can build a new world, a world of peace, a world of justice, a world of independence for all nations.

If we succeed in working together where we can find common ground, if we can find the common ground on which we can both stand, where we can build the bridge between us and build a new world, generations in the years ahead will look back and thank us for this meeting that we have held in this past week. Let the great Chinese people and the great American people be worthy of the hopes and ideals of the world, for peace and justice and progress for all.

In that spirit, I ask all of you to join in a toast to the health of Chairman Mao, of Prime Minister Chou En-lai, and to all of our Chinese friends here tonight, and our American friends, and to that friendship between our two peoples to which Chairman Chang has referred so eloquently.

PRESIDENT RICHARD M. NIXON RESIGNS
FROM OFFICE
9 August 1974

Five months before Election Day in 1972, seven men entered the offices of the Democratic National Committee at the Watergate office and apartment complex in downtown Washington. The predawn trespassers were discovered, arrested, and identified—at first vaguely—as associates of President Nixon's re-election organization. All of the men remained silent and no evidence directly linked them to the Committee to Re-elect the President or to the White House itself, so the odd incident soon began to fade from public view. Nixon's re-election campaign proved a rousing success. He routed Democratic nominee George McGovern on 7 November, and turned his attention back to the intractable war in Vietnam. Six months later, in March 1973, one of the accused Watergate burglars, James McCord, talked—claiming that the break-in had been ordered by Nixon's campaign chairman, John Mitchell, a former Attorney-General and close presidential confidant. With the dam of silence broken, the Watergate Crisis occupied the next eighteen months, providing political bombshells and high constitutional drama on a regular basis. In April 1973, the FBI Director admitted destroying relevant Watergate evidence at the urging of White House aides. Ten days later, the President's closest advisors, H. R. Haldeman, John Erlichman and John Dean, resigned under pressure. In May, a Senate Select Committee began televised hearings. Dean testified that the President had ordered "hush money" paid to the Watergate burglars. The most startling testimony occurred on 16 July when White House aide Alexander Butterfield told the Senate Committee and a national television audience that a taping system automatically recorded all of the President's meetings and telephone conversations. The Senate subpoenaed this evidence, the President claimed Executive Privilege, and for an entire year the nation watched the constitutional, political and personal struggle of Richard Nixon to retain his office. The President's troubles intensified in October when Vice President Spiro Agnew resigned after acknowledging guilt in an income tax case, becoming the only vice president in American history to leave office in a criminal matter. As successor, Nixon appointed House Republican Leader Gerald R. Ford, a popular conservative and strong supporter of the President and his policies. The constitutional struggle over the Presidential tapes continued while many leading Nixon associates received indictments for obstruction of justice. In the summer of 1974, the President took two extended international tours designed to burnish his image as a world leader. But neither the Middle Eastern tour nor the ensuing summit meeting in Moscow would equal in impact the decision of the Supreme Court on 24 July. The Justices unanimously ordered the White House to turn over all subpoenaed materials to Watergate Special Prosecutor Leon Jaworski. Three days later, the Judiciary Committee of the House of

Representatives issued two articles of impeachment against the President. On 5 August, with the tapes now available for scrutiny, Nixon acknowledged that he had committed "a serious act of omission" by failing to disclose that six days after the break-in, he had ordered the FBI to halt its investigation. On 8 August the President went before the nation to announce his resignation, effective at noon the following day. Years later, in 1997, came the publication of additional tapes long withheld from public view through legal maneuvers directed by Nixon and his partisans. They clearly indicate the President's knowledge of the elaborate cover-up and participation in obstruction of justice, which Nixon never acknowledged as he left office. On 9 August 1974, before leaving the White House for the last time as President, he spoke to an impromptu assemblage of family, friends, and staff.

I think the record should show that this is one of those spontaneous things that we always arrange whenever the President comes in to speak, and it will be so reported in the press, and we don't mind, because they have to call it as they see it.

But on our part, believe me, it is spontaneous.

You are here to say goodby to us, and we don't have a good word for it in English—the best is *au revoir*. We will see you again.

I just met with the members of the White House staff, you know, those who serve here in the White House day in and day out, and I asked them to do what I ask all of you to do to the extent that you can and, of course, are requested to do so: to serve our next President as you have served me and previous Presidents—because many of you have been here for many years— with devotion and dedication, because this office, great as it is, can only be as great as the men and women who work for and with the President.

This house, for example—I was thinking of it as we walked down this hall, and I was comparing it to some of the great houses of the world that I have been in. This isn't the biggest house. Many, and most, in even smaller countries, are much bigger. This isn't the finest house. Many in Europe, particularly, and in China, Asia, have paintings of great, great value, things that we just don't have here and, probably, will never have until we are 1,000 years old or older.

But this is the best house. It is the best house, because it has something far more important than numbers of people who serve, far more important than numbers of rooms or how big it is, far more important than numbers of magnificent pieces of art.

This house has a great heart, and that heart comes from those who serve. I was rather sorry they didn't come down. We said goodby to them upstairs. But they are really great. And I recall after so many times I have made speeches, and some of them pretty tough, yet, I always come back, or after a hard day—and my days usually have run rather long—I would always get a lift from them, because I might be a little down but they always smiled.

And so it is with you. I look around here, and I see so many on this staff that, you know, I should have been by your offices and shaken hands, and I would love to have talked to you and found out how to run the world—everybody wants to tell the President what to do, and boy, he needs to be told many times—but I just haven't had the time. But I want you to know that each and every one of you, I know, is indispensable to this Government.

I am proud of this Cabinet. I am proud of all the members who have served in our Cabinet. I am proud of our sub-Cabinet. I am proud of our White House Staff. As I pointed out last night, sure, we have done some things wrong in this Administration, and the top man always takes the responsibility, and I have never ducked it. But I want to say one thing: We can be proud of it—5½ years. No man or no woman came into this Administration and left it with more of this world's goods than when he came in. No man or no woman ever profited at the public expense or the public till. That tells something about you.

Mistakes, yes. But for personal gain, never. You did what you believed in. Sometimes right, sometimes wrong. And I only wish that I were a wealthy man—at the present time, I have got

to find a way to pay my taxes—[*laughter*]—and if I were, I would like to recompense you for the sacrifices that all of you have made to serve in government.

But you are getting something in government—and I want you to tell this to your children, and I hope the Nation's children will hear it, too—something in government service that is far more important than money. It is a cause bigger than yourself. It is the cause of making this the greatest nation in the world, the leader of the world, because without our leadership, the world will know nothing but war, possibly starvation or worse, in the years ahead. With our leadership it will know peace, it will know plenty.

We have been generous, and we will be more generous in the future as we are able to. But most important, we must be strong here, strong in our hearts, strong in our souls, strong in our belief, and strong in our willingness to sacrifice, as you have been willing to sacrifice, in a pecuniary way, to serve in government.

There is something else I would like for you to tell your young people. You know, people often come in and say, "What will I tell my kids?" They look at government and say, sort of a rugged life, and they see the mistakes that are made. They get the impression that everybody is here for the purpose of feathering his nest. That is why I made this earlier point—not in this Administration, not one single man or woman.

And I say to them, there are many fine careers. This country needs good farmers, good businessmen, good plumbers, good carpenters.

I remember my old man. I think that they would have called him sort of a little man, common man. He didn't consider himself that way. You know what he was? He was a streetcar motorman first, and then he was a farmer, and then he had a lemon ranch. It was the poorest lemon ranch in California, I can assure you. He sold it before they found oil on it. [*Laughter*] And then he was a grocer. But he was a great man, because he did his job, and every job counts up to the hilt, regardless of what happens.

Nobody will ever write a book, probably, about my mother. Well, I guess all of you would say this about your mother—my mother was a saint. And I think of her, two boys dying of tuberculosis, nursing four others in order that she could take care of my older brother for 3 years in Arizona, and seeing each of them die, and when they died, it was like one of her own.

Yes, she will have no books written about her. But she was a saint.

Now, however, we look to the future. I had a little quote in the speech last night from T.R. As you know, I kind of like to read books. I am not educated, but I do read books—[*laughter*]—and the T.R. quote was a pretty good one.

Here is another one I found as I was reading, my last night in the White House, and this quote is about a young man. He was a young lawyer in New York. He had married a beautiful girl, and they had a lovely daughter, and then suddenly she died, and this is what he wrote. This was in his diary.

He said, "She was beautiful in face and form and lovelier still in spirit. As a flower she grew and as a fair young flower she died. Her life had been always in the sunshine. There had never come to her a single great sorrow. None ever knew her who did not love and revere her for her bright and sunny temper and her saintly unselfishness. Fair, pure and joyous as a maiden, loving, tender and happy as a young wife. When she had just become a mother, when her life seemed to be just begun and when the years seemed so bright before her, then by a strange and terrible fate death came to her. And when my heart's dearest died, the light went from my life forever."

That was T.R. in his twenties. He thought the light had gone from his life forever—but he went on. And he not only became President but, as an ex-President, he served his country, always in the arena, tempestuous, strong, sometimes wrong, sometimes right, but he was a man.

And as I leave, let me say, that is an example I think all of us should remember. We think sometimes when things happen that don't go the right way; we think that when you don't pass the bar exam the first time—I happened to, but I was just lucky; I mean, my writing was so poor the bar examiner said, "We have just got to let the guy through." We think that when someone dear to us dies, we think that when we lose an election, we think that when we suffer a defeat that all is ended. We think, as T.R. said, that the light had left his life forever.

Not true. It is only a beginning, always. The young must know it; the old must know it. It must always sustain us, because the greatness comes not when things go always good for you, but the greatness comes and you are really tested, when you take some knocks, some disappointments, when sadness comes, because only if you have been in the deepest valley can you ever know how magnificent it is to be on the highest mountain.

And so I say to you on this occasion, as we leave, we leave proud of the people who have stood by us and worked for us and served this country.

We want you to be proud of what you have done. We want you to continue to serve in government, if that is your wish. Always give your best, never get discouraged, never be petty; always remember, others may hate you, but those who hate you don't win unless you hate them, and then you destroy yourself.

And so, we leave with high hopes, in good spirit, and with deep humility, and with very much gratefulness in our hearts. I can only say to each and every one of you, we come from many faiths, we pray perhaps to different gods—but really the same God in a sense—but I want to say for each and every one of you, not only will we always remember you, not only will we always be grateful to you but always you will be in our hearts and you will be in our prayers.

Thank you very much.

PRESIDENT GERALD R. FORD PARDONS
RICHARD M. NIXON
8 September 1974

President Richard Nixon's resignation took effect at noon on 9 August 1974. Three minutes later, Gerald R. Ford took the oath of office from Chief Justice Warren Burger. The new President faced a country and Congress politically exhausted from the months of Watergate, and immediately delighted the nation with his unpretentious all-American qualities. Ruggedly handsome at the age of sixty-one, he still resembled the University of Michigan football star he had been in the early 1940s. In his first public appearances, Ford spoke slowly and plainly in support of honesty and traditional values. A burst of affection spontaneously arose at the news that he made his own toast for breakfast. At the same time, while Washington remained a political minefield, Ford possessed shrewd instincts honed over a twenty-five-year career in the House of Representatives and quickly moved on two significant fronts. The wounds of Vietnam remained open, and Ford had been a leading "hawk" throughout the ordeal. The vice presidency was again vacant, engendering bitter infighting among the Republicans. Ford moved swiftly and surprisingly. Received tumultuously at the Chicago convention of the hawkish Veterans of Foreign Wars on 19 August, the President indicated that his approach toward draft evaders and military deserters would be "leniency." The veterans, stunned, remained polite. The next day, Ford greatly disappointed conservative Republicans with the announcement that his choice as vice president would be Nelson A. Rockefeller, progressive Governor of New York and the favorite enemy of the Republican right wing. Perhaps the greatest problem remained the political specter of Richard Nixon, whose legal status lay between possible indictment by the Watergate Special Prosecutor and presidential pardon. Congressman Ford had supported Nixon for a quarter of a century, and when he was named vice president in December 1973 to replace the disgraced Spiro Agnew, the appointment produced speculation about an ultimate "deal" should Nixon be forced from office. At an 28 August press conference, the President seemed to indicate that there would be no decision regarding his predecessor until the Special Prosecutor acted. Ford's honeymoon period continued despite his controversial decisions, for on 1 September the Gallup Poll revealed an outstanding 71 percent favorable rating, made up of 77 percent Republicans and 68 percent Democrats. From this politically privileged position came news that the President had granted his predecessor "a full, free and absolute pardon. . . ."

I have come to a decision which I felt I should tell you and all of my fellow American citizens, as soon as I was certain in my own mind and in my own conscience that it is the right thing to do.

I have learned already in this office that the difficult decisions always come to this desk. I must admit that many of them do not look at all the same as the hypothetical questions that I have answered freely and perhaps too fast on previous occasions.

My customary policy is to try and get all the facts and to consider the opinions of my countrymen and to take counsel with my most valued friends. But these seldom agree, and in the end, the decision is mine. To procrastinate, to agonize, and to wait for a more favorable turn of events that may never come or more compelling external pressures that may as well be wrong as right, is itself a decision of sorts and a weak and potentially dangerous course for a President to follow.

I have promised to uphold the Constitution, to do what is right as God gives me to see the right, and to do the very best that I can for America.

I have asked your help and your prayers, not only when I became President but many times since. The Constitution is the supreme law of our land and it governs our actions as citizens.

Only the laws of God, which govern our consciences, are superior to it.

As we are a nation under God, so I am sworn to uphold our laws with the help of God. And I have sought such guidance and searched my own conscience with special diligence to determine the right thing for me to do with respect to my predecessor in this place, Richard Nixon, and his loyal wife and family.

Theirs is an American tragedy in which we all have played a part. It could go on and on and on, or someone must write the end to it. I have concluded that only I can do that, and if I can, I must.

There are no historic or legal precedents to which I can turn in this matter, none that precisely fit the circumstances of a private citizen who has resigned the Presidency of the United States. But it is common knowledge that serious allegations and accusations hang like a sword over our former President's head, threatening his health as he tries to reshape his life, a great part of which was spent in the service of this country and by the mandate of its people.

After years of bitter controversy and divisive national debate, I have been advised, and I am compelled to conclude that many months and perhaps more years will have to pass before Richard Nixon could obtain a fair trial by jury in any jurisdiction of the United States under governing decisions of the Supreme Court.

I deeply believe in equal justice for all Americans, whatever their station or former station. The law, whether human or divine, is no respecter of persons; but the law is a respecter of reality.

The facts, as I see them, are that a former President of the United States, instead of enjoying equal treatment with any other citizen accused of violating the law, would be cruelly and excessively penalized either in preserving the presumption of his innocence or in obtaining a speedy determination of his guilt in order to repay a legal debt to society.

During this long period of delay and potential litigation, ugly passions would again be aroused. And our people would again be polarized in their opinions. And the credibility of our free institutions of government would again be challenged at home and abroad.

In the end, the courts might well hold that Richard Nixon had been denied due process, and the verdict of history would even more be inconclusive with respect to those charges arising out of the period of his Presidency, of which I am presently aware.

But it is not the ultimate fate of Richard Nixon that most concerns me, though surely it deeply troubles every decent and every compassionate person. My concern is the immediate future of this great country.

In this, I dare not depend upon my personal sympathy as a long-time friend of the former President, nor my professional judgment as a lawyer, and I do not.

As President, my primary concern must always be the greatest good of all the people of the United States whose servant I am. As a man, my first consideration is to be true to my own convictions and my own conscience.

My conscience tells me clearly and certainly that I cannot prolong the bad dreams that continue to reopen a chapter that is closed. My conscience tells me that only I, as President, have the constitutional power to firmly shut and seal this book. My conscience tells me it is my duty, not merely to proclaim domestic tranquillity but to use every means that I have to insure it.

I do believe that the buck stops here, that I cannot rely upon public opinion polls to tell me what is right.

I do believe that right makes might and that if I am wrong, 10 angels swearing I was right would make no difference.

I do believe, with all my heart and mind and spirit, that I, not as President but as a humble servant of God, will receive justice without mercy if I fail to show mercy.

Finally, I feel that Richard Nixon and his loved ones have suffered enough and will continue to suffer, no matter what I do, no matter what we, as a great and good nation, can do together to make his goal of peace come true.

"Now, therefore, I, Gerald R. Ford, President of the United States, pursuant to the pardon power conferred upon me by Article II, Section 2, of the Constitution, have granted and by these presents do grant a full, free, and absolute pardon unto Richard Nixon for all offenses against the United States which he, Richard Nixon, has committed or may have committed or taken part in during the period from 20 July (January) 1969 through 9 August 1974."

"In witness whereof, I have hereunto set my hand this eighth day of September, in the year of our Lord nineteen hundred and seventy-four, and of the Independence of the United States of America the one hundred and ninety-ninth."

PRESIDENT JIMMY CARTER RETURNS THE CANAL ZONE TO PANAMA
1 February 1978

Jimmy Carter's unlikely victory in the 1976 election produced a one-term presidency of ambiguous content. He won by running against the Washington establishment yet appointed many of its mainstays to prominent positions, including Cyrus Vance and Zbiegniew Brzezinski to oversee American foreign policy. While Carter proudly sported his born-again Baptist faith his unfortunate confession in Playboy magazine that he frequently "committed adultery in my heart" raised questions both about that statement and the propriety of his choice of magazine. Similar contradictions seemed to mark his polit-ical and policy judgments. In staking out initiatives on inflation, energy and tax cuts, in each case the President's original intentions were overtaken by considerations that forced alterations and general policy confusion. In foreign affairs, Carter came to Washington vowing a fundamental change in America's role in world affairs. His new agenda featured an emphasis on human rights as a basic criterion for relations, thoroughgoing nuclear disarmament and curtailed American arms sales abroad. None of the plans found much measure of success in Carter's term, although human rights remains as an ideal and dis-armament has followed the end of the Cold War. Carter's diplomacy, ironically, found its most notable success through paths of conventional diplomacy. The idea of returning the Panama Canal to Panama, begun in the Johnson Administration and continued under Presidents Nixon and Ford, came to fruition in the late 1970s, with President Carter leading the fight. Among the proponents' arguments was the righting of the naked power used by Theodore Roosevelt to seize the Canal seventy years earlier. Throughout the cen-tury, the United States had operated without restriction or restraint within another sov-ereign country. Panamanian resentment at real and perceived slights within the Zone produced periodic uprisings, and added to the general Latin resentment of "Yankee im-perialism." Opponents of returning the Canal, including Ronald Reagan and conservative forces from both parties, cited the loss of American honor and will in the sacrifice of "our" property, and the consequent jeopardy of national security. The long-simmering debate dominated Congress for eight months in 1977, with speeches of impressive rhetoric on both sides echoed in editorials and talk shows across the country. In April 1978, with one vote to spare, the Senate passed the treaty and President Carter enjoyed one of the high-lights of his term. Prior to the vote, Carter explained his case in a nationally televised address from the Oval Office.

Seventy-five years ago, our Nation signed a treaty which gave us rights to build a canal across Panama, to take the historic step of joining the Atlantic and Pacific Oceans. The results of the agree-ment have been of great benefit to our-selves and to other nations throughout the world who navigate the high seas.

The building of the canal was one of the greatest engineering feats of history. Although massive in concept and con-struction, it's relatively simple in design and has been reliable and efficient in operation. We Americans are justly and deeply proud of this great achievement.

The canal has also been a source of pride and benefit to the people of Panama—but a cause of some continu-ing discontent. Because we have con-trolled a 10-mile-wide strip of land across the heart of their country and because they considered the original terms of the agreement to be unfair, the people of Panama have been dissat-isfied with the treaty. It was drafted here in our country and was not signed by any Panamanian. Our own Secretary of State who did sign the original treaty said it was "vastly advantageous to the United States and . . . not so advantageous to Panama."

In 1964, after consulting with former Presidents Truman and Eisenhower, President Johnson committed our Nation to work towards a new treaty with the Republic of Panama. And last summer, after 14 years of negotiation under two Democratic Presidents and two Republican Presidents, we reached and signed an agreement that is fair and beneficial to both countries. The United States Senate will soon be debating whether these treaties should be ratified.

Throughout the negotiations, we were determined that our national security interests would be protected; that the canal would always be open and neutral and available to ships of all nations; that in time of need or emergency our warships would have the right to go to the head of the line for priority passage through the canal; and that our military forces would have the permanent right to defend the canal if it should ever be in danger. The new treaties meet all of these requirements.

Let me outline the terms of the agreement. There are two treaties—one covering the rest of this century, and the other guaranteeing the safety, openness, and neutrality of the canal after the year 1999, when Panama will be in charge of its operation.

For the rest of this century, we will operate the canal through a nine-person board of directors. Five members will be from the United States and four will be from Panama. Within the area of the present Canal Zone, we have the right to select whatever lands and waters our military and civilian forces need to maintain, to operate, and to defend the canal.

About 75 percent of those who now maintain and operate the canal are Panamanians; over the next 22 years, as we manage the canal together, this percentage will increase. The Americans who work on the canal will continue to have their rights of employment, promotion, and retirement carefully protected.

We will share with Panama some of the fees paid by shippers who use the canal. As in the past, the canal should continue to be self-supporting.

This is not a partisan issue. The treaties are strongly backed by President Gerald Ford and by Former Secretaries of State Dean Rusk and Henry Kissinger. They are endorsed by our business and professional leaders, especially those who recognize the benefits of good will and trade with other nations in this hemisphere. And they were endorsed overwhelmingly by the Senate Foreign Relations Committee which, this week, moved closer to ratification by approving the treaties, although with some recommended changes which we do not feel are needed.

And the treaties are supported enthusiastically by every member of the Joint Chiefs of Staff—General George Brown, the Chairman, General Bernard

Rogers, Chief of Staff of the Army, Admiral James Holloway, Chief of Naval Operations, General David Jones, Chief of Staff of the Air Force, and General Louis Wilson, Commandant of the Marine Corps—responsible men whose profession is the defense of this Nation and the preservation of our security.

The treaties also have been overwhelmingly supported throughout Latin America, but predictably, they are opposed abroad by some who are unfriendly to the United States and who would like to see disorder in Panama and a disruption of our political, economic, and military ties with our friends in Central and South America and in the Caribbean.

I know that the treaties also have been opposed by many Americans. Much of that opposition is based on misunderstanding and misinformation. I've found that when the full terms of the agreement are known, most people are convinced that the national interests of our country will be served best by ratifying the treaties.

Tonight, I want you to hear the facts. I want to answer the most serious questions and tell you why I feel the Panama Canal treaties should be approved.

The most important reason—the only reason—to ratify the treaties is that they are in the highest national interest of the United States and will strengthen our position in the world. Our security interests will be stronger. Our trade opportunities will be improved. We will demonstrate that as a

large and powerful country, we are able to deal fairly and honorably with a proud but smaller sovereign nation. We will honor our commitment to those engaged in world commerce that the Panama Canal will be open and available for use by their ships—at a reasonable and competitive cost—both now and in the future.

Let me answer specifically the most common questions about the treaties.

Will our Nation have the right to protect and defend the canal against any armed attack or threat to the security of the canal or of ships going through it?

The answer is yes, and is contained in both treaties and also in the statement of understanding between the leaders of our two nations.

The first treaty says, and I quote: "The United States of America and the Republic of Panama commit themselves to protect and defend the Panama Canal. Each Party shall act, in accordance with its constitutional processes, to meet the danger resulting from an armed attack or other actions which threaten the security of the Panama Canal or [of] ships transiting it."

The neutrality treaty says, and I quote again: "The United States of America and the Republic of Panama agree to maintain the regime of neutrality established in this Treaty, which shall be maintained in order that the Canal shall remain permanently neutral. . . ."

And to explain exactly what that means, the statement of understanding says, and I quote again: "Under (the Neutrality Treaty), Panama and the United States have the responsibility to assure that the Panama Canal will remain open and secure to ships of all nations. The correct interpretation of this principle is that each of the two countries shall, in accordance with their respective constitutional processes, defend the Canal against any threat to the regime of neutrality, and consequently [shall] have the right to act against the Canal or against the peaceful transit of vessels through the Canal."

It is obvious that we can take whatever military action is necessary to make sure that the canal always remains open and safe.

Of course, this does not give the United States any right to intervene in the internal affairs of Panama, nor would our military action ever be directed against the territorial integrity or the political independence of Panama.

Military experts agree that even with the Panamanian Armed Forces joined with us as brothers against a common enemy, it would take a large number of American troops to ward off a heavy attack. I, as President, would not hesitate to deploy whatever armed forces are necessary to defend the canal, and I have no doubt that even in a sustained combat, that we would be successful. But there is a much better way than sending our sons and grandsons to fight in the jungles of Panama.

We would serve our interests better by implementing the new treaties, an action that will help to avoid any attack on the Panama Canal.

What we want is the permanent right to use the canal—and we can defend this right through the treaties—through real cooperation with Panama. The citizens of Panama and their government have already shown their support of the new partnership, and a protocol to the neutrality treaty will be signed by many other nations, thereby showing their strong approval.

The new treaties will naturally change Panama from a passive and sometimes deeply resentful bystander into an active and interested partner, whose vital interests will be served by a well-operated canal. This agreement leads to cooperation and not confrontation between our country and Panama.

Another question is: Why should we give away the Panama Canal Zone? As many people say, "We bought it, we paid for it, it's ours."

I must repeat a very important point: We do not own the Panama Canal Zone. We have never had sovereignty over it. We have only had the right to use it.

The Canal Zone cannot be compared with United States territory. We bought Alaska from the Russians, and no one has ever doubted that we own it. We bought the Louisiana Purchases—Territories from France, and that's an integral part of the United States.

From the beginning, we have made an annual payment to Panama to use their land. You do not pay rent on your own land. The Panama Canal Zone has always been Panamanian territory. The U.S. Supreme Court and previous American Presidents have repeatedly acknowledged the sovereignty of Panama over the Canal Zone.

We've never needed to own the Panama Canal Zone, any more than we need to own a 10-mile-wide strip of land all the way through Canada from Alaska when we build an international gas pipeline.

The new treaties give us what we do need—not ownership of the canal, but the right to use it and to protect it. As the Chairman of the Joint Chiefs of Staff has said, "The strategic value of the canal lies in its use."

There's another question: Can our naval ships, our warships, in time of need or emergency, get through the canal immediately instead of waiting in line?

The treaties answer that clearly by guaranteeing that our ships will always have expeditious transit through the canal. To make sure that there could be no possible disagreement about what these words mean, the joint statement says that expeditious transit, and I quote, "is intended . . . to assure the transit of such vessels through the Canal as quickly as possible, without any impediment, with expedited treatment, and in case of need or emergency, to go to the head of the line of vessels in order to transit the Canal rapidly."

Will the treaties affect our standing in Latin America? Will they create a so-called power vacuum, which our enemies might move in to fill? They will do just the opposite. The treaties will increase our Nation's influence in this hemisphere, will help to reduce any mistrust and disagreement, and they will remove a major source of anti-American feeling.

The new agreement has already provided vivid proof to the people of this hemisphere that a new era of friendship and cooperation is beginning and that what they regard as the last remnant of alleged American colonialism is being removed.

Last fall, I met individually with the leaders of 18 countries in this hemisphere. Between the United States and Latin America there is already a new sense of equality, a new sense of trust and mutual respect that exists because of the Panama Canal treaties. This opens up a fine opportunity for us in good will, trade, jobs, exports, and political cooperation.

If the treaties should be rejected, this would all be lost, and disappointment and despair among our good neighbors and traditional friends would be severe.

In the peaceful struggle against alien ideologies like communism, these treaties are a step in the right direction. Nothing could strengthen our competitors and adversaries in this hemisphere more than for us to reject this agreement.

What if a new sea-level canal should be needed in the future? This question has been studied over and over throughout this century, from before the time the canal was built up through the last few years. Every study has reached the same conclusion—that the best place to build a sea-level canal is in Panama.

The treaties say that if we want to build such a canal, we will build it in Panama, and if any canal is to be built in Panama, that we, the United States, will have the right to participate in the project.

This is a clear benefit to us, for it ensures that, say, 10 or 20 years from now, no unfriendly but wealthy power will be able to purchase the right to build a sea-level canal, to bypass the existing canal, perhaps leaving that other nation in control of the only usable waterway across the isthmus.

Are we paying Panama to take the canal? We are not. Under the new treaty, any payments to Panama will come from tolls paid by ships which use the canal.

What about the present and the future stability and the capability of the Panamanian Government? Do the people of Panama themselves support the agreement?

Well, as you know, Panama and her people have been our historical allies and friends. The present leader of Panama has been in office for more than 9 years, and he heads a stable government which has encouraged the development of free enterprise in Panama. Democratic elections will be held this August to choose the members of the Panamanian Assembly, who will in turn elect a President and

a Vice President by majority vote. In the past, regimes have changed in Panama, but for 75 years, no Panamanian government has ever wanted to close the canal.

Panama wants the canal open and neutral—perhaps even more than we do. The canal's continued operation is very important to us, but it is much more than that to Panama. To Panama, it's crucial. Much of her economy flows directly or indirectly from the canal. Panama would be no more likely to neglect or to close the canal than we would be to close the Interstate Highway System here in the United States.

In an open and free referendum last October, which was monitored very carefully by the United Nations, the people of Panama gave the new treaties their support.

The major threat to the canal comes not from any government of Panama, but from misguided persons who may try to fan the flames of dissatisfaction with the terms of the old treaty.

There's a final question—about the deeper meaning of the treaties themselves, to us and to Panama.

Recently, I discussed the treaties with David McCullough, author of "The Path Between the Seas," the great history of the Panama Canal. He believes that the canal is something that we built and have looked after these many years; it is "ours" in that sense, which is very different from just ownership.

So, when we talk of the canal, whether we are old, young, for or against the treaties, we are talking about very deep and elemental feelings about our own strength.

Still, we Americans want a more humane and stable world. We believe in good will and fairness, as well as strength. This agreement with Panama is something we want because we know it is right. This is not merely the surest way to protect and save the canal, it's a strong, positive act of a people who are still confident, still creative, still great.

This new partnership can become a source of national pride and self-respect in much the same way that building the canal was 75 years ago. It's the spirit in which we act that is so very important.

Theodore Roosevelt, who was President when America built the canal, saw history itself as a force, and the history of our own time and the changes it has brought would not be lost on him. He knew that change was inevitable and necessary. Change is growth. The true

conservative, he once remarked, keeps his face to the future.

But if Theodore Roosevelt were to endorse the treaties, as I'm quite sure he would, it would be mainly because he could see the decision as one by which we are demonstrating the kind of great power we wish to be.

"We cannot avoid meeting great issues," Roosevelt said. "All that we can determine for ourselves is whether we shall meet them well or ill."

The Panama Canal is a vast, heroic expression of that age-old desire to bridge the divide and to bring people closer together. This is what the treaties are all about.

We can sense what Roosevelt called "the lift toward nobler things which marks a great and generous people."

In this historic decision, he would join us in our pride for being a great and generous people, with the national strength and wisdom to do what is right for us and what is fair to others.

PRESIDENT JIMMY CARTER PRESIDES OVER THE PEACE TREATY BETWEEN EGYPT AND ISRAEL
26 March 1979

Throughout the Carter Administration American foreign policy interests attracted their strongest challenges in the Middle East. Iran, Lebanon, Yemen, Iraq, and the Soviet invasion of Afghanistan provided the sites of separate crises. Instability treatening the Persian Gulf jeopardized Saudi Arabia, the key to the industrial world's supply of oil. In the center of this volatile arena, the venomous hostility between Israel and surrounding Arab states characterized the world's most troubled region. Diplomacy under President Carter concentrated on bringing about a peace treaty between Egypt and Israel. The Egyptian President, Anwar al-Sadat, the most prestigious of the Arab leaders, had astonished the world by going to Israel in November 1977 to offer terms for a peace. Months passed without significant progress before President Carter invited Sadat and his Israeli counterpart Prime Minister Menachem Begin to a summit meeting at Camp David, the presidential retreat near Washington. From 5 to 17 September 1978, the three men engaged in difficult and exhausting negotiations, with Carter by turns brandishing both carrots and sticks—pleading and threatening, offering financial favors, drafting new terms, supporting each side against the other—and finally prevailing on a framework for a treaty. The next spring, the President visited both Cairo and Tel Aviv to sustain the initiative, and succeeded. On 26 March 1979, on the lawn of the White House, the three leaders signed the treaty, the first ever between Israel and an Arab state. The day marked the high point in the foreign policy of President Jimmy Carter.

During the past 30 years, Israel and Egypt have waged war. But for the past 16 months, these same two great nations have waged peace. Today we celebrate a victory—not of a bloody military campaign, but of an inspiring peace campaign. Two leaders who will loom large in the history of nations, President Anwar al-Sadat and Prime Minister Menahem Begin, have conducted this campaign with all the courage, tenacity, brilliance, and inspiration of any generals who have ever led men and machines onto the field of battle.

At the end of this campaign, the soil of the two lands is not drenched with young blood. The countrysides of both lands are free from the litter and the carnage of a wasteful war. Mothers in Egypt and Israel are not weeping today for their children fallen in senseless battle. The dedication and determination of these two world statesmen have borne fruit. Peace has come to Israel and to Egypt.

I honor these two leaders and their government officials who have ham-mered out this peace treaty which we have just signed. But most of all, I honor the people of these two lands whose yearning for peace kept alive the negotiations which today culminate in this glorious event.

We have won at last the first step of peace, a first step on a long and difficult road. We must not minimize the obstacles which still lie ahead. Differences still separate the signatories to this treaty from one another, and also from some of their neighbors who fear what they have just done. To overcome these differences, to dispel these fears, we must rededicate ourselves to the goal of a broader peace with justice for all who have lived in a state of conflict in the Middle East.

We have no illusions—we have hopes, dreams, and prayers, yes, but no illusions.

There now remains the rest of the Arab world, whose support and whose cooperation in the peace process is needed and honestly sought. I am convinced that other Arab people need and want peace. But some of their leaders are not yet willing to honor these needs and desires for peace. We must now demonstrate the advantages of peace and expand its benefits to encompass all those who have suffered so much in the Middle East.

Obviously, time and understanding will be necessary for people, hitherto enemies, to become neighbors in the best sense of the word.

Just because a paper is signed, all the problems will not automatically go away. Future days will require the best from us to give reality to these lofty aspirations.

Let those who would shatter peace, who would callously spill more blood, be aware that we three and all others who may join us will vigorously wage peace.

So let history record that deep and ancient antagonism can be settled without bloodshed and without staggering waste of precious lives, without rapacious destruction of the land.

It has been said, and I quote, "Peace has one thing in common with its enemy, with the fiend it battles, with war; peace is active, not passive; peace is doing, not waiting; peace is aggressive—attacking; peace plans its strategy and encircles the enemy; peace marshals its forces and storms the gates; peace gathers its weapons and pierces the defense; peace, like war, is waged."

It is true that we cannot enforce trust and cooperation between nations, but we can use all our strength to see that nations do not again go to war.

All our religious doctrines give us hope. In the Koran, we read: "But if the enemy incline towards peace, do thou also incline towards peace, and trust in God; for He is the One that heareth and knoweth all things."

And the prophet Isaiah said: "Nations shall beat their swords into plowshares and their spears into pruning-hooks: nation shall not lift up sword against nation, neither shall they learn war any more."

So let us now lay aside war. Let us now reward all the children of Abraham who hunger for a comprehensive peace in the Middle East. Let us now enjoy the adventure of becoming fully human, fully neighbors, even brothers and sisters. We pray God, we pray God together, that these dreams will come true. I believe they will.

PRESIDENT JIMMY CARTER ANNOUNCES THE FAILURE OF THE IRANIAN HOSTAGE RESCUE MISSION
25 April 1980

The seemingly endless Iranian hostage crisis blighted the last year of the Carter presidency and seriously impaired his chances for re-election in 1980. Fifty-three Americans, seized by Revolutionary Guards inspired by Ayatollah Ruhollah Khomeini on

4 November 1979, spent 444 days in captivity. They returned home in January 1981, just after Ronald Reagan entered the White House. The Iranian militants, deeply committed to a form of Islam that prizes ancient tradition and rejects modernization, associated the United States with the figure of their greatest hatred, Mohammad Reza Pahlavi, the Shah of Iran who had been overthrown by Khomeini's movement. The Shah, long supported and maintained by the United States and the West as a central participant in Cold War struggles with the Soviet Union, had earned the enmity of traditionalist Iranians because of his lavish personal habits as well as his attempts to transform Iran into a secular Westernized nation. A few days before the seizure of the hostages, the Shah, wracked with cancer, was permitted to enter the United States to seek treatment at a hospital in New York. "Death to the Shah! Death to Carter! Death to the United States!" shouted the hostage-takers as they seized the American Embassy. Diplomacy failed to affect the situation, and plans emerged in Washington for freeing the men and women from their arduous imprisonment. The dramatic attempt at rescue authorized by President Carter was launched on 25 April 1980, when a team of 130 U.S. Army raiders deployed in a remote salt desert site 265 miles southeast of Teheran. Almost immediately, the raid commander decided to abort the mission because of the malfunctioning of three helicopters. In their haste to depart, a maneuvering helicopter struck a loaded supply plane, engulfing both craft in flames. Eight men died. The next evening, a somber President Carter faced the nation.

Late yesterday, I cancelled a carefully planned operation which was underway in Iran to position our rescue team for later withdrawal of American hostages, who have been held captive there since 4 November. Equipment failure in the rescue helicopters made it necessary to end the mission.

As our team was withdrawing, after my order to do so, two of our American aircraft collided on the ground following a refueling operation in a remote desert location in Iran. Other information about this rescue mission will be made available to the American people when it is appropriate to do so.

There was no fighting; there was no combat. But to my deep regret, eight of the crewmen of the two aircraft which collided were killed, and several other Americans were hurt in the accident. Our people were immediately airlifted from Iran. Those who were injured have gotten medical treatment, and all of them are expected to recover.

No knowledge of this operation by any Iranian officials or authorities was evident to us until several hours after all Americans were withdrawn from Iran.

Our rescue team knew and I knew that the operation was certain to be difficult and it was certain to be dangerous. We were all convinced that if and when the rescue operation had been commenced that it had an excellent chance of success. They were all volunteers; they were all highly trained. I met with their leaders before they went on this operation. They knew then what hopes of mine and of all Americans they carried with them.

To the families of those who died and who were wounded, I want to express the admiration I feel for the courage of their loved ones and the sorrow that I feel personally for their sacrifice.

The mission on which they were embarked was a humanitarian mission. It was not directed against Iran; it was not directed against the people of Iran. It was not undertaken with any feeling of hostility toward Iran or its people. It has caused no Iranian casualties.

Planning for this rescue effort began shortly after our Embassy was seized, but for a number of reasons, I waited until now to put those rescue plans into effect. To be feasible, this complex operation had to be the product of intensive planning and intensive training and repeated rehearsal. However, a resolution of this crisis through negotiations and with voluntary action on the part of the Iranian officials was obviously then, has been, and will be preferable.

This rescue attempt had to await my judgment that the Iranian authorities could not or would not resolve this crisis on their own initiative. With the steady unraveling of authority in Iran and the mounting dangers that were posed to the safety of the hostages themselves and the growing realization that their early release was highly unlikely, I made a decision to commence the rescue operations plans.

This attempt became a necessity and a duty. The readiness of our team to undertake the rescue made it completely practicable. Accordingly, I made the decision to set our long-developed plans into operation. I ordered this rescue mission prepared in order to safeguard American lives, to protect America's national interests, and to reduce the tensions in the world that have been caused among many nations as this crisis has continued.

It was my decision to attempt the rescue operation. It was my decision to cancel it when problems developed in the placement of our rescue team for a future rescue operation. The responsibility is fully my own.

In the aftermath of the attempt, we continue to hold the Government of Iran responsible for the safety and for the early release of the American hostages, who have been held so long. The United States remains determined to bring about their safe release at the earliest date possible.

As President, I know that our entire Nation feels the deep gratitude I feel for the brave men who were prepared to rescue their fellow Americans from captivity. And as President, I also know that the Nation shares not only my disappointment that the rescue effort could not be mounted, because of mechanical difficulties, but also my determination to persevere and to bring all of our hostages home to freedom.

We have been disappointed before. We will not give up in our efforts. Throughout this extraordinarily difficult period, we have pursued and will continue to pursue every possible avenue to secure the release of the hostages. In these efforts, the support of the American people and of our friends throughout the world has been a most crucial element. That support of other nations is even more important now.

We will seek to continue, along with other nations and with the officials of Iran, a prompt resolution of the crisis without any loss of life and through peaceful and diplomatic means.

PRESIDENT RONALD REAGAN DENOUNCES THE SOVIET UNION AS AN "EVIL EMPIRE"
8 March 1983

Ronald Reagan entered the White House with a fixed view of the world. Global upheavals great and small—terrorism, espionage, civil wars, arms escalation, and the threat of nuclear destruction—began, he insisted, with the Russian Revolution of 1917 and continued through the century under the successors of Lenin and Trotsky. Throughout the twenty-five years prior to his election in 1980, Reagan metamorphosed from Hollywood actor to political leader. He delivered thousands of speeches to friendly conservative audiences who shared his assurances that world affairs simply reflected the biblical struggle between the forces of good and evil. Reagan's partisans have always insisted that this seemingly-simplistic world view actually masked Reagan's political genius. That he chose to communicate in stark terms the better to be understood. In fact, this emotionally insulated man remains an enigma in history as in life, both venerated and lampooned. Characteristically, he dealt with the Soviets both with bellicose rhetoric and traditional diplomacy. Reagan entered office in a world controlled to a large extent by the two super powers, each with vast resources, far-flung alliance systems of client states, and ever-costlier arms systems constantly stimulated by technological innovations. While he would later engage in intense diplomatic and strategic relationship highlighted by four summit conferences between the President and the Soviet leadership, Reagan also freely offered his assessment of the Soviet Union as an "evil empire" at a meeting of Evangelicals in 1983.

. . . There is sin and evil in the world, and we're enjoined by Scripture and the Lord Jesus to oppose it with all our might. Our nation, too, has a legacy of evil with which it must deal. The glory of this land has been its capacity for transcending the moral evils of our past. For example, the long struggle of minority citizens for equal rights, once a source of disunity and civil war, is now a point of pride for all Americans. We must never go back. There is no room for racism, anti-Semitism, or other forms of ethnic and racial hatred in this country.

I know that you've been horrified, as have I, by the resurgence of some hate groups preaching bigotry and prejudice. Use the mighty voice of your pulpits and the powerful standing of your churches to denounce and isolate these hate groups in our midst. The commandment given us is clear and simple: "Thou shalt love thy neighbor as thyself."

But whatever sad episodes exist in our past, any objective observer must hold a positive view of American history, a history that has been the story of hopes fulfilled and dreams made into reality. Especially in this century, America has kept alight the torch of freedom, but not just for ourselves but for millions of others around the world.

And this brings me to my final point today. During my first press conference as President, in answer to a direct question, I pointed out that, as good Marxist-Leninists, the Soviet leaders have openly and publicly declared that the only morality they recognize is that which will further their cause, which is world revolution. I think I should point out I was only quoting Lenin, their guiding spirit, who said in 1920 that they repudiate all morality that

proceeds from supernatural ideas—that's their name for religion—or ideas that are outside class conceptions. Morality is entirely subordinate to the interests of class war. And everything is moral that is necessary for the annihilation of the old, exploiting social order and for uniting the proletariat.

Well, I think the refusal of many influential people to accept this elementary fact of Soviet doctrine illustrates an historical reluctance to see totalitarian powers for what they are. We saw this phenomenon in the 1930's. We see it too often today.

This doesn't mean we should isolate ourselves and refuse to seek an understanding with them. I intend to do everything I can to persuade them of our peaceful intent, to remind them that it was the West that refused to use its nuclear monopoly in the forties and fifties for territorial gain and which now proposes 50-percent cut in strategic ballistic missiles and the elimination of an entire class of land-based, intermediate-range nuclear missiles.

At the same time, however, they must be made to understand we will never compromise our principles and standards. We will never give away our freedom. We will never abandon our belief in God. And we will never stop searching for a genuine peace. But we can assure none of these things America stands for through the so-called nuclear freeze solutions proposed by some.

The truth is that a freeze now would be a very dangerous fraud, for that is merely the illusion of peace. The reality is that we must find peace through strength. . . .

A number of years ago, I heard a young father, a very prominent young man in the entertainment world, addressing a tremendous gathering in California. It was during the time of the cold war, and communism and our own way of life were very much on people's minds. And he was speaking to that subject. And suddenly, though, I heard him saying, "I love my little girls more than anything—" And I said to myself, "Oh, no, don't. You can't—don't say that." But I had underestimated him. He went on: "I would rather see my little girls die now, still believing in God, than have them grow up under communism and one day die no longer believing in God."

There were thousands of young people in that audience. They came to their feet with shouts of joy. They had instantly recognized the profound truth in what he had said, with regard to the physical and the soul and what was truly important.

Yes, let us pray for the salvation of all of those who live in that totalitarian darkness—pray they will discover the joy of knowing God. But until they do, let us be aware that while they preach the supremacy of the state, declare its omnipotence over individual man, and predict its eventual domination of all peoples on the Earth, they are the focus of evil in the modern world.

It was C. S. Lewis who, in his unforgettable "Screwtape Letters," wrote: "The greatest evil is not done now in those sordid 'dens of crime' that Dickens loved to paint. It is not even done in concentration camps and labor camps. In those we see its final result. But it is conceived and ordered (moved, seconded, carried and minuted) in clear, carpeted, warmed, and well-lighted offices, by quiet men with white collars and cut fingernails and smooth-shaven cheeks who do not need to raise their voice."

Well, because these "quiet men" do not "raise their voices," because they sometimes speak in soothing tones of brotherhood and peace, because, like other dictators before them, they're always making "their final territorial demand," some would have us accept them at their word and accommodate ourselves to their aggressive impulses. But if history teaches anything, it teaches that simple-minded appeasement or wishful thinking about our adversaries is folly. It means the betrayal of our past, the squandering of our freedom.

So, I urge you to speak out against those who would place the United States in a position of military and moral inferiority. You know, I've always believed that old Screwtape reserved his best efforts for those of you in the church. So, in your discussions of the nuclear freeze proposals, I urge you to beware the temptation of pride—the temptation of blithely declaring yourselves above it all and label both sides equally at fault, to ignore the facts of history and the aggressive impulses of an evil empire, to simply call the arms race a giant misunderstanding and thereby remove yourself from the struggle between right and wrong and good and evil.

I ask you to resist the attempts of those who would have you withhold your support for our efforts, this administration's efforts, to keep America strong and free, while we negotiate real and verifiable reductions in the world's nuclear arsenals and one day, with God's help, their total elimination.

While America's military strength is important, let me add here that I've always maintained that the struggle now going on for the world will never be decided by bombs or rockets, by armies or military might. The real crisis we face today is a spiritual one; at root, it is a test of moral will and faith. . . .

I believe we shall rise to the challenge. I believe that communism is another sad, bizarre chapter in human history whose last pages even now are being written. I believe this because the source of our strength in the quest for human freedom is not material, but spiritual. And because it knows no limitation, it must terrify and ultimately triumph over those who would enslave their fellow man. For in the words of Isaiah: "He giveth power to the faint; and to them that have no might He increased strength. . . . But they that wait upon the Lord shall renew their strength; they shall mount up with wings as eagles; they shall run, and not be weary. . . ."

Yes, change your world. One of our Founding Fathers, Thomas Paine, said, "We have it within our power to begin the world over again." We can do it, doing together what no one church could do by itself.

God bless you, and thank you very much.

President Ronald Reagan Announces the "Star Wars" Missile Defense Concept
23 March 1983

Early Reagan Administration foreign policy featured the futuristic concept of the "Strategic Defense Initiative," popularly known as Star Wars, after the then-current science fiction film. This notion promised to secure the United States against incoming intercontinental missiles with an extraterrestrial shield. "Perfect security," as claimed by its political, military, and industrial sponsors, would, in effect, end the threat of nuclear war. President Reagan remained committed to Star Wars throughout his term, despite its apparent consequences. Research and development of the lasers and satellites projected extraordinary expenses, even as astrophysicists continued to argue over the fundamental question of its very feasibility. Moreover, Star Wars threatened to quicken the arms race and damage the negotiations on limitations with the Soviets, which had continued throughout the Ford and Carter administrations. This specter of a costly and dangerous new round of the arms race energized a mass anti-nuclear movement in Europe and the United States. In 1982, an estimated one million "freezniks" assembled in New York City's Central Park to demand the halt of nuclear buildup. While his Administration resumed arms control talks with Moscow, President Reagan continued to extol Star Wars.

My fellow Americans, thank you for sharing your time with me tonight.

The subject I want to discuss with you, peace and national security, is both timely and important. Timely, because I've reached a decision which offers a new hope for our children in the 21st century, a decision I'll tell you about in a few minutes. And important because there's a very big decision that you must make for yourselves. This subject involves the most basic duty that any President and any people share, the duty to protect and strengthen the peace. . . .

There was a time when we depended on coastal forts and artillery batteries, because, with the weaponry of that day, any attack would have had to come by sea. Well, this is a different world, and our defenses must be based on recognition and awareness of the weaponry possessed by other nations in the nuclear age.

We can't afford to believe that we will never be threatened. There have been two world wars in my lifetime. We didn't start them and, indeed, did everything we could to avoid being drawn into them. But we were ill-prepared for both. Had we been better prepared, peace might have been preserved.

For 20 years the Soviet Union has been accumulating enormous military might. They didn't stop when their forces exceeded all requirements of a legitimate defensive capability. And they haven't stopped now. During the past decade and a half, the Soviets have built up a massive arsenal of new strategic nuclear weapons—weapons that can strike directly at the United States. . . .

When I took office in January 1981, I was appalled by what I found: American planes that couldn't fly and American ships that couldn't sail for lack of spare parts and trained personnel and insufficient fuel and ammunition for essential training. The inevitable result of all this was poor morale in our Armed Forces, difficulty in recruiting the brightest young Americans to wear the uniform, and difficulty in convincing our most experienced military personnel to stay on.

There was a real question then about how well we could meet a crisis. And it was obvious that we had to begin a major modernization program to ensure we could deter aggression and preserve the peace in the years ahead. . . .

If the Soviet Union will join with us in our effort to achieve major arms reduction, we will have succeeded in stabilizing the nuclear balance. Nevertheless, it will still be necessary to rely on the specter of retaliation, on mutual threat. And that's a sad commentary on the human condition. Wouldn't it be better to save lives than to avenge them? Are we not capable of demonstrating our peaceful intentions by applying all our abilities and our ingenuity to achieving a truly lasting stability? I think we are. Indeed, we must.

After careful consultation with my advisers, including the Joint Chiefs of Staff, I believe there is a way. Let me share with you a vision of the future which offers hope. It is that we embark on a program to counter the awesome Soviet missile threat with measures that are defensive. Let us turn to the very strengths in technology that spawned our great industrial base and that have given us the quality of life we enjoy today.

What if free people could live secure in the knowledge that their security did not rest upon the threat of instant U.S. retaliation to deter a Soviet attack, that we could intercept and destroy strategic ballistic missiles before they reached our own soil or that of our allies?

I know this is a formidable, technical task, one that may not be accomplished before the end of this century. Yet, current technology has attained a level of sophistication where it's reasonable for us to begin this effort. It will take years, probably decades of effort on many fronts. There will be failures and setbacks, just as there will be successes and breakthroughs. And as we proceed, we must remain constant in preserving the nuclear deterrent and maintaining a solid capability for flexible response. But isn't it worth every investment necessary to free the world from the threat of nuclear war? We know it is.

In the meantime, we will continue to pursue real reductions in nuclear arms, negotiating from a position of strength that can be ensured only by modernizing our strategic forces. At the same time, we must take steps to reduce the risk of a conventional military conflict escalating to nuclear war by improving our nonnuclear capabilities.

America does possess—now—the technologies to attain very significant improvements in the effectiveness of our conventional, nonnuclear forces. Proceeding boldly with these new technologies, we can significantly reduce any incentive that the Soviet Union may have to threaten attack against the United States or its allies.

As we pursue our goal of defensive technologies, we recognize that our allies rely upon our strategic offensive power to deter attacks against them. Their vital interests and ours are inextricably linked. Their safety and ours are one. And no change in technology can or will alter that reality. We must and shall continue to honor our commitments.

I clearly recognize that defensive systems have limitations and raise certain problems and ambiguities. If paired with offensive systems, they can be viewed as fostering an aggressive policy, and no one wants that. But with these considerations firmly in mind, I call upon the scientific community in our country, those who gave us nuclear weapons, to turn their great talents now to the cause of mankind and world peace, to give us the means of rendering these nuclear weapons impotent and obsolete.

Tonight, consistent with our obligations of the ABM treaty and recognizing the need for closer consultation with our allies, I'm taking an important first step. I am directing a comprehensive and intensive effort to define a long-term research and development program to begin to achieve our ultimate goal of eliminating the threat posed by strategic nuclear missiles. This could pave the way for arms control measures to eliminate the weapons themselves. We seek neither military superiority nor political advantage. Our only purpose—one all people share—is to search for ways to reduce the danger of nuclear war.

My fellow Americans, tonight we're launching an effort which holds the promise of changing the course of human history. There will be risks, and results take time. But I believe we can do it. As we cross this threshold, I ask for your prayers and your support.

PRESIDENT RONALD REAGAN ADDRESSES THE NATION ON THE *CHALLENGER* TRAGEDY
28 JANUARY 1986

Ronald Reagan's "Great Communicator" reputation rested on his outstanding ability to use television to genuinely touch a mass audience. However much he relied on the precise reading off a TelePrompTer of the words of his talented speech writers, Reagan's presentation invariably conveyed a sense of his emotional belief in a message usually resonating with traditional themes of simple virtue and patriotism. In 1986, when the space shuttle Challenger *shockingly exploded, killing its seven-person crew, the President rose to the bitter occasion in a nationally televised speech.*

Ladies and gentlemen, I'd planned to speak to you tonight to report on the state of the Union, but the events of earlier today have led me to change those plans. Today is a day for mourning and remembering. Nancy and I are pained to the core by the tragedy of the shuttle *Challenger*. We know we share this pain with all of the people of our country. This is truly a national loss.

Nineteen years ago, almost to the day, we lost three astronauts in a terrible accident on the ground. But we've never lost an astronaut in flight; we've never had a tragedy like this. And perhaps we've forgotten the courage it took for the crew of the shuttle. But they, the *Challenger* Seven, were aware of the dangers, but overcame them and did their jobs brilliantly. We mourn seven heroes: Michael Smith, Dick Scobee, Judith Resnik, Ronald McNair, Ellison Onizuka, Gregory Jarvis, and Christa McAuliffe. We mourn their loss as a nation together.

For the families of the seven, we cannot bear, as you do, the full impact of this tragedy. But we feel the loss, and we're thinking about you so very much. Your loved ones were daring and brave, and they had that special grace, that special spirit that says, "Give me a challenge, and I'll meet it with joy." They had a hunger to explore the universe and discover its truths. They wished to serve, and they did. They served all of us. We've grown used to wonders in this century. It's hard to dazzle us. But for 25 years the United States space program has been doing just that. We've grown used to the idea of space, and perhaps we forget that we've only just begun. We're still pioneers. They, the members of the *Challenger* crew, were pioneers.

And I want to say something to the schoolchildren of America who were

watching the live coverage of the shuttle's takeoff. I know it is hard to understand, but sometimes painful things like this happen. It's all part of the process of exploration and discovery. It's all part of taking a chance and expanding man's horizons. The future doesn't belong to the fainthearted; it belongs to the brave. The *Challenger* crew was pulling us into the future, and we'll continue to follow them.

I've always had great faith in and respect for our space program, and what happened today does nothing to diminish it. We don't hide our space program. We don't keep secrets and cover things up. We do it all up front and in public. That's the way freedom is, and we wouldn't change it for a minute. We'll continue our quest in space. There will be more shuttle flights and more shuttle crews and, yes, more volunteers, more civilians, more teachers in space. Nothing ends here; our hopes and our journeys continue. I want to add that I wish I could talk to every man and woman who works for NASA or who worked on this mission and tell them: "Your dedication and professionalism have moved and impressed us for decades. And we know of your anguish. We share it."

There's a coincidence today. On this day 390 years ago, the great explorer Sir Francis Drake died aboard ship off the coast of Panama. In his lifetime the great frontiers were the oceans, and an historian later said, "He lived by the sea, died on it, and was buried in it." Well, today we can say of the *Chal-*

lenger crew: Their dedication was, like Drake's, complete.

The crew of the space shuttle *Challenger* honored us by the manner in which they lived their lives. We will never forget them, nor the last time we saw them, this morning, as they prepared for their journey and waved goodbye and "slipped the surly bonds of earth" to "touch the face of God."

PRESIDENT RONALD REAGAN ANNOUNCES ARMS CONTROL AGREEMENT WITH THE SOVIET UNION
1 December 1987

Shortly after Ronald Reagan's triumphal reelection in 1984, Mikhail Gorbachev came to power in the Soviet Union. This new leader in Moscow initially inspired no great expectations, given his decades within the deadening conformity of Soviet bureaucracy. Yet Gorbachev recognized the crumbling state structure over which he now presided. The brutal costs of the arms race combined with torpid economic growth and a repressive social system propelled the Soviet Union toward disaster. Attracted by Gorbachev's reformist concepts of glasnost (openness) and perestroika (restructuring), the Reagan administration moved toward accommodation. Ultimately, the leaders would visit each other's capitals, hold four summit meetings, and agree on arms limitation on a basis heretofore unthinkable. In December 1987, the leaders signed a pact eliminating all American and Soviet intermediate-range nuclear forces from Europe, marking the first actual reduction in the arsenal of both sides. President Reagan explained its significance to a group of high school students in Jacksonville, Florida.

. . . In just a few days, I'll meet with General Secretary Gorbachev of the Soviet Union. We will sign the first arms reduction agreement in the history of relations between our two countries . . .

For many years critics around the world have insisted that it would be impossible to get an agreement along the lines we've now worked out. Six years ago, when I proposed the elimination of an entire category of U.S. and Soviet intermediate-range missiles, they sneered and said I couldn't be serious. It was a sure sign, they said, that I was against arms reductions altogether, and they added that I ought to offer something the Soviets would agree to, even if I didn't believe it was in America's best interests. And yet we—and I mean here you and all Americans who supported rebuilding our national defense and our determination that it was better to have no arms agreement than a bad arms agreement—all of us stuck together. We set goals. We made plans. We worked hard.

Many of those same critics also said that it was provocative to tell the truth about repression in the Soviet Union, about Soviet overseas adventures, about Soviet violations of past agreements. We said that the United States of America must never be afraid to tell the truth about anyone. Well, now, as a result of lots of hard work and patience, we're about to sign an agreement that will do just what I proposed 6 years ago and that the critics said was impossible. For the first time in history, we will wipe an entire category of American and Soviet nuclear weapons from the face of the Earth.

After the summit, we'll keep our negotiators working on an agreement that could lead to cutting the U.S. and Soviet long-range nuclear arsenals in half and reducing the disparities in conventional forces, that is, the armies that face each other in Europe. Those disparities favor the Soviets. With the Intermediate-range Nuclear Forces agreement, we take a first step across the open frontier toward a safer world for you and your children. And my plan—our plan—should be to keep right on marching.

But in the excitement of the summit, the treaty signing, and all the rest, we must not forget that peace means more than arms reduction. More than a decade ago, there was a warming in

U.S.-Soviet affairs that we called détente. But while talking friendship, the Soviets worked even faster on the largest military buildup in world history. They stepped up their aggression around the world. They became more repressive at home. We do not want mere words; this time we're after true peace.

One Eastern European dissident thinker has written that "respect for human rights is the fundamental condition and the sole guarantee of true peace." Well, I believe he's right. True peace and freedom are indivisible. That's why it's important to all of us that the Soviets have released over 200 political prisoners over the past year and that they appear to have eased censorship somewhat in the arts and media.

It's also why we're concerned that many more political prisoners remain in jail, internal exile, and psychiatric hospitals. As many as 10,000 Jews await permission to emigrate. Persecution of religious believers continues. Some, including Ludmilla Andrushenko and Father Alsonsas Svarinskas, wait in prison. Their only crime: They wanted to practice their religion and worship God as they pleased. Well, Mr. Gorbachev and I are going to have a few words about that.

We're also going to have words about Soviet expansionism around the world, for example, in Afghanistan. Since the Red Army invaded 8 years ago, the Afghan people have suffered a million casualties, and at least 4 million others have been driven to exile, as freedom fighters have taken up arms against the invader.

Who are these freedom fighters? Well, many of them would be your classmates if they lived here in Jacksonville. That's how young they are. They've taken up arms against one of the largest and best equipped armies in the world, because they've seen what Communist oppression means. To some it means being prevented from living by the rules of their religions. To others it means parents murdered and crops, and even entire villages, destroyed in random and repeated Soviet raids. Or it means a little brother or sister whose hand was blown off by Soviet mines disguised as toys. Oppression means many things. There are many reasons to fight for freedom. The simple people of Afghanistan pose no threat to Soviet territory. They don't now. They never have. The Soviet Union has no legitimate purpose in this war. And I will tell Mr. Gorbachev it is time for the Soviets to set a date certain for withdrawal, to talk with the freedom fighters, and to allow the people of Afghanistan to determine their own destiny.

I will also say it's time for them to leave Cambodia, Ethiopia, Angola, and Nicaragua. Even as the five Central American countries search for peace, the Soviet bloc continues to pour billions of dollars in guns, planes, bullets, tanks, and other assistance into Nicaragua. Why? To quote one of our leading national strategists, Zbigniew

Brzezinski: "Potentially at stake in Central America is America's capacity to defend Western interests throughout the world." And he adds: "If the Soviet-Cuban presence in Nicaragua destabilizes the entire region, the United States will inevitably pull back" from Europe and the Pacific to defend our own border.

Well, I want my meeting with Mr. Gorbachev to help build a true peace that will last for your lifetime and that of your children and of their children. And that's why we will review our areas of agreement, but also emphasize our points of disagreement. Some say it will be impossible for the Soviets to listen. But we've come a long way already by being strong, steady, and determined. We Americans set our goals. We were realistic about how to go after them. We kept on working, in good times and bad. We believed in America's strength and in America's ability to use its strength to make the world better. For the last 7 years, through us, through all of us here today and millions of others, America has said, I can. And around the world, because of that, peace is more secure and freedom more widely shared. At home, because of that, we're in the longest peacetime economic expansion on record, and unlimited opportunities are waiting for you after graduation. Think of what those two words, "I can," have meant to the story of our nation and the world in our time. . . .

PRESIDENT GEORGE BUSH ANNOUNCES
WAR IN THE PERSIAN GULF
16 January 1991

The triumphal military exercise known as Desert Storm formed the focal point of George Bush's Presidency. Tiny oil-rich Kuwait, invaded and subsequently occupied by Iraq beginning in August 1990, was freed six months later by a United States-led coalition of troops from many nations. The brief war featured massive air strikes on Baghdad and military and industrial infrastructure throughout Iraq. President Saddam Hussein was initially compelled to accept UN peace terms that included reparations to Kuwait and comprehensive international inspection of Iraqi weapons, including alleged chemical and biological stores. Despite the indisputable military outcome, the war nevertheless left this vital region unsettled, and the role of Iraq unresolved. Cobbled together from disparate and often belligerent peoples, Iraq spent most of the twentieth century as a pawn of outside interests attracted to its lucrative oil deposits, first identified in 1927. While Iraq achieved nominal independence in 1930, British influence remained controlling until the 1950s. By then, Pan-Arab nationalism dominated the often-violent political landscape in Baghdad, including a 1956 coup that attracted the presence of the nineteen-year-old Saddam Hussein. By the late 1960s, Saddam possessed great influence, and by the late 1970s, control of Iraq. Throughout the 1980s the United States backed Saddam in a vicious war against Iran, deemed by Washington to be the greater Middle Eastern threat. Early in 1990, the festering Iraqi problems with Kuwait again recurred. Iraq had always considered Kuwait its "19th province," cut away by the British in 1897 to serve their own strategic interests in the Persian Gulf. This desolate 6,177 sq. mi. desert plot, ruled for centuries by the al-Sabah dynasty, produced a huge percentage of the world's oil and sat atop an ocean of proven reserves. There the al-Sabah's presided in medieval lavishness while the Iraqis, totally dependent upon their own oil revenue, struggled to overcome the painful costs of the Iranian war. Saddam Hussein and other Middle Eastern leaders resented not only the ostentation and corruption of the Kuwaitis but also their habit of over-producing oil, thus driving down the world price and penalizing other oil producers. At the end of July 1990, with Baghdad's irritation rising, a State Department spokesman noted that "we do not have any defense treaties with Kuwait." Saddam Hussein summoned the American Ambassador, who cited Secretary of State James Baker's policy that the United States had "no opinion on Arab-Arab conflicts, like your border disagreement with Kuwait." On 2 August, Iraqi forces crossed the border, seized Kuwait, and installed a puppet regime. The initial responses of the United States, like the neighboring Middle Eastern powers, consisted of moderate calls for diplomacy and compromise. After brief reflection, President Bush decided to treat the event as an aggression on a major scale that violated the covenants of international law. On 6 August, with the announcement of Operation Desert Shield, American military troops were committed to the Saudi Arabian border to prevent further Iraqi advances. By November, American forces in the Gulf totaled 230,000. Through the autumn and early winter, Bush skillfully used the United Nations to create an alliance of the world's leading powers, who were attracted to U.S. leadership by a mixture of motives. Some nations may have acted on the principle of opposing aggression, many Arab neighbors feared Saddam Hussein's regional objectives, and all parties silently acknowledged the primacy of oil. Further, the willingness of the United States to expend major resources wherever needed brought to bear key United Nations votes, producing a vast international alliance against Iraq. With Saddam defying all demands to capitulate, the first Allied air attacks on Baghdad began on 17 January 1991. On 23 February, with the collapse of Soviet efforts to find a compromise, the American-led alliance invaded Iraq in Operation Desert Storm. To general surprise, the war ended in about one hundred hours with the rout of Iraqi forces. Geopolitical considerations of creating a huge power vacuum prevented the United States from attempting the conquest and problematical military occupation of Iraq, however. Saddam Hussein retained power, and the strategic questions in the region remain in flux. President Bush presented the case for war in a nationally-televised broadcast from the Oval Office on 16 January 1991.

Just two hours ago, allied air forces began an attack on military targets in Iraq and Kuwait. These attacks continue as I speak. Ground forces are not engaged.

This conflict started 2d August when the dictator of Iraq invaded a small and helpless neighbor. Kuwait—a member of the Arab League and a member of the United Nations—was crushed; its people, brutalized. Five months ago, Saddam Hussein started this cruel war against Kuwait. Tonight, the battle has been joined.

This military action, taken in accord with United Nations resolutions and with the consent of the United States Congress, follows months of constant and virtually endless diplomatic activity on the part of the United Nations, the United States, and many, many other countries. Arab leaders sought what became known as an Arab solution, only to conclude that Saddam Hussein was unwilling to leave Kuwait. Others traveled to Baghdad in a variety of efforts to restore peace and justice. Our Secretary of State, James Baker, held an historic meeting in Geneva, only to be totally rebuffed. This past weekend, in a last-ditch effort, the Secretary-General of the United Nations went to the Middle East with peace in his heart—his second such mission. And he came back from Baghdad with no progress at all in getting Saddam Hussein to withdraw from Kuwait.

Now the 28 countries with forces in the Gulf area have exhausted all reasonable efforts to reach a peaceful resolution—have no choice but to drive Saddam from Kuwait by force. We will not fail.

As I report to you, air attacks are underway against military targets in Iraq. We are determined to knock out Saddam Hussein's nuclear bomb potential. We will also destroy his chemical weapons facilities. Much of Saddam's artillery and tanks will be destroyed. Our operations are designed to best protect the lives of all the coalition forces by targeting Saddam's vast military arsenal. Initial reports from General Schwarzkopf are that our operations are proceeding according to plan.

Our objectives are clear: Saddam Hussein's forces will leave Kuwait. The legitimate government of Kuwait will be restored to its rightful place, and Kuwait will once again be free. Iraq will eventually comply with all relevant United Nations resolutions, and then, when peace is restored, it is our hope that Iraq will live as a peaceful and co-operative member of the family of nations, thus enhancing the security and stability of the Gulf.

Some may ask: Why act now? Why not wait? The answer is clear: The world could wait no longer. Sanctions, though having some effect, showed no signs of accomplishing their objective. Sanctions were tried for well over 5 months, and we and our allies concluded that sanctions alone would not force Saddam from Kuwait.

While the world waited, Saddam Hussein systematically raped, pillaged, and plundered a tiny nation, no threat to his own. He subjected the people of Kuwait to unspeakable atrocities—and

among those maimed and murdered, innocent children.

While the world waited, Saddam sought to add to the chemical weapons arsenal he now possesses, an infinitely more dangerous weapon of mass destruction—a nuclear weapon. And while the world waited, while the world talked peace and withdrawal, Saddam Hussein dug in and moved massive forces into Kuwait.

While the world waited, while Saddam stalled, more damage was being done to the fragile economics of the Third World, emerging democracies of Eastern Europe, to the entire world, including to our own economy.

The United States, together with the United Nations, exhausted every means at our disposal to bring this crisis to a peaceful end. However, Saddam clearly felt that by stalling and threatening and defying the United Nations, he could weaken the forces arrayed against him.

While the world waited, Saddam Hussein met every overture of peace with open contempt. While the world prayed for peace, Saddam prepared for war.

I had hoped that when the United States Congress, in historic debate, took its resolute action, Saddam would realize he could not prevail and would move out of Kuwait in accord with the United Nation resolutions. He did not do that. Instead, he remained intransigent, certain that time was on his side.

Saddam was warned over and over again to comply with the will of the

United Nations: Leave Kuwait, or be driven out. Saddam has arrogantly rejected all warnings. Instead, he tried to make this a dispute between Iraq and the United States of America.

Well, he failed. Tonight, 28 nations—countries from 5 continents, Europe and Asia, Africa, and the Arab League—have forces in the Gulf area standing shoulder to shoulder against Saddam Hussein. These countries had hoped the use of force could be avoided. Regrettably, we now believe that only force will make him leave.

Prior to ordering our forces into battle, I instructed our military commanders to take every necessary step to prevail as quickly as possible, and with the greatest degree of protection possible for American and allied service men and women. I've told the American people before that this will not be another Vietnam, and I repeat this here tonight. Our troops will have the best possible support in the entire world, and they will not be asked to fight with one hand tied behind their back. I'm hopeful that this fighting will not go on for long and that casualties will be held to an absolute minimum.

This is an historic moment. We have in this past year made great progress in ending the long era of conflict and cold war. We have before us the opportunity to forge for ourselves and for future generations a new world order—a world where the rule of law, not the law of the jungle, governs the conduct of nations. When we are successful—and we will be—we have a real chance at this new world order, an order in which a credible United Nations can use its peacekeeping role to fulfill the promise and vision of the U.N.'s founders.

We have no argument with the people of Iraq. Indeed, for the innocents caught in this conflict, I pray for their safety. Our goal is not the conquest of Iraq. It is the liberation of Kuwait. It is my hope that somehow the Iraqi people can, even now, convince their dictator that he must lay down his arms, leave Kuwait, and let Iraq itself rejoin the family of peace-loving nations.

Thomas Paine wrote many years ago: "These are the times that try men's souls." Those well-known words are so very true today. But even as planes of the multinational forces attack Iraq, I prefer to think of peace, not war. I am convinced not only that we will prevail but that out of the horror of combat will come the recognition that no nation can stand against a world united, no nation will be permitted to brutally assault its neighbor.

No President can easily commit our sons and daughters to war. They are the Nation's finest. Ours is an all-volunteer force, magnificently trained, highly motivated. The troops know why they're there. And listen to what they say, for they've said it better than any President or Prime Minister ever could.

Listen to Hollywood Huddleston, Marine lance corporal. He says, "Let's free these people, so we can go home and be free again." And he's right. The terrible crimes and tortures committed by Saddam's henchmen against the innocent people of Kuwait are an affront to mankind and a challenge to the freedom of all.

Listen to one of our great officers out there, Marine Lieutenant General Walter Boomer. He said: "There are things worth fighting for. A world in which brutality and lawlessness are allowed to go unchecked isn't the kind of world we're going to want to live in."

Listen to Master Sergeant J.P. Kendall of the 82d Airborne: "We're here for more than just the price of a gallon of gas. What we're doing is going to chart the future of the world for the next 100 years. It's better to deal with this guy now than 5 years from now."

And finally, we should all sit up and listen to Jackie Jones, an Army lieutenant, when she says, "If we let him get away with this, who knows what's going to be next?"

I have called upon Hollywood and Walter and J.P. and Jackie and all their courageous comrades-in-arms to do what must be done. Tonight, America and the world are deeply grateful to them and to their families. And let me say to everyone listening or watching tonight: When the troops we've sent in finish their work, I am determined to bring them home as soon as possible.

Tonight, as our forces fight, they and their families are in our prayers. May God bless each and every one of them, and the coalition forces at our side in the Gulf, and may He continue to bless our nation, the United States of America.

PRESIDENT BILL CLINTON PROCLAIMS THE NORTH ATLANTIC FREE TRADE AGREEMENT
8 December 1993

On 8 December 1993, President Bill Clinton signed into law the North American Free Trade Agreement (NAFTA). This treaty embodied concepts that committed the United States for the first time to the creation of a global marketplace for production and exchange of goods and services. The Agreement came only after a bitter quarrel that erupted over the political landscape, splitting both parties and posing a serious political threat in Clinton's first term. Negotiations to create a low-or free-tariff market including Canada, the United States, and Mexico began during the Reagan administration and were completed by President George Bush, who joined Mexican president Carlos Salinas de Gortari and Canadian Prime Minister Brian Mulroney to sign the pact on 17 December 1992. The real fight, left to President Clinton, came in the Congress, where powerful forces sought to defeat the Agreement and the thinking behind it. Central to NAFTA and all other regional trading agreements is the elimination or sharp reduction of tariffs among the partners, thus making goods and services flow freely across borders, enlarging the markets of all participants to include the consumers of all other participants. Thus does the European Union function from Ireland and Britain to the nations of Western Europe and on to Greece. In the United States, the idea of free trade was central to the vision of President Woodrow Wilson, who believed that trade expanded and spread wealth to its producers, invigorated consumption, and promoted prosperity, stability, and an ever-expanding job market. From prosperity came stability and world peace. Both NAFTA and the other regional and global partnerships which have continued to emerge became timely only after the fall of the Soviet Union, whose economic premises and global political influence sharply constricted the advance of capitalism. Even so, Clinton's success in passing NAFTA came only after a bruising challenge. Opposition arose from generalized fear that American industries and their jobs would be inevitably drawn southward, where, in Mexico, cheap labor and casual environmental enforcement dramatically lowered the cost of production. Goods manufactured under these conditions, opponents held, could be sold on the great American consumer market at prices that American manufacturers, paying union wages and observing environmental laws, could never compete with. This nightmare scenario dominated the position of the AFL/CIO and its political supporters within the Congress, particularly among Democrats, whose leader, the president, stood against them. NAFTA became a dominant issue in the 1992 presidential campaign, particular when third-party candidate Ross Perot consistently reminded his huge army of supporters of "that great sucking sound" of American jobs moving south. President Bush, up for reelection, had signed the bill. Candidate Clinton approached the issue with great care, speaking artfully about the need for "side agreements" on labor and the environment. Vice-Presidential candidate Al Gore met Perot in a widely viewed television debate on the subject and easily prevailed, thus reducing the issue in the campaign if not in Congress. President Clinton spent virtually all of the three weeks preceding the November vote focused on the issue. He talked to innumerable audiences of the virtues of NAFTA and "the larger trading universe" beyond. Like-minded supporters risked often- arcane references to the General Agreement on Tariffs and Trade (GATT), which envisioned the global market on the horizon. The President also dealt behind the scenes with members from both parties who demanded special protection for commodities like sugar, peanuts and wheat. The deals were made. In the crucial House vote on 17 November, NAFTA prevailed by 234–230, with more Republican supporters than the President's own party. Upon signing the Agreement into law the President confidently proclaimed an historic achievement.

. . . I believe we have made a decision now that will permit us to create an economic order in the world that will promote more growth, more equality, better preservation of the environment, and a greater possibility of world peace. We are on the verge of a global economic expansion that is sparked by the fact that the United States at this critical moment decided that we would compete, not retreat.

In a few moments, I will sign the North American free trade act into law. NAFTA will tear down trade barriers between our three nations. It will create the world's largest trade zone and create 200,000 jobs in this country by 1995 alone. The environmental and labor side agreements negotiated by our administration will make this agreement a force for social progress as well as economic growth. Already the confidence we've displayed by ratifying NAFTA has begun to bear fruit. We are now making real progress toward a worldwide trade agreement so significant that it could make the material gains of NAFTA for our country look small by comparison.

Today we have the chance to do what our parents did before us. We have the opportunity to remake the world. For this new era, our national security we now know will be determined as much by our ability to pull down foreign trade barriers as by our ability to breach distant ramparts. Once again, we are leading. And in so doing, we are rediscovering a fundamental truth about ourselves: When we lead, we build security, we build prosperity for our own people.

We've learned this lesson the hard way. Twice before in this century, we have been forced to define our role in the world. After World War I we turned inward, building walls of protectionism around our Nation. The result was a

Great Depression and ultimately another horrible World War. After the Second World War, we took a different course: We reached outward. Gifted leaders of both political parties built a new order based on collective security and expanded trade. They created a foundation of stability and created in the process the conditions which led to the explosion of the great American middle class, one of the true economic miracles in the whole history of civilization. Their statecraft stands to this day: the IMF and the World Bank, GATT, and NATO.

In this very auditorium in 1949, President Harry Truman signed one of the charter documents of this golden era of American leadership, the North Atlantic Treaty that created NATO. "In this pact we hope to create a shield against aggression and the fear of aggression," Truman told his audience, "a bulwark which will permit us to get on with the real business of Government and society, the business of achieving a fuller and happier life for our citizens."

Now, the institutions built by Truman and Acheson, by Marshall and Vandenberg, have accomplished their task. The cold war is over. The grim certitude of the contest with communism has been replaced by the exuberant uncertainty of international economic competition. And the great question of this day is how to ensure security for our people at a time when change is the only constant.

Make no mistake, the global economy with all of its promise and perils is now the central fact of life for hard-working Americans. It has enriched the lives of millions of Americans. But for too many those same winds of change have worn away at the basis of their security. For two decades, most people have worked harder for less. Seemingly secure jobs have been lost. And while America once again is the most productive nation on Earth, this productivity itself holds the seeds of further insecurity. After all, productivity means the same people can produce more or, very often, that fewer people can produce more. This is the world we face.

We cannot stop global change. We cannot repeal the international economic competition that is everywhere. We can only harness the energy to our benefit. Now we must recognize that the only way for a wealthy nation to grow richer is to export, to simply find new customers for the products and services it makes. That, my fellow Americans, is the decision the Congress made when they voted to ratify NAFTA.

I am gratified with the work that Congress has done this year, bringing the deficit down and keeping interest rates down, getting housing starts and new jobs going upward. But we know that over the long run, our ability to have our internal economic policies work for the benefit of our people requires us to have external economic policies that permit productivity to find expression not simply in higher incomes for our businesses but in more jobs and higher incomes for our people. That means more customers. There

is no other way, not for the United States or for Europe or for Japan or for any other wealthy nation in the world.

That is why I am gratified that we had such a good meeting after the NAFTA vote in the House with the Asian-Pacific leaders in Washington. I am gratified that, as Vice President Gore and Chief of Staff Mack McLarty announced 2 weeks ago when they met with President Salinas, next year the nations of this hemisphere will gather in an economic summit that will plan how to extend the benefits of trade to the emerging market democracies of all the Americas.

And now I am pleased that we have the opportunity to secure the biggest breakthrough of all. Negotiators from 112 nations are seeking to conclude negotiations on a new round of the General Agreement on Tariffs and Trade; a historic worldwide trade pact, one that would spur a global economic boon, is now within our grasp. Let me be clear. We cannot, nor should we, settle for a bad GATT agreement. But we will not flag in our efforts to secure a good one in these closing days. We are prepared to make our contributions to the success of this negotiation, but we insist that other nations do their part as well. We must not squander this opportunity. I call on all the nations of the world to seize this moment and close the deal on a strong GATT agreement within the next week.

I say to everyone, even to our negotiators: Don't rest. Don't sleep. Close the deal. I told Mickey Kantor the other day that we rewarded his laborious effort on NAFTA with a vacation at the GATT talks. [*Laughter*]

My fellow Americans, bit by bit all these things are creating the conditions of a sustained global expansion. As significant as they are, our goals must be more ambitious. The United States must seek nothing less than a new trading system that benefits all nations through robust commerce but that protects our middle class and gives other nations a chance to grow one, that lifts workers and the environment up without dragging people down, that seeks to ensure that our policies reflect our values.

Our agenda must, therefore, be far reaching. We are determining that dynamic trade cannot lead to environmental despoliation. We will seek new institutional arrangements to ensure that trade leaves the world cleaner than before. We will press for workers in all countries to secure rights that we now take for granted, to organize and earn a decent living. We will insist that expanded trade be fair to our businesses and to our regions. No country should use cartels, subsidies, or rules of entry to keep our products off its shelves. And we must see to it that our citizens have the personal security to confidently participate in this new era. Every worker must receive the education and training he or she needs to reap the rewards of international competition rather than to bear its burdens.

Next year, our administration will propose comprehensive legislation to transform our unemployment system into a reemployment and job retraining system for the 21st century. And above all, I say to you we must seek to reconstruct the broad-based political coalition for expanded trade. For decades, working men and women and their representatives supported policies that brought us prosperity and security. That was because we recognized that expanded trade benefited all of us but that we have an obligation to protect those workers who do bear the brunt of competition by giving them a chance to be retrained and to go on to a new and different and, ultimately, more secure and more rewarding way of work. In recent years, this social contract has been sundered. It cannot continue.

When I affix my signature to the NAFTA legislation a few moments from now, I do so with this pledge: To the men and women of our country who were afraid of these changes and found in their opposition to NAFTA an expression of that fear—what I thought was a wrong expression and what I know was a wrong expression but nonetheless represented legitimate fears—the gains from this agreement will be your gains, too.

I ask those who opposed NAFTA to work with us to guarantee that the labor and side agreements are enforced, and I call on all of us who believe in NAFTA to join with me to urge the Congress to create the world's best worker training and retraining system. We owe it to the business community as well as to the working men and women of this country. It means greater productivity, lower unemployment, greater worker efficiency, and higher wages and greater security for our people. We have to do that.

We seek a new and more open global trading system not for its own sake but for our own sake. Good jobs, rewarding careers, broadened horizons for the middle class Americans can only be secured by expanding exports and global growth. For too long our step has been unsteady as the ground has shifted beneath our feet. Today, as I sign the North American Free Trade Agreement into law and call for further progress on GATT, I believe we have found our footing. And I ask all of you to be steady, to recognize that there is no turning back from the world of today and tomorrow. We must face the challenges, embrace them with confidence, dead with the problems honestly and openly, and make this world work for all of us. America is where it should be, in the lead, setting the pace, showing the confidence that all of us need to face tomorrow. We are ready to compete, and we can win.

PRESIDENT BILL CLINTON DENIES WHITE HOUSE AFFAIR
26 January 1998

In 1994 stories out of Little Rock reached the attention of the national media with reports that, while Governor, Bill Clinton had used state troopers to lure women to him. Among those identified was a low-level state employee named Paula Corbin Jones. As soon as Ms. Jones decided to file suit against the President "to regain her good name," a small network of influential lawyers politically and personally opposed to Clinton began to help, mostly behind the scenes. Among several others the prominent Republican lawyer Kenneth Starr quietly provided advice to Jones' supporters. In August 1994, Starr, recommended by a panel of judges, was appointed by Attorney-General Janet Reno as Independent Council to investigate the Clinton's alleged improprieties in Arkansas commercial ventures, an extended inquiry which came to be immortalized as "Whitewater." Meanwhile, the Jones case endured several phases, alternately neglected and derided in the media as successive teams of lawyers came and went. In 1997 the case blossomed on 27 May when the Supreme Court unanimously ruled that this—the first civil complaint filed against a sitting President—could go forward. Ms. Jones refused an offer of $700,000 to settle, and forged ahead, abetted by skilled legal talent drawn from long-standing conservative Clinton opponents whose legal briefs convinced Arkansas Judge Susan Webber Wright to consider evidence emphasizing Clinton's supposed philandering, and to allow the Jones case to *continue. In all this time, the efforts of Independent Council Starr had failed to produce in-dictments on Whitewater—or subsequent political uproars christened "Travelgate" and "Filegate." In the fall of 1997, a New York literary agent named Lucianne Goldberg re-ported a tale which soon reached the conservative lawyers who still remained quietly in-volved in the Jones case. The story featured Ms. Goldberg's friend, a former White House employee named Linda Tripp, who possessed hours of taped conversations with a young woman named Monica Lewinsky who for months had carried on a clandestine sexual re-lationship with President Clinton in the White House. Almost immediately a strategy un-folded to make Ms. Tripp and Ms. Lewinsky witnesses in the Jones case. Simultaneously, on 12 January 1998, the Tripp-Lewinsky tapes found their way to Kenneth Starr, as did Ms. Tripp herself. Five days later, President Clinton testified in the Jones lawsuit and denied a sexual relationship with Ms. Lewinsky. By this time a chorus of whispers about the affair began to pass from obscure internet web sites to radio talkshows and all-news television cable programs. On 26 January, the President felt compelled to address the issue.*

I want to say one thing to the American people: I did not have sexual relations with that woman, Miss Lewinsky. I never told anybody to lie, not a single time. Never. These allegations are false. Now I have to get back to work for the American people.

PRESIDENT BILL CLINTON'S COMMENTS AT THE END OF THE ATTEMPT TO REMOVE HIM FROM OFFICE
12 February 1999

For more than a year American politics had but one subject, the Clinton-Lewinsky sex scandal. From its public revelation in January 1998 to the end of the impeachment trial on 12 February 1999, Washington throbbed with salacious gossip while radio, television and newspapers sent the nation the unraveling facts, rumors and allegations. Some of the newly established cable news networks adopted programming seemingly based on "all Monica, all the time." Critics and defenders of the President used all media outlets to joust. Periodically, as allegation became sensational fact, interest soared. Throughout the year Independent Council Kenneth Starr deposed and brought before Grand Juries a parade of witnesses, including President Clinton, who responded with elaborated replies to questions regarding Monica Lewinsky. On 9 September, Starr informed House leaders that he had found "substantial and credible information . . . that may constitute grounds for impeach-

ment." A month later, the President agreed to an $850,000 settlement with Ms. Jones, without admission of crime or apology. Meanwhile, House Judiciary Committee Hearings, nationally televised, quickly devolved into a partisan brawl, with the Republican majority able to bring impeachment charges to the House floor. This precipitated an even larger political quarrel and the eventual passage, on 19 December, of two articles of impeachment, one charging that the President perjured himself in sworn testimony, the other that he had obstructed justice. The nation faced a political crisis the of a type not encountered for 131 years. In 1868, Andrew Johnson, the vice president who entered the White House after the assassination of Abraham Lincoln, had survived in office by one vote after a brutally-partisan United States Senate trial. In January 1999, Clinton, the first elected President ever impeached, faced a Senate trial in different circumstances. While the Republicans enjoyed a 55–45 Senate majority, two-thirds, or 67, votes were needed to convict. Yet several Republicans were likely to cross over and the Democrats were united in support of the President, and his popularity in public opinion poll soared to 70 percent. Nonetheless, the presentation of the case by the thirteen House prosecutors (or "Managers") recounted again and again all the lurid details of the affair and insisted that the President's perjury and obstruction fell within the Constitutional definition of "high crimes and misdemeanors." On 12 February, the Senate voted. The perjury charge was defeated, 55–45, with ten Republicans joining all the Democrats. The obstruction of justice charge also failed, with a 50–50 vote including five Republican defections. The results represented a political anticlimax. The outcome was predetermined and polls indicated a strong public aversion to the entire proceedings. While Clinton supporters quickly pointed to the failure of either article of impeachment to achieve even a majority vote, the President's adamant opponents continued to vilify him. The effect, the polls indicated, had produced a loss of personal respect for the President, for the office, and for politics and politicians in general. Shortly after the Senate adjourned, Clinton appeared in the Rose Garden alone with only the media present and spoke only five sentences.

Now that the Senate has fulfilled its constitutional responsibility, bringing this process to a conclusion, I want to say again to the American people how profoundly sorry I am for what I said and did to trigger these events and the great burden they have imposed on the Congress and the American people.

I also am humbled and very grateful for the support and the prayers I have received from millions of Americans over this past year.

Now I ask all Americans—and I hope all Americans—here in Washington and throughout our land—will rededicate ourselves to the work of serving our nation and building our future together.

This can be and this must be a time of reconciliation and renewal for America.

Thank you very much.

INDEX